JOHN CLIMACUS

John Chryssavgis explores the ascetic teaching and theology of St John Climacus, a classical and formative writer of the Christian medieval East and the author of the seventh-century *Ladder of Divine Ascent*. This text proved to be the most widely used handbook of the spiritual life in the Christian East, partly because of its unique and striking symbol of the ladder that binds together the whole book. It has caught the attention of numerous readers in East and West alike through the ages and is a veritable classic of medieval spirituality, whose popularity in the East equals that of *The Imitation of Christ* in the West.

Chryssavgis follows the development and influence of earlier desert literature from Egypt through Palestine into Sinai, and includes a discussion of the theology of tears, the concept of unceasing prayer, as well as the monastic principles of *hesychia* (silence) and *eros* (love).

John Climacus

From the Egyptian Desert to the Sinaite Mountain

JOHN CHRYSSAVGIS

ASHGATE

Published by
Ashgate Publishing Limited
Gower House
Croft Road
Aldershot
Hants GU11 3HR
England

Ashgate Publishing Company
Suite 420
101 Cherry Street
Burlington, VT 05401-4405
USA

Ashgate website: http://www.ashgate.com

British Library Cataloguing in Publication Data
Chryssavgis, John
    John Climacus: from the Egyptian desert to the Sinaite mountain
    1. John, Climacus, Saint, ca. 579–ca. 649 – Contributions in the theology of man
    2. Man (Christian theology) – History of doctrines – Early church, ca. 30–600
    I. Title
    233′.092

Library of Congress Cataloging-in-Publication Data
Chryssavgis, John.
    John Climacus: from the Egyptian desert to the Sinaite mountain / John Chryssavgis.
        p. cm.
    Includes bibliographical references and index.
    ISBN 0–7546–5040–5 (alk. paper)
    1. Christian life – Orthodox Eastern authors. 2. John, Climacus, Saint, 6th cent.
    I. Title.

BX382.C49 2004
270.2′092–dc22
                                                                2004002021

ISBN 0 7546 5040 5

Printed on acid-free paper

Typeset by Tradespools, Frome, Somerset
Printed and bound in Great Britain by Antony Rowe Ltd, Chippenham, Wilts

Contents

Chronological Table

Agathon	d. 370
Am(m)oun	d. 350
Anastasius of Sinai	d. *c.* 700
Antony	251–356
Arsenius	*c.* 360–*c.* 449
Athanasius of Alexandria	*c.* 296–373
Augustine of Hippo	354–430
Barsanuphius	d. *c.* 543
Basil of Caesaria	330–379
Clement of Alexandria	*c.* 150–*c.* 215
Cyril of Scythopolis	fl. *c.* 524–558
Diadochus of Photice	*c.* 400–*c.* 486
Dionysius the Areopagite	*c.* 500
Dorotheus of Gaza	*c.* 506–*c.* 570
Ephraim the Syrian	*c.* 306–373
Euthymius	376–473
Evagrius	*c.* 345–399
Evergetinos, Paulos	d. 1054
Gregory of Nazianzus	329–379
Gregory of Nyssa	*c.* 330–395
Gregory Palamas	*c.* 1296–1359
Gregory of Sinai	*c.* 1265–*c.* 1337
Hesychius of Sinai	7th–8th century
Hilarion	*c.* 291–*c.* 371
Isaac the Syrian	late 7th century
Isaiah of Scetis	d. *c.* 489
John Cassian	360–435
John Chrysostom	347–407
John the Dwarf	*c.* 339–*c.* 407
John of Lycopolis	d. 395
John Moschus	*c.* 545–619
John, the 'Other Old Man'	d. *c.* 543
Macarian Homilies	mid-5th century
Macarius of Alexandria	293–393
Macarius of Egypt	*c.* 300–*c.* 390
Mark the Monk	early 5th century
Maximus the Confessor	*c.* 580–682
Melanie the Elder	342–411

Melanie the Younger	380–*c.* 439
Nilus of Ancyra	5th century
Origen of Alexandria	185–*c.* 254
Pachomius	292–347
Palladius of Helenopolis	*c.* 363–*c.* 431
Pambo	304–373
Paul of Thebes	*c.* 235–*c.* 341
Paula the Elder	347–404
Paula the Younger	b. *c.* 397
Peter the Iberian	d. *c.* 490
Philotheus of Sinai	9th–10th century
Poemen	d. *c.* 450
Porphyry of Gaza	d. 420
Sabas	439–532
Serapion of Thmuis	d. *c.* 370
Seridos	d. *c.* 543
Silvanus	d. *c.* 412
Sisoes	d. 429
Symeon the Stylite	d. 459
Symeon the New Theologian	949–1022
Syncletica	380–*c.* 460
Theodore the Studite	759–826
Thalassius the Libyan	7th century
Theodoret of Cyrus	*c.* 393–466
Xanthopoulos, Kallistos and Ignatios	mid-13th–early 14th century
Zeno, of Silvanus	d. 451
Zosimas (*Reflections*)	fl. 475–525

List of Illustrations

Acknowledgements

I am grateful to the Holy Transfiguration Monastery in Brookline MA for the gracious support of the brotherhood throughout the preparation of this publication, as well as for permission to quote from their translation of the *Ladder*. An icon of St John Climacus from the same monastery is also included in this book.

Ms Elizabeth Williams has, yet again, proved generous in her friendship, granting permission for and use of her photographs, which adorn this book.

A sabbatical fellowship at the Center of Theological Inquiry at Princeton in the spring of 2002 provided the necessary resources – both the academic leisure and the spiritual pleasure – for the re-writing and revision of my book.

JC
Easter 2004

Abbreviations

CSCO	Corpus Scriptorum Christianorum Orientalium
DB	Dictionnaire de la Bible, 5 volumes, Paris: 1895–1912
DS	Dictionnaire de Spiritualité, Paris: 1937f.
DTC	Dictionnaire de Théologie Catholique, 13 volumes, Paris: 1903–36
ERE	Encyclopaedia of Religion and Ethics, 13 volumes, New York: 1908–21
GCS	Die Griechischen Christlichen Schriftsteller der Ersten Jahrhunderte, Leipzig/Berlin: 1897f.
JTS	Journal of Theological Studies, London: 1899–1949; New Series: 1950f.
NCE	New Catholic Encyclopedia, 17 volumes, Washington: 1967–79
OCA	Orientalia Christiana Analecta, Rome: 1935f.
OCP	Orientalia Christiana Periodica, Rome: 1923f.
PG	Patrologia Graeca, cursus completus, 161 volumes, Paris: 1857–66
PL	Patrologia Latina, cursus completus, 221 volumes, Paris: 1844–64
PO	Patrologia Orientalis
RAM	Revue d' Ascetique et de Mystique, volumes 1–47, Toulouse: 1920–71
SC	Sources Chrétiennes (Paris)
TDNT	Theological Dictionary of the New Testament, 9 volumes, ed. G. Kittel and G. Bromiley, Grand Rapids, MI: Eerdmans, 1964–74
TEE	Threskeutike kai Ethike Enkyklopaideia, 12 volumes, in Greek, Athens: 1962–68
TU	Texte und Untersuchungen

Author's Note

Scriptural translations are based on the Revised Standard Version, with slight modifications. Text and numbering may differ, in accordance with The Septuagint.

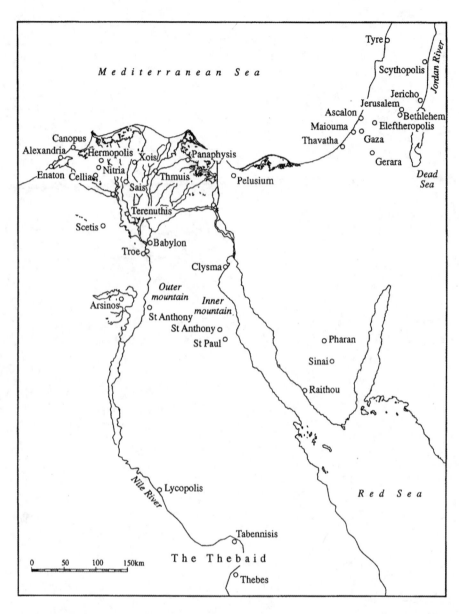

The Sinaite peninsula and neighboring Egypt and Palestine
(Map: the author)

Introduction

It occurred to my mind, once when I was
sitting in my humble cell not far from
Alexandria ... that I would undertake a
journey to Palestine ... Having turned a
little aside, however, I devoted myself to the
desert, with other people who feared God,
who were going there to pray. We arrived,
by the grace of God, in eighteen days ...
There was a certain fortress in that
neighborhood, where the abbot was
Doulas ... very near to the Holy
Mountain.

(Abba Ammonius)

We came on foot to a certain place where
the mountains opened out ... There, across
the valley, appeared Sinai, the Holy
Mountain of God. On reaching that spot,
the holy guides told us: 'The custom is that
prayer should be made from this place,
where the mountain of God is first seen.'

(Etheria, *Diary*)

The high mountain system of Sinai stands somewhat apart from the rest of the monastic world of the Eastern Mediterranean, although near enough to Egypt and Palestine to be influenced by both.[1] It is an impressive landscape of profound paradoxes. Its fierce geography will daunt even the most disinterested traveler. Yet, at the same time, its fascinating landscape will overwhelm the most apathetic pilgrim. Moreover, its forbidding distance, for a visitor in the fifth or sixth centuries, involved many and dangerous days of travel. Nonetheless, its accessibility to those wishing to take refuge in the deserted spaces or else to take counsel from the desert elders of the Sinaite peninsula invited pious travelers from the earliest of times. Sinai was always a popular place of sacred pilgrimage, at least when historical and political circumstances allowed, with an international character no less marked than that of Jerusalem. More so than either of the other Abrahamic traditions, Christianity has long been fascinated with this site as 'a landscape of terror

---

[1] See R. Devreesse, 'Le christianisme dans le Péninsule Sinaïtique, des origins à l'arrivée des Musulmans,' *Revue Biblique* 49 (April 1940), 205–23.

and theophany … a place that sacramentally conveys the grandeur of God's majesty.'[2]

Sinai could take pride in its own tradition and expression of monasticism, independent of and even unrelated to the monasticism of its neighboring regions of Egypt, Palestine and Syria. It could even claim biblical revelations and proto-monastic patriarchs in the Exodus scene and the figure of Moses. While one may choose to overlook or discredit such spiritual 'origins' of monasticism, there or elsewhere, yet it does remind us of the reality of 'asceticism as bursting forth simultaneously in myriad places … It was the spirit of the times and the new Christian faith that produced the explosion, and as it welled forth from below, it burst onto the plane of history independently throughout the empire.'[3]

As early, however, as the middle of the fourth century, the Syrian ascetic, Julian Saba, arrived in 'the inaccessible desert of the Sinaite mountain' and founded a small church on the Holy Peak of Moses' mountain, 'where the supreme Prophet Moses hid in order to be counted worthy to see God.' Thereafter, Julian returned to Syria.[4] Theodoret also tells of another Syrian, Symeon the Ancient, who visited Sinai during the fourth century in order to see the place where Moses encountered God; not – as Theodoret claims – because God is not found everywhere, but because 'those who passionately love do not only desire their lovers' countenance but worship even their lovers' places of abode.'[5]

When the much-traveled Etheria recorded her visit to Sinai (*c.* 383–4) some two decades later, toward the end of the fourth century, the picture offered is of a loose collection of hermit cells gathered around the main mountain, at its foot and in its neighborhood. Nevertheless, the ascetics are by no means exclusively Syrian. The vision is already of a more international presence, imposed by the geography itself:

> From that place [i.e., 'the central mountain'], we could see Egypt and Palestine and the Red Sea and the Parthenian Sea, which leads to Alexandria and the boundless territories of the Saracens, all so close there below us as to be scarcely credible, but the holy men pointed each one of them out to us.[6]

---

[2] Cf. B. Lane, *The Solace of Fierce Landscapes: exploring desert and mountain spirituality*, Oxford: Oxford University Press, 1998, 100 and 112.

[3] Cf. G. E. Goehring, 'The Origins of Monasticism,' in H. W. Attridge and G. Hata (eds), *Eusebius, Christianity and Judaism*, Leiden: 1992, 235–55 (see 250).

[4] See Ephraim, *Hymni de Juliano Saba* XIX and XX (ed. T. Lamy, *Hymni et Sermones*, Mechliniae, 1882–1902, vol. III, pp. 907–14) and Theodoret, *Historia Religiosa* II PG82.1316.

[5] Cf. *Historia Religiosa* VI PG82.1360–1364, esp. 1361BC.

[6] See *Itinerarium Aetheriae* in *Sources Chrétiennes* 21, Paris: 1948, 108. For the citation at the outset of this chapter, see 97–9. Translation modified.

Indeed, another, anonymous, pilgrim from Placentia arrived in the region in 570 described three of the monks there who could speak Latin, Greek, Syriac, Coptic and Bessic, as well as numerous interpreters of various languages.[7] The monastery library to this day reflects the same international history.

The first text, cited above, claims to be written in the fourth century but is in fact a sixth-century document, entitled *The Forty Martyrs of the Sinai Desert and Raithou* and written by a certain Ammonius.[8] The picture that is presented is somewhat romanticized, but the connection drawn between Egypt and Sinai is not to be overlooked. As we shall see below, some well-known Egyptian elders moved to Sinai with their disciples toward the end of the fourth century. The above hagiographical account also makes reference to 'the fortress' that the Emperor Justinian built in the wilderness of that region, at the request of the renowned Palestinian monastic founder, Sabas (439–532), quite possibly during the latter's visit to Constantinople in 531.[9] The *castrum* was completed in 556–7, during which time Doulas was the abbot of the community. Undoubtedly, the monks of that region would have remembered Sabas and his own communities daily.

During the late fourth and throughout the fifth centuries, some of the key representatives of Egyptian monasticism began to disperse, for a variety of reasons, to the neighboring regions of Palestine and Sinai. Such an event may have been the result of the close of the foundational and formative era of the first generation of monks that took flight into the desert of Egypt. Alternatively, it may have been caused by the persecution of the more intellectual representatives of the contemplative life. Perhaps, however, it was also the consequence of a general trend and growing movement of migration throughout the seminal lands of monasticism. Monks now began to travel

---

[7] See Geyer (ed.), *Itinera Hierosolymitana*, Leipzig–Prague, 1898, 184–6. See also J. Wilkinson, *Egeria's Travels to the Holy Land*, London: 1971; Jerusalem: 1981; and *Jerusalem Pilgrims before the Crusades*, Jerusalem: 1977, 78–89.

[8] Translation modified. Greek text in *Ammonii monachi relatio de sanctis patribus barbarorum incursione in monte Sina et Raithu peremptis*, in Combefis (ed.), *Illustrium Christi martyrum lecti triumphi*, Paris: 1660, 88–122. For the Palestinian Syriac version, published with an English translation (completed from the Greek), cf. A. S. Lewis, 'The Forty Martyrs of the Sinai Desert,' *Horae Semiticae* IX, Cambridge: 1912. See also F. Nau, 'Rezension der von A. S. Lewis edierten westaramäischen Version der Ammonius Legende,' *Revue de l'Orient Chrétien* 17 (1912), 445. For the Aramaic version, cf. C. Muller-Kessler and M. Sokoloff (eds), *The Forty Martyrs of the Sinaite Desert, Eulogios the Stone-Cutter, and Anastasia*, in *Corpus of Christian Palestinian Aramaica*, vol. 3, Groningen: Styx Publications, 1996. A similarly interesting but historically unreliable source of this period is attributed to the monk Nilus (see his *Narrations* in PG79.589–601), but this is not to be identified with the early fifth-century Nilus of Ancyra.

[9] See Procopius, *De Aedificiis* V, 8, in H. B. Dewing (ed.), *Procopius of Caesarea: Wars, Buildings and Anecdota*, London: Loeb Classical Library, 1914–40. See also Eutychius of Alexandria, *Annales* PG111.1071–72. The *Ladder* refers to the central monastery as 'fortress' in 6.20 (797A).

eastward. Nevertheless, they did not travel alone; at any rate, they did not have the feeling of innovating, at least in the way that Antony's biographer and Pachomius' biographical accounts appear to imply about these men. By this time, monasticism was well established throughout the empire, and some of the main texts were already available. Nor were these migrating monastics alone in two other ways: first, they often traveled with their disciples; and, second, they brought with them an entire tradition of 'stories' and 'sayings' that shaped their understanding of the ascetic way.

This was the age in which the *Apophthegmata Patrum* flourished, when the words of the elders of former times were retained in the hearts of disciples and in the memories of admirers. To begin with, they were still precisely that: recollections of sayings. Yet, with this fluid monastic transmigration, the *Sayings* began to circulate not only in Egypt but also in Palestine and in the Sinaite peninsula. Already Evagrius of Pontus and John Cassian included several of these aphorisms in their influential writings.[10] Both of these authors admit their profound indebtedness to the Desert Fathers. They were neither the only ones nor the first to do so. The biography of Hilarion, written by Jerome in 390, endeavors to forge a connection between Hilarion in Palestine and Antony in Egypt. Hilarion, it seems, spent several months in the circle of Antony and his friends. This possibly occurred – possibly, that is, because Jerome is a good storyteller – during the time of Antony's first emergence from the desert around 304 or 305. Antony reportedly inspired Hilarion to return to Palestine where his parents had died. And it was Antony that Hilarion envisioned as his exemplar when he gave away his inheritance, albeit at the tender age of fifteen, in order to lead a life of complete renunciation.

Egypt constituted a kind of model for those who aspired to a life of seclusion and silence. If Jerome is correct, then Hilarion marks the beginning of a long journey and significant connection between the ways and words of the Egyptian elders and the rules and writings of their successors in Palestine and Sinai. Indeed, the *Sayings of the Desert Fathers* include the names of other Palestinian monks, whether by origin or by adoption: Gelasius, Epiphanius, Theodore of Eleftheropolis, Hilarion, Cassian, Phocas and Philagrios. Another personality from this period, Porphyry, spent some five years in Scetis, returning in 377 in order to inhabit a cell in the valley of the Jordan and, later, to become bishop of Gaza (395–420).[11]

---

[10] Evagrius toward the end of his *Praktikos* and in chapters 106–12 of his treatise *On Prayer*; Cassian in his *Institutes* V, 24–41.

[11] See Mark the Deacon's *Life of St. Porphyry of Gaza*, translated by C. Rapp, in T. Mead (ed.), *Medieval Hagiography: An Anthology*, New York and London: Garland Publishing, 2000, 53–75. On accessibility and travel between Egypt, Palestine and Sinai, see P. Figueras (ed.), *From Gaza to Palestine: Materials for the Historical Geography of North Sinai and Southwestern Palestine* (Beer-Sheva Studies, vol. 14: Beer-Sheva, 2000) and R. Jullien, *Sinaï et Syrie*, Lille: Desclée, 1893.

The *Sayings* also actually record several bonds between the desert of Egypt and the desert of Sinai. Following the death of Antony (d. 356), Abba Sisoes also left Scetis and moved eastward, choosing however to settle no farther east than Antony's inner mountain. There he remained for seventy-two years. This would bring us to the year 429. From there, Sisoes would not have very far to travel to Clysma, very close in fact to the opening of the Sinaite desert. Clysma was situated at the very tip of the Red Sea, on the side of the Suez Gulf. Sisoes would sometimes even meet at that crossroad with elders from the Sinaite region. For example, he had occasion to meet a certain Ammoun of Raithou, who came to Sisoes for advice.[12] A road existed, certainly from Egeria's time, from Pelusium through Clysma to Pharan. From there, a paved path led to the Holy Mountain itself. Indeed, the monks of Raithou would frequently visit Clysma for purposes of commercial exchange and social contact, especially as they were by far the most isolated of the Sianite inhabitants.[13] There is a *Saying* about Abba Joseph of Pelusium, who stayed for a while on Sinai;[14] another *Saying* describes Abba 'Nicon, who lived on Mt. Sinai.'[15] Yet another refers to Abba Megethios, 'who lived on the river bank at Sinai;'[16] Abba Xoios the Theban 'one day visited the mountain of Sinai.'[17]

The relationship between Egypt, Sinai and Palestine becomes more evident when Abba Silvanus and his disciples leave their desert for the dunes of Gaza, settling near Gerara in the very early part of the fifth century. Abba Silvanus, a Palestinian by birth and one of the renowned elders of the Egyptian desert, moved with his twelve disciples temporarily to Sinai and, finally, to Palestine. Silvanus may have moved to Sinai toward the end of the fourth century, possibly even as early as 380. However, Silvanus possibly remained in the Sinaite desert for an extended period of up to a decade, certainly long enough for his monastic family to acquire significant reputation there. Indeed, people would visit him from as far away as Egypt.[18]

---

[12] This is not, however, the Ammoun of Nitria. References to Clysma are found in *Sayings*, Sisoes 17, 21, 26 and 50. *Sayings* 17 and 26 refer to his meeting with this Ammoun. For Sisoes' long sojourn there, see *Sayings* 28. References to Sisoes' sojourn in that region may be found in *Sayings* 3, 7–9, 15, 18, 25, 28 and 48. Cf. also *Sayings*, Tithoes 5 and Pistos 1. For the English translation of the *Sayings* quoted throughout this book, cf. B. Ward (ed.), *The Sayings of the Desert Fathers. The Alphabetical Collection*, London–Oxford: Mowbrays, 1975. In places, I have modified this translation.

[13] Cf. U. Dahari, *Monastic Settlements in South Sinai in the Byzantine Period: the archaeological remains*, Jerusalem: Israel Antiquities Authority, 2000, 113–46.

[14] *Sayings*, Cronius 5.

[15] *Sayings*, Nicon 1.

[16] *Sayings*, Megethios 2.

[17] *Sayings*, Netras 1.

[18] *Sayings*, Silvanus 5.

In Scetis, this Abba Silvanus lived with his disciples in a semi-eremitic manner, with scattered cells around his own dwelling and a central church for worship on Saturday and Sunday. The same lifestyle was later adopted on Sinai as well as in Gerara. We know the names of four of Silvanus' disciples: Zaccharias, Mark, Netras and Zeno. Zaccharias was perhaps the first and closest of the disciples, who also succeeded Silvanus as spiritual elder on the death of the latter. Mark has become known as the exemplar of desert obedience. 'The old man [Silvanus] loved Mark because of his obedience.' He is the one who heard his elder calling him and left the letter 'omega' which he was writing incomplete; he was a copyist.[19] Netras became bishop of Pharan in the Sinaite peninsula, while Zeno was the youngest of the group.[20]

This small group was quite probably also refined and cultivated. From the *Sayings* attributed to them, we have already noted that they had one copyist among them; Zaccharias knew Hebrew; Netras was qualified to be ordained to the episcopate; they liked to entertain visitors; and – at least in Sinai – these monks even tended a garden. In addition, Mark's mother was wealthy. These may be among the reasons that they left Egypt in the first place during the first Origenist crisis. After a brief sojourn at Sinai, they moved to Palestine, near Gerara and the river that flowed in that area.[21] The fifth *Saying* of Mark records Mark's wish not to accompany the group to Palestine but to remain in Sinai, where he died. This means that two of the above four disciples of Silvanus spent the remainder of their lives in the Sinaite desert. Indeed, Mark seems always to have had a special attraction and attachment to Sinai, apparent already in the fourth *Saying*.

Silvanus died in Palestine before 414 and was succeeded by Zaccharias, his foremost disciple. Another of his disciples, Zeno the Prophet, enjoyed a considerable role in the first half of the fifth century, largely as a result of his own disciple, Peter the Iberian, who became the non-Chalcedonian bishop of Maiouma. The historian Sozomen was born in Bethelea near Gaza (*c.* 380) and, while writing in Constantinople around 440, recalls the influence of monks such as Hilarion on the region around Thavatha but also the impact of monks such as Silvanus and his group on his own family and on his own

---

[19] *Sayings*, Mark 1.

[20] See *Sayings*, Silvanus 1–2, Mark 1 and Netras 1. For a detailed account of the lifestyle and movements of this group, cf. M. Van Parys, 'Abba Silvain et ses disciples' in *Irénikon* 61, 1988, 315–30.

[21] Silvanus, *Sayings* suppl. 1, in J.-C. Guy, *Recherches sur la tradition grècque des Apophthegmata Patrum*, Brussels, 1984 (2nd edn), 47. While the *Sayings of the Desert Fathers* provide much material for someone hoping to reconstruct the daily routine and the general development of the group around Silvanus, Sozomen offers the clearest historical evidence outside of the monastic milieu. See his *Historia Ecclesiastica* VI, 32, 8 in J. Bidez and G. C. Hansen (eds.), *GCS* 50, Berlin: 1960, 288–9.

life.[22] Thavatha, of course, was to become familiar as the site of the monastery of Abba Seridos.

Another well-known monk and monastic author in this area was Abba Isaiah of Scetis. A later emigrant from Egypt, Isaiah had spent many years in a monastery but also in the desert of Scetis. He moved to Palestine, fleeing fame, between 431 and 451. He first settled near Eleftheropolis, moving finally to Beit Daltha near Gaza, some four miles from Thavatha. There he stayed for several decades, serving for his contemporaries and visitors as a living example of the old Scetiote ascetic life, until his death in 489.[23] In his *Ascetic Discourses*, Isaiah inserts numerous *apophthegmata*, both recognizable and original. Moreover, he possibly also regarded himself as somehow responsible for preserving and promoting the words of the elders with whom he was personally acquainted in Egypt.

It is not the last that we hear of these places or even of the *Sayings*. For Gaza and its environs will be indelibly marked by the presence of two remarkable elders in the next century, Barsanuphius and John, and by the products of their teaching, both their *Letters: Questions and Answers* as well as their disciples, especially Dorotheus. Indeed, the city of Thavatha is mentioned on the Madeba Map, a mosaic map from a church in Madeba (modern Jordan) dating from the latter part of Justinian's era[24] and therefore almost coinciding with the latter part of the lives of Barsanuphius, John and Seridos.

One of the most likely places that these *Sayings* were recollected and then collected was in Palestine. This diffusion of the *Apophthegmata* on the one hand, together with the emigration of the *Patres* on the other, cannot be unrelated. Already, Lucien Regnault has demonstrated how the *Sayings of the Desert Fathers*, in both their alphabetical and anonymous or systematic collections, are found in fundamental texts of this period. Such texts include: *The Life of Saint Melanie the Younger* (d. 439), attributed to her confidant and chaplain Gerontius and dating to the middle of the fifth century; *The Life of Saint Euthymius* (d. 473), written by Cyril of Scythopolis in the latter half of the sixth century; and the *Reflections* of Zosimas, who founded a community in the first half of the sixth century. Indeed, Zosimas' reference to the *apophthegmata*

---

[22] The *Life of Hilarion* may be found in PL23.29–54. Sophronius, a contemporary of Jerome, translated it into Greek. See also Sozomen, *Historia Ecclesiastica* I, 12–13 PG67.896–900 and V, 14–15, *Sources Chrétiennes* 306, Paris: 1983, 215–16.

[23] More on Abba Isaiah in J. Chryssavgis and P. R. Penkett, *Abba Isaiah of Scetis: Ascetic Discourses*, Kalamazoo, MI: Cistercian Publications, 2002. See also by the same, *In the Footsteps of the Lord: the ascetic teaching of Abba Isaiah of Scetis*, Oxford: Fairacres Press, 2001.

[24] See C. A. M. Glucker, *The City of Gaza in the Roman and Byzantine Periods*, BAR International Series 325, Oxford: 1987, 18–20; and M. Avi-Yonah, *The Madeba Mosaic Map*, Jerusalem: 1954, 16–18.

ton agion geronton[25] is perhaps the earliest such characterization of the *Sayings* with this specific title.

In particular, Fr Regnault highlights the role of the monasteries of Seridos and of Dorotheus in the Gaza region, together with the *Correspondence* of Barsanuphius and John as well as the *Works* of their disciple Dorotheus, all of which offer the richest documentation in this regard.[26] The *Letters* of Barsanuphius and John, again dating to the first half of the sixth century, frequently quote or evoke the *Sayings*. There are at least eighty references to the *Apophthegmata* themselves, while numerous phrases recommend these as a basis for spiritual practice and progress, sometimes by name (sixteen times) but mostly implicitly (thirty-four times). On other occasions, the Old Men adopt alternative phrases (twenty-six times). There are at least fifty-five references from the *Sayings of the Desert Fathers* in the writings of Dorotheus alone. He also seems to be the first writer to designate the *Apophthegmata* as *to Gerontikon*.[27] Might, therefore, this circle of monks also be responsible for the collection of the *Sayings* themselves? Certainly, Dorotheus is the only ancient witness to the single saying attributed to Basil in the alphabetical collection of the *Sayings of the Desert Fathers*,[28] while both Barsanuphius and Dorotheus refer to the *Rules* of Saint Basil.

In addition to these connections between Egypt and Palestine, writers of the sixth and seventh centuries tend to share certain characteristics, which may or may not always be evident in earlier texts. For instance, Barsanuphius and John in Palestine, and John Climacus on Sinai, deliberately address their audience in a balanced and un-polemical manner with reference to rules or counsels. In this way, they have much in common also with the disposition of their Egyptian predecessors. Therefore, the *Sayings*, the *Letters* and the *Ladder* do not in general reveal the confessional rifts that affected so much of Christendom from

---

[25] Cf. *Discourses*, ch. 12, Avgoustinos edition: Jerusalem, 1913, 17. Also found in John Moschus, *Spiritual Meadow*, ch. 212 PG87.3104–05. On Zosimas, see my *In the Heart of the Desert: The Spirituality of the Desert Fathers and Mothers*, Bloomington, IN: World Wisdom Books, 2003, which contains a translation of the full text of the *Reflections*, hereafter referred to by the Latin name used by J.-P. Migne, namely *Alloquia*.

[26] L. Regnault, 'Les *Apophtegmes des Pères* en Palestine aux Ve et VIe siècles,' *Irénikon* 54, 1981, 320–30. A complete English translation of Barsanuphius and John will soon appear by J. Chryssavgis. A selection of this important correspondence, translated and introduced by John Chryssavgis, has been published by St Vladimir's Seminary Press, New York: 2003, entitled *Letters from the Desert*. For the critical edition, see L. Regnault, *Barsanuphe et Jean de Gaza: Correspondance*, volume I, tomes I–II, *Sources Chrétiennes* 426–7 and 451–2, Paris: 1997–2002. Critical text, notes and index by F. Neyt and P. de Angelis-Noah.

[27] See his *Teachings* I, 13 PG88.1633C in *SC* 92, Paris: 1952. G. W. H. Lampe's *Patristic Lexikon*, Oxford: Oxford University Press, 1991, 313 refers to a letter by Nilus; however, this is not an authentic letter by this author.

[28] See L. Regnault, 'Les *Apophtegmes* des Pères,' 328; and Dorotheus, *Teachings* 24 in *SC* 92, 182–4.

the fourth to the seventh centuries. They are far less militant than other representatives of both the Chalcedonian and non-Chalcedonian circles during the fifth and sixth centuries. Other contemporary ascetics, such as Sabas (d. 532), while compassionate and non-judgmental in their outlook, are nevertheless more directly, deliberately and defensively concerned with confessional doctrine.

Yet the Gaza and Sinaite elders also differ somewhat from their Egyptian counterparts, inasmuch as they are on the whole educated and widely read. This more intellectual aspect may not be unknown among the Desert Fathers, but it is on the whole exceptional. Barsanuphius' responses to questions about Origenist tendencies among certain representatives of the monastic tradition, in *Letters* 600–07, together with John's explanations of the Great Old Man's words, reveal an elder who accepts and appreciates fine intellectual discourse and distinctions without at the same time being absorbed by these. John Climacus, too, manifests a wide appreciation for learning and literature, evident not only in the content but also in the style of his *Ladder*. At the same time, both the *Letters* and the *Ladder* do not normally encourage abstract speculation among their disciples.[29]

At some point in time, between the work of Abba Isaiah of Scetis in the fifth century and the correspondence of the two Old Men of Gaza in the sixth century, there appears to have occurred a shift in the appreciation of the *Sayings*. Abba Isaiah senses that he is a part of the tradition of the Desert Fathers, that he has transplanted this tradition from the chosen land to an adopted land, and that he is obliged to keep that memory alive in his new homeland. Abba Barsanuphius and his disciples, particularly the gifted Dorotheus, sense that they are a part of a new tradition, closely linked to the past and yet at the same time clearly looking to a different experience and working within a different environment. Abba Isaiah's attitude is backward-looking to the golden age of Egypt; Barsanuphius and Dorotheus are forward-looking to the diverse monastic population that they are addressing and the diverse monastic culture that they are confronting. In fact, their presence in the region of Gaza, that renowned intersection and cross-section of peoples and pilgrims, may well be the reason why the alphabetical collection of the *Sayings of the Desert Fathers* bring together so many disparate elements from the worlds of Egypt, Sinai, Palestine, Asia Minor, Syria, and as far east as Persia. The region also numbered Arabs, Greeks, Latins, Armenians, Georgians and others. And the monks of this region were deeply influenced by a sense of openness, defined in Barsanuphius' attitude toward foreigners and imposed by a dynamic of positive interaction in the region.[30] Indeed, Barsanuphius was quite clear about the role of his contemporaries; it was, as he determines in

---

[29] See, for example, *Letters* 151 and 167; for the *Ladder*, cf. Step 4,30 (700B).
[30] See *Letters* 686, 733 and 777.

Letter 569, to pray for the salvation of the whole world, orthodox and non-orthodox, pious and pagan:

> There are three men, perfect in God, who have exceeded the measure of humanity and received the authority to loose and bind, to forgive and hold sins. These stand before the shattered world, keeping the whole world from complete and sudden annihilation. Through their prayers, God combines His chastisement with His mercy. And it has been told to them, that God's wrath will last a little longer. Therefore, pray with them. For the prayers of these three are joined at the entrance to the spiritual altar of the Father of lights. They share in each other's joy and gladness in heaven. And when they turn once again toward the earth, they share in each other's mourning and weeping for the evils that occur and attract His wrath. These three are John in Rome and Elias in Corinth, and another in the region of Jerusalem. I believe that they will achieve His great mercy. Yes, they will indeed achieve it. Amen.

This was undoubtedly also the open-minded outlook of John Climacus in a region that was likewise to become the center of a variety of cultures and the site for numerous pilgrims of three major monotheistic religions: Christianity, Judaism, and – at least by the time John of the *Ladder* was writing – also Islam.

The chapters that follow seek to place the *Ladder* of John, arguably the masterpiece of Byzantine spiritual guidance,[31] within the ascetic context of his monastic predecessors. In particular, emphasis will be placed on John's spiritual and textual indebtedness to the Desert Fathers of Egypt, especially as their *Apophthegmata* were received, preserved and transmitted through the Palestinian tradition of the monastic representatives living in Gaza. While John's knowledge and appropriation of a broader range of monastic literature should not be overlooked, it is this line of thought – from the foundational teachings of the Egyptian desert, through the formative counsel of the Gaza elders – that John bequeathed to his Sinaite successors. It will also become apparent throughout this study that John is, in a remarkably ingenious way, able to transform the teachings that he has received into a particular form and unique voice that would be identified as Sinaite and forever shape monastic thought and writing. The monastic authority of the Egyptian desert and the Palestinian dunes that John invoked from the immediate past allowed him to speak with an authentic monastic assurance within his own Sinaite desert and in his own time, while simultaneously enabling him to provide for the future a monastic author of unparalleled importance and influence. This becomes immediately apparent with a simple comparison of John's impact on Byzantine writers, such as Symeon the New Theologian in the tenth century, and on the Hesychast representatives of the fourteenth century.

---

[31] Cf. P. Brown, *Body and Society*, 237. Brown also remarks: 'John wrote with three centuries of spiritual wisdom behind him' (240). The importance and influence of these three centuries on the *Ladder* form a central focus of my book.

The present study is concerned with John's ascetic teaching, and in particular his understanding of the human person, or, more specifically, of personhood itself.[32] The anthropological question is one of the most neglected in classical patristic literature, which addressed itself in the main to matters of Trinitarian and Christological doctrine, although a Christian anthropology is, naturally, latent in such doctrine and depends on it. The ascetic literature offers wider and more concrete opportunities for discovering the inner world of human personhood than do some of the more discursive and doctrinal patristic writings. John Climacus, whatever his Egyptian or Palestinian monastic predecessors and influences, is one of the most important to provide insights of remarkable subtlety into the spiritual and, indeed, the psychological life of the inner being. The *Ladder* is an extraordinary Christian response to the precept adopted by Socrates from the oracle of Delphi: 'Know yourself!'

It is these insights that I have tried to examine in a discussion of the three constituent parts or self-revelations of the human person – the body, the heart and the intellect – centered on their common purpose of divine-human fulfillment and finding in that fulfillment the essence, or the humanity, of personhood.

Whether Climacus' views, let alone my attempt to interpret them, are sufficient ground for a definition and understanding of the human person as a unique relational being may be questioned. At any rate, they provide an answer to the endemic problem of the dissociation of human nature into fragments, each more or less autonomous and governed by extrinsic influences. Such an answer is not of a theoretical order for Climacus, but something with practical validity. It indicates a way of life, predominantly or paradigmatically a monastic way of life, rather than a way of thinking, yet for all that having no less relevance than the conclusions of doctrinal anthropological teachings.

The three chapters that follow on tears, on struggle and on prayer reveal precisely how Climacus envisages this reintegration of the human person as a practice, as the act, or series of acts, of living in accordance with the true essence of personhood, in an 'ascending' fashion.

The heart of the matter resides in the link between the 'practice' and 'theory' of the nature of the human person. And the identification or illumination of this link

---

[32] This book is based on a doctoral dissertation originally submitted to the University of Oxford in 1983 and later published by Holy Cross Orthodox Press, Brookline, MA: 1987, with the title *Ascent to Heaven: the theology of the human person according to St. John Climacus*. The book has long gone out of print and is rewritten here with major revisions and substantial changes. Meanwhile, the explosion in the last two decades of crtical texts, but especially of secondary sources relating to monastic literature and ascetic thought, has rendered necessary the reconsideration of the teaching of John Climacus in light of his own sources. In addition, I have also endeavored to set John in a historical and literary context so that the reader may better appreciate his place and role in the wider monastic and later Byzantine tradition.

constitutes the most significant and valuable contribution by John Climacus to Christian anthropology. Seeing that John's primary concern is a reaffirmation of the wholeness of the human person as a basis for understanding ourselves, it may be asked whether he has in fact successfully and consistently achieved this aim. Has he, for instance, managed to avoid that tendency which is never far from the surface of Christian asceticism: the notion that one's corporeal existence is suspect – not necessarily in any ostensibly Manichean sense, but in the sense of a barely, grudgingly tolerant attitude towards it? There may be readers for whom the *Ladder* will come naturally and neatly to hand for the purpose of repressing the body and even to some extent the affective strains in human nature, while the affirmative statements – notably those on *eros* – might give the impression that the sensuousness of human nature remains as a dangerous and abiding competitor, sublimated rather than confirmed and restored.

Two comments suggest themselves in this connection. First, Climacus has a very distinctive style of writing and thinking alike. The writing is terse, aphoristic and uncoordinated. The thinking is 'dialectical.' In the words of Peter Brown:

> A guide for souls, John had been content to sketch the mere outline of a trajectory, leaving the resolution of the paradoxes to which he alluded to the experience of his charges.[33]

As can be seen from many quotations in this study, he is a master of the ambivalent, of saying and unsaying the same thing. It is a way of having it both ways. This, after all, may well be the divine way, at any rate of a God who is both divine and human. Whatever the implications, this certainly does not conjure up a shadowy parallel world – parallel with our ordinary one – into which one might withdraw in some nihilistic escape or even in sublimation.

Second, John is far removed from ferocious monastic misanthropists, who use the wicked and the worldly as a scapegoat loaded perhaps with the detestable acts they have been tempted to commit themselves. He is also an ascetic writer for whom life is a way of giving. And to give, in acts of even the most extreme renunciation and mortification, was to give to others, by virtue of an undefined – or undefinable – law of generosity. To give away and expect nothing – nothing whatever in return – to embrace all things in self-giving love, is the air that John of the *Ladder* breathes. He leaves, it is true, evil in its demonic shape, and demonology is an irksome, extremist approach, which we shall also examine. But then, without extremes, in dialectical affirmation and negation, one would probably not know what the human person really is supposed to be.

---

[33] *Body and Society*, 240.

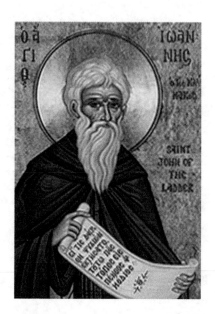

John Climacus
(Holy Transfiguration Monastery, Brookline, MA)

CHAPTER 1

John Climacus and the *Ladder*

Your tears and your words have spoken of
ascents to divine love and beauty.
(Menaion, March 30)

Exile is separation from everything in order
to hold onto God totally.
(John Climacus, Step 3)

Life of St John of the *Ladder*

The life and condition of the monks in the Sinaite desert are well described in the *Spiritual Meadow* of John Moschus, published by his friend and pupil Sophronius. Therein, John informs his readers a series of incidents and stories that seemed to him noteworthy. Another source of information is the collection of forty *Narratives* attributed to Anastasius of Sinai, published by F. Nau.[1] These documents offer us a picture of monks who enjoyed a high reputation, with an atmosphere and tradition of their own, distinct from that of Palestine or of Egypt yet at the same time blending both in an austere but balanced ethos. It is in these mountains that Moses encountered God; it is here that Elijah heard God; and it is here that John Climacus, or John of the *Ladder*, recorded his experiences of God.

The principal source, apart from the writings of John himself, is the *Life* of John written by a monk named Daniel of Raithou, whose biographical dates and origin are equally uncertain.[2] Daniel writes as an eyewitness, or at the very least as a contemporary of the Sinaite ascetic and author of the *Ladder*. Yet we cannot be entirely sure of this; after all, in his *Life*, which resembles an edifying eulogy, Daniel too is imprecise. He does not, for example, provide any chronology and explicitly states that he does not even know John's place of origin (596A). All other information, apart from the evidence mentioned below, goes no further than Daniel's: such includes the *Menaion* for March 30,

---

[1] Cf. Skrobucha, *Sinai*, 29 and Chitty, *Desert*, 168–72.

[2] Daniel's *Life* is found in J.-P. Migne, *Patrologia Graeca*, vol. 88, immediately before the *Ladder*. For an account of Climacus' life, see also H. Delehaye, *Synaxarium*, 571–4. Beck believes that Daniel lived on Sinai several years after Climacus: cf. Beck, *Kirche*, p. 466. Petit, 'Saint John Climaque,' *DTC*, 8, 690, says that Daniel may be a contemporary of Climacus. Nevertheless, one cannot be confident of this, since, as we have noted, Daniel's factual knowledge of Climacus' biography is scanty and vague.

the day of John's repose, as well as other *synaxaria* and *menologia* such as the
tenth-century *Life* in the *menologion* of Emperor Basil.[3]

The precise dates of the period during which John, the author of the *Ladder of
Divine Ascent,* lived are hard to determine with any certainty, owing to the lack
either of sources or else of detailed information in the few sources available.
However, it is possible to reconstruct a basic outline of John's life using the
evidence of the *Ladder* itself, which while limited is nonetheless authentic, the
information provided by Daniel's *Life,* which, despite its vagueness one may
accept as basically reliable, and the above-mentioned *Narratives* of Anastasius,
although with the reservations highlighted in the appendix to this chapter. How,
then, does John's biographical sketch emerge from these sources?

John of the *Ladder* is also known as John 'the Scholastic' (596A) or
'Scholar,' an indication that he was not unlettered, as earlier scholars have
supposed.[4] Possibly born into a noble family some time around or before the
year 579, John enjoyed a good education, which his biographer describes as
'wide learning' (597B), a phrase denoting an all-round education that may or
may not include higher learning. However, the fact that John was only sixteen
years of age when he arrived at Sinai, as will be seen below, may rule out the
last possibility, but need not imply that he had no education at all. The *Ladder*
is a skillfully written work, from a stylistic point of view, and is not the work of
a semi-literate person. Naturally, John may have acquired much of his
knowledge *after* entering the monastic life.

It is not known where John was born (596A), but his biographer tells us that
he arrived at Sinai when he was only sixteen.[5] John appears to have been
exceptionally mature already at this early age (597A). He immediately and
humbly placed himself under the obedience of a spiritual guide, referred to as
'Abba Martyrius' (600B), who tonsured John on the Holy Peak (608B) at the
age of twenty (608C). Interesting accounts have come down to us of prophecies
by certain elders living in the Sinaite desert at the time. On descending from the
Holy Mountain after John's profession, Martyrius led his disciple to a certain
abbot (*hegoumenos*) called Anastasius.[6] This may have been the abbot of the
central monastery. Anastasius predicted that John would one day become

---

[3] Both the *Life* and the account from the *Menaion* are found in PG88.596A–608A and 609C–
12A. In referring to these two sources, the column number from Migne will be given in parentheses
within the main body of the text. Parenthetical references in the footnotes signify the column in
Migne (for Climacus) or the page number in the edition mentioned in the bibliography (for other
authors).

[4] Cf. Beck, *Kirche,* 451.

[5] Cayré believes that Climacus was born in Syria, but there is no evidence for this. Cayré
appears to make other clear errors, such as claiming that Climacus later probably became Bishop of
Sinai: cf. F. Cayré, *The First Spiritual Writers,* English translation: London, 1959, 86.

[6] Basing his view on *Narrative* 34, Chitty (in *Desert,* 178, n. 34) says that, if this Anastasius could
be identified with the one who became Patriarch of Antioch in 559, and his hegumenate placed

abbot – a prediction fulfilled forty years later. The fact that Martyrius is called 'abba,' a term which does not necessarily denote the office of abbot, whereas Anastasius is called *hegoumenos*, which clearly means 'abbot' in the narrower sense – coupled with the fact that Anastasius encounters John for the first time – seems to indicate that our John did not originally have the experience of living inside the main monastery. This may be a further reason why John was so impressed by the monastery he later visited in Alexandria. Soon after this meeting with Anastasius, and perhaps even on the very same expedition, Martyrius and John also visited John the Sabbaite, who lived some fifteen miles away in the wilderness of Goudda[7] and who, having washed John's feet, informed his own disciple that, although he did not know whose feet he had washed, he sensed that this person would one day become abbot (608B). Abba Strategius, too, on the day of John's profession, 'prophesied about him that he would be revealed as a great star' (608C).

At the age of thirty-five and after Martyrius' death (597B), John lived as a hermit at a place called Tholas (597C, *Menaion* 609C), some five miles from the central monastery itself.[8] Although Daniel explicitly uses the phrase 'removes himself' to describe John's action, it was not a 'move out' of the nearby monastic community, since in all probability he was never a novice or monk there. Above all, however, it was not a 'move away' from social interaction on John's part. For he continued to see and to counsel numerous visitors (650A),[9] even to the point that, out of envy, he was accused of being a chatterbox (604D–605A)! Indeed, it was only when his accusers themselves pleaded for him to return to his former way of life that he once more agreed to receive visitors (605A). In a meaningful and profound way, then, John's silence as well as his talking, his flight from the world and his retreat into the solitary life were not an escape from people, but rather a result of his burning love (600A) for others as well as for God (601C). After a time, Climacus assumed the third way of monasticism, the middle or intermediate path, also known as the semi-

---

before this and not during his exile from Antioch (570–93), then Climacus could be the same as the correspondent of Gregory the Great. This would certainly fit well with Petit's theory, but Chitty contends that it would be difficult to adapt other evidence from the *Narratives* to this argument.

[7] *Narrative* 6. These predictions about John parallel those by Euthymius concerning Sabas and by Markianus regarding Theodosius: cf. Cyril of Scythopolis, *Life of Efthymios*, 21 (50, 1f.) and *Life of Theodosios* (237, 16–26).

[8] Daniel's account, together with that of the *Menaion*, is not clear at this point: it could mean either 'at the age of nineteen' or 'nineteen years after his profession.' The former meaning appears to be more probable. The cell attributed to John lies some 150 meters west of Tholas, beside a waterfall and beneath a large boulder. To this day, the remains of a Byzantine orchard survive. Tholas, today known as 'Et-Tlah,' is first mentioned by Nilus in *Narrative* 6 PG79.664. See Dahari, *Monastic Settlements*, 67–9.

[9] The *Oikos* in the *Triodion* calls him 'a teacher.' Such liturgical texts, while not necessarily historical evidence, nevertheless provide invaluable illustrations.

cenobitic or semi-eremitic way,[10] where small groups lived as a close-knit cluster of families, each under the immediate guidance of a spiritual director. Accordingly, John accepted a disciple, Moses, to live with him (601B). The normal custom in eastern monasticism is to treat the community as a preparation for the desert.[11] The alternative view of Basil, however, regards the cenobitic life as superior and even actively discourages the eremitic way.[12] Evagrius of Pontus and his disciple, John Cassian, refer to the temptations and dangers of solitude, although Evagrius does not actually express a preference for the cenobitic life;[13] in any case, he himself was a solitary, and not a cenobite. As regards John, he did not enter a *cenobium* initially, precisely because the preparation for the solitary life may take place equally in the cenobitic and in the semi-eremitic life. On the whole, John agrees with the former view, which is also in general the Palestinian line, although passages to the contrary may also be found in the *Ladder*.[14]

As a man of sincere *ascesis* and intense love (600B), at least according to the esteem of Daniel, John was also known to have worked miracles through prayer (604A, 608–12A):[15] he was recognized as a healer of body and soul (604C). According to John Cassian, who both appreciated and appropriated the desert tradition of Egypt, the further that ascetics move from people and the closer they are to God, the more visitors inevitably will approach them. This certainly proved true of John, for, while in the desert, as we have already seen, he received many visitors, often including lay people.[16] Moreover, John himself visited other sick solitaries. He tells us that he also visited monasteries and scetes on the outskirts of Alexandria.[17] He may even have visited Scetis and Tabennisis, although the evidence for this is not altogether clear. John

---

[10] All the three ways – the cenobitic, the eremitic and the semi-eremitic – are mentioned together in the *Ladder* 1.47 (641D).

[11] Cf. *Apophth*. Rufus 2 (PG65.389C).

[12] Basil, *Sermo Asceticus* 3 (PG31.873 CD) and *Reg. Fus. Tract*. 7, 1–3 PG31.928C–32D.

[13] Cf. Evagrius, *Prakt*. 5 (504). For Cassian's view of the cenobitic life as inferior to the anachoretic, cf. *Inst*. 5. 36. 1 (246–8); 10.1 (384); 5. 4. 1 (194), where he stresses the dangers involved in solitude in *Conf*. 19.6 (43–5). A sixteenth-century manuscript in the monastery of Dionysiou on Mt Athos (*Codex* 17) contains a eulogy to John by Niketas the Rhetorician and chronicler of Paphlagonia (d. *c*. 890) and mentions that John was in fact tonsured within the monastery. Similar manuscripts are also found in the monasteries of Great Lavra and Philotheou on Athos. These manuscripts, however, offer no further details or evidence for this claim.

[14] Cf. 4.72 (712C) for the importance of a *cenobium*, and 26.ii,61 (1073B) for the difficulties in a cenobitic monastery. For the Palestinian view, cf. Cyril of Scythopolis, *Life of John the Hesychast* (206, 7–10).

[15] Cf. also *Narrative* 16 and 1.38 (640C). This is also illustrated in the *Triodion*, Canon Ode 9, *Troparion* 1.

[16] Cf. 1.38–40 (640C–41A). For the reference to Cassian, cf. *Conf*. 24.19 (190–92).

[17] 4.16–17 (685AC); 5.5 (776B) and *Shep*. 100 (1200). Concerning his visits to sick solitaries, cf. 6.20 (797AB) and 26.16 (1017D).

states that there are more 'luminaries' among the Scetiotes than among the Tabennisiotes, but he does not give any reason for this.[18] While he mentions both places, he may never have actually visited them. A visit to Scetis is certainly possible, however, and is more likely because it is closer to Alexandria than Tabennisis. Moreover, John describes yet another voyage during which he met with various troubles.[19] Indeed, the *Ladder* generally provides significant historical information about the cenobitic monasteries in Alexandria, about the eremitic dwellings in Egypt and, above all, about contemporary monasticism pertaining to all three forms of asceticism at Sinai itself.

John's monastic life would not be complete without an experience of the first way of monasticism, the cenobitic path. After forty years in the desert, his monastic colleagues compelled him (605A, *Menaion* 612A) to become abbot,[20] an event foreseen, as we have already observed, on the day of his profession. John's love of God and his ascetic struggles remained for the most part a secret between himself and God, unknown to others (604AB). He spent days and nights in an unknown cave (which Daniel, nevertheless, claims to have known [601A] and which, by tradition, can be visited to this day), there shedding many tears (600C). Yet, on the day of his installation as abbot, some six hundred pilgrims arrived at the monastery. It was on this occasion that John noticed the prophet Moses 'going about, authoritatively giving orders to the cooks, cellarers, stewards, and other servants' (608C).[21] His admirers regarded John as a 'newly appeared Moses' who 'saw God' (605AB, 624B).[22] He was considered a second Jacob for seeing and describing the ladder leading to heaven (625A, *Prologue* 628D), and even declared a second David for his meekness.[23] It is not surprising that many admired John as a holy and loving hermit (625A); John even complains of this in the *Ladder*.[24] A fresco in the church of the monastery to this day depicts him with a square halo, which suggests that it was painted while the saint was still alive or soon after his

---

[18] 27.ii,3 (1105C). One possible explanation can be found in *Apophth.* Amoun of Nitria 1 (PG65.128B).

[19] 26.43 (1028C).

[20] This in no way implies that John was also an ordained priest. Petit translates *abba* as *prêtre* (cf. 'Saint Jean Climaque,' in *DTC* 8, 691), but this is no more than a generalization of classical terms. In fact, the word itself hardly contains the notion even of holding the office of superior (cf. J. Pargoire, *L'église byzantine*, 69); its usual meaning is that of a monk advanced in perfection. If it sometimes also means 'abbot,' it is not on account of the word itself, but because in fact the abbot is also a holy man (cf. Hausherr, *Direction*, 37). In any case, even an 'abbot,' in the institutional sense, need not necessarily be a priest. Pachomius was not ordained, and there is no evidence that Benedict was in orders.

[21] Cf. also *Narrative* 7.

[22] Cf. also *Narrative* 5 and 7.

[23] Cf. *Triodion*, Canon Ode 4, *Troparion* 2.

[24] 27.ii,10 (1109AB).

death. This halo need not imply sanctity, but could be indicative of an important office held. The earliest surviving icon portraying John with a round halo is a miniature in a tenth-century manuscript.[25]

John of the *Ladder* is sometimes said to have been both figuratively and spiritually dominated by two mountains: Sinai and Tabor (2 Pet. 1.18).[26] Sinai – because he lived close to it, and the rough surroundings must often have reminded the hermit of the scene in Exodus 20; Tabor – as the place of the prefiguration of Christ's glory, the scene of the vision of Christ's Transfiguration (Mt. 17.1). A majestic mosaic in the apse of the monastery basilica, built almost a century before John and surviving to this day, was dedicated to the Transfiguration. Climacus as abbot must have spent many hours gazing at it from his stall during the long services. His entire life, so it was felt by those who knew him, was a prayer offered to God, an exemplary life of love (601A). The light that he radiated reflected the light seen by Moses on Mount Sinai and beheld by the three Apostles on Mount Tabor. John himself withdrew from the world out of love for God, much as Moses and the three Apostles withdrew from their peers, but the divine light experienced by these seers could not remain concealed (Mt. 5.14–15) out of love for the world. In John's life, as in that of many holy hermits, there can be seen a creative tension between solitude and service to the world.

Finally, John returned, for an unascertainable period, to the eremitic life, having appointed his brother George to the abbacy (609A). This George predicted that he would die within a year of John's own death, around or after the year 654. The prediction was fulfilled within ten months of the saint's demise.[27]

The Ladder of Divine Ascent

When already quite advanced in age, John accepted to write the *Ladder* at the request of another John, Abba of Raithou (624AB).[28] Abbot John's *Letter* is

---

[25] Cf. Martin, *Illustration*, p. 19. Daniel provides additional evidence of John's reputation for saintliness.

[26] Ware, *Introduction*, pp. 1–2. The monastery was originally dedicated to the Mother of God, the Holy Bush seen as a 'type' of her: cf. Chitty, *Desert*, p. 169. It was only in the fourteenth century that the enthusiasm for the cult of the virgin-martyr Catherine, whose tomb is still preserved in the monastery, wrought the change of name: cf. Skrobucha, *Sinai*, 65.

[27] George had complained to John about the fact that the saint was to die before him, leaving him alone to be abbot of a monastery (609B). Perhaps – and it is no more than surmise – this is an allusion to the fact that George was older than John and expected to die first. If *Narrative* 32 in fact refers to John, this explains his retirement, leaving the abbacy to his bishop and brother George, and his continued spiritual connection with George and the monastery even after his retirement.

[28] Raitho(s) or Raithou lies north-west of the Sinaite peninsula, some 125 miles from the present Suez Canal. Today it is called el-Tor and has always been a region of deep, fertile valleys chosen by

addressed to 'John the Sinaite,' perhaps implying that John was still a solitary monk in the region at the time of writing. Yet the title of both Rader's and Sophronius' editions, as will be seen below, explicitly refers to the author of the *Ladder* as 'Abba John, abbot of the monks of Mount Sinai.' It is likely that John is being referred to as the 'the Sinaite' in his role as abbot of the large monastery. It is in this capacity that the abbot of a smaller nearby community approaches him. The original title of his work was 'Spiritual Tablets,' as many manuscripts indicate – derived from the parallel between John and Moses (624B). In the end, it was the title 'Ladder' that prevailed.

The *Ladder* consists of thirty steps, as a supplement to which John also authored a short treatise entitled *To the Shepherd*, describing the task of the abbot or spiritual elder, and likewise addressed to John of Raithou.[29] The surviving manuscripts of the *Ladder* are numerous and, unfortunately, no critical edition exists as yet. Rader's edition of 1633, reprinted in *Patrologia Graeca* of Migne,[30] is usable and, at least for general purposes, the textual variations between this and other editions are neither numerous nor significant. Another edition, independent of that by Rader, is by the Athonite monk Sophronius, published in Constantinople in 1883. (More recently, in 1978, this edition was published in Athens by Archimandrite Ignatios of the monastic community of the 'Paraclete' in Oropos in Attica, which has subsequently been

---

men and women who sought God in solitude and silence; monks and hermits have frequented this area since the fourth century, when the well-known Abba Ammonius was abbot at the monastery destroyed and later rebuilt by Justinian in 540. This John of Raithou could be John the Cilician, *hegoumenos* of Raithou, mentioned in the *Spiritual Meadow* of John Moschus (cf. ch. 115 and 117, PG87.2980BC and 3048A) and in the *Apophthegmata Patrum* under the name of John the Eunuch (cf. *Saying* 3, PG65.233AB). Chitty, however, contends that we cannot be sure of this: cf. *Desert*, 173.

[29] For the Greek text, see *Shep.* 1–100 (1165–208). A recent translation of this remarkable document may be found in J. Chryssavgis, *Soul Mending* (2000) 176–93. Although the *synaxarion* of the *Triodion* mentions that Climacus 'left many other works,' this seems doubtful and there is no reason to attribute other works to him apart from the *Ladder* and the treatise *To the Shepherd* – which in the Constantinople edition is given as chapter 31 of the *Ladder*, whereas in Migne it immediately follows the *Ladder* as a separate work – and the letter, being in effect a brief reply to Abba John of Raithou. All three works, then, are addressed to the same John of Raithou. There is no justification for attributing to Climacus: (1) the commentary on Matthew and Luke, (2) a number of letters to monks, (3) a letter to Pope Gregory I, and (4) the *Scholia* found in Migne at the end of each step. None of the first three is preserved, and one can only speculate about their existence. The attribution of the Gospel commentary was refuted as early as the eighteenth century by P. Lambecius, *Commentarius de Bibliotheca Caesarea Vindobonensi* 304 (Vindobonae, 1776), 423. The letters to the monks are only mentioned by Tresvian, but without any reference to sources: cf. *Introduzione* in *S. Giovanni Climaco, Scala Paradisi*, 25. The letter to Pope Gregory is unlikely to have existed, since John was writing his *Ladder* a generation after Gregory's death in 604. Finally, as will be seen towards the end of this introduction, a number of the *scholia* have already been identified as the work of persons either prior to or after John Climacus.

[30] PG88.632–1161.

revised and reprinted.) The Migne edition, which in this study will be cited in parentheses after the relevant step and paragraph numbering of the Constantinople edition, bears a similar but shorter title than the edition of Sophronius: 'An ascetic treatise by Abba John, Abbot of the monks of Mount Sinai, sent by him to Abba John, Abbot of Raithou, at whose request it was written.'[31]

In translating the text, on the whole it is the English version, *Saint John Climacus, the Ladder of Divine Ascent*, published in 1978 by the Holy Transfiguration Monastery in Brookline, that I have followed with the kind permission of the Monastery. This is a revised edition of the 1959 translation by Lazarus Moore; in the revision, a Sinai manuscript (*Codex* 421) was additionally consulted. While this is not the only translation of the *Ladder* (see the Conclusion), I have chosen it inasmuch as it is quite faithful to the original Greek and, therefore, more helpful to the student of the *Ladder*. There are, however, certain modifications which I felt were necessary in many of the cited passages, and so the translation has been appropriately edited.

John did not at first wish to write anything at all, regarding himself as 'a pauper and a beggar in the virtues' and considering the task to be 'beyond [his] strength.' He finally acceded to the request of Abba John, doing so under 'the yoke of holy obedience, the mother of all virtues.' He felt that John of Raithou should have asked this of the 'well-experienced' because he believed that he was 'still among the learners' (625BC). The task was 'beyond [his] power' (625D), and he only undertook it 'with fear and love.'

> With my poor and scanty knowledge, and in my stammering way, I have sketched in ink alone the bare outline of living words (628A).

Humbly acknowledging his limitations and ignorance, his own work appears to him as rather clumsy and uninspiring.[32] The fact of the case proved to be the precise opposite.

The immediate recipients of the *Ladder* were the cenobites under John of Raithou. John is quite explicit on this point: he sends it to none other than 'to the God-called community who, together with me, are learning under you, O best of teachers' (628B). The audience, then, is clearly a monastic one: the *Ladder* is the work of a former solitary writing for cenobites. Yet it is the work of a former hermit who also had personal contact with monks living in community and who now, as a recognized spiritual elder and perhaps already

---

[31] Cf. PG88.632A. The full title of Sophronius' edition is: '*Ladder of Divine Ascent*, that is, an ascetic treatise by Abba John, Abbot of the monks of Mount Sinai, sent by him to Abba John, Abbot of Raithou. It is divided into thirty chapters similar to the rungs of a ladder, which lift those who follow it from the lower to the higher places. This is why the book has been named *Ladder*.' For other translations of the *Ladder*, see the Conclusion.

[32] Cf. 3.35 (669B), 5–10 (777C), 15.44 (889AB) and 27.ii,2 (1105BC).

abbot, understood well the tribulations faced by such monks. The modern reader must keep all this in mind and not suppose that John intended people to be put off by, for instance, the fifth step relating to repentance, and especially by the horrendous account of the monastic penitentiary of Alexandrian Prison in the same step.[33]

Chitty believes that writers of John's generation seem to have an instinct that they were living at the end of an epoch, one which summed up the teaching of the preceding centuries[34] but which was at the same time open-minded, forward-looking and somewhat unprecedented. This claim, as already observed, in many ways provides the fundamental focus of this book. However, for John's purposes, this meant that before he could even proceed to write down a teaching intended specifically for monks, he needed first to proclaim the universality of the creator God.[35] He felt the urge to underline the fact that salvation was for all, and that marriage is in no way an impediment in the spiritual life,[36] although a married person must not expect to equal the attainments of a monk.[37] He understood that chastity is by no means a monastic monopoly – and here John quotes the apostle Peter as an example.[38]

Two related points, then, should be kept in mind when reading the *Ladder*. First, the *Ladder* was written specifically for monks in a *cenobium*.[39] And, second, the work is relevant to lay people, too; the *Ladder* has indeed over centuries influenced many monks and married people alike. Symeon the New Theologian finds the *Ladder* in the library of his father, a layman of the tenth-century aristocracy.[40] It must be remembered that the monastic way of life is essentially 'the life according to the Gospel.'[41] All are invited to respond to Christ's call to salvation. While the circumstances of the response may vary externally, nevertheless the path is effectively one. In the spiritual life, there is no sharp distinction between monastics and non-monastics: the monastic life is simply the Christian life, lived in a particular way. Monks are Christians who have discovered special possibilities of imitating Christ and transcending

---

[33] Cf. 5.5–7 (764D–77B). Cf. also Chitty, *Desert*, 174. For further proof that throughout the centuries people have understood the *Ladder* as addressed to monks in a *cenobium*, cf. *Menaion*, Canon Ode 1, *Troparion* 4 and Ode 4, *Troparion* 2; cf. also Triodion, Canon Ode 3, *Troparion* 1. A fourteenth-century manuscript of the *Ladder* at the Monastery of Stavronikita on Mt Athos (*Codex* 915. f.50) contains a miniature depicting John writing his book *within* the walls of the monastery.

[34] Chitty, *Desert*, 173.

[35] 1.4 (633A).

[36] 2.7–9 (656BC).

[37] 2.15 (657B) and 1.38 (640C). Climacus' line is very similar to that of *Apophth.* Antony 19 (PG65.81BC).

[38] 15.66 (893D–96A).

[39] 27.ii,7 (110BC).

[40] Cf. Hausherr, *Vie* 6, p. 12.

[41] Basil, *Ep.* 207, 2 (PG32.761B). Cf. also Athanasius, *Life of Antony* 23 (PG26.876C–77A).

normal conditions:[42] 'l'hésychaste, c'est le chrétien fait prière.'[43] Viller-Rahner may accuse Climacus of having rendered narrower the evangelical way (Mt. 7.13) through his strict ascetic teaching,[44] but this 'way' is no more than another, or an alternative, relationship with God. Other 'ways' may seem wider and easier but may bear little or no relation to the experience of the victory over death, which characterizes the Christian life, the goal at which the *Ladder* aims. Such a clarification is paramount for an appreciation of the *Ladder*. 'The *Ladder* is an invitation to pilgrimage,'[45] an invitation extended to all those who wish to be saved (*Prologue* 628C), provided they sincerely seek salvation (625A).

John admits that he primarily wants to write down an account of his own personal experience during his forty-year stay in the Sinaite desert, an account that is supposed to stimulate a parallel personal experience in those who read the *Ladder*. This is precisely why it is, indirectly, addressed to all readers. It is personal experience, then, that Climacus continually emphasizes in eliciting a response, in provoking his readers to a leap of faith, in bringing them to the point of personal commitment and encounter.[46] For John, the meaning of the ascetic life lies much deeper than mere acceptance of certain doctrines and rules:

> Just as it is impossible to learn to see by word of mouth, because seeing depends on one's own natural sight, so it is impossible to learn the beauty of prayer from the teaching of others.[47]

The aim is clearly spiritual and pastoral, rather than didactic or normative. John usually refrains from giving detailed instructions about liturgical offices,

---

[42] 26.53–5 (1029D). On silence and community, cf. G. Gould, *The Desert Fathers on Monastic Community*, esp. 88–106, and 139–66.

[43] Hausherr, 'Théologie du monachisme,' 376. On the urbanization of asceticism, cf. S. Elm, '*Virgins of God*,' esp. 311–72. Throughout the patristic tradition, there is an understanding that monasticism is not essentially different from the lay or married life of a Christian: cf. Basil, *Sermo Asceticus* 1 (PG31.881B); Chrysostom, *Adversus oppugnatores vitae monasticae* 3.14 (PG47.374–75); *Mac. Hom.* 38.1 (271); Palladius, *Hist. Laus.*, Paisius and Isaiah 15 and 16 (cf. ed. Butler, 37–8); Mark Monk, *Disp. cum quodam causidico* 1 (PG65.1072B) and Symeon the New Theologian, *Cat.* 22 (382–4) and *Cat.* 28 (138). The ways of salvation could not be restricted to one outward form: cf. Palladius, *Hist. Laus.*, Pambo 15–16 (ed. Butler, 38–9); Cassian, *Conf.* 13–15 (174–6). Men and women alike could be sanctified: cf. Theodoret, *Phil. Hist.*, Peter, 9.12, p. 428 (1385B), and abstention from marriage was by no means regarded as an end in itself: cf. Greg. Nyssa, *De Virg.* 18 (PG46.393A). In fact, lay people can often acquire greater virtues than monks: cf. *Hist Monachorum*, 14, Paphnutius 5, 10 and 18 (103, 105 and 108). For more detailed discussion, see Ware, 'The Monk.'

[44] *Aszese*, p. 158. Cf. also Viller, *Spiritualité*, 89.

[45] G. Florovsky, *Questions disputées*, Paris: 1935, 105–106.

[46] Cf. Ware, *Introduction*, 10.

[47] 28.63 (1140C). Cf. also 25.1 (988AB) and *Shep.* 1 (1165C).

techniques of prayer, methods and hours of *ascesis*, or foods from which to abstain. He offers no intellectual or moral regulations,[48] but instead provides a path of initiation, a way of life consisting ultimately of erotic ascent towards God.[49] What matters for him are not external, physical rules of asceticism as such but the interior disposition, not an uncompromising obedience to ethical demands but humility and purity of heart:

> David did not say, 'I have fasted,' 'I have kept vigil,' or 'I have lain on the bare earth,' but 'I humbled myself, and straightaway the Lord saved me.' (Ps. 114:6).[50]

As regards the external rules, Climacus knows that he is writing for monks, who would already know about these from their life in the monastery. He takes it for granted that the monks will already be aware of these, and does not discuss this aspect. His purpose is always to indicate the inner spirit and meaning behind and beyond the outward rule.

The *Ladder* is an existential work, concerned with concrete experience, intended for monks but equally relevant to every reader, laypersons included, who are resolved to ascend. 'Only those who read it existentially will appreciate its value.'[51]

Style and Structure

The style and structure of the *Ladder* give an impression of certain disjointedness. The Greek of the original is rough, reflecting somewhat the arid desert in which it was conceived. Yet there is a certain subtlety to it, too, together with a conscious artistry all its own. Ehrhard believes that its style is 'popular and free from all oratorical flourish;'[52] but there are also traces of a more cultivated rhetoric. There is a deliberate word-play in many passages,[53] and one also discovers a freshness, spontaneity and purity reminiscent of the *Apophthegmata* of the desert elders during the

---

[48] 7.69 (816C), 26.20 and 37 (1020B, 1025B).

[49] 1.48 (644A), 7.35 (813B).

[50] 25.14 (992D). If, for example, John does not mention the sacrament of Communion at all, it is not because he ignores or undermines it but because he takes it for granted. Nevertheless, the sacraments, and more particularly Communion, are certainly implied in 28.52 (1137C).

[51] Ware, *Introduction*, p. 8. The *Ladder* also offers many interesting parallels, which cannot be discussed here, with existential philosophy and depth-psychology. See the article by Georgoulis in the bibliography and, to a lesser extent, Hausherr, 'Théologie du monachisme,' 377; cf. also the articles by Kornarakis and Sumner in the bibliography; Bogdanovic, *Jean Climaque*, 99–126; *Introduction* (ed. Paraclete), 7.

[52] Quoted in Krumbacher, *Geschichte*, p. 143.

[53] 5.5 (772) and 15.2–3 (880D). On Climacus' enigmatic and proverbial phrases, cf. K. Krumbacher, *Mittelgriechische Sprichwörter*, Munich: 1893, 227–34 and S.G. Mercati, 'Pretesi versi politici in Giovanni Climaco e Giovanni Mosco,' *Byzantinische Zeitschrift*, 33 (1933), 32.

third and fourth centuries. The *Ladder* even contains a number of its own anecdotes and sayings, which make up a small *Gerontikon*.[54] John also displays a monastic sense of humour in many of his illustrations, which are quaint in character: 'like a man who is swimming and wants to clap his hands.'[55]

The strong personality of the author, his high spiritual culture and the homogeneity of his conviction make this work at once traditional and original, a work belonging to a particular school yet, at the same time, to the whole world.[56] The author's character clearly emerges in the course of the book: he has a sharp eye for the weaknesses of his fellow-monks, a balanced sense of humour, and a surprisingly compassionate realism, combined with an awareness of divine grace. Often John is intentionally puzzling – and in this he follows the parables of the Gospels, the *Sayings of the Desert Fathers*, and also resembles the Zen masters and their koans, or the Sufis and their 'scatter' technique. Yet John also delights in the use of cryptic phrases, such as: 'I shall be silent about what follows,'[57] deliberate negations which aim to stress an affirmation,[58] and imagery from diverse domains of life, including family,[59] royalty,[60] courts of law,[61] medicine,[62] military,[63] countryside,[64] garden,[65] sea,[66] school,[67] and even married life.[68] The metaphorical forms used are many: one example is the personification of various passions.[69] In fact, the numbers and letters themselves have a symbolical character in the *Ladder*: the thirty steps, to take but one example, symbolize the perfect age of Christ's maturity, namely

---

[54] Cf. 4.21 (689AC), 25 (693C–96A), 26 (696BD), 29 (697B–700A), 111 (720A–21A); and 6.20 (796C–97B).

[55] 6.12 (796A).

[56] Couilleau, 'Saint Jean Climaque,' *DS* 8, 372.

[57] 1.19 (636C) and 27.ii,6 (1108AB). Cf. also 25.16 (993A); 26.24 (1021A) and 27.3 (1105C).

[58] Cf. especially Step 5; for example 5.5 (765A–77A). Only representative examples are given in each of the following cases.

[59] 3.2 (665D–68A); 7.51 (813A) and 8.17 (829CD).

[60] 25.55 (1001A); 7.40 (808D–09A) and 15.78 (901AB).

[61] 8.31 (833D–36A); 15.83 (901C–04B) and 28.1 (1129AB).

[62] 5.12 (777D); 8.8 (828D) and 10.1 (845BC).

[63] 4.68 (712A); 14.5 (864D–65A) and 15.10 (381BC).

[64] 10.17 (848D); 12.1 (853D) and 15.39 (888D).

[65] 4.32 (701BD). A garden, possibly dating to Byzantine times, still exists in the region of John's cell: see Dahari, *Monastic Settlements*, 69.

[66] 4.52 (708BC); 6.12 (796A). Sea imagery – together with the medical and countryside images – is the most prevalent. It is possible to conclude from this that Climacus' early years must have been spent near the coast (cf. Rabois-Bousquet and Salaville, 'Saint Jean Climaque,' 442–3) and, in view of his being well educated, perhaps on a large country estate of a rich family. His estate may have overlooked the sea. These suggestions, however, remain speculative.

[67] 26.14 (101AC).

[68] 26.ii,35 (1065D).

[69] 13.10 (860D–61A) and 14.32 (869B–72A).

Christ's hidden life before his baptism, and consequently the spiritual maturity of the monk (*Prologue* 629C);[70] and in Step 26 John lists two 'alphabets' of the ascetic life.[71] Climacus' prose at times acquires a rhythmic and even poetic quality.[72] A strict and rough prose-writer, although the abruptness is often deliberate, John is also an impressive and inspired artist.

Rhythmical, paradoxical, ironic,[73] his language is at the same time intricately theological:[74] the imagery can be Triadological or Christological.[75] Dogma is constantly paralleled or even identified with ethics; doctrinal themes appear to overflow into practical ones;[76] the purely ascetic is continually being raised to the deeply mystical and even intricately theological level.[77] Nevertheless, the explicitly theological statements are not very frequent.

Hausherr observes that the *Ladder* portrays 'un véritable essai de systématisation, comme son titre même l'indique.'[78] Although John refers to himself as a 'second-rate architect,'[79] the doctrines are well linked and consequential: he always explains the position of each saying, the significance of each digression. However, while the logical gradation and method of the development in the principal theme can be shown, the composition is not rigorously faithful to it, and John tends to be less systematic and often rather repetitive. Whatever deliberate patterns may be discerned in his work, there is no systematization in any formal discursive sense.

The basic image used in the *Ladder* is that found in Genesis 28.12.[80] The use of the 'ladder' in the spiritual life is not unknown in earlier Christian authors and even in antiquity,[81] but it is far more fully developed in John. In fact, it is precisely this image that gives the entire book its distinct flavour and unity. In this respect, its use in John's work is entirely unprecedented. It also influenced

---

[70] Brief *Summary* (1161A).

[71] 26.14 (1017AC). On the importance of alphabets in the ascetic tradition, cf. F. Noah (de Angelis-), 'La méditation de Barsanuphe sur la lettre *êta*,' *Byzantion* 53 (1983), fasc. 2, 494–506.

[72] Cf. Bogdanovic, *Jean Climaque*, 222.

[73] 17.3 (932B–33A) and 19.9 (941AB).

[74] 25.4 (992D).

[75] 6.4 (793BC).

[76] Cf. Bogdanovic, *Jean Climaque*, 218.

[77] Cf. Archim. Sophrony, 'Trois renoncements,' 395.

[78] Cf. *La Méthode*, 136.

[79] 27.ii,2 (1105B).

[80] 30.18 (1160BD).

[81] Origen was first among Christian authors to use this image as a symbol of spiritual progress: cf. *Comm. on Joh.* 19.6 (ed. Preuschen, in *GCS* 4, 304–35). Cf. also Greg. Naz., *Or.* 43.71 (PG36.529D); Chrysostom, *Hom. on Joh.* 83.5 (PG59.454–55); Theodoret, *Phil Hist.* 27 (PG82.1484C); Barsanuphius 85. Cf. A. B. Cook, *Zeus: A Study in Ancient Religion*, Cambridge: Cambridge University Press, 1925, 114–40; E. Bertand and A. Rayez, 'Echelle spirituelle,' *DS* 4, Paris: 1958, 62–86.

later iconography in monastery churches and refectories, especially from the eleventh century onwards.[82]

In regard to structure, the *Ladder* can be separated into three unequal parts:

Steps 1–3: the break with the 'world,' or renunciation;
Steps 4–26: the 'active life,' or practical way; and
Steps 27–30: the 'contemplative life,' or 'theoria.'

The second section can likewise be divided into two parts:

Steps 4–7: the four fundamental virtues – obedience, repentance, remembrance of death and joyful sorrow;
Steps 8–26: the passions and their contrasting virtues.

The general scheme is as follows:

A   BREAK WITH THE WORLD

1	Renunciation
2	Detachment
3	Exile

B   VIRTUES AND PASSIONS

Fundamental Virtues

4	Obedience
5	Repentance
6	Remembrance of Death
7	Joyful Sorrow

The Struggle against the Passions

(a) Passions that are predominantly Non-Physical

8	Anger
9	Malice
10	Slander
11	Talkativeness
12	Falsehood
13	Despondency

---

[82] Cf. Martin, *Illustration* and Heppell, *Introduction*, 29–31.

(b) Passions that are predominantly Physical and Material

14   Gluttony
15   Lust
16–17   Avarice

(c) Passions that are predominantly Non-Physical and Spiritual

18–20   Insensitivity
21   Fear
22   Vainglory
23   Pride (including Blasphemy)

Higher Virtues of the 'Active Life'

24   Simplicity
25   Prayer
26   Discernment

C UNION WITH GOD

27   Stillness
28   Prayer
29   Dispassion
30   Love[83]

As for the Evagrian distinction between the active life (*praxis*) and the contemplative life (*theoria*), John accepts this but does not adhere to it with any consistency, as will be shown in the following section of this chapter. In his mind, there can really be no sharp differentiation between the two; they are all but identical: *praxis* and *theoria* are interdependent, two aspects of a single reality. Indeed, the active and the contemplative are regarded as equivalents of repentance and theology. For John, then, even the 'ladder' image is intended not literally, but figuratively and dynamically. One may find oneself on the first rung, and yet one may achieve other heights. Or again, one may be very close to the top of the ladder but, for example, be required to mourn unceasingly.[84] Perhaps a way of interpreting the ladder in John's sense would be to say that one can reach the top in the ascent, even while still working one's way up lower

---

[83] I have followed the pattern of Ware (*Introduction*, 12–13), which I find the most appropriate and helpful. This pattern in turn follows Couilleau, 'Saint Jean Climaque,' DS 8, col. 373.

[84] 7.73 (816D). Cf. also Greg. Nyssa, *De Vita Moysis* 2 (PG44.401B).

down; and, by the same token, one may still be on the lower rungs and yet have reached the top.[85]

In addition to the above general structure, most steps in turn have an internal substructure, their own composition organized according to the following principles:

(i)   a brief introductory statement, often metaphorical in character;
(ii)   a series of short definitions, reminiscent of those in Aristotle;
(iii) an exposition of the theme at hand – a more detailed analysis, usually accompanied by several illustrative anecdotes, which add vivacity to the work;
(iv)   a terminal summary of the chapter, the conclusion of the step, normally comprising an exhortation through which the author attempts to encourage and inspire.

On examining the text more closely, one may actually recognize that the structure of the *Ladder* is fairly precise and even presents several skillfully balanced contrasts.[86] *Prima facie*, for instance, the total effect of the book may give a negative impression. Sixteen out of the thirty steps deal with vices to be avoided and, of the remaining fourteen, some are again seemingly negative: repentance, sorrow and dispassion. Nevertheless, this initial impression could be misleading, because the sixteen steps dealing with the

---

[85] Other commentators divide the *Ladder* into two separate and unequal sections:

(i)   Steps 1–23: the difficulties which one undergoes in the spiritual life; and
(ii)   Steps 24–30: the moral and theological values involved.

This structural pattern is suggested by Krumbacher (*Geschichte*, 143) and assumed also by Altaner (*Patrologie*, 468). The latter contends that the first section describes the vices, while the second describes the virtues. However, such a pattern is misleading in that the first section, Steps 1–23, does not in fact deal only with 'difficulties' but also, among other things, with the concepts of repentance, remembrance of death, joyful sorrow and meekness.

[86] Ware (cf. *Introduction*, p. 14), drawing on Couilleau (cf. 'Saint Jean Climaque,' *DS* 8, cols 373–4), gives two good examples:

(a)   I (Steps 1–3) balances III (Steps 27–30).
       II i (Steps 4–7) balances II iii (Steps 24–26).
       III ii b (Steps 14–17), which concerns physical passions, is flanked by two balancing sections, each of six steps, which deal with passions of a less physical character: II ii a (Steps 8–13) and II ii c (Steps 18–23).
(b)   Here are some examples of the 'type–antitype' structure:
       Step 2 (detachment)   Step 29 (dispassion)
       Step 4 (obedience)   Step 26 (discernment)
       Step 5 (repentance)   Step 25 (humility)
       Step 13 (despondency)   Step 18 (insensitivity).

vices deal at the same time with their corresponding virtues and are much shorter than the other fourteen, which are also not as negative as they may at first appear.

We have already mentioned the fact that John at least nominally adopts the *praxis–theoria* distinction of Evagrius. Why, then, should he say little on the contemplative life, deliberately concentrating on the active life, on the vices to be avoided and the virtues to be acquired? It is clear that John would like his readers to seek humility and repentance,[87] and not to aim at visions and ecstasies. In fact, the *Ladder* displays a marked sobriety with its cautions about dreams[88] and with its insistence on obedience (Step 4) and discernment (Step 26) – these two steps are in fact the longest of the entire book and clearly echo his Palestinian spiritual inheritance. John would prefer his readers to acquire continual tears[89] – his own mourning was exceptional. He possessed, as Daniel puts it, 'the fountain of tears, which we see in so few' (600C). However, he is also aware how dangerous tears can be, and how he himself was once deceived on this account.[90] When, on another occasion, in the Alexandrian *cenobium*, Climacus attempted to initiate a conversation about inner silence (*hesychia*), he was swiftly rebuked by the monks, who said:

> We, Father John, being material, live a material life, preferring to wage war according to the measure of our weakness ... considering it better to struggle with men ... than with demons.[91]

Hesychia is only for 'very few;'[92] theology is not for all.[93] John's reticence, then, on several matters is deliberate. He speaks at length about the warfare and struggle of the ascetic but avoids mentioning, or gives only few subtle hints about, the transfiguration of the ascetic or about the vision of divine light. Even on the subject of vices and virtues, which he does expound in detail, Climacus avows his limitations;[94] he is cautious in his advice and humbly defers to others, preferring instead to consult other ascetics.

Sources

The *Ladder* is a work reflecting a direct and personal experience on the author's part. Step 28 is a case in point, although Climacus never actually mentions that

---

[87] 14.8 (865B).
[88] 3.35–45 (669B–72B).
[89] 7.73 (816D).
[90] 15.39 (888D).
[91] 4.30 (700B).
[92] 4.21 (725C).
[93] 27.9 (1097C).
[94] 5.10 (777C).

his basis here is empirical. It is this that gives the book its originality. At the same time, however, it is also a book impregnated with tradition, a work of synthesis. While being one of Christian antiquity's most original spiritual books, it integrates into a single whole many distinct strands of previous tradition.[95] John certainly does borrow from earlier authors, but what he borrows he makes his own, rather than slavishly adhering to these authorities. A brief examination of the sources will suffice at this point, because throughout this study references will be made to parallels with or borrowings from other writers.

John makes explicit references to certain authors but, as is often the case in antiquity, without giving precise information where his passages or quotations are derived. There is clear evidence of his wide reading,[96] even where he admits knowledge through personal experience or that the purpose of the spiritual struggle is to be learned not by books.[97] For example, he explicitly names Origen[98] and Evagrius,[99] both with obligatory disapproval, as well as John Cassian,[100] Gregory the Theologian,[101] and Ephraim whom John simply calls 'the Syrian.'[102]

Apart from explicit and implicit references to other authors, John further alludes to certain elders, who are his contemporaries and whom he either knows personally or else has heard about. In this connection, we learn of John the Sabbaite,[103] George of Arselaũm,[104] the monk Menas and the Archdeacon Macedonius at Alexandria, together with other monks, such as Hesychius the Chorebite,[105] at the *cenobium* in Alexandria.[106] 'Some told me very honestly,' 'a certain person related to me,' and 'I heard from someone' are not unusual expressions in the *Ladder*.[107]

Let us look more carefully now at John's debt to his sources. If we examine the *Ladder* closely, we can first discover references to classical philosophy, although these are rare. John refers to 'meditation on death,' but his statement

---

[95] Viller, *Spiritualité*, 88; and Ware, *Introduction*, 59, 66.

[96] 26.29 (1021C–24B).

[97] 26.29 (1021C–24B) and *Shep.* 5 (1165BC).

[98] 5.29 (780D) and he implies him in 14.5 (865D) and 6.11 (798A).

[99] 14.8 (865A) and he implies him in 13.8 (860C); 16.24 (929BC); 21.1 (948D–49A); 26.2 (1013AB), 29 (1021C–24B) and 27.ii,9 (1109A).

[100] 4.105 (717B).

[101] 21.1 (948D–49A); 26.ii,19 (1064A) and he implies him in 28.52 (1137C); 15.1 (880D) and 29 (885D). The passage in 21.1 (949A) referring to the seven, not eight, passions probably refers to Gregory the Great, *In Caput 39 B.Job* 87 (PL76.621A), since one looks in vain for such a passage in Gregory of Nazianzus.

[102] 29.5 (1148D).

[103] 4.111 (720A–21A).

[104] 27.ii,22 (1112B).

[105] 6.20 (796C–97A).

[106] 4.29 (697C) and 26 (696B) and 5.5 (765A–77A).

[107] 7.50; 7.54; and 22.6 (965CD). Cf. also 15.58 (892CD) and *Shep.* 17 (1172D).

is fairly general and need not imply a direct influence by Plato.[108] The tripartite division of the human soul into *pathos* (*pathetikon*), *thymos* (*thymikon*) and *logos* (*logistikon*) in the treatise *To the Shepherd* is another case of the use of philosophical propositions. Nevertheless, this too might be taken not directly from pagan writers but from Christian sources, such as Gregory the Theologian or Evagrius.[109]

It is the Bible that John quotes most abundantly. Situated closer to Jerusalem than to Athens – geographically, theologically and spiritually – John considers the Bible to be his fundamental source.[110] Indeed, what characterizes John is the adaptation of biblical texts, by either adding or omitting words, so as to make them fit appropriately into a particular context or concept.[111] The end of Step 30 can easily be placed alongside Saint Paul's hymn of love (1 Cor. 13).[112]

There is no certainty as to whether Climacus had any direct knowledge of the fourth-century theologians, such as Basil the Great (329–79) or John Chrysostom (*c.* 347–407).[113] However, Gregory Nazianzus (329–79) is explicitly mentioned in the *Ladder* and greatly influenced its author. This can be clearly seen even in passages which do not actually refer to Gregory by name but which betray an obvious acquaintance with his writing.[114] Elsewhere, John refers to Gregory simply as 'the theologian'[115] or shows that he was directly influenced by some Gregorian doctrine, as for example in the matter of the connection between prayer and respiration; in the latter case, while in Gregory the meaning is merely metaphorical, in John it is both metaphorical and literal.[116] In another passage, Gregory is again not mentioned by name but there is an unmistakable reference to him in the *Scholia*.[117] One may also say with some assurance that John was familiar with the works of Gregory of

---

[108] Compare 6.26 (797C) with Plato, *Phaedo* 67e. However, Climacus' more probable source is the *Apophthegmata*: cf. Sarah 6 (PG65.421A); Rufus 1 (389BC) and Nau 1182 (1908, p. 271).

[109] *Shep.* 100 (1205B).

[110] Cf. 7.26 (805CD) and 26.ii,44 (1069AB). On the role and influence of Scripture in the quest for holiness in the ascetic tradition, cf. D. Burton-Christie, *The Word in the Desert*.

[111] Cf. 4.20 (688D); 26.ii,38 (1068B), 44 (1069AB); 27.ii,13 (1109C) and 28.28 (1133C).

[112] Cf. Paschos, *Eros*, 453.

[113] Compare, however, Basil, *Ep.* 2 (PG32.228A) – concerning the intellect and its return to God – with 27.5 (1097B) and 28.16–17 (1132C); and Chrysostom, *De Pascha* (PG59.721–24) – concerning death and resurrection – with 4.43 (705B).

[114] Compare 15.83 (901D–04B) with *Or.* 14,7 (PG38.65BC); 27.9 (1097C) with *Or. Theol.* 1,3 (PG36.12C–16A) and *Or.* 20,1 and 3 (PG35.1065B–168A and 1069A); 27.ii,34 (1113B) with *Or.* 40,45 (PG36.421D–25A); 28.52 (1137C) with *Or.* 40,36 (PG36.409C–12B) and 15.1 (880D) with *Or.* 45,8 (PG36.632C–33B).

[115] 28.52 (1137BD).

[116] Compare 27.ii,26 (1112C) with *Or.* 27,4 (PG36.16B). This issue is further discussed in Chapter 7 on prayer.

[117] 15.29 (885CD) and *Scholion* 18 of Step 15 (909A).

Nyssa (*c.* 330–95), who may have proved influential on such topics as the human person,[118] the passions,[119] dispassion and salvation,[120] the vision of God,[121] deification,[122] death,[123] as well as the relationship between body and soul.[124] This Gregory's notion of *epektasis* is implied in several passages of the *Ladder*,[125] although without mention of the specific term itself. One may, however, find traces of this doctrine in Step 29, on dispassion, where it is found in the form of *epekteinomenos*, although here John is thinking primarily of Philippians 3.13.[126]

John of the *Ladder* is familiar with the more intellectualist tradition, earlier, of Origen (185–254) and, later, Evagrius (349–99). There are even particular traces of influence by the latter, even though Climacus only mentions him once and with disapproval.[127] It would, however, be wrong to say that Climacus belongs to an Evagrian 'school.' The *Ladder* analyses in some detail the eight vices and speaks of mother – or, correspondingly, of daughter – virtues and vices. This analysis may disclose many obvious similarities between the two authors. Yet the similarities are not due to any common philosophical or Origenist assumptions but rather to a common spiritual experience found in the desert tradition and in the discipline of *ascesis*.[128] It is a gross simplification

---

[118] Compare 15.83 (901C–04B) with *De an. et resurr.* (PG46.124C); 15.1 (880CD) with *De hom. opif.* 17 and (PG44.188A–92A and 204B–09A).

[119] Compare 26.41 (1028A) and 26.ii,41 (1068CD) with *De hom. opif.* 18 (PG44.193B).

[120] Compare 29.5 (1148D) with *De vita S. Patris Ephraem Syri* (PG46.820–49). Cf. also *De beat.* 2 (PG44.1280CD).

[121] Compare 29.3 (1149C) and *Shep.* 100 (1025A) with *De Vita Moysis* (PG44.297B).

[122] Compare 29.3 (1149CD) with *De beat.* (PG44.1280CD).

[123] Compare 4.43 (705B) with *Cat. Or.* 35 (PG45.88D–89A).

[124] Compare 15.73 (896C–97C) and 26.54 (1029D) with *De hom. opif.* 12 and 15 (PG44.160 and 177).

[125] 26.37–38 (1068AB) and 30.18 (1160B). For this notion in Gregory, cf. J. Daniélou, *Platonisme et théologie mystique. Doctrine spirituelle de Saint Grégoire de Nysse*, Paris: 1953, 291–307; J. Daniélou, 'La colombe et la ténèbre dans la mystique byzantine ancienne,' *Eranos Jahrbuch* 23 (1954), 403; *From Glory to Glory*, ed. H. Mursurillo, London: 1962, 46f.; and E. Ferguson, 'Progress in Perfection: Gregory of Nyssa's *Vita Moysis*,' *Studia Patristica* 14 (Berlin, 1976), 307–14.

[126] 29.2 (1148C). In any case, Gregory of Nyssa himself uses the term only once in a mystical sense. Although the 'theology of *epektasis*,' implicit in Climacus, is a fundamental concept in Gregory's thought, it is more a development of Jean Daniélou: cf. A. Louth, *The Origins of the Christian Mystical Tradition from Plato to Denys*, Oxford: Clarendon Press, 1981, 89–90.

[127] 14.8 (865A). Cf. Lot-Borodine, 'Déification,' 527, who says that Climacus' spiritual roots clearly lie in Evagrius.

[128] Cf. C. Yannaras, *Metaphysike*, 60. In his book, a doctoral dissertation, Yannaras comes perhaps closest to the subjects examined in the present study. Although the approach is neither systematic nor analytical, and, with few exceptions, Yannaras does not focus attention on John's sources or influences, nevertheless Yannaras' book is a vibrant, contemporary dialogue with the ascetic theology of an early monastic author.

to classify the *Ladder* as a 'system' analogous to the Evagrian. In fact, the *Ladder* as a whole is not susceptible of 'systematization.' John borrows ideas and vocabulary from Evagrius; but he does not borrow any methodology or system. Similarities can thus be detected in the description of the temptations[129] and in the second alphabet of virtues,[130] in the development of the notions of 'insensitivity' and 'dispassion,' as well in the stress upon the 'laying aside of concepts.'[131] Likewise John's demonology and his analysis of the vices is influenced by Evagrius' work *De octo spiritibus malitiae* that survives in the *corpus* of Nilus.[132] But John does not follow the Evagrian classification of vices, nor any other scheme for that matter, with any degree of accuracy.[133] The Sinaite ascetic may agree with Evagrius in closely linking dispassion and love,[134] but he completely discards the Evagrian cosmology and gnosiology. For John, love is the primary virtue,[135] whereas for Evagrius *gnosis* is superior to love. Evagrius' influence upon Climacus may be more aptly described as terminological or, at most, merely formal. Even the terminological affinities are far less pronounced than, for instance, in Maximus the Confessor. For Evagrius, the return to oneself is an entirely intellectual act; for Climacus it involves body, intellect and soul.[136] As we have already seen, even the fundamental Evagrian distinction between *praxis* and *theoria* is not followed consistently by John,[137] who, while stressing the active rather than the contemplative life, neither questions their unity nor makes any attempt to separate the two. There are, of course, two sides to Evagrius himself: on the one hand, there is the Origenist, more speculative Evagrius; and on the other, there is his more apophthegmatic, practical side. The Evagrian influence on John is present but not profound, and it is predominantly from the latter side of Evagrius that John borrows. And, in that respect, both authors may have more in common with the desert tradition of Egypt than with each other.

---

[129] 15.73 (896C–97B). Völker seems to overemphasize the influence of Evagrius (as of Cassian) on John, but the parallels he discovers between the author of the *Ladder* and Maximus the Confessor are of interest.

[130] 26.14 (1017BC).

[131] Compare 27.ii,17 (1112A) with *De or.* 70 (PG79.1181C).

[132] PG 79.1145–64.

[133] Ware, *Introduction*, 63–4, especially n. 242–3 concerning the Evagrian scheme and n. 244–7 concerning the sevenfold scheme.

[134] For Evagrius, cf. *Prakt.* Prologue and 81 (482–94 and 670).

[135] 30.18 (1160D).

[136] 27.5 (1097B) and 28.6–20 (1132). For the influence of Evagrius on Maximus, cf. M. Viller, 'Aux sources de la spiritualité de S. Maxime: les oeuvres d'Evagre le Pontique,' *RAM* 2 (1930), 156–84 and 239–68; H. U. von Balthasar, *Kosmische Liturgie. Das Weltbild Maximus' des Bekenners*, 2nd edn, Einsiedeln: 1961, 482–643. Cf. also Meyendorf, *Palamas*, 150–51.

[137] Cf. 4.2 (677D) and 26.25 (1021B).

John's use of and indebtedness to the *Sayings of the Fathers* (fourth–fifth centuries) is very apparent throughout the work but especially, for example, in Step 29 on dispassion. His discussion of the spiritual father uses sayings of Abba Antony,[138] whom John also mentions explicitly,[139] together with *Sayings* by Paul the Simple[140] and Arsenius the Great.[141] Elsewhere, the *Ladder* can only be understood by referring to the *Apophthegmata*; thus John asks why there were not as many luminaries among the holy Tabennisiotes as among the Scetiotes, but provides no answer.[142] The answer is provided by the first *Saying* of Abba Amoun of Nitria: 'Abba Antony answered, "it is because I love God more than you".'[143] The connection with the desert of Egypt will be underlined throughout my study. It is precisely one of the aims of this study to indicate the direct influence of the *Sayings* on the *Ladder*.

In fact, at least as Daniel describes it, John's whole life in many ways reflected the Desert Fathers' *Sayings*: 'He ate of everything that is allowed by the monastic vow, but he ate extremely little (600A).'[144] If any of John's utterances appear 'foolish,' such as those describing the Alexandrian Prison,[145] they nonetheless reflect the same peculiarity of the *Apophthegmata*[146] and, ultimately, the 'folly' of the Cross (1 Cor. 1.18). It is clear that John was familiar with the early desert tradition, including the *Sayings* themselves, as well as other formative sources, such as Pachomius' *First Greek Life* (c. 390),[147] Palladius' *Lausiac History* (419–20),[148] John Moschus' *Spiritual Meadow* (615–19),[149] *The Story of Thais* (fifth century),[150] and the *Life of Saint Pelagia*.[151]

---

[138] *Sayings* 37–8 (PG65.88B). On obedience and spiritual direction in the *Ladder*, see J. Chryssavgis, *Soul Mending* (2000). Compare also 18.6 (937D) with Antony 1 (76AB); 15.27 (885BC) with Antony 14 (80AC); 29.5 (1148D) with Antony 32 (85C); 27.ii,29 (1112D) with Arsenius 7 (89AB); *PTO* 15.76 (900D) with Ammonas 7 (121A) and Elias 7 (184D–85A); 4.106 (717C) with John the Theban (240AB); 26.ii,25 (1064C), with Simon 1 (412CD); 29.3 (1148) with Tithoes 1 (428B); 26.ii,25 (1064C) with Timothy (429AB) and 15.48 (889C) with Nau 291 (1909, pp. 376–7).

[139] 15.27 (885BC) and 18.6 (937D).

[140] 24.13 (984C).

[141] 27.ii,29 (111CD).

[142] 27.ii,3 (1105C).

[143] PG 65.128B.

[144] Compare Daniel's words with *Apophth*. Ammonas 4 (120BC) and Poemen 31 (329C).

[145] 5.5–7 (764D–77B).

[146] Cf. *Apophth*. Antony 25 (84C); Arsenius 37 (104AB); Ammonas 9 (121C); Nau 61 (1907, p. 181).

[147] Compare 27.ii,54 (1117A) with the *Vita Prima* 6 (pp. 4–5, p. 162).

[148] Compare 24.13 (984C) with *Hist. Laus.* 23 (pp. 62–3) and 25.40 (997C) with 37 (1098D–99B). Cf. also *Introduction* (ed. Paraclete), 426, n. 2.

[149] Compare 26.10 (1016AB) with *Pratum* 112 (2977AB).

[150] Compare 26.ii,25 (1064C) with *Thais*, in *Annales du Musée Guimet*, 30.51.

[151] Compare 15.58 (892CD) with *Vita S. Pelagiae* 3 (PL73.665AC).

John also explicitly refers to John Cassian (*c.* 365–*c.* 435), whom he calls 'great.'[152]

Moreover, there are affinities, if these are not sufficiently strong for us to speak of direct influences, even with the *Macarian Homilies* (fourth–fifth centuries),[153] especially in the anthropological monism of the Macarius, with the notion of the heart as the center of the human person[154] and the primacy attributed there to love. Although the Holy Spirit is referred to less frequently than in Macarius, John seems to be opposed both to an extreme spiritualism and an extreme intellectualism alike, thereby achieving a kind of synthesis between Evagrius and Macarius – a task inaugurated already by Mark the Monk and Diadochus of Photice.

While there is no reference to either Mark the Monk (early fifth century) or Diadochus of Photice (mid-fifth century) by name, John was probably familiar with their writings. The relationship with Mark is more certain than with Diadochus. From the former, John drew his analysis of temptation in Step 15.[155] Phrases and certain terms such as *pararripismos noos*[156] or *protonoia*,[157] as well as the analogies in Step 26, indicate the same source.[158] From the latter, John derived such elements as his aforementioned reservation in respect of dreams,[159] his understanding of prayer without mental images,[160] the invocation 'Lord Jesus' in prayer,[161] his view of dispassion as something positive,[162] and his concept of the 'spiritual senses.'[163] Diadochus also speaks of the withdrawal of God's grace, even adopting the same metaphor of the mother with the child.[164] Nevertheless, although the parallels with Diadochus

---

[152] 4.105 (717B). Compare 21.1 (984D–49A) with *Inst.* 11,1 (428); 4.105 (717BC) with *Conf.* 2,10 (120–21); 13.10 (861A) with *Conf.* 17,6 (253). Cassian's influence can also be seen in 2.9 (657A); 7.40 and 42 (808D–09A); 21.30 (956B); 22.1,6 and 10 (965BD and 968A). Climacus was also perhaps influenced by a compilation of Cassian, *De octo vitiosis cogitationibus*, translated into Greek and attributed to Nilus (PG79.1435–72). Cf. also Archim. Sophrony, 'Trois renoncements.'

[153] Cf. Yannaras, *Metaphysike*, 172 who quotes *Mac. Hom.* 43,7 (p. 289) as an example. Cf. also Bogdanovic, *Jean Climaque*, 222 and Ware, *Introduction*, 60–61.

[154] Compare 28.57 (1140) and 7.18 (805A) with *Mac Hom.* 15,20 (p. 139).

[155] 15.73 (896C–97C).

[156] Compare 15.73 (897B) with *Ad Nic.* 7 (1040B).

[157] 26.76 (1036AB). Compare 22.6 (965D) with *De lege spir.* 146 (921C) and 28.57 (1140A) with *De his* 139 (952B).

[158] Compare 26.iii,20f. (1088A) with *De his* 73f. (941).

[159] Compare 3.35–45 (669B–72B) with *Cent.* 36–38 (pp. 105–107).

[160] Compare 27.ii,17 (1112A) with *Cent.* 59 (p. 119). But this could be from Evagrius: compare 18.5 (937CD) with *De or.* 8 and 114–19 (PG79.1169AB and 1192D–93A).

[161] Compare 28.9 (1132B) and 15.51 (889D) with *Cent.* 31 (p. 101), 59 (p. 119), 61 (pp. 120–21), 85 (pp. 144–5), 88 (pp. 147–8), 97 (pp. 159–60).

[162] Cf. *Cent.* 17 (pp. 93–4).

[163] Cf. G. Horn, 'Sens de l'esprit d'après Diadoque de Photicé,' *RAM* 8 (1927), 404, n. 3.

[164] Compare 5.10 (777C) and 7.57 (813C) with *Cent.* 86–7 (pp. 154–7).

are interesting, they are not altogether convincing, especially since the most striking one – namely, the use of the expression 'Lord Jesus' – could possibly be borrowed from Barsanuphius.[165]

John's style of biblical exegesis, the manner in which he freely quotes and changes quotations from the Old and New Testament, is probably influenced by Nilus of Ancyra (fifth century). The influence is apparent in a number of passages, as already noted,[166] especially in connection with such subjects as sin,[167] the erotic relationship between God and humanity,[168] death and resurrection.[169] Nilus also speaks of the connection between prayer and breathing, although here, as in Gregory the Theologian, the meaning is metaphorical.[170]

Like Macarius, Dionysius the Areopagite (*c.* 500) is never mentioned by name in the *Ladder* and no distinct influences can be discovered here. Nevertheless, there are certain parallels – probably due to common sources rather than direct influence – as regards the themes of *eros*[171] and passions.[172] There is no explicit development of apophatic theology, but this underlies John's thinking and, in a way, his whole ascetic experience may be described as apophatic. The clearest apophatic statement made by John is found at the beginning of the thirtieth step on love, where John rejects any definition of God, except that of God as love.[173]

Obviously much indebted to the Palestinian school of Gaza (early sixth century), John could be seen as a deliberate continuator or direct successor of this school of spirituality. From this, and through this from the Egyptian desert, John inherited the significant idea and critical role of the spiritual elder, as well as a discriminating use of Evagrian terminology. Moreover, the unsystematic presentation of the *Ladder* is typical especially of Abba Dorotheus. The spiritual and linguistic affinity of John's doctrine to that of Barsanuphius, John the Prophet, and their disciple Dorotheus may be clearly detected in their common interpretation of the Pauline 'bear one another's

---

[165] Cf. Chapter 7, on 'Prayer.' Bogdanovic attaches too much importance to the influence of Macarius and Diadochus on Climacus while invalidating that of Barsanuphius and overlooking entirely that of Dorotheus: cf. *Jean Climaque*, 153–6. For the influence of Diadochus upon John, also see L. Bouyer, *Le Consolateur. Esprit-Saint et vie de Grâce*, Paris: 1980, 310.

[166] Cf. also *Shep.* 17 (1172D), mentioned in a *scholion* cited in *Ladder* (ed. Paraclete), 434, n. 3. Compare also 29.14 (1149BC) with *Liber monastica* 51 (PG79.781D).

[167] Compare 26.41 (1028AB) and 26.ii,41 (1068CD) with *Ep.* 2,229 (PG79.348D–49A).

[168] Compare 7.1 (801CD) and 30.1 (1153D–56A) with *Ep.* 3,169 (464A).

[169] Compare 4.43 (705B) with *Ep.* 2,78 (236AB).

[170] Compare 27.ii,6 (1112C) with *Ep.* 1,239 (169D).

[171] *De div. nom.* 4 (PG 3.712AB).

[172] *De div. nom.* 4 (720BC).

[173] 30.2 (1156AB). Cf. also 7.53 (813B), where it is clear that apophatic theology is not merely a 'style' of writing that Climacus uses.

burdens' (Gal. 6.2).[174] It is, as already stated, one of the purposes of this study to indicate the similarities between John and these authors. Another Palestinian writer, not however explicitly cited, on whom John seems to draw is Abba Isaiah of Scetis (d. 489); both have similar views on what is 'according to nature.'[175]

There are interesting parallels between John and Maximus the Confessor (*c.* 580–682). However, while the two are contemporaries, there is no evidence of any direct influence in either direction. Both, nevertheless, speak of the primacy of love and describe the character of the passions,[176] sin,[177] and even the two natures of Christ[178] in similar fashion. Though any watertight distinctions between modes of theology are often fruitless, one might say that John expressed in ascetic terminology what Maximus formulated in dogmatic theology. (See the biographical appendix below.)

It might be said that John lays the foundations for a new spiritual school, the 'Sinaite school,' which is commonly restricted to Hesychius (?seventh–eighth century) and Philotheus (?ninth–tenth century). The Sinaite tradition clearly and deeply influences the fourteenth–century Hesychasts, but they cannot in any strict sense be deemed part of the same school, otherwise the term 'Sinaite spirituality' may be misleading, ignoring fundamental geographical considerations.[179] Certainly, however, John shaped his immediate past in a unique way that would profoundly affect his successors, creating refreshing perspectives and even coining fresh terminology for the spiritual life, especially on such issues as tears and silence. Nonetheless, the shifting from one 'school' of spirituality, as that of Palestine, to another, as that of Sinai, is ultimately immaterial since what in fact is at stake is the appropriation of the deeper sources of spiritual life. Although it may be misleading to refer to a Sinaite 'school' as such, nevertheless the *Ladder* is undoubtedly responsible for fashioning a new synthesis, at once reminiscent of its Egyptian inheritance,

---

[174] Compare 4.18 (685D) with Barsanuphius 168–9 and Dorotheus, *Instr.* 4,56–7, (24–44) and 7,79 (288–90). Compare also 15.51 and 76 (889D and 900D) with Barsanuphius 39, 126, 255, 268, 446, 659 and Dorotheus, *Life of Dositheus* 10 (138). On Palestinian monasticism generally, cf. J. Binns, *Ascetics and Ambassadors of Christ*.

[175] Compare, for instance, 26.41 (1068CD) with *Logos* 2 (4–6). See J. Chryssavgis and P.R. Penkett, *Abba Isaiah of Scetis: Ascetic Discourses* (2002).

[176] Cf. *De ambig.* (PG91.1317AB) and *Cap. de car.* 3, 98 (PG90.1048A).

[177] Cf. *Schol. in div. nom.* 32 (PG4.305B).

[178] For Climacus' teaching, see 6.4 (793BC).

[179] For the broad sense of the term, 'Sinaite spirituality,' cf. Hausherr, 'Grands courants,' 132f. Nevertheless, Fr Hausherr later changed his mind and even criticized Fr Lev Gillet for speaking of a 'Sinaite school' in too wide a sense: cf. Hausherr, *Noms du Christ*, 247–8. Indeed, long before the appearance of this book, Hausherr had modified and toned down his original argument and was surprised that Gillet ignored this: cf. Hausherr, *Traité de Oraison*, 169f.

characteristic of its Sinaite environment, and influential on its Byzantine posterity.

Finally, some reference must be made to the *scholia*, which are placed together with their Latin translation at the conclusion of each step in the edition of Migne. Matthew Rader discovered these in the margins of his manuscripts. The *scholia* have in fact nothing to do with the humble Abbot of Raithou, John, although they have been attributed to him. Many have not as yet been identified[180] and, as a *corpus*, remain perhaps as the only trace in the Migne collection of an entire literature of translations originating in Franciscan evangelism. These *scholia* are especially influenced by the work of the Franciscan 'spiritual' Angelo Clareno (Angelo de Cingoli) who, around the year 1300, translated the *Ladder* when in exile and while living with the monks of Meteora in central Greece.[181] In addition to Angelo's collection and that found in Migne, another collection should be noted here: it is a rather voluminous commentary compiled by Elias of Crete which remains unpublished. Elias lived some time during the eighth century, but J. Darrouzès places him in the late eleventh to early twelfth century.[182] A brief but illuminating survey of the *scholia* found in Migne, even though some refer to authors who lived after Climacus and others are not even accurately attributed to their proper authors, reveals the number of times various authors may have been used or, at least, the frequency with which particular parallels can be drawn. The proportion, rather, between the authors cited probably reflects to a large extent the personal tastes and reading of the scholiast, rather than the standpoint of John the *Ladder*.

Isaac of Nineveh – 39 times

Mark the Monk – 22: under Mark's name, the commentator evidently includes many statements by Evagrius, which are somewhat ambiguous.

Maximus the Confessor – 22

Basil the Great – 14

Isaiah of Scetis – 10

John Chrysostom – 9

Evagrius of Pontus – 8: usually the quotations attributed to him are not in any way controversial theological statements but merely general points of interest.

---

[180] As early as 1918, Mariott had identified two *scholia* as coming from Macarius: cf. G. L. Mariott, *Macarii Anecdota. Seven Unpublished Homilies of Macarius*, in *Harvard Theological Studies* 5, Cambridge, MA: Harvard University Press, 1918, 44–5. But the majority of these identifications were to appear several years later: cf. articles by Peterson and Hofman in the bibliography.

[181] Cf. Gribomont, 'La *Scala Paradisi*,' 345–58.

[182] Cf. 'Elie de Crète,' *DS* 4,1 (1960), 574–5.

Photius the Great – 8
Amma Syncletica – 5
Thalassius – 5
Gregory of Nyssa – 4
Diadochus – 4
John of Carpathus – 4
Gregory the Theologian – 4
Nilus of Ancyra – 4: here, again, sayings of Evagrius are concealed.
Theodore of Edessa – 3
Abba Dorotheus – 2: the overall importance of the Gaza school for John's
    Ladder scarcely emerges from this comparison.
Isidore of Pelusium – 2
Abba Antony – 2
Abba Barsanuphius – 2: but in fact the similarities with Barsanuphius are far
    greater than this in the *Ladder*.
John Damascene – 2
Abba Elias – 1
Athanasius the Great – 1
Ephraim the Syrian – 1
Gabriel of Latrum – 1
Theodoret of Cyrus – 1
Abba Josephus – 1
Aristotle – 1

One may draw additional parallels to those indicated in this introduction, for example with John's contemporary ascetic bishop of Nineveh, Isaac the Syrian (late seventh century), and others. As for influences, after all, the very idea of spiritual life being like rungs on a ladder of mystical ascent goes back to at least Origen. I shall return to the matter in the main body of the work to show that the *Ladder* draws from many sources, but cannot be reduced to, and does not duplicate, any one of them. In a way, the whole exercise of detecting influences, however illuminating these may be within certain limits and however much attention I may find it necessary to give them in this study, is a form of divination. What is important is to consider such influences, borrowings, assimilations and parallels in the light of that which makes them possible. For, beyond them all, there is the unity of the underlying experience and way of life which is at the root of the mystical and ascetical tradition, and which also accounts for John's own inspiration. This is what concerns me most in the discussion that follows.

Appendix

Biographical note

The *Menaion* states in a simple but express manner that John died in 603 at the age of eighty. Following the *Menaion*, in the nineteenth century, Krumbacher believed that John was a sixth-century author and placed him between the years 525 and 600.[183] It was not until the beginning of the twentieth century that F. Nau was able to contest this view on the basis of hitherto unused sources. Basing his argument on anonymous fragments – and of these especially on *Narrative* 32 – which he attributed to the Sinaite monk Anastasius and for which he gave the year 650 as the *terminus post quem*, Nau supposed that John died in or after 649 because the *Narratives* mention that he died a year before their composition.[184] Nau's theory is largely speculative and has not gained universal acceptance. It seems, however, to be at least partly corroborated by the fact that no abbot of Sinai named John of the *Ladder* is mentioned in the *Spiritual Meadow*. John Moschus wrote this latter work around 615–19. It records his sojourn at Sinai around 580–90 and does in fact mention other Sinaite Fathers. If our John was born around 525, then Moschus would have mentioned him; indeed Climacus must have been the abbot of the monastery during the time of Moschus' visit to Sinai. If again John was born around 569, as Nau would imply, he would have been far too young either to be a monk, or to be known for his virtue, while John Moschus was journeying through the Sinaite desert – arguments from silence, but arguments nonetheless.

Petit treats Nau's theory with much reserve and sees in it confusion in chronology or, worse, a misidentification of persons – of John Climacus and John the Sabbaite. The latter must have been much older, and if the manuscripts, especially those containing *Narrative* 32, are reliable, then the two persons are clearly distinct.[185] In any case, many of Nau's *Narratives* speak of

---

[183] Krumbacher, *Geschichte*, 143, 651. This theory is also accepted by Sakkos, *Peri Anastaseon*, 180, 237. Benesevic claims Climacus was born before 532 and died before 596: cf. Benesevic, 'Sur la date,' 168–9. The opinion expressed in the introduction to the Holy Transfiguration Monastery edition of the *Ladder* is drawn from the *Menaion*; cf. xxxi.

[184] Nau, 'Note sur la date' and Nau's edition of the Narratives in *Oriens Christianus*. There is, however, some doubt as to how much of this material in Anastasius actually refers to Climacus, as we shall see below. Nau's theory is accepted by Ball, *Byzant. Christentum*, 23. Beck, who places Climacus' death as late as 670–80, fundamentally agrees with Nau: cf. Beck, *Kirche*, 451.

[185] Petit, 'Saint Jean Climaque,' *DTC* 8, 690. Cf. also Chitty, *Desert*, 178, n. 36, where it is claimed that the John the Sabbaite mentioned in *Narrative* 32 can hardly be the same as John the Sabbaite of the other *Narratives*. All we can say with any degree of certainty is that it was John the Sabbaite who died one year before the *Narratives* were written, namely 649. With this Petit, too, would agree (col. 690).

the 'old' John the Sabbaite[186] and of the 'young' John who was appointed abbot of Sinai. Petit thinks Climacus must have died around 680, or at the earliest around 670.

However, before leaving Petit's discussion, one must examine another interesting point about the aforementioned *Spiritual Meadow*. As already noted, in the manuscripts of the *Ladder*, John is also referred to as 'Scholastic,' a term which, although Daniel makes use of it in his *Life* (596A), is not explained by him except to say that John was a learned monk (597B). In the *Spiritual Meadow* one reads of a certain 'Abba, the Scholastic'[187], whom, in his *Miracles of Saints Cyrus and John*, Sophronius describes as 'John the Rhetorician.'[188] At that time, certainly, the two words 'scholastic' and 'rhetorician' were similar in meaning, both denoting 'scholar.' Now Sophronius also says that this person was married,[189] and Petit believes that this explains Daniel's silence about the details of Climacus' life before his profession as a monk. In my opinion, this is again no more than conjecture, since Daniel omits many other details of John's later life, which are no less important and which John himself explicitly mentions.[190] Petit's theory is by no means established as a certainty or even a probability – as he would claim[191] – but remains, if anything, a remote possibility. Nevertheless, the evidence from Moschus might imply that John was born as early as 579 and that Moschus was familiar with his existence as a hermit on Sinai.

Accepting Nau's theory, though only with the reservations expressed by Petit, Dimitrije Bogdanovic places John's birth before 579 and his death after 654.[192] If Bogdanovic is correct, then the question arises as to how it is that John makes no allusion whatsoever to the Arab occupation of Cairo in 640 (21

---

[186] A *geron* need not always be old in years. John the Sabbaite was a *geron*, just as George of Arselaum was. This holy man George – not to be confused with Climacus' brother – is often mentioned in the *Narratives*: cf. *Narratives* 9 and 12 which also offer an account of his death. He is also known to John of Raithou: cf. 27.ii,22 (1112B). At all events, the greatest proof that Climacus is not the same person as the Sabbaite is Climacus' reference to the latter as having originated in Asia Minor, having spent some time on Mar Saba before coming to Sinai: cf. 4.111–13 (720A–24B).

[187] Ch. 70 (PG87.2960).

[188] Ch. 70 (PG87.3673A). On the *Pratum Spirituale* and Sophronius, cf. H. Chadwick, 'John Moschos and his Friend Sophronios the Sophist,' *Journal of Theological Studies*, 25 (1974), 41–74.

[189] Ch. 62 (PG87.3640B).

[190] Among the fundamental data concerning Climacus' life, to which not so much as an allusion is made in the *Life* are, for example, Climacus' visits to Egyptian monasteries which Climacus himself describes in 5.5 (764D) and 27.ii,3 (1105C).

[191] Cf. col. 692.

[192] Bogdanovic, *Jean Climaque*, 216–17. The reservations of Petit are also mentioned by Benesevic, 'Sur la date,' 168–9, and by Viller-Rahner, *Aszese*, 155–6. The theory of Bogdanovic is somewhat similar to Altaner's view, according to which Climacus was born before 597 and died around 649: cf. Altaner, *Patrologie*, 468. Yannaras seems to take no stand in this debate, though he expresses a certain favor towards the theory of Bogdanovic: cf. Yannaras, *Metaphysike*, 51–2. This

December) – a reason certainly in favor of placing John in the sixth century. Nevertheless, this argument from silence is once again not decisive. Right down to the Crusades, we have no details at all of the Sinaite monastery from the Arab period, and we can only presume that the monks must have succeeded in securing the continued survival of the monastery and in reaching a tolerable understanding with their Muslim overlords.[193]

In fact, John may have died as late as 680, when, around the time of the Sixth Ecumenical Synod held in Constantinople, many monks entered the Sinaite peninsula. As a result of this move, we know that the bishop of Pharan came to live permanently within the monastery itself, which was formerly within the confines of his eparchy, assuming from that time onward the title 'Bishop of Sinai.' Another reason for this shift of the diocesan see was perhaps the impending threat of the Arab occupation in Pharan. It is known that lack of security accounts largely for Bishop Theodore's move to the monastery after the Sixth Ecumenical Synod, at which he was condemned for Monothelitism. It is also known that John's brother, named George, became bishop of Sinai. He may in fact have been the first to move from Pharan to the monastery.[194]

Finally, one must mention the view expressed by Derwas Chitty and Kallistos Ware, who regard John of the *Ladder* as a contemporary of Maximus the Confessor (*c.* 580–662) and consider the *Ladder* as an ascetic synthesis comparable to the theological synthesis of Maximus. There are passages in John, which are reminiscent of the language used by the Confessor,[195] and this view is plausible not so much as a decisive argument but as a confirmation of the Bogdanovic hypothesis. It seems more reasonable, then, to treat John as an author of the seventh rather than the sixth century. His dates should be placed between *c.* 579 (or possibly as late as 599) and *c.* 659 (or perhaps as late as 679).

---

is, more or less, also the view of Couilleau, who gives *c.* 575–*c.* 650 as John's dates: cf. Couilleau, 'Saint Jean Climaque,' *DS* 8, 372. Völker, *Scala Paradisi*, 1, agrees that the middle of the seventh century is the approximate period of Climacus' death.

[193] Cf. Skrobucha, *Sinai*, 57.

[194] *Narrative* 32. Cf. also Bogdanovic, *Jean Climaque*, 12, especially n. 15; Bogdanovic is assuming here that John the Sabbaite in *Narrative* 32 is the same as John Climacus.

[195] Cf. especially 6.4 (793BC). Cf. Chitty, *Desert*, 173 and Ware *Introduction*, 3, 18, and 57–8. Cf. also Bogdanovic, *Jean Climaque*, 218–19, where Bogdanovic states that John developed a notion of *synergeia*, although the word itself is not explicitly used.

The peaks of Mt Sinai and St Catherine on the horizon
(Photograph: Elizabeth Williams)

CHAPTER 2

Soma–Sarx: The Body and the Flesh

> When you speak of the body, first make the
> sign of the cross.
> > (S. S. Harkianakis)

> Kill the flesh in order to acquire a body.
> > (Fr Sergei Bulgakov)

Introduction

All definitions of the human being are bound to fail, or are at least destined to
remain only tentative, provisional attempts at identification, depending on
one's view of human nature. For the Greek ascetic Fathers, who never offered,
nor claimed to offer, a comprehensive account of the matter, there always
remained an element of mystery attached to the human person. This was due
largely to their underlying idea of man or woman as an irreducible pneumato-
psycho-physical being, of which both the material and immaterial constituents
are mysteriously conjoined and are essential for a properly integrated personal
existence. The mysterious unity of the human person was regarded as the sign
of infinity and even of divinity. To divide body and soul, or perhaps body and
mind, or again mind and heart, is to inaugurate an expanding series of division.
John Climacus, using as he often does symbolical images rather than exact or
even cogent theoretical explanations, speaks of 'defeating the three tyrants, or
to put it more clearly, conquering the body, the soul, and the spirit.'[1] This may
give the impression of an implied trichotomy in a quasi-Platonist sense. In fact,
his approach shows a much more nuanced and integrated idea of the complex
nature of human personality, which reflects the traditional patristic as well as
the biblical view (cf. 1 Thess. 5.23). In the chapters that follow, I shall try,
under the separate headings of 'the body,' 'the heart' and 'the intellect,' to
demonstrate how John of the *Ladder* saw these complexities in their conflicting
yet intimately related aspects that characterize the nature of the human person.
A discerning master and guide of the soul's complexities, John Climacus is
unafraid to address the paradoxes of human nature.

Any study of the human body cannot avoid ambiguities. Such ambiguity is
not absent from patristic literature, especially where Platonist terminology is
used or Platonist associations of ideas occur. The ambiguity begins when the

---

[1] *Shep.* 100 (1205B).

body – or the heart, or the intellect, for that matter – is seen as a distinct object rather than a subject, as some-thing rather than as some-*one*, as an *id* rather than an *is*. For Gregory the Theologian: 'A human being cannot be detached from matter without ceasing at the same time to be human.'[2] Any separatist view implies an abstract point of observing objects, as it were from outside. The least authentic way to treat a person is to do so as if one is not a person oneself. It is a way of unreality. John Climacus does not hesitate to call it 'hypocrisy':

> Hypocrisy is soul and body in a state of opposition to each other (*enantia katastasis*), intertwined with every kind of invention.[3]

The body–soul antithesis evokes the general tendency that we have as human beings to oppose in order to understand. Yet this is not the only way that people have thought about human nature, and a primary focus of this study will be to present an alternative anthropology as this is suggested by the ascetic tradition of the early Christian era. To think of the body as separate from the soul – as soul-less or anti-soul – is to make an object of it, denying its mystical dimension and presence. In reality, when we think, we often think of two.[4] Consequently, it is from philosophers and religious or mystical abstractionists – as in Orphism and Pythagoreanism – that we first hear of a separation between soul and body, leading ultimately to contempt for the latter, or to viewing it as something of little or no consequence, or even as a mere burden. However, a philosophy of disembodiment is a philosophy of death. Genuine philosophy reflects upon aspects of life in its entirety, and the compartmentalization of human nature into 'body' and 'soul,' each self-contained, is a symptom of a loss of wholeness, resulting in a variety of dualistic philosophies.

The Pythagorean view, with its play on the words *soma–sema*, which describes the body as a form or structure rather than a reality, is as divisive as Plato's idea of the body as a prison or, at best, a 'garment of the soul,' and of the soul 'descending' into the body. The same may be said about Epicurean 'atomism' and the Stoics' 'indifferent' human mind impinged upon by the extraneous material world – even in the Latin, more practically oriented, versions of Marcus Aurelius and Seneca. Moreover, this applies to Plotinus' 'idealism,' in which phenomena in time are ephemeral copies of incorporeal reality: thus Plotinus was 'ashamed' of his body.[5] Admittedly, these are broad

---

[2] *Or.* 26,13 PG35.1245B.

[3] 24.20 (981B).

[4] Cf. M. Midgley, 'The soul's successors: philosophy and the body,' in S. Coakley (ed.), *Religion and the Body*, 53–68. See also the enlightening essay by B. S. Turner, 'The body in Western society: social theory and its perspectives,' in S. Coakley, *Religion and the Body*, 15–41.

[5] Porphyry, *Vita Plotini* 1. Cf. also Plato, *Phaedo* 64e–66a and 82e. For Plato's sources, cf. Zaehner, *Sundry Times*. For the notions of *soma* and *sarx* in the Greek world, also see *TDNT*,

and generalized comparisons, which require qualification. It is not difficult to find conflicting strains in Plato, the Stoics and Plotinus alike. For instance, the idea of *eros* in Plato's *Symposium* allows more reality to the sensible world and reflects a more integrated view of human nature than, say, the approach found in *Phaedo* and *The Republic*. The Stoic appeal to life 'according to nature' and the theme that the soul – and, indeed, God – are corporeal realities implies a more monistic view of humanity. Even Plotinus' adherence to distinct 'levels of being' did not exclude the presence of these levels everywhere and in everyone, while the 'Gnostic' tone of his thought did not prevent him from being an opponent of extreme, dualistic (Chaldean) Gnosticism. Still, by and large, there was a pervasive trend to regard the individual, earthly human body as a hindrance to the intellectual and spiritual life, weighing us down and hampering us in our ascent. This suspicion of the body – seen as enemy, or the anti-body – is easily transformed into its opposite, into an inflation of the body. The body is, as a result, either despised or made absolute. The two derivative extremes originate in the same primary assumption of a dissociated human being.

In reality, the human person – whether called body or soul – transcends any such dualism.[6] Any dichotomy of the self damages both the body and the soul. Extreme asceticism ('encratism') and excessive spiritualism ('gnosticism') represent only a partial truth, but to assert partial truth is to harm or destroy the human person. The teaching of Christianity in this respect seems clear: Christ came to glorify the entire human person and made nonsense of dualism or partiality. No such body–soul differentiation can be found in the Old Testament: human nature there is spoken of in its totality.[7] The Hebrew mind saw things in their entirety and in relation to God, and saw the human person as a unity (cf. Gen. 2.24; 6.17; 7.16 and 21; Job 14.22 and 34.25, Ps. 62.2 and 135.25).

The New Testament similarly speaks of the human person as a unified, unfragmented being related to God. Even the 'divine' humanity of Christ is revealed in that relation. Grounded in the Old Testament, the New Testament spells a vision of the human body glorified by Christ. Paul's theology, too, follows this pattern. He speaks of the body as the 'outer person' (2 Cor. 4.16) or, by analogy, of the soul as the 'inner person' (Rom. 7.22; 2 Cor. 4.16; Eph.

1025–44 and 99–105, esp. 102. On Platonist asceticism, cf. J. Dillon, 'Rejecting the Body, Refining the Body,' in Wimbush and Valantasis, *Asceticism*, 80–87. On Manichean asceticism, cf. J. Beduhn, 'The Battle for the Body in Manichaean Asceticism,' in *Asceticism*, 513–19.

[6] Cf. P. Tillich, *Systematic Theology*, London: 1978, vol. 1, 250. Tillich's use of the word 'spirit' seems, in many ways, to correspond with the patristic notion of 'personhood' (*hypostasis – prosopon*).

[7] Cf. Tresmontant, *La pensée Hébraïque*, 88. See also L. Jacobs, 'The body in Jewish worship: three rituals examined,' in S. Coakley, *Religion and the Body*, 71–89.

3.16), although this perhaps oversimplifies the problem. There is, in the Hebrew and Christian Scriptures, a certain hierarchical subordination of the body to the soul (Mt. 10.28; Lk. 12.4) and even a supposition of the provisional character of the earthly body (Mk. 12.25). Nevertheless, there is no clear, whether direct or indirect, indication that the two are taken in dissociation. For Paul, body and soul are ontologically united.[8] His flesh–spirit dualism is existential, that is to say related to a concrete, behavioral situation rather than an ontological state. The human person is a stricken, fallen being. It is its sinful condition, otherwise known as 'the flesh' – that separates the person from the spirit. 'Body' is not to be equated with 'flesh,' nor again 'soul' with 'spirit.'

Unity in the human person, unity in the human race: the Greek Fathers in general share this essentially biblical attitude towards the body.[9] There are exceptions to this view but, as will be seen below, it is the predominant understanding in Greek patristic thought, at least in its ascetic expression. One cannot discount the influence of Platonism on the patristic literature,[10] but the Hebraic sythesizing, psychosomatic attitude ultimately prevails. In the end, 'Jerusalem' appears to triumph over 'Athens,' even in the more platonically minded writers. It is a case of the Christianization of Hellenism rather than the Hellenization of the Gospel. The Greek Fathers assimilated the Platonist and Stoic anthropological idiom without becoming either Platonists or Stoics. They could, in fact, more properly be said to incline toward the Aristotelian notion of the person as indivisible (*a-tomon*) rather than towards Platonist dualism.

---

[8] For the need to beware of oversimplified equations in the New Testament, see Robinson, *Body*, 18 and Bultmann, *Theology*, 201–02. An oversimplistic contrast, however, between the Hebrew and Greek conceptions of the human person ought to be avoided: cf. J. Barr, *The Semantics of Biblical Language*, Oxford: 1961, 12–14 and 34–7; J. Barr, *Old and New in Interpretation. A Study of the Two Testaments*, London: 1966, 50–53.

[9] See J. Behr, *Asceticism and Anthropology in Irenaeus and Clement*, Oxford: Oxford University Press, 2000, with special reference to sexuality and the body in Irenaeus of Lyons and Clement of Alexandria. Cf. also J. Bonsirven and M. Viller, 'Chair,' *DS* 2 (1953), 443f. See the balance between body and soul in *Apophth.* Nau 269 and 272 (1909, p. 370). For the notion of solidarity with the human race, cf. Basil, *Hom. in quadraginta martyres* 2 (PG31.509C) and Greg. Nyssa, *De hom. opif.* 16 (PG44.185BC) and *De paup. amand. or.* 1 (PG46.465B) and 2 (476CD). Gregory is probably directly indebted to the Stoics. Also, cf. Greg. Palamas, *First Treatise on the Procession of the Holy Spirit* 40 (1, p. 70).

[10] Cassian speaks not of a body–soul opposition but rather of a battle between '*carnis et animae,*' cf. *Inst.* 5, 11,2 (208). And in other authors, the body is seen as less precious than the soul: cf. Athanasius, *Vita Ant.* 45 (PG26.909AB); Dorotheus, *Instr.* 14, 158 (444); Mark the Monk, *De Paenitentia* 4 (PG65.969–72); Greg. Naz., *Or.* 37, 22 (PG36.308A) and Climacus' contemporary, Isaac the Syrian, *Mystic Treatises* (222). In fact, often a case is made against the body: Evagrius, *De or.* 105 (PG79.1189CD) does not seem to find any positive role for it, except perhaps in regard to tears, cf. *De or.* 5–10 (PG79.1168D–69C). The body ought to be put to death by *ascesis*: cf. Cyril of Scythopolis, *Life of Sabas* 62 (163, 17–18); John Moschus, *Pratum*, Barnabas 10 (PG87.2860B) and *Apophth.* Daniel 4 (PG65.156B). See also A. Pettersen, *Athanasius and the Human Body*, Bristol: Bristol University Press, 1990.

The Alexandrian tradition is clearly more Platonist, and it may be asked to what degree Origen or even Evagrius influenced John Climacus. Origen was an Alexandrian Platonist deeply steeped in Philo; such writers as Methodius of Olympus and Eustathius of Antioch contested his views in the fourth century. Yet, in the same century, Origen's views were espoused by Didymus the Blind, Evagrius and Priscillian of Spain, although the first two were condemned together with their master in 553. However, Origen's emphasis on the eternal soul is found in Gregory of Nyssa's *Life of Saint Macrina the Virgin*, while Origen himself opposed excessive spiritualism.[11]

Certain representatives of the Greek patristic tradition may likewise show, following in a measure the biblical tradition, some affinity with the Stoics, especially as Stoicism was itself a reaction against Platonist ideas or abstract forms that serve to disembody humanity's existence.[12] Where some ascetic writers expressed extremist views of quasi-Platonist character, when examined more carefully, their comments are indicative of an urgent struggle against sin and not against human nature, against the fallen flesh and not the body as such, against passions and not the person. It is a case of intensity rather than division; it is a case of the 'folly of the Cross' (1 Cor. 1.18). Some comments in the *Sayings of the Desert Fathers*, the *Lausiac History* of Palladius or Theodoret's *Philotheos History* are equivocal, if taken at their face value.[13] Yet any body–soul distinction in the monastic tradition often belongs to an entirely different experience from that underlying dualist philosophy. The early ascetic authors share the language of the philosophers, so some would say. However, in so doing, they apply the language haphazardly and inconsistently. They do not tend to distinguish various parts of the human person as objective entities. As has been noted, they always see the human person, above all, as a mystery. The very oneness of human nature and of human personhood is regarded as a mystery, a 'paradox.' At the same time, it is something both natural and good because that is how God created and intended humanity.[14] If the Greek ascetic

---

[11] For Gregory of Nyssa's *Life of Saint Macrina the Virgin*, cf. PG46960–1000. For Origen's more positive statements on the body, cf. *Contra Celsum* 3, 42 and 4, 65–6 (ed. Koetschau, 237–8 and 335–6) and contrariwise in *Contra Celsum* 7, 38 (188–9) and *De princ.* 8, 4 (102–04).

[12] Cf. G. Florovsky, 'Eschatology in the Patristic Age: An Introduction,' *Studia Patristica* (Berlin: 1957), 246f. For the Stoic viewpoint, see Spanneut, *Stoicisme*, 349–85. For a fundamental study of the body in classical Greek thought, see D. Martin, *The Corinthian Body*, New Haven, CT: Yale University Press, 1995.

[13] See, for instance, *Apophth.* Antony 33 (PG65.85C); 'despise the flesh': *Hist. Laus.* Dorotheus 2 (16–17), which is reproduced by Climacus in 5.5 (769D); Macarius of Alexandria 19–20 (pp. 55–6); Benjamin 13 (35–6) and Alexandra 5 (20). Extreme ascetic feats are advocated in *Phil. Hist.*, Theodosius, 10, 2, p. 438 (1389A); Romanos, 11, 1, p. 454 (1393C) and 3, p. 458 (1396A); Marcianus, 3, 21, p. 286 (13337D) and 3, p. 250 (1325B).

[14] 27.5 (1097B). Although this passage refers strictly to the action of the hesychast, the latter may be seen, for the purposes of this discussion, as the authentic human person; cf. also 26.ii,54 (1072).

writers do make any distinction, they distinguish rather between the levels of
kata physin (humanity as created by God), *para physin* (humanity as fallen),
and *hyper physin* (humanity as deified). This distinction is articulated clearly in
Abba Isaiah of Scetis, when he speaks of the effect of the incarnation on
human nature:

> Nature, which had become contrary to nature (*para physin*), returned to its
> natural state (*kata physin*).[15]

The same distinction is found also in Climacus:

> One who has conquered the body has conquered nature; and one who has
> conquered nature has certainly risen above nature (*hyper physin*).[16]

We gain a clear view of what the body truly is in Christian anthropology
when we link it with the creation of humanity in God's 'image and likeness'
(Gen. 1.27), even while bearing in mind that for most of the Greek Fathers the
'image' is in fact connected with the soul.[17] Sometimes, writers assume that the
concepts of image and likeness are the same, but often the two are
distinguished. In the latter case, the image is seen as the initial endowment
in creation, that potentiality which is not an end in itself, but a capability
pointing forward. Likeness indicates the final aim, the realization of the
eschatological hope. Though John himself does not make this particular
distinction, the idea is certainly implicit in his dynamic doctrine of the human
person. Through the divine act of creation, the human body is directly related
to God the creator. Indeed, in its natural condition, humanity – the whole
person and, by extension, also the body – seeks God. One is what one is in
relation to God. In this relation, the body is seen as 'holy' and united to God,
filled with the Holy Spirit (1 Cor. 6.19).[18] The body is meant to share in the
sanctification and glorification of the whole human being in its relationship
with the creator. Our enduring purpose is to transform the world, nature, our
own very body, in which we have our being as priests and prophets. Invited to
theosis and summoned to become God (2 Pet. 1.4), our aim is to raise nature
above its own level, to offer it to God in, as it were, a gesture of thanksgiving
and love. When the body is offered back – or, up – to God it is, for John
Climacus, *in statu ante peccatum*, 'incorruptible.' The human person, now as
priest, 'faces the person of our Lord' and, although still a creature, rises 'above'

---

[15] *Logos* 25, 15 (167). Cf. also *Logos* 2,1 (4–5); Mark the Monk, *De his* 83 (PG65.941C) and
Evagrius, *Cent.* 1, 64 and 4, 83 (ed. Frankenberg, 105 and 417).

[16] 15.70 (896C).

[17] Cf. Origen, *Ad Mart.* 12 (*GCS*, 13). Abba Isaiah, *Logos*, 2, 1 (p. 4) speaks of the body as
created good by God; see also Gregory Palamas (in fact, Michael Choniates), *Prosopopoeiae*
(PG150–1361).

[18] For the sanctification of the body, cf. Gregory Nyssa, *Comm. in Cant. Cant.* 11 (PG44.1005A).

all creatures.[19] The body is to be converted into a means of relating to God. Our purpose is to 'present' God with the beauty of the body as an act of prayer to the One who originally presented it to us as a gift of love. We return it as priests (in a eucharistic attitude), glorifying God (in a doxological act)[20] in the body which at all times remains God's own 'temple' (1 Cor. 3.16 and Jn 2.21).

It must be made clear that *soma* is distinguishable from *sarx*, the former being basically descriptive as corporeity, while the latter has an evaluative connotation and expresses the condition and the function of the former, in reference to its fallen and unfallen state. John implies this distinction without in fact explicitly adopting this terminology in any precise or consistent fashion. An altogether narrowly linguistic interpretation of his text would be misplaced. What is important is the context of the language used and the ultimate aim of John's vision.

Soma – the Body

Positive Statement

The subject-matter of this section is epitomized in the following quotations from the *Ladder*:

> Naturally it is impossible for a bodiless (*asomaton*) being to be confined by a body (*somatos*).[21]

> A hesychast is one who strives to confine the incorporeal (*asomaton*) being within one's bodily (*somatikon*) house, paradoxical as this may be.[22]

The entire human person, as known to the Sinaite hesychast, is referred to in the *Ladder* as a 'most paradoxical mystery.' The body is not treated with contempt or scorn; it is not an object of revulsion or a foe. Contrary attitudes

---

[19] 29.2 (1148B). For the concept of the human person as king over the animal creation – a concept not developed explicitly by Climacus himself – cf. K. Ware, 'Saints and Beasts: The Undistorted Image,' *The Franciscan* 5,4 (1963), 144–52 and Benedicta Ward, '"Signs and Wonders": Miracles in the Desert Tradition,' *Studia Patristica* 17 (Berlin: 1982), 539–42. The goal is deification: cf. Greg. Naz., *De Moderatione in disputando* 15 (PG36.192B); Isaac the Syrian notes that asceticism 'makes the human person a God on earth' (cf. *Mystic Treatises*, 64) and Symeon the New Theologian speaks of the *theosis* of the entire human person, 'body and soul:' cf. *TGP* 3.59 (98); cf. also Gregory Palamas, *Antirrhetikos* 2, 17 (3, pp. 143–4). The notion of the body as incorruptible in creation is clearly found in Barsanuphius 246.

[20] The doxological implication is evident in Abba Isaiah, *Logos* 25, 7 (158): 'Having glorified Christ in the body.' 'The body is for Him who made it,' says Amma Theodora in *Apophth. Theodora* 4 (PG65.201D–04A), and Evagrius, too, gives the body some positive meaning by linking it with its Creator: cf. *Prakt.* 53 (620).

[21] 26.52 (1029C).

[22] 27.5 (1097B). Cf. also 1.10 (6338).

are heresies to be militated against. Indeed, the body as such is a thing of beauty. John relates a well-known story that he once heard:

> 'A certain man, on seeing a beautiful woman, thereupon glorified the creator; and from that one look he was moved to the love of God and to a fountain of tears. And it was wonderful to see how what could have been a cause of destruction for one person became the supernatural cause of a crown for another.' If such a person always feels and behaves in this way on similar occasions, then he has risen immortal before the general resurrection.[23]

Far from being any cause for 'shame,' the body is reason for the glorification of God and the sanctification of the human person. The above story refers to Saint Nonnus, bishop of Helioupolis; the beautiful woman was a prostitute, who later came to be known as Saint Pelagia.[24] How ironic it is that Christians, as the adherents to a religion of the body and inheritors of such legends, could also, over the centuries, be blamed for the 'scars' left on the body, which make it appear to be unseemly. While the early desert hermits are often criticized for their dualistic tendencies, in fact fourth-century patristic commentaries of Scripture understood that the 'garments of skin' (Gen. 3.21) did not refer to the body.[25] The latter is, on the contrary, an object of admiration and marvel, a revelation of divine love and wisdom. John Climacus, too, can only but marvel at the body. He says he cannot explain its creation or its role 'logically.' For him, it is a mystery evoking a sense of awe, of the *tremendum* and *majestas*.[26]

Negative Statement

The supreme affirmation of the body seems to have an almost ominous counterpart in the very same authors and sometimes within the very same texts. This might be taken as implying dualistic conclusions, although, in my view,

---

[23] 15.58 (892D–93A). Compare also the article by P. Cox Miller, 'Dreaming the Body: An Aesthetics of Asceticism,' in Wimbush and Valantasis, *Asceticism*, 281–300.

[24] Cf. *Vita Sanctae Pelagiae*, Greek text in *Legenden der heiligen Pelagia*, ed. H. Usener, Bonn: 1897, 1–16; Latin text in PL73.663–72. The same story is also quoted in Niketas Stethatos, *Contemplation on Paradise* 37 (in *SC* 81: Paris, 1961), 200, and it is very likely that Niketas' source is in fact Climacus. First, the wording is so similar; and, second, Niketas was certainly familiar with Climacus, while further being aware of the influence of the *Ladder* on his own spiritual father, Symeon the New Theologian: cf. Hausherr, *Vie* 6 (12).

[25] Gregory of Nyssa is in fact the first to interpret Gen. 3.21 in this fashion: cf. *De Virginitate* 12 (PG46.376B); *De anima et resurr.* (PG46.248C); *Or. Cat.* 8 (PG45.33C); *Or. dom.* 5 (PG44.1184B); *Hom.* 2 in *Cant. Cant.* (PG 44.800D). For the reference to 'garments of skin' in the *Ladder*, cf. 15.76 (900b).

[26] 26.ii,14 (1061B); 26.ii,14 (1061B); although in this passage Climacus is referring to the fallen state of the body, his professed 'ignorance' can equally apply to the human person. Cf. also 26.52 (1029C); 15.83 (901C–04B) and 58 (1032AB): in context, the word 'wonder' refers not just to the body as such but to its dynamic potential; it may be the cause of sin and of purity alike.

such conclusions would not be justified either textually or in the light of the main burden of the *Ladder*'s approach. For instance, John advises the spiritual elder continually to wipe clean the 'souls, but *especially the bodies*' of his spiritual children in view of their salvation.[27] This could contain a subtle hint of dualism, and conflicts with a number of contrasting statements about the 'beauty' and the positive significance of the body. However, John is merely reminding us that an unbalanced, divisive view of the human person is a pitfall to all, whether this takes the form of strict discipline or that of disengaged indifference. In this particular instance, John is reminding the spiritual father of the community that several of his dependents may very well hold separatist opinions which will be reflected in their attitude to their body through their practice of discipline. For the spiritual father to attend '*especially* to the bodies' implies that he should help the monks to acquire a proper, harmonious attitude to the body and the soul in their mutual interrelation. It is not difficult, then, to find negative statements about the body in the *Ladder*, but one should at all times seek to determine to what level of the human condition John is addressing his comments. Is it to the body in its authentic, natural and unfallen state, or else to the body in its unauthentic, unnatural and fallen state, or again to the body as restored and redeemed in Christ? Thus John writes:

> The person who pets a lion may tame it, but the person who cuddles the body makes it ravenous. A monster is this gross and savage body. Treat your body as an enemy . . .[28]

Of the approximately seventy times that John employs the term *soma*, more than half the passages refer to the body in its stricken condition, just under a third actually refer to it as it was created by God or redeemed in Christ, and only on about twelve occasions is the meaning doubtful.[29]

Soma – Sema

John, then, can be found to say seemingly contradictory things. Yet, like many other Christian ascetics, he ultimately reaffirms the Hebraic, unitary viewpoint.

---

[27] *Shep.* 72 (1193B). Cf., however, *Shep.* 61 (1189D).

[28] 14.3 (864D); 26.13 (1016D); 9.8 (841C).

[29] Passages where the body is seen as fallen include: 1.20 (636D); 2.17 (657C); 3.20 (668A); 7.7 (804A), 31 (808B) and 40 (809A); 9.8 (841C); 14.3 (864D), 9 (865B) and 24 (868C); 15.1 (880D), 2 (880D), 20 (929A), 13 (1016D) and 82 (1036C); 26.2,1 (1105A); 28.28 (1133C), 52 (1137C) and 57 (1140A); 29.9 (1149A); *Shep.* 61 (1189D), 72 (1193B) and 100 (1205B). Positive statements regarding the body are found in: 1.10 (633C) and 16 (636B); 14.24 (868C) and 31 (869B); 15.32 (888B), 49 (889C), 58 (892D–93A) and 74 (897C); 22.16 (968C); 24.20 (981B); 25.2 (982B), 26.1 (1013A) and 16 (1020A); 26.2, 20 (1064AB) and 26 (1065A); and *Shep.* 100 (1204C). Passages where *soma* is doubtful: 3.32 (668D); 11.6 (852D); 14.1 (865C) and 23 (868B); 15.13 (881D); 20.8 (945D); 21.16 (952D); 25.59 (1001B); 26.32 (1024C) and 59 (1032B); 26.iii,45 (1089B) and 30.11 (1157B).

The implication is relevant not only for 'beginners,' but equally important for those who have reached the higher degrees of the spiritual life. Any 'standard, rule, and law' concerns human nature in its entirety. While John surprisingly enough refers to the body as the 'cell' (*kella*) of the hesychast, by apparent analogy with the Platonist prison cell, the meaning is altogether different. For the ascetic trained in the desert tradition of Egypt, the cell is the 'dwelling-place of knowledge.'[30] John, then, may ostensibly reflect the views of certain dualist philosophers, but the underlying experience is quite different. Mark the Monk provides the reason for this: before the incarnation, he observes, 'repentance was impossible.'[31] Barsanuphius, like John, can therefore describe the monastic cell as both a 'cemetery' and as the 'dwelling-place of God;' it is a place of mortification, but also of 'sanctification.'[32] And John's younger contemporary, Isaac the Syrian, offers a more Sinaite image: 'The cell of a solitary is the cave of the rock in which God spoke with Moses.'[33] Climacus himself is more explicit; for him, the cell is a grave from which shines forth the light of the resurrection:

> Let the place where you are be your tomb before the tomb. For no one will come out of the grave until the general resurrection.[34]

Within the cell, and by analogy within the body, one knows oneself and one knows God (Mt. 6.6); therein God dwells (Lk. 17.21) and one is known by God (Gal. 4.9). This is why John advises the hesychast to 'shut the door of the cell to the body.'[35] The body, then, is not considered apart from the human person; and still less does it constitute an evil part. It is so intimately linked with human nature as to be identical with it. Thus, a seemingly dualistic language denotes ultimately a unitary conception. If there is any 'separation' – as in the case of death – it is only temporary. This adds an eschatological dimension to John's ascetic thought. For we await our ultimate restitution at the universal resurrection of the dead. It is God's prerogative alone to divide the human

---

[30] 27.10 (1097C). 26.14 (1017B) for the above reference. For the body as divine dwelling-place, cf. 27.5 (1097B); Diadochus, *Cent.* 78 (pp. 135–6); *Mac. Hom.* 30, 7 (244–5) and 49, 4 (317–19) and Isaiah, *Logos* 15,1 (83). For a positive view of the cell, cf. *Apophth.* Daniel 5 (PG65.156B), Moses 6 (284C), Paphnutius 5 (380CD) and Nau (1908, p. 279). Symeon the New Theologian echoes this doctrine when he says that Christ 'enters our body as if into a tomb' and resurrects it: cf. *Cat.* 13 (194). Basil says that the body does not imprison but frees us: cf. *Praevia Institutio Ascetica* 2 (PG31.621B). Abba Isaiah calls the world a 'prison' but he is referring to a fallen, Godless world: cf. *Logos* 25, 10 (160) and Isaac the Syrian, *Mystic Treatises* (85) also reflects this view. For the link between the 'cell' and the 'prison,' cf. also *Apophth.* Poemen 2 (317B).

[31] *Adv. Nest.* 18 (ed. Kunze, 19).

[32] Barsanuphius 72 and 73. For the *Ladder*, cf. 27.ii,39 (1113D).

[33] *Mystic Treatises* (121).

[34] 4.39 (716B).

[35] 27.17 (1100A).

person,[36] and this is what, temporarily, occurs at the moment of separation in death. This leads Climacus to profess ignorance, if not awe; he cannot understand why this is so, unless it be a miracle:

> And it is wonderful how the soul can exist outside the body in which it received its being.[37]

Our 'spiritual' nature neither exists independently nor can it be examined in itself, cut off from the body – a line of thought curiously echoed in modern psychology and medicine.

Redemption of the Body

A Christian ascetic can only speak of the body with reference to the incarnation, transfiguration, passion, resurrection and ascension of the divine Word. The human body is closely linked with the body of Christ, who is our archetype. In the words of Abba Isaiah, 'Christ became our type, in order that we may follow in his footsteps.'[38] Just as he acted 'in a divine–human manner,' we too should act 'in a manner combining body and soul, following the example of the God–Man Christ,' says Anastasius of Sinai,[39] who lived shortly before Climacus but shared the same desert and the same kind of experience as Climacus. We are to love the body, just as Christ did in assuming a human body.[40] This, however, does not allow for any complacency. The fact that Christ assumed a human body at the incarnation is reason enough for Abba Isidore of Pelusium never to give his own body any rest.[41] John Climacus, too, is aware of Christ's expectations:

> Inasmuch as the Lord is incorruptible and incorporeal (*asomatos*), so too does He rejoice in the purity and incorruptibility of our body.[42]

---

[36] 26.ii,54 (1072C). Cf. also *Apophth.* Poemen 184 (PG65.386A) and Evagrius, *Prakt.* 52 (618): although Climacus' words echo Evagrius, the attitude of the latter towards the body is ambivalent since in this passage he speaks of disincarnation as the spiritual way. On resurrection, cf. 15.30 (888A) and *Shep.* 100 (1205B).

[37] 26.79 (1036B). This echoes the advice given by Pachomius to his disciples in *Vita Prima* 93 (62–3 and 207–08). Cf. also *Apophth.* Elias 1 (PG65.184A) and Theophilus 4 (200A–01A).

[38] *Logos* 27, 1 (188). Cf. also the entire *Logos* 13 (74–8).

[39] *Secundum imaginem* (PG89.1148D–9A). Cf. also *Sermo* 3 (1161C).

[40] 2.17 (657C): although Climacus is making a somewhat different point in this passage, it remains a fact that love for God and love for the body must be balanced. Regarding the incarnation and its significance for the body, cf. Mark the Monk, *Disp. cum quodam causidico* 20 (PG65.1100B) and *De Melch.* 4–5 (PG65.1121C–24C); cf. also Dorotheus, *Instr.* 16, 170 (466).

[41] *Apophth.* Isidore of Pelusium 5 (PG65.220D–21A). In this respect, we can understand *Apophth.* Poemen 38 (332B) and 57 (336A).

[42] 15.32 (888B).

The ascetic is called 'to make incorruptible that which has received an incorruptible nature.'[43] Nevertheless, 'the acquisition of a bodiless nature' is itself nothing but a bodily action, since it is identified with the concept of 'purity of body.'[44] The monk is defined, among other attributes adopted by Climacus, as 'a purified body.'[45]

As Christ raised human nature to the heavens, the ascetic too must deify it by divine grace. Through the body, through its natural beauty – of which one ought not to be ashamed but proud of as having been granted by the creator and assumed by the Word – one should glorify God. The body is a means whereby the ascetic glorifies God and catches a glimpse of the divine glory. This, too, constitutes a mystery; for, it reflects God's beauty and love for humanity.[46] Symeon the New Theologian describes the same mystery in poetic language: 'My hand is Christ, my foot is Christ, wretched though I am.'[47] The purpose of humanity is to raise the body to the level to which Christ raised it:

> We ought to use every means to raise this clay, so to speak, and seat it on the throne of God. And let no one make excuses for not undertaking this ascent, because the way and door are open.[48]

Symeon the New Theologian further develops the notion of raising the body:

> And now let us rise up and ascend to the heavens with him, or rather may he raise us up and glorify us with him.[49]

Our body, as a fact of personification, is found on God's throne in the person of Christ. This point may not be explicit in John's *Ladder* but it is certainly implied when he writes that we, too, have the potential to raise the 'clay vessel,' this body described as 'clay' or 'earthen.'[50] The Greek Fathers understood that Christ's victory over death returned to human nature what it had lost as a consequence of the Fall, namely life – immortality and indestructibility, which humanity will receive again, no longer in potentiality but in actuality, at the resurrection of the dead (1 Cor. 15.54). Through the incarnation, Christ sanctified the whole material creation, including the human body, which thereby became a channel of divine grace. In the phraseology of the *Macarian Homilies*:

---

[43] 15.83 (901C). Cf. Diadochus, *Cent.* 90 (150–52).

[44] 15.2 (880D).

[45] 1.10 (633C). On the notion of 'purity,' see G. S. Gasparro, 'Asceticism and Anthropology,' in Wimbush and Valantasis, *Asceticism*, 127–46.

[46] 15.58 (829D).

[47] *Hymn* 15 (298).

[48] 26.ii,20 (1064AB). Cf. also 1.16 (636) and 27.ii,13 (1109B).

[49] *Cat.* 7 (82).

[50] 26.ii,20 (1064AB). Barsanuphius 165 employs the word 'tile.'

> This was the very purpose of the coming of our Lord Jesus Christ, to give us ... a new mind, and a new soul, and new eyes, and new ears, a new spiritual tongue, and in short to make us new persons altogether.[51]

It may be hard to offer up the body. John claims that this requires 'force' and 'toil.'[52] Still, 'the door has been opened' by Christ and, what is more, 'the way' has been shown, the road trodden by others.

This theme of the glorified body is central to patristic and ascetic spirituality. It is also, for example, relevant to John's attitude to sexual relations. These, too, are to be transfigured in terms of our relation with God. The ways of the transfigured and ascended body of Christ are also to be found in human love.[53] In deprecating sex, one deprecates the body. It is all a part of the alienation, isolation and objectification of human nature, which inevitably turns into idolatry. Nevertheless, love, even sexual love, restores a sense of wholeness to humanity, subsumed in the love of God and of all humankind. One establishes a true relationship to oneself and to one's body through love of God and of others. Like Plato, John underscores the critical significance of *eros* as a unifying element in the human person, whose ultimate aim is to love God.[54] This concept will be examined more closely in the chapter on the ascetic struggle. Here it is sufficient to quote John's words: 'As it is with the body, so it is with the bodiless bodies.'[55]

The Body in Ascetic Struggle

Just as Christ used his body in order to defeat the devil, sin and death, so we too can use our body to fight certain aspects of the 'body.'[56] Evagrius claims that one can only attain 'to purity of heart by means of the body,' which 'the monk should always treat as if he were to live on with it for many years to come.'[57] Climacus adopts a similar attitude: 'If I strike the body down, I have nothing with which to obtain virtues.' The body is, therefore, 'a friend,' 'an ally,' 'an assistant' and 'a defender.'[58] Climacus' theology in no way subverts the body. Indeed, one cannot function without it; one cannot be saved without

---

[51] *Mac. Hom.* 44.1 (291).

[52] 1.16 and 17 (636BC). Cf. also Dorotheus, *Instr.* 10,104 (336–8).

[53] 15.1 (880D). Already Pachomius seems to identify bodily and spiritual resurrection with love: cf. *Vita Prima* 57 (39–40, 190). For the relationship between language, anatomy and sexuality, see T. Laqueur, *Making Sex: Body and Gender from the Greeks to Freud*, Cambridge, MA: Harvard University Press, 1990, 1–24.

[54] 26.31 (1024B).

[55] 30.6 (1156D).

[56] 14.23 (868A). Cf. also 27.17 (1100A) and Barsanuphius 240.

[57] *Prakt.* 53 (620) and 29 (566–8). Cf. also *Apophth.* Nau 71 (1908, p. 66); Barsanuphius 518 and 524. See also Ps. Athanasius, *Life of Syncletica*, ch. 19 (PG28.1496C) and ch. 100 (1549B).

[58] 15.83 (901D).

it; hence, grace cannot be afforded to anyone if it is not also accorded to the body:

> For the spiritual things are achieved by means of sensory things. [59]

> The virtue of the soul is modelled on outward behaviour and ... the soul becomes like its bodily occupations. It conforms itself (*typoutai*) to its activities and takes its shape (*schematizetai*) from them.[60]

In fact, each ascetic struggle is but a reaffirmation of the incarnation. Therefore, the earthly may be used in order to challenge the earthly, in order to prevent the body from dominating us, and in order to transfigure the body. The earthly finds, however, its full meaning only in divine glory. To look for ultimate meaning in material creation itself, apart from God, to absolutize the relative, is to disable it tragically. Being relative, the body is related to both God and other people:

> If I bind the body by fasting, yet by condemning my neighbour I am handed over to it again.[61]

It is no less than a true miracle, a thing of wonder, to witness the polluted body being cleansed and purified again by the same body:

> It is not surprising for the immaterial to struggle with the immaterial. However, it is truly surprising for a person inhabiting matter and in conflict with this hostile and crafty matter, to put to flight immaterial foes.[62]

Yet there is, in John, no trace of Messalianism and no inclination to any form of 'mystical sensuality' or materialism. If bodily sin seems to be stressed,[63] it is because the Christian ascetic does not fight mere ideas or theories. The struggle should be seen as a fight for survival, not an attempt to escape. John wants the body to be treated with discernment, with delicacy and love,[64] even when confronting its aberrations. The body embodies sin; but it is not in itself sinful. The body is not sacred; but it is to be sanctified. This point will emerge more fully in the later treatment of tears.

---

[59] 13.2 (860A). Mark the Monk, *De lege spir.* 162 (PG65.925A) adopts similar terminology when referring to the origin of sin. Symeon the New Theologian, *Thanks.* 1 (318) speaks of the body sharing in God's grace, and uses similar phraseology.

[60] 25.54 (1000D–01A). Cf. also 28.25 (1133B).

[61] 15.83 (901D).

[62] 15.71 (896C). Cf. also 14.24 (868C), 22 (868B); and 26.16 (1020A).

[63] Cf. 2.17 (657C); 13.5 (860BC); 15.1 (880D), 47–8 (889C) and 67 (896A); 21.16 (952D) and 26.iii,23 (1088A). The term 'mystical sensuality' is from A. Guillaumont, 'Les Messaliens,' *Mystique et Continence* (Etudes Carmélitaines, 31ème année: 1952), 138.

[64] 26.33 (1024D). Climacus recommends that one could fast only when it does not impair one's health: cf. 26.ii,26 (1065A). This echoes Barsanuphius, *Letter* 23.

We have seen how, through divine grace, one may attain the *kata physin* from the *para physin* condition. Nevertheless, bodily nature is very deceptive and demons can easily exploit it. One should never trust the body but rather struggle continually for its transfiguration. Climacus writes:

> Throughout your life, do not trust your clay body, and do not rely on it until you meet Christ.[65]

He does not, however, spell out whether we shall encounter Christ only at the time of death or in fact earlier. To see Christ in this life may still be possible. Elsewhere John observes:

> We shall be faced by toil of this kind until the divine fire enters into our sanctuary (Ps. 72.16).[66]

Resurrection of the Body

To speak of resurrection of the dead may prove a scandal for some. Yet an even greater scandal may be caused by speaking of a resurrection *before* death as an indication of the resurrection after death, a resurrection of the *living* as a prefiguration of the resurrection of the dead, a resurrection *here* and *now*, which would offer a glimpse of the eschatological resurrection (cf. Ps. 26.13). It is precisely the monks, according to Abba Serapion, who desire to anticipate, and who enjoy hearing about, this resurrection.[67] Although John does not, in fact, refer anywhere to Christ's transfiguration as an anticipation of the final resurrection, the idea of an anticipated resurrection is clearly implied in his statements regarding the 'resurrection of the soul before the general resurrection,'[68] which reveal the potential spirituality of created nature and also reflect the function of monks as prophets of the mysteries of the age to come. Mark the Monk observes that such a resurrection in no way detracts from the uniqueness of resurrection on the last day:

---

[65] 15.13 (881D). On the 'crafty' nature of the body, cf. 15.71 (896C).

[66] 26.7 (1013C).

[67] *Ep. ad monachos* 7 and 10 (PG40.932D and 936D). Cf. also Pachomius *Vita Prima* 56 (38–9, 189), *Apophth.* Theodora 10 (ed. Guy, 23), Barsanuphius 607, and John Moschus, *Pratum*, Kosmas 171 (PG87.3040B). For more examples, see *Apophth.* Pambo 12 (PG65.372A) and Nau 235 (1909, p. 362); Mark the Monk, *Cap. de temp.* 26 (PG65.1068AB) and Abba Isaiah, *Logos* 29, 1 (198).

[68] 29. title (1148A), 2 and 4 (1148BD); 15.58 (892D) and 6.20 (796C–97B). The distinction between the two stages of resurrection – first of the soul and later of the body – is also found in Evagrius: cf. *Gnostic Chapters* 5, 19 and 22 (327). For similar references, cf. Chrysostom, *Ad Theodorum lapsum* 1,13 (PG47.295); Basil, *In Ps.* 44 (PG29.400CD); *Mac. Hom.* 5, 8 and 9 (60–61); 11, 1 (69–97); 15, 38 (149–50); 32,2 (252); 34,2 (261); 36, 1 (264): in this passage, Macarius speaks of 'a twofold resurrection of souls and bodies;' Mark the Monk, *De baptismo* (PG65.1009BC). Cf. also Symeon the New Theologian, *TGP* 1.76 (62); *Cat.* 8 (100); Greg. of Sinai, *Chapt.* 38 and 47 (36 and 38); Kallistos/Ignatios, *Cent.* 16 (214), 100 (294), 67 (261) and 96 (292).

> We have said these things neither excluding the future events nor limiting the universal retribution to the present life.[69]

In the words of Isaac the Syrian, one is able to 'breathe from here the air of that resurrection.'[70] Symeon the New Theologian was to take up John's terminology and speak of 'the spiritual rebirth and resurrection of the dead souls in a spiritual manner.'[71] Yet both he and John, while not denying the resurrection of the body, are certainly not as explicit about this as Gregory Palamas was in the fourteenth century.[72]

For John, it is precisely the person who reveals a comprehensive attitude towards the body, who also has a vision of God's splendour in the body, and who can be said to 'have risen incorruptible before the general resurrection.'[73] John's distinction between the two resurrections is not on the level of body–soul but rather on the level of before and after death. The body tends to denote the entire person; so, too, does the soul. In the above phrase from the *Ladder*, John simply informs his readers that transfiguration is possible here and now. While yet alive on this earth, one can place one's body on God's throne – 'one is rapt as though in heaven.'[74] These passages are found in the twenty-ninth step of the *Ladder*, which concerns dispassion (*apatheia*). This context is significant because, like dispassion, resurrection is something for which the ascetic continually strives, something of which one can have a foretaste but which one always anticipates.

Even as Christ is divine–human in heaven, one can become human–divine, by God's grace, on earth, though subject to death. An angel relates to Climacus that he cannot reach the state where Christ is because he does not possess the 'fire of incorruption.'[75] It appears that 'incorruption' in this life may only be tasted partially, or incipiently, as the first fruits or a pledge. Upon reaching dispassion, one has clearly attained this kind of incorruptibility.[76] However, it seems that this is not a permanent state. John is not particular in explaining what the resurrection of the last day will resemble, as distinct from the

---

[69] *De his.* 137 (PG65.952A). Cf. also Athanasius, *Vita Ant.* 91 (PG26.972B) and Barsanuphius 607.

[70] *Mystic Treatises* (211; cf. also 305 and 377).

[71] *Cat.* 6 (p. 46).

[72] *Triads* 1, 3, 33. For Gregory Palamas, too, the 'first resurrection is that of the soul:' cf. *Hom.* 16 (PG 151.217A) and *Ad Xenam de mentali quietudine* (PG150.1049D). Baptism is often regarded as a prelude to bodily resurrection: cf. Mark the Monk, *De bapt.* (PG65.1009AB); Nilus, *Ep.* 3, 135 (PG79.445D) and *De vol. paup.* 50 (PG79.1033B). Cf. also J. Daniélou, *Platonisme et théologie mystique. Doctrine spirituelle de Saint Grégoire de Nysse*, Paris: 1953, 57.

[73] 15.58 (893A).

[74] 29.3 (1148C). The emphasis on the word 'rapture' (*ekstasis*) shows that it is a result of outgoing love for God.

[75] 27.ii.13 (1109C). Cf. also P. Brown, *The Body and Society*, 237–8.

[76] 29.2 (1148BC).

resurrection that we experience now. What matters for John is that here and now, from this earthly life, one can transfigure the human body and human nature, as well as the whole created universe, into a positive, a 'fiery' gift. It may seem a morbid thought, but for the ascetic Fathers, the anticipation of the resurrection is paralleled by the anticipation of death.[77] In this regard, John emphasizes the significance of the remembrance of death (*mneme thanatou*), which renounces the fallen body.[78]

What has been said so far also sheds light on the veneration, particularly in the Eastern Orthodox Churches, of the relics of saints and of pieces of their clothing. There is no sharp distinction between the two in the Christian East. In the Book of Acts, for instance, Peter performed many miracles in the early years of the Church (Acts 3), but we are also told of other wonders effected by his shadow alone (Acts 5.15). The woman with the issue of blood was healed by touching Christ's garment (Mt. 9.20). In the *Life of Saint Antony* many people sought to touch Antony, and in the *First Greek Life* it is written of Pachomius that a woman with an issue of blood 'touched the cowl on his head and was healed immediately.'[79] The idea is the same when John Climacus describes the condition of the monk Menas whose body, after death, gives off a sweet-smelling fragrance:

> The whole place where the saint was resting was filled with fragrance ...
> We all saw that fragrant myrrh was flowing like two fountains from his precious feet.[80]

Climacus' theology of the body enables him to see, in the transfiguration of the dead monk, a resurrection before the final resurrection. This is pointed out still more strikingly in the example of the empty tomb of Hesychius the Chorebite (cf. Gen. 5.24).[81] The monk Menas' sweat and toil became like 'myrrh' anointing his body:

---

[77] Regarding death of the soul, cf. Basil, *Hom. quod Deus non est auctor malorum* 7 (PG31.345A). Cf. also Greg. of Sinai, *Chapt.* 34 and 37 (p. 36) and Greg. Palamas, *On Divine and Divinising Participation* 8 (2, p. 144).

[78] 16.20 (929A).

[79] Ch. 41 (25–6, 181). The reference to the *Vita Ant.* by Athanasius is 70 (PG26.941C); cf. also 92 (972C–73A). Cf. also Theodoret, *Phil. Hist.* Palladios, 7, 4, p. 370 (1365D); Aphraate, 8, 13, p. 400 (1376D) and Peter, 9, 15, p. 434 (1388B); *Hist. Monachorum*, 8, Apollo 6 (49); 13 John 9 (p. 100); Palladius, *Hist. Laus.* Domnenos 84 (113–14); Barsanuphius 123 and 174; Cyril of Scythopolis, *Life of Sabas*, 13 (164.14–20) and *Life of Euthymios*, 40 (60.20–21); John Moschus, *Pratum*, Kosmas 40 (PG87.2893A) and John 87 (2944CD); *Apophth.* Arsenius 42 (PG65.105D–08B). On relics in the later patristic tradition, cf. Greg. Palamas, *Ad Dionysium* 5 (2, p. 497) and *Triads* 2, 12.

[80] 4.29 (697C). Chrysostom describes the effect of grace on the bodies of the saints: 'It flows from the soul to the body, and from the body to the clothes, and from the clothes to the sandals, and from the sandals to the shadows.' Cf. *Dicta postquam reliquiae martyrum* 1 (PG63.469–70).

[81] Cf. 6.20 (797A).

> The sweat of his toils was offered as myrrh to God, and it was truly accepted as myrrh by God.[82]

Barsanuphius notes of such ascetics: 'They laboured, they were magnified, they were glorified, they were illumined, they lived because they first died.'[83] In this respect, these ascetic writers transcend the Platonist *soma–sema* scheme in an extreme, yet effective, manner. For the monk does not treat the body as a tomb; rather, together with the body, the monk is completely entombed in order to be completely risen – body and soul. Thus death gives way to resurrection, which is linked to, though not confounded with, the resurrection of the dead on the last day.

Although the transfiguration of the body, of the bodies of those who have been resurrected before the resurrection, is not permanent, they are nonetheless in a position to see much more than a mere glimpse of the uncreated light. They experience yet other first fruits of the last things, other gifts that were lost with the Fall. This will be understood more clearly in considering an important section of the thirtieth step. There, John describes the effect of God's loving grace on the human body. God's love, he declares, can entirely consume and ravish the heart (S. of S. 4.9). In so doing, God's loving action can also be the cause of a bright and cheerful countenance.[84] John's ascetic proclamations are at one with his doctrinal claims. Following the earlier desert tradition, he closely links faith and moral behavior.[85] He knows very well that corruptibility is a result of the Fall. Technical though it may seem, this doctrinal point is vital for spirituality. It implies that, to the extent that one overcomes sin, in transformation through grace, corruptibility and mortality can in fact diminish. Here and now, the 'outer' person experiences the same as 'the soul.' The relationship between the two resembles 'a mirror' (*esoptron*):

> Even one's outward appearance in the body, as a kind of mirror, reveals the spendour of the soul.[86]

The classic example of this process in early monastic literature is found in the *Life of Antony*, where Athanasius relates how Antony's body had not deteriorated even after twenty years of austere ascetic discipline and that his health was in good condition right up until the end of his long life. The effect of God's grace, we are told, literally shone on Antony's face: 'For, since his soul was undisturbed, so too were his outer senses; and even his face shone as if from the joy of his soul.'[87] Moreover, in this state, the ascetic may no longer

---

[82] 4.29 (697C).

[83] Barsanuphius 120. Cf. also Theodoretos, *Phil. Hist.*, Symeon the Elder, 6, 9, p. 358 (1361D).

[84] 30.11 (1157AC).

[85] Cf. also 30.14 (1157C).

[86] 30.11 (1157AC). A similar notion is found in Isaac the Syrian, *Mystic Treatises* (349).

[87] *Vita Ant.* 67 (PG26.940AB); cf. also 14 and 93 (864C and 973AB). There are similar examples in other writers: cf. *Mac. Hom.* 12, 8 (110–11) and 17, 2 (167–8). Theodoretos, *Phil. Hist.*,

even wish to eat. This does not mean that the body is treated as less significant than the soul or as a trivial part of the human person. Rather, the whole person is directed by *eros* to God, an action impelling one to 'forget' to eat or even rendering food unnecessary. To understand this, we only have to look at bodily *eros* and how it affects lovers.[88] Barsanuphius says of such ascetics:

> They are not grieved by hunger, thirst, or by any other earthly thing; for they have been set free from every crime, passion, and sin in life. Their food and drink and clothing is the Holy Spirit.[89]

Sleep, too, does not hinder one's union with God in deification when one has acquired what, as we have already observed, John calls 'bodiless bodies' (*asomata somata*).[90] This occurs when the bodies are transfigured:

> I sleep because my nature requires this; but my heart is awake (S of S 5.2) in the abundance of my love.[91]

The seemingly dualistic statements in the *Ladder*, then, are to be seen in light of the New Testament distinction between flesh and spirit, rather than in the light of any body–soul dichotomy. Even while using predominantly negative language, John's is basically a unitary view. To be more precise, it is dialectical: the body is an adversary, but it is also a friend. Although marred by the Fall, the body remains God's creation and, following Christ's incarnation, it is called to share in the glory of the resurrection. It can be seen that the consideration of 'the body' shows a configuration of divine and human acts in which Christ's incarnation opens the way to the monk's conquest over the

---

Markianos, 3, 18, p. 282 (1337A) and Julian Sabas, 2, 14, p. 224 (1317A); *Hist. Monachorum* 2 Abba Or 1 (35); 6, Theon 1 (44); 8, Apollo 52 (67); 1, John of Lykopolis 46 (27); 11, Skourous 6 (91) and 17, Isidore 3 (114), which is also mentioned in Palladius, *Hist. Laus.* 71 (PG34.1177D–78A); Diadochus, *Cent.* 25 (96–7); Cyril of Scythopolis, *Life of Sabas*, 5 (89.15f); 24 (108.27–109.1); 17 (184.11–13); 173.19–24; *Life of Euthymios*, 40 (59.21–22). Cf. also Kallistos/Ignatios, *Cent.* 90 (284). My account has centered largely on the spiritual dimensions of the body. For a general account of the hermeneutics – and especially the 'political' and 'social' function – of the human body in relation to early Christian monasticism, see R. Valantasis, 'A Theory of the Social Function of Asceticism,' in Wimbush and Valantasis, *Asceticism*, 544–52; see also S. Rubenson, 'Christian Asceticism and the Emergence of the Monastic Tradition,' in ibid., 49–57. For attitudes and practices in regard to the body in late antiquity, see P. Brown, *The Body and Society*, esp. Part Two entitled 'Asceticism and Society in the Eastern Empire,' 210–338.

[88] 30.11 (1157AC). Cf. also *Apophth.* Nau 149–50 (1908, p. 51) and 175 (1908, pp. 266–8); *Hist. Monachorum*, Prol. 7 (7); *Vita Prima* 89 (128, 206); John Moschus, *Pratum*, Theodore 54 (PG87.2908D–09A). Cf. also Symeon the New Theologian, *Eth.* 1 (296). The subject of *eros* is examined in Chapter 6, but the reader is also directed to P. Brown, *The Body and Society*, 238–9.

[89] Barsanuphius 173 and 78. Cf. also Barsanuphius 36; *Hist. Monachorum*, 1, John of Lykopolis 17 and 46 (15 and 27); and Apollo 5 (48). See *Life of John the Hesychast*, p. 211.1–14. Cf. also *Hist. Monachorum*, 11, Skourous 5 (91) and 12, Helle 15 (97), where an angel feeds the ascetics.

[90] 30.6 (1156D).

[91] 30.7 (1156D).

body in *ascesis* and offers hope for the restoration of the stricken body in the final resurrection.

Sarx – the Flesh

Sarx *in the Christian Scriptures*

The word 'flesh' – *bâsâr* in Hebrew, *sarx* in the Septuagint and the New Testament – can sometimes signify the body (cf. Lk. 24.29), but more often it has the meaning of the 'carnal mind' described by Paul (Rom. 8.6–7).[92] It must be understood at the outset that, first, the flesh is not to be regarded as sinful in itself, since Christ assumed it at the incarnation; and, second, unlike the body, which is something particular, *sarx* refers to human nature as a whole. As has been noted, for the ascetic tradition, human nature must be described not in terms of any body–soul opposition but rather on the level of *kata physin* and *para physin*, of humanity before the Fall and humanity as fallen. Both the body and the soul are natural when they coinhere with God's will. Curiously, they are ours only when they are fully God's. The 'temple of God' (1 Cor. 3.16, 2 Cor. 6.16), the monk's entire person is the 'property' of God. John says quite emphatically and categorically:

> For the body does not belong to you; it is a creation of God.[93]

One must also keep in mind once again the distinction in Greek ascetic literature between *physis* and *hyper physin*, between the natural and the supernatural within the human person.[94] Elsewhere John even contrasts the monolithic nature of *physis* with the ecstatic, loving nature of the human person.[95] Fallen human nature, often simply referred to as *sarx*, is contrary to our natural way of life, which is spiritual or 'according to the spirit.' Yet, no matter how polluted human nature may be, the human person always remains 'extremely beautiful,' says John. It exists in the image of divine beauty and glory. A human being is never self-sufficient, determined by its own fallen nature, but rather has the capacity to move out in an act of personal, ecstatic love towards another person – whether divine or human. And, for John, one has this capacity no matter how deeply one is steeped in sin.[96]

---

[92] The variety of meanings attached to the term 'flesh' in the Scriptures is taken up by Cassian, *Conf.* 4, 10 (174) and Isaac the Syrian, *Mystic Treatises* (16).

[93] 22.16 (986C).

[94] 15.70 (896C).

[95] 30.7 (1156D).

[96] 26.72–73 (1033CD).

In the New Testament, then, the word 'flesh' refers – in agreement also with Hebraic thinking – to our entire human nature.[97] When the term is found in opposition to other aspects of the human person, this indicates either the limitations of human nature *vis-à-vis* divine nature, the distinction between the creature and the creator, or else human nature's fallen state. On the contrary, where the term is used in isolation, it does not suggest any moral implications. For the New Testament writers, it is – with very few exceptions (see, for example, 2 Pet. 2.18) – quite clear that *sarx* does not refer solely to the body, since the sins attributed to the flesh are not only bodily sins (Gal. 5.19–21). Instead, the term assumes a moral value. Jesus reminds the Jews that fleshly or evil thoughts come from the heart (Mt. 5.28). Similarly, 'spirit' is not confined to those aspects that are not bodily.[98] There is no contradiction between 'spirit' and 'body' on the ontological level. Nor is this a matter of mere intellectual distinctions on the part of Paul. It refers to an existential condition, as we have already seen, a conflict that is experienced personally and profoundly. For Paul, *sarx* includes his whole life prior to his conversion; it involves all that against which he must struggle in the aftermath of his conversion. With his conversion (Acts 9.1–19), it is not just his attitude to his body that changes, but his entire life. This is signified by his being blinded, then by having his sight restored, as well as by the changing of his name from 'Saul' to 'Paul.' In his epistles, 'flesh' denotes the *whole* person *qua* fallen, while 'spirit' denotes the *whole* person *qua* redeemed. *Sarx* is the 'old person' that must be laid aside in order for one to put on the 'new person' (Eph. 4.22 and Col. 3.9).[99]

Sarx: *Varieties of Meaning*

As with the term *soma*, each reference in the *Ladder* to the term *sarx* must be examined carefully and separately because John employs *sarx* with different connotations. Of the approximately thirty times that John mentions *sarx*, over half refer to fallen human nature. John speaks of 'hating one's own flesh.'[100] And the monks in the Alexandrian Prison 'exhorted one another, saying: "Let us run, brothers ... and not spare this our foul and wicked flesh".'[101]

---

[97] Cf. Tresmontant, *La pensée Hebraïque*, 96; J. Bonsirven, 'Chair,' *DS* 2 (1953), 439. Cf. also Athanasius, *Contra Arianos* 3, 30 (PG26.388AC); Symeon the New Theologian, *Cat.* 3 (282); Niketas Stethatos, *Cent.* 2,3–5 (298–9) and 15 (pp. 301–02); Greg. Palamas, *Triads* 2, 9: 'And it is the whole of person that is called *sarx*.'

[98] Cf. 15.83 (901Cf.) and 71 (897C). Cf. esp. Greg. Palamas, *Triads* 2,9: 'And spirit, too, is the whole person.'

[99] *Cap. de temp.* (PG 65.1061D). For the imagery of the 'old person,' cf. also Greg. Nyssa, *De Virginitate* 5, 12 and 13 (PG 46.348B, 376BD); In *Cant. Cant.* 11 (PG 44.1004D–05A) and *Mac. Hom.* 48, 5 (pp. 314–15).

[100] 2.1 (653C). Cf. *Apophth.* Antony 33 (PG65.85C).

[101] 5.5 (769D).

A less negative sense of *sarx* is conveyed elsewhere, when Climacus speaks of it in a more neutral way. At times, he almost identifies *sarx* with *soma*, indicating the physical members of the body.[102] There is even one instance where *sarx* is referred to as God's creation.[103] The New Testament sense of *sarx* as equivalent to the human person itself (cf. Jn 1.14) is nowhere to be found in the *Ladder*, except possibly in one passage when Climacus quotes one of the Psalms (cf. Ps. 27.7).[104]

Despite, then, certain passages with positive connotations, the *Ladder* gives the impression of a rather negative attitude towards the flesh. It is not even always evident that John has in mind the fallen flesh. Seemingly, he adopts a dualistic view eschewing the flesh as evil. In fact, however, his is the traditional asceticism, which exposes the evil that is found in the condition of the flesh, rather than pointing to the flesh itself as evil. John's stance is dialectical: like the body, the *sarx* too is both good and bad, natural and unnatural alike, 'our partner' – as he describes it – but one which is to be 'observed at all times,'[105] an 'enemy' but a foe who is described as 'domestic.'[106] Hence, also, the ambivalent designation of the flesh as 'an ungrateful and wicked friend'[107] or, in a phrase which illustrates clearly John's view of *sarx*, as 'my beloved adversary, the flesh.'[108] There are, therefore, several passages in which the meaning of *sarx* is ambiguous. And it is in this genuine self-questioning that John emerges as a monk in the authentic tradition of the Christian East:

> How can I hate him when my nature disposes me to love him? How can I break away from him when I am bound to him forever? How can I escape from him when he is going to rise with me? How can I make him incorrupt when he has received a corruptible nature?
>
> He is my helper and my enemy, my assistant and my opponent, a protector and a traitor ... I embrace him. And I turn away from him ... How can I be my own friend and my own enemy?[109]

Thus *sarx* is not evil in itself; it is merely liable to evil. And *ascesis* is by no means directed against the flesh, which is God's creation. It is the flesh as a bundle of passions, which must be fought against, not the flesh itself. In the

---

[102] Cf. 9.8 (841C); 18.1 (937A); 26.14 (1017B); 26.iii,7 and 8 (1085B); 29.3 (1148C) and 15 (1149C).

[103] 24.7 (984A).

[104] 30.11 (1157B).

[105] 27.ii,11 (1109B).

[106] 15.39 (888D).

[107] 9.8 (841C).

[108] 15.29 (885D).

[109] 15.83 (901C–04B). Cf. also 26.ii,14 (1061B). In the passage quoted, Climacus is in fact referring to *soma* but the ambiguity can only be understood in the light of the *soma–sarx* distinction.

words of Abba Poemen: 'We have not been taught to kill our bodies, but to kill our passions.'[110] *Sarx*, understood as the fallen human person, draws John's attention to the monks in the Alexandrian Prison who, as he says, obviously echoing Abba Dorotheus of Gaza, 'kill the flesh, just as it has killed them.'[111] In the chapter on ascetic struggle it will be claimed that, for John, the struggle is not ultimately leveled against the passions but only engaged for the purpose of the direction of the passions, or of their redirection, towards God.

The proper sense of sin in this connection is well understood by Dorotheus: 'Evil is not partial, nor is it spatial; but it is found in the entire body; it contains the soul and controls all of its powers.'[112] And Abba Isaiah sums up the whole matter by stating: 'Sin is not just one thing but the entire "old person" is called sin.'[113] It could be said that to fight the body as if it were evil is to identify *soma* with *sarx* – an identification, however, that is itself but another consequence of the 'works of the flesh.' The correct intention, as will be seen below, is to put the flesh to death in order to resurrect the body. Abba Alonius says: 'If I had not destroyed myself completely, I should not have been able to rebuild and reshape myself again.'[114] And Barsanuphius repeatedly advises: 'Die fully in order that you may live fully in Christ Jesus our Lord! Die ... and you will be comforted! Mortify yourself and become alive!'[115] Similarly, John, resuming as it were the Pauline argument (Rom. 7.24), writes:

> If the flesh ... is death, whoever has conquered it undoubtedly does not die. But who is the one that shall live and not see the death (Ps. 88.46) of the impurity of his flesh?[116]

John therefore advises the spiritual guide 'to be crucified with Christ (Gal. 5.24) ... in order to be risen with him.'[117]

John of the *Ladder* would also claim that such phrases as 'the polluted brick-making of the clay ... that red and burning sea,' and others referring to human sinfulness, do not in fact apply to the body itself, but to the *sarx*, to the entire fallen nature. If they were to be applied to the body, then everyone would stand condemned before God. After all, he says, since our very existence is a bodily existence, there would be no point to any ascetic struggle. Nonetheless, evidently referring to those whose flesh has already been

---

[110] *Apophth.* Poemen 184 (PG 65.368A). Cf. also Basil, *Ad Adolesc.* 7 (PG31.581), and Dorotheus, *Instr.* 15, 162 (450).

[111] 5.5 (769D). Cf. also 15.29 (885CD). For Dorotheus' words, cf. Palladius *Hist. Laus.*, Dorotheus 2 (17).

[112] *Instr.* 1, 3 (150).

[113] *Logos* 21, 2 (p. 121).

[114] *Apophth.* Alonius 2 (PG65.133A).

[115] Barsanuphius 37, 52 and 207.

[116] 15.30 (885D).

[117] *Shep.* 100 (1205B).

transfigured, John says that not all but *most* people are involved in such a confusion of concepts.[118] The danger can be overcome. It is the 'thickness' of our sinful condition that covers or conceals our true personality.[119] Very often, however, our bodily actions may help us to understand how we must treat the *sarx*. For example, carnal *eros* shows us how we should direct our flesh toward God in a passionate act of divine *eros*: it should be a movement away from our self to another person, away from any self-regarding attitude toward an 'ecstatic' relationship.[120] Earlier, Mark the Monk had written that a sinful attitude or 'ill-disposition' towards the body is overcome precisely by one's desire for God.[121]

How is one to turn away from the sinful desires of the *sarx*? In a way, this question is wrongly stated. John would say that we do not turn away from the *sarx* itself but instead turn the flesh, as a manifestation of the fallen state, towards God. It is then 'seized' from the earth-bound level and ceases to be *sarx*, whereupon one comes to live 'in heaven' and no longer 'on earth.' John says: one is 'rapt *as if* in heaven.'[122] And Abba Zosimas says of such persons: 'They walk on earth but have no earthly thoughts.'[123] The goal, therefore, of the ascetic life is for one to be 'rapt as if in heaven.' John observes that 'the tyrant of despondency' attacks the monk's flesh especially when the monk has 'forgotten about the things that are above.'[124] We do not shake off the *sarx*, for it is our 'partner for life.' It is in fact, John says, our 'spouse,'[125] and therefore inseparable from us. Without it, we are not ourselves; without it, we are not fully human.

Climacus prefers to speak of 'the inclinations and alterations' (*ropai kai tropai*) of the *sarx* which, again, are not evil in themselves but impel us to struggle, by turning away from our stricken self towards God. This underlies John's understanding of the passions. There must be no 'idio-tropy' (self-ward turn) but rather a 'theo-tropy' (or God-ward tendency), to adopt John's terminology. This comes about 'through the Holy Spirit' in cooperation with our own will.[126] The purpose is to become 'immaterial material persons,'[127] to be inside yet outside matter, in the world but not of the world (Jn 1.10), with a

---

[118] *Shep.* 100 (1204AB).

[119] 30.18 (1160D); 26.40 (1025C) and 13 (1016D) and 26.ii,14 (1061AC).

[120] 26.31 (1024BC) and 2.17 (657C).

[121] *Cap. de temp.* 26 (PG65.1064C).

[122] 29.3 (1148C). The word 'as' gives Climacus the benefit of the doubt regarding his realism; one is not *in* heaven but '*as if* in heaven.'

[123] *Alloquia* 1 (PG78.1681C). Cf. also Basil, *Praevia Institutio Ascetica* (PG31.620–25).

[124] 13.10 (860D–61A).

[125] 27.ii, 11 (1101A).

[126] Ibid. Cf. also Greg. Nyssa's play on the words 'pleasure-loving' and 'God-loving' in *De Virginitate* 8 (PG46.357A); cf. also Mark the Monk, *De bapt.* (PG65.993D).

[127] 27.26 (1101A).

body but without lowly fleshly desires. There is a certain ambiguity, here, similar to the one arising in connection with the term *pathos*, which will be discussed in a separate chapter. *Pathos* may signify a fallen reality, a neutral or physical motion, or else an attraction toward God. A move away from God could cost us our life. John warns us not to exchange gold for mud; in the words of his contemporary, Isaac the Syrian, describing the degrees of knowledge, we are not to exchange 'a pearl of great price for a copper coin.'[128]

A passion or 'illness' may have either a positive or else a negative effect, depending on its aim or direction. By our 'clay' we sin; and it is again by our 'clay' that we are cleansed.[129] When, however, a natural inclination is directed toward God, John no longer uses the term *pathos*.[130] Only in our estrangement from God is the *sarx* called a 'beast,' 'heavy' and 'wild,' and 'illogical (*alogon*).'[131] This is not the case when the monk is turned toward God, when the flesh finds its *logos*, namely its original and final meaning in God. To quote Abba Dorotheus, who also adumbrates the central image adopted by John:

> Imagine two ladders: one leading up to heaven, and the other down to Hades, and then imagine yourself standing on earth between the two ladders.[132]

For John, the saint is preeminently the person who can climb the ladder leading to God, thereby 'transfiguring (*metapoiesei*) and sanctifying' the *sarx*. This implies a kind of re-creation (*poiesis*) of the flesh through its transformation (*meta-poiesis*), a return to the original condition created by God. The process, therefore, implies a 're-directing' (*metaphora*) of the *sarx* towards God, the 're-grafting' into the source of life, which is God.[133] The flesh is to be guided towards God in order that the body may be transfigured, so that it may be enhanced or endowed with the good 'mutation (*alloiosis*),' to adopt alternative patristic terminology. This reality is certainly possible and achievable, says John in another context that reveals sacramental overtones:

> If a body is changed in its activity from contact with another body, then how can one remain unchanged who touches the body of God with innocent hands?[134]

---

[128] *Mystic Treatises* (245).

[129] 26.16 (1020A).

[130] Cf. 26.2, 41 (1068CD).

[131] 26.13 (1016D). Cf. also 1.20 (636D).

[132] *Instr.* 14, 154 (432).

[133] 15.49 (889C); 21.23 (953AB) and 24.8 (984AB). Peter Brown examines the role of the body and its redirection or transformation: cf. *Body and Society*, 238–9.

[134] 28.52 (1137C). For the use of the term 'change' in the Greek Fathers, cf. Hausherr, *Méthode*, xxxii.

By attaining the state of the *hyper physin*, in effect one is returning to the natural condition of communion with God.[135] What seems supernatural or metaphysical is ultimately and really only 'physical,' namely quite natural. The struggle is against the fallen nature, the state of the *para physin*, of the un-natural, the condition in which we are no longer human but in fact 'inhumane' (*apanthropos*).[136] It is natural for our flesh to move in some direction, but its natural inclination is to move towards God.[137] Unfortunately, our predicament (Gal. 5.16–17) is that the flesh moves away from God, following 'the contestations of nature.'[138] Hence the perennial struggle against it,[139] since the 'taming' of the flesh 'is not ultimately resolved this side of the grave.'[140] Meanwhile, the various forms of ascetic struggle are ways of directing, ultimately of deceiving the flesh:

> And does not the flesh desire flesh too? Yet we who constrain nature, and desire to take the kingdom by force, try various tricks to deceive this deceiver.[141]

Despite the fact that fasting, for example, is a way in which the sinful flesh is 'weakened' and 'melted,'[142] it is a way ultimately leading to the healthy reintegration or to the integral health of the human person.[143]

Ways of Struggle Against Sarx

John speaks of three different, yet fundamentally similar, ways of carrying out this ascetic struggle. First, *sarx*, according to him, embraces a multitude of worldly matters: 'money,' 'material possessions,' 'worldly glory,' 'friends,' 'relatives' (cf. Mt. 10.36) and, in general, 'earthly matters.' He stresses the need to avoid treating these things as ends in themselves. Only when one is denuded, 'having stripped oneself of all clothing and care ... and always looking heavenward,'[144] can one also direct the *sarx* towards God. John's advice is to move away visibly from 'all those who are relatives and friends.'[145] In the

---

[135] 15.70 (896BC) and 29.2 (1148BC).

[136] 15.23 (884B).

[137] 27.17 (1100A).

[138] 15.83 (901C).

[139] 1.45 (641C); 15.17 (884A) and 29.4 (1148D). Cf. also Dorotheus, *Instr.* 16.167 (460).

[140] 14.6 (865A).

[141] 15.23 (884C).

[142] 18.1 (937A) and 23.14 (980A). For a challenging exploration into the religious symbolism of food and fasting in medieval asceticism, cf. C. Bynum, *Holy Feast and Holy Fast*, Berkeley: University of California Press, 1987, 48–69. Prof. Bynum deals predominantly with representatives of the Western Christian tradition, and primarily of centuries much later than John Climacus.

[143] 14.31 (869B).

[144] 2.1 (653C).

[145] 3.22 (668D). Cf. 15.15 (881D).

ascetic tradition, the words 'world' (Jn 17.16), 'flesh' and 'family' (Mt. 10.37) have a wider than merely moral meaning. To adopt Rudolf Otto's term, these concepts have undergone a certain 'schematisation.' So John will write:

> Certain learned elders have defined renunciation well by saying that it is hostility to the body.[146]

Yet such renunciation – *xeniteia* or *apotagi* – has a broader and deeper significance because John also stresses the importance of love. Flight from the world is only the negative, but not an inevitable side of *xeniteia*, which, in its positive sense, denotes a consonance with God's will. It is the learning of a new or foreign (*xenos*) language, that of the divine way and will. The exodus into the desert is less of a movement *away* than a movement *into* the realm where one encounters one's true self and God. Jesus begins his ministry with such a withdrawal *into* the desert (Mt. 4.1; Lk. 4.1–2); and the early monks believed that Paul, too, retreated to the desert after his conversion (Gal. 1.17). The retreat and withdrawal, however, are not an escape but an encounter that ensues in the desert, a fierce confrontation and struggle against the demons. The desert, according to the *Life of Antony*, becomes a source of life for the monk, just as the water of the sea is for fish:[147] a monk moves out into the desert in a zealous search for the deeper source of life. For John, intense faith and extreme *xeniteia* are closely linked:

> No one has surrendered oneself to exile (*xeniteia*) to such an extent as that great man [Abraham], who heard: 'Go forth out of your land, and out of your kindred, and out of the house of your father' (Gen. 12.1). And then, he was called into a barbarous land that spoke another tongue.[148]

One moves away from the earthly, fallen self, towards the unknown in order to find the unknowable God. Here again, John's ascetic teaching complements the doctrinal teaching about knowing the unknowable God. The apophatic tradition is wonderfully fostered in the mountainous desert of Sinai, as it was in the mystical formulations of the more intellectual writers, such as Evagrius. John's conviction reflects Moses' vision on the same mountain. John says:

---

[146] 15.15 (881D). On the meaning of *xeniteia*, cf. Guillaumont, 'Le dépaysement,' in *Aux Origines*.

[147] Athanasius, *Vita Ant.* 85 (PG26.961C–64A). See also *Sayings*, Antony 10. For the understanding of the desert, cf. Guillaumont, 'La conception du désert.' For the positive side of 'renunciation,' cf. Greg. Nyssa, *De Virginitate* 9 (PG46.360AB); *Apophth.* Theodore of Pherme 14 (PG65.189D–92A); Isidore the Priest 2 (236A); Moses 7 (284D–85A); Arsenius 13 (92A); *Mac. Hom.* 49, 1 (315–16); *Hist. Monachorum*, 1, John of Lykopolis 26 (18); Cassian, *Inst.* 5, 36, 1 (246–8) and 10, 1 (384); Mark the Monk, *Cap. de temp.* 20 (PG65.1061BC) and *De his* 107 (945B); Barsanuphius 348; Cyril of Scythopolis, *Life of Euthymios* 7 (14.27–15.1); *Life of Abraamios* (245. 30–31); Abba Isaiah, *Logos* 4, 2–3 (17–18) and Isaac the Syrian, *Mystic Treatises* (1, 151 and 294).

[148] 3.28 (668C).

Firm faith is the mother of renunciation ... Love of God is the fountain of exile.[149]

Xeniteia, therefore, is a genuine act of love and faith. One risks life, and is prepared to surrender one's life, in exchange for divine life. Isaac the Syrian shares this experience: 'Lord,' he says, 'make me worthy of hating my life, for the sake of life in you.'[150] In the *Ladder*, *xeniteia* is seen as a result of 'true love for the Lord and genuine seeking after the future kingdom.'[151]

Another way of ascetic struggle against the flesh aims at becoming what we are created to be, namely kings and priests. The ascetic does not suppress the flesh but instead 'educates' it;[152] the aim is to rule over it (Mt. 8.9), rather than allow it to rule as a 'tyrant.'[153] 'Become like a king,'[154] John says, 'and treat your body like a slave.'[155] At the same time, as priests, we should offer the flesh up to God knowing that God alone is the king who 'governs,' who alone can transfigure and fill the emptiness that entered into the world when we moved away from Godliness.[156] The same royal concept underlies the statement by Abba Joseph of Panephysis: 'I am king today, for I reign over the passions.'[157] However, this is further qualified by Gregory the Theologian, who contends that God originally created each person 'as ruler over all that is on earth, though as a ruler that is ruled from above.'[158] Thus, as kings, we order our flesh to be deified, to be redirected and offered eucharistically – in accordance with the priestly order – to the king of kings (1 Tim. 6.5; Rev. 19.16). John identifies such regal subjection of the flesh with the highest of virtues, namely

---

[149] 26.iii,1 (1084C).

[150] *Mystic Treatises* (292).

[151] 2.1 (653B).

[152] 11.6 (852D).

[153] 7.40 (809A). Cf. *Apophth*. Isidore of Pelusium 6 (PG65.224B) and Abba Isaiah, *Logos* 29, 3 (200).

[154] 7.40 (808D).

[155] 3.20 (668A).

[156] 29.15 (1149C); 7.40 (808D–09A) and 29.2 (1148B). Cf. also Mark the Monk, *De bapt.* (PG65.1008B); *Mac. Hom.* 15, 20 (139) and Greg. of Sinai, *Chapt.* 133 (61). For the notion of man as king, ruling over his passions, cf. Athanasius, *Vita Ant.* 52–3 (PG26.917C–20B); Greg. Nyssa, *Adv. castigat.* (PG46.308BC); Greg. Naz., *In laudem S. Cypriani* 15 (PG35.1188AC); Barsanuphius 80 and 204; Dorotheus, *Ep.* 1 (112); *Instr.* 1, 14 (152) and 16, 170 (464); John Moschus, *Pratum,* Leon 112 (PG87.2976C); *Apophth*. Paul of Thebes 1 (PG65.380–81) and Pambo 12 (372A); Niketas Stethatos, *Cent.* 2.37 (306) and 3, 15 (330). For the notion of the human person as king but subservient to God, cf. Basil, *Praevia Institutio Ascetica* 3 (PG31.624C); Chrysostom, *Ad Theod. lapsum* 2, 3 (PG47.312–13); *Comparatio regis et monarchi* 2 (PG47.388) and *De compunctione* 2, 5 (PG47.419); Zosimas, *Alloquia* 1 (PG78.1681B) and 5 (1689B); Dorotheus, *Life* 8 (134) and *Ep.* 8, 193 (514); Isaiah, *Logos* 22, 6 (138) and 26, 4 (186); and Isaac the Syrian, *Mystic Treatises* (243). For 'priestly' imagery, cf. Greg. Nyssa, *De Virginitate* 24 (PG46.413D) and Isaiah, *Logos* 5, 3 (37).

[157] *Apophth*. Joseph of Panephysis 10 (PG65.232AB).

[158] *Or.* 38, 11 (PG36.324A).

purity.[159] John implicitly suggests both the priestly and the royal function of the human person when he claims that one who has reached such purity is not merely a king but an imitator of Peter, who, 'having become pure, himself carries the keys of the kingdom.'[160]

Finally, in a third way of struggle against the flesh, we are told to 'mortify' the flesh, to put it to death in order that it may rise again.[161] John Climacus says that we must become 'eunuchs' (Mt. 19.12).[162] He is not implying the obliteration of the *sarx* or the annihilation of the passions, but rather the 'double death' – as he describes it – that is to be undergone. It is a 'death' which follows and which gives meaning to death, namely the resurrection of a spiritual person, or in Abba Longinus' words, the act of 'giving blood in order to receive the Spirit.'[163] While the monks in the Alexandrian Prison may appear to contemporary readers like 'fools' for Christ, yet they know that if they have not undergone death and resurrection in order to live truly, they will in fact remain dead. Their effort to teach something very fundamental through their extreme, even eccentric, acts of 'folly' is a way of being punished for their sins in this life so as not to suffer the pains of hell thereafter (cf. Tobit 13.2). They are aware that, after all, they live in hell here and now. But as one anticipates hell and lives in it, one may also anticipate and live in paradise, in the light of resurrection.

An Athonite hermit, who had spent several years in a desert cell on Mt Sinai, once told me that the ascetic wears out the body in order to tear away the flesh from the earthly and sinful desires. And in this act of 'wearing out,' in the continual struggle – day in and day out, through endless services, hundreds of prostrations, much fasting, and bodily labour – one finally senses that 'something heavenly is occurring, even within the body.' Death feels as if it is being conquered in the here and now. And then, the same death becomes life-giving; then, one lives out Holy Friday and the Sunday of the Resurrection all in one. This monk was simply acknowledging what hundreds of monastics have experienced throughout the centuries. It is what John lived in the desert of Sinai. This is the experience of the flesh crucified with Christ, buried, and taken down to Hades; there, it becomes as odorous as 'the four day old' corpse of Lazarus (Jn 11.39), so as to acquire the fragrant myrrh of the grace of resurrection (Rom. 6.6–11; Gal. 2.20). Resurrection, for John Climacus, is 'three days old.' Or, elsewhere, he describes it as 'threefold,' which signifies a

---

[159] 15.6 (881B).

[160] 15.66 (896A).

[161] 26.iii, 8 (1085B); 14.15 (865D); 5.5 (764Df); 26.iii,48 (1089C); 15.29 (885CD) and 28 (885C); 15.39 (888D), where Climacus implies a 'suppression' of one's enemies, again adopting a 'royal' image.

[162] 14.15 (865D); 15.17 (884A); 14.14 (865D).

[163] *Apophth.* Longinus 5 (PG65.257B).

victory not only over the body, but over the entire flesh, over one's entire fallen nature – body, soul and spirit.[164] John challenges his reader:

> Consider this question. Who is greater? One who dies and rises again? Or one who does not die at all? Those who extol the latter are deceived; for, Christ both died and rose.[165]

In other words, one's way of life should imitate that of Christ, who is always the archetype. The idea is reflected in earlier authors. Barsanuphius, for instance, says that Christ is our 'type;' and Christ wants the ascetic to ascend the cross in an act of imitation.[166] The monk's life is a life lived out on the cross; and the monk is the authentic 'crusader.' Abba Dorotheus of Gaza asks: 'What else is the cross, but complete mortification achieved through faith in Christ?'[167] In the same vein, Symeon the New Theologian invites challengingly: 'Die and live. Do you not want to? Well, then you are already dead.'[168] This offers a concise and pithy conclusion to John's own view about the significance of the body and the flesh as revelations of the divinely ordained fullness of the human person, and at the same time as realms of its liability to corruption. The body is an instrument of life (such are the implications of *soma*) as well as of death (such are the consequences of *sarx*). And one may be fully alive even while being dead, just as one can be truly dead even while being alive.

---

[164] *Shep.* 100 (1205B). Cf. also Dorotheus, *Instr.* 17.177 (482).
[165] 15.30 (888A).
[166] Barsanuphius 156 and 48. Cf. also Mark the Monk, *Ad Nic.* 7 (PG65.1040A).
[167] *Instr.* 1, 17 (172).
[168] *Eth.* 11 (332).

The monastery of St Catherine from the basin of Elijah
(Photograph: Elizabeth Williams)

CHAPTER 3

Kardia: The Heart

The deep calls unto the deep.

(Psalm 41.8)

Cor ad cor loquitur.

(Cardinal Newman's motto)

Introduction

While in Plato there may be a strong contrast between head and heart, and the real person is always identified more closely with the *nous* or intellect, so that the center of the human person is the head, other classical writers do not emphasize this contrast as much. Homer, for example, claims that one thinks and feels with one's diaphragm (*phrenes*), and a similar view is found among other poets such as Hesiod and the tragedians, who uphold an undifferentiated view regarding personhood, as do Virgil and Lucretius. Aristotle, too, in contrast to Plato, sees the heart as the pivot of the entire human person, and the early Stoics, together with Cicero, tend to agree with him on this point.

In the Old Testament, too, the term heart (*leb, lebab*) is normally used in an all-embracing sense. It signifies not only the emotions, the feelings and the affections, but also the spiritual center of the human person. It is even the seat of thought and reason.[1] The New Testament reflects the Semitic rather than the Platonist approach. After the incarnation, for example, Mary is said to have kept everything in her heart (Lk. 2.19) like a treasure (Mt. 6.21). Moreover, evil thoughts arise from the heart (Mk 7.21; Rom. 1.24), which is seen as the moral center of the human person, the determinant of action. Furthermore, as the inner person (Eph. 3.16–17), the heart signifies the center of the spiritual life of grace (Gal. 4.6).

When the early ascetic writers speak of the human person, they are very hesitant to break it up into various parts or members. Rather, the approach is biblical – even if at times there appears to be a tension between 'Athens' and 'Jerusalem' – and here their attitude resembles perhaps that of the Stoics.[2] This implies a synthesis or even a Christ-centered 'monism,' in accordance with Paul's *nous Christou* (in 1 Cor. 2.16) and *kardia Christou* (in Eph. 3.17), in contrast to any dualist notions. Writers with a stronger Platonist tendency,

---

[1] Cf. Guillaumont, 'Coeur,' 47; and Tresmontant, *La pensée Hebraïque*, 117–23.

[2] Cf. Meyendorff, *Palamas*, 147.

such as Origen, Evagrius and Dionysius, tend to neglect the heart but as a result seem to lose the richness of Hebraic conceptions. This is not the case with John Climacus, who, in any case, as already indicated, has no rigidly defined doctrine of the human person.

John's writings enable us to identify a number of insights, which, together, offer a comprehensive and anthropologically valid unity. For instance, John clearly perceives the way in which sin arises from thought, or even within the intellect itself, and through the heart reaches the body, but he has no mystical doctrine of the heart. At times, he seems to link the heart closely with the soul and even to identify the two:

> The beginning of freedom from anger is silence on the lips when the *heart* is agitated; the middle is silence of the thoughts when the *soul* is slightly agitated.[3]

At other times, John draws a subtle, though imprecise, distinction between heart and soul. The former has a more 'tender,' somewhat 'lighter' sense – if these are adequate words to describe the center of human consciousness – and its connotation is more religious, suggesting the concrete human person in relation to God. The latter is more philosophical, and suggests a somewhat shadowy existence, namely one's natural faculties. However, the distinction is indeed subtle and in some passages *kardia*, *psyche* and even *nous* appear as almost synonymous and are used indiscriminately.[4] In fact, already in the Septuagint, these terms are often interchangeable. Nevertheless, there seems to be no basic confusion between *kardia* and *nous*, despite their close connection. Abba John of Gaza, also known in Palestinian monastic circles as 'the other *geron*' in order to distinguish him from 'the great *geron*' Barsanuphius, writes: 'To guard the heart means to keep sober and pure the intellect of the person at war [i.e., with the demons].'[5] The distinction here implies that the preservation of the intellect's soberness and purity is helpful for the guarding of the heart.

It is perhaps the term *psyche* which is the least constant and concise in use, being closely linked at times with *nous* and at other times with *kardia*. The 'soul' usually implies one's entire 'spiritual' being in an abstract way, in contrast to one's 'bodily' aspect. Still, John of the *Ladder* does not aim at defining exactly the constituent elements of the human person, but shows the

---

[3] 8.4 (828C). Cf. also 8.6 (828D).

[4] Cf. 15.73–74 (896D). Cf. 27.2 (1097AB), where body and heart are distinguished, whereas the term 'soul' is used in place of *nous*. The three terms – heart, soul and intellect – are very close in Diadochus, *Cent.* 33 (102–04), 59 (p. 119) and 79 (137). *Nous* and *kardia* are very close in Diadochus, *Cent.* 16 (92–4). Cf. also Ps. Chrysostom, *Ep. and mon.* (PG60.751).

[5] Barsanuphius 91. While the Liturgy of Chrysostom says 'Let us lift up our hearts,' the Syriac form – called the Liturgy of Saint James – says 'Let us lift up our intellects and our hearts.' Cf. also Cyril of Scythopolis, *Life of Euthymius* 29 (46.16). *Nous* seems to have the same meaning as *kardia* in Evagrius, *Prakt.* 47 (606).

'method' by which one may act, by which one may struggle against the demons and acquire God's grace. In this respect, the heart acquires an all-embracing significance, as distinct from the *nous* or the more abstract *psyche*.

At any rate, there is a reciprocal relationship between body, intellect (and even soul) and heart.[6] *Nous, logismos, kardia, soma, pathos* are interactive aspects of personhood. Each of them, when integrated, leads to God. At the same time, the demons also use every possible way in order to tempt us. If we conquer them in the intellect, says John, they attack the body; and if we conquer them there, they try to enter the heart.[7] The body influences the heart, and the heart in turn influences the body: 'a joyful heart renders the body beautiful' (Prov. 15.13).[8] For Isaac the Syrian, the heart *is* the body; the heart is the central organ, the sense of senses, the intermediary between the psychic (*psyche*) and the physical (*soma*).[9] In the fourteenth century, Gregory Palamas would refer to the heart as 'the innermost body within the body.'[10] At times, a clearer distinction is made in the *Ladder* between the various elements constituting the human person, especially between *kardia* and *nous*.[11] It is a graver sin – in the sense that it is more difficult to overcome – to sin in the heart. Hence the intellect must guard the heart against all evil imaginings by bravely defending its entrance.[12] The intellect is the 'eye' of the heart, there ruling as sovereign. In contrast to this visual dimension of the intellect, the heart's function is more sacramental. As the unifying organ of the entire person, it must offer the human person to God. The first (*nous*) is in need of purification through ascetic struggle; the second (*kardia*), in its natural condition, merely awaits illumination through God's grace.[13]

The discussion that ensues is concerned, first, with the *status* of the heart as the center of the human person, with its susceptibility of both evil and good. Second, it will consider certain particular functions and operations of the heart, such as conscience, prayer, humility and love. Finally, it will examine the heart

---

[6] See 7.66 (816B); 8.4 (828C); 14.17 (868A); 19.3 (940D); 15.82 (901C); 6.14 (796B); 7.18 (805A); 15.80 (901B); 19.3 (940D).

[7] 15.76 (900AD).

[8] This passage from Proverbs is quoted in 30.11 (1157B). For the heart influencing the body, cf. also Abba Isaiah, *Logos* 10 (67). For the body influencing the heart, cf. Abba Isaiah, *Logos* 16, 2 and 6 (89 and 94) and Isaac the Syrian, *Mystic Treatises* (150).

[9] *Mystic Treatises* (20 and 148). For the heart as the central organ, cf. Greg. Nyssa, *De opif. hom.* 15 and 8 (PG44.177B and 145C) quoted in Greg. Palamas, *Triads* 2, 2, 28. Cf. Meyendorff, *Palamas*, 147; and A. Bloom, 'Contemplation et ascèse,' in *Etudes Carmélitaines* 28 (1949), 49–67.

[10] *Triads* 1, 2, 3.

[11] 27.2 (1097AB); 26.ii, 69 (1064A) and the end verse of 26.ii (1076B). Although Climacus himself did not in fact write these end verses, they are often illuminatory of his remarks. For the above distinction, cf. also 27.ii,6 (1108A) and 28.52 (1137BC).

[12] 27.2 (1097B).

[13] 28.52 (1137BC). Cf. also *Mac. Hom.* 15, 20 (139).

as the ground of the vision of divine light. The underlying conception is of the heart as the essence of the human person. There is no question of restricting it to the emotions and affections, or indeed to any one individual part of personhood. The burden of the argument is to show how John Climacus, echoing the Scriptures and earlier ascetic writers, views the heart as the spring of life and also the seat of the highest spirituality.

The Heart as Center of the Human Person

John Climacus sees human life as being lived with 'feeling of heart.'[14] The heart is the center and source of the human person, and therefore virtually synonymous with it:

> 'I have cried with my whole heart,' says the Psalmist (Ps. 118.145), that is, with body, soul and spirit.[15]

To discover one's heart is an act of reintegration, a recovery of the mystery of one's primal unity. The heart is not only the central organ, but also the organ of organs.[16] As a physical organ, it is but a symbolic point of convergence, integrating us within ourselves and, through this, with others and indeed with the cosmos at large. There should be no reason for reserve towards such localization or material representation. The openness to God is a way into and out of the world. The heart must not be ruffled by worldly distractions; in the words of Mark the Monk: 'The comfort of the heart is hope in God; its discomfort is bodily care.'[17] Such an utterance, though mainly concerned with protecting the heart from external turmoil, implies a view of the heart as at one with the total person.

The human person is a mystery. So, too, is the human heart. No one but God knows the heart. God is, in the significant phrase familiar already in the Scriptures, the one who knows the heart's secrets.[18] Therefore, God knows us most intensely and intimately (1 Sam. 16.17; Lk. 16.15). Mark the Monk calls God 'the knower of hearts,' and Abba Isaiah says that only God can know the depth of our heart.[19] One can never fully comprehend the heart of one's fellow human being, and such ignorance disqualifies one from judging others (Mt. 7.1; Lk. 6.37; Jn 7.24).[20] Can one 'accomplish a diligent search,' as God does? For

---

[14] 7.31 (808B) and 27.2 (1097AB).

[15] 28.59 (1140B).

[16] Cf. Greg. Nyssa, *De opif. hom.* 15 and 8 (PG44.177B and 145C).

[17] *De his.* 107 (PG65.945B).

[18] 21.16 (925B); 24.9 (984B); 26.2,39 (1068C).

[19] Mark the Monk, *De his.* 15 (PG65.932D) and Abba Isaiah, *Logos* 4, 7 (23) and 15, 1 (83).

[20] 21.16 (952B); 24.9 (984B) and 26.ii,39 (1086C).

'the heart is deep' (Ps. 63.7). The devil may know a lot, says John; yet the devil knows only those thoughts which he himself planted in our heart, whether these be evil or good.[21] The demons act '*as if* they know what is in our heart,'[22] but in fact only God possesses such knowledge. For God alone sees the human person whole – by seeing the human heart.[23] And God would never attribute the course of evil to the human heart.[24]

The Heart as Battlefield of Good and Evil

Yet the demons are constantly at work. They may address any 'part' of our person and are capable of presenting to us both good and evil thoughts. Nevertheless, however evil, 'shameful' thoughts always remain something foreign to the heart. John refers to them as 'chance' or 'foreign' thoughts,[25] which, like thieves,[26] try to gain access to our hearts.[27] They must not only be turned away but ultimately destroyed.[28] Similarly, the *Spiritual Meadow*, which in many ways succinctly expresses Sinaite spirituality, advises:

> Become the doorkeeper of your heart so that no foreigner may enter, and ask, 'Are you on our side or with the enemy?'[29]

Such thoughts are not natural but alien because they are caused by the demons. Sin is the extreme opposite of our natural state, which is love and humility of heart,[30] as will be seen below. Abba Orsisios says:

> I think that if a person does not guard his heart well ... the enemy finding room in the heart, will overthrow that person.[31]

For John, curiously, as we shall see in later chapters, the best way to fight evil thoughts may in fact be 'to disregard them altogether.'[32]

---

[21] 26.ii,39 (1068C).

[22] 21.16 (952B).

[23] 24.9 (984B).

[24] 23.4 (976D).

[25] 15.73 (896D) and 22.26 (969B).

[26] 7.18 (805A) and 22.26 (969B).

[27] 15.74 (897C).

[28] 22.22 (969A) and 27.2 (1097B).

[29] John Moschus, *Pratum* 110 (PG87.2976A). Cf. also Anastasius the Sinaite, *Questiones* 1 (PG89.329C); and Abba Isaiah, *Logos* 1, 1 (1) and 17, 3 (105).

[30] 10.1 (845BC); 22.7 and 8 (965D) and 25.32 (993C).

[31] *Apophth.* Orsisios 2 (PG65.316CD). Ascetic writers speak of 'guarding the heart;' cf. Athanasius, *Vita Ant.* 6 (PG26.849A); Pachomius, *Vita Prima* 18 (11–12, pp. 167–8); *Apophth.* Poemen 20 (PG65.328A); *Mac. Hom.* 11,11 (103–04) and 15, 13 (133–5).

[32] 15.82 (901C). Cf. similar 'indirect strategy' condemned by Athanasius, *Vita Ant.* 23 (PG26.877A) and 42.904B–05C); *Apophth.* Theodora 8 (ed. Guy, 23), and Barsanuphius 91.

In reference to the effect of the demons on the heart, however, the result of their onslaught is very frequently 'hard-heartedness.' Certain writers refer to this as 'painlessness;' others tend to speak of a 'heaviness' of heart. John usually prefers the notion of 'hardness,' because he sees the struggle as an aggressive or violent procedure, not as a speculative or entertaining pastime.[33] Mark the Monk, in a similar vein, says:

> A finer word of knowledge is of no benefit to the hard-hearted person, because that person accepts no pains of repentance except fear.[34]

According to John, in this state, the heart grows hard, unable to feel the gentleness of God's presence. To regain that feeling one's heart must again become 'softened.'[35] There is, here, a play on the words *apalotēs* (softness) and *aplotēs* (simplicity), which will be further discussed later. John develops a biblical theme found in Ezekiel, who identifies God's action with the 'softening' of the hard heart: 'A new heart I will give you ... and I will take out ... the heart of stone and give you a heart of flesh' (Ezek. 36.26).

There are many ways by which the demons harden the heart, and so one must be vigilant. Their most frequent device is gluttony. This is a difficult vice to guard against. Gluttony has a 'naturally' deceptive quality because, by nature, we need food to sustain ourselves. Our own nature is, in a way, working against us, as John says elsewhere.[36] John cannot find words harsh enough to describe 'hard-heartedness' and 'painlessness;' these are slavery to the devil and the mother of all evil.[37]

This hardened state causes the heart to grieve, to suffer pain. The heart by nature seeks God but, instead, encounters its own hardness, which only God can obviate (Ezek. 11.19–21). The heart seeks God 'madly,' says John in what resembles a mystical confession, crying out in pain (Ps. 50.10) as if for its lover:

---

[33] 6.14 (796B); 14.32 (869D); 27.2,8 (1108D). This 'hardness' (*sklerotis*) clearly differs from the terminologically similar notion in *Apophth.* Euprepios 4 (PG65.172C), which refers to stability of intention: 'acquire for yourself a heart of iron.' Climacus also speaks of 'heaviness' (*varūtes*) in 10.1 (845C) of 'insensitivity' (*anaisthesia*) in 17.5 (933D) and of 'depth' (*vathos*) of heart in 24.17 (981C). Cassian's version is *cordis gravitas:* cf. *Inst.* 12, 29.2 (p. 494) and a similar notion is found in Mark the Monk, *De his.* 66 and 196 (PG 65.940C and 961A); cf. also *De lege spir.* 18 (908B) and Abba Isaiah, *Logos* 14, 3 (p. 80) and 17, 2 (p. 103). 'Painlessness' (*analgesia*) is mentioned in Mark the Monk, *De his.* 122 (948C) and Greg. Palamas, *Triads* 2, 2, 7 who says that most Fathers refer to it as 'hardness' (*pōrōsis*).

[34] *De lege spir.* 149 (PG65.924B).

[35] 19.3 (940D).

[36] 15.83 (901C).

[37] 27.ii, 8 (1108D) and 17.5 (933C).

A sorrowing heart ever madly seeks that for which it thirsts; and when it fails in its quest, it painfully pursues it, and follows in its wake grievously lamenting.[38]

Such 'holy sorrow' actually 'guards' and 'oversees' the heart, having the effect of focusing it on the authentic object of its love, on the one who 'has nailed' this *penthos* to the heart's hardness, to adopt John's own imagery. This condition entails an attitude (*diathesis*)[39] of the whole person and for this reason reciprocally affects the body too. The *Ladder* provides other 'extreme examples' (*akrotaton oron*)[40] of such repentance, which aim solely at breaking the hardness of the heart. For, as John well knows, 'a broken and contrite heart God will not reject' (Ps. 50.19).

The Dwelling-place of God

The heart is the depth (Ps. 63.7)[41] wherein one is able to encounter God personally, as person to person. One should aim to master the heart (Prov. 4.23), allowing nothing foreign within it. The *Macarian Homilies* claim that, 'if the heart at all times desires God, then God is the Lord of the heart.'[42] As John assures us, in the meek of heart, God feels 'at home' (Gal. 4.6).[43]

The human person is 'a world within a world,' according to Nilus of Ancyra,[44] and, by analogy, the human heart includes the subconscious, conscious and supraconscious levels. To quote again from the *Macarian Homilies*:

> There [in the heart] is God, there are angels, there is life and the kingdom, there is light and the Apostles, there are the treasures of grace, there is everything.[45]

---

[38] 7.1 (801CD). Cf. also 7.2 (801D) and Nilus, *Ep.* 3, 169 (PG79.464AB).

[39] 7.1 (801CD).

[40] 7.66 (816B). Cf. also 5.5–6 (764D–77A).

[41] The words of the psalmist are also found in Diadochus, *Cent.* 59 (119) and *Mac. Hom.* 15, 32 (145–6). The 'depth' of the heart sometimes has a negative connotation, signifying the 'abyss of sin;' cf. 24.17 (981C).

[42] *Mac. Hom.* 43, 3 (286–7).

[43] 24.3 (981A). Cf. also 21.16 (952B) and *Shep.* 43 (1185A). In the tenth century, Symeon the New Theologian speaks of 'an indwelling of the divinity;' cf. *TGP* 1.7 (42). And, later, the hesychasts write of 'the heart as a heaven wherein Christ dwells:' Cf. Kallistos/Ignatios, *Cent.* 52 (252).

[44] *Ep.* 2, 119 (PG79.252BC). Cf. also Greg. Naz., *De moderatione in disputando* 27 (PG36.204D–05C) and *Or.* 38, 11 (PG36.324A). Symeon the New Theologian, *Cat.* 28 (160) and *Eth.* 4 (64) inherited this notion from Gregory the Theologian. The notion, however, of the human person as microcosm is very old and may be traced back to Philo: cf. H. Chadwick, 'Philo and the Beginnings of Christian Thought,' *The Cambridge History of Later and Early Medieval Philosophy*, ed. A. H. Armstrong, Cambridge: Cambridge University Press, 1967, 139, n. 3.

[45] *Mac. Hom.* 43.7 (289). Cf. also 11, 5 (98–9).

John, too, speaks of 'the earthly heaven of the heart.'[46] The heart, then, is not only a kind of microcosm that contains the whole world, but also a mediator between human nature and divine nature. John prefers a more traditional expression, which, although fully developed by Maximus the Confessor, is already adumbrated in the *Life of Antony*: 'we do not need to travel abroad for the kingdom of heaven.'[47] However, in order to encounter God in one's heart one must primarily avoid, in the words of the Desert Fathers, 'that which does not satisfy one's heart.'[48] This, for John, requires manifesting one's thoughts; to leave the heart polluted, to ignore evil thoughts within, means ultimate inability to discern God within the heart. This condition is not only unnatural but also 'illogical.' Since there is an interrelation between heart, intellect and body, the human person can actually end up in utter confusion, in a kind of madness, if pushed to the extremity of this condition.[49]

There is no way of stating in the abstract what the heart actually is since, as has already been noted, it always retains its mysterious dimension. John and the ascetic tradition would readily agree with the *Macarian Homilies* when they say: 'the heart contains an unfathomable depth ... In it, is death; in it, is life.'[50] In the heart there are unknown depths, stretching out into space, time, and even beyond. One should feel a sense of awe before the human heart; human anthropology cannot but be aphophatic in nature, just as all genuine theology must be. To speak about the heart in positive terms is to consider how it functions in one's personal inwardness, what purpose it serves, rather than what its essence actually is.

---

[46] This rendering is found in Rader's text and also in that of Sophronius: cf. 15.2 (880D). It is not, however, found in Rader's own translation, which gives the rendering: 'the earthly shield of the heart' (879D).

[47] Athanasius, *Life of Antony* 20 (PG26.873A). Cf. Maximus, *Ambigua* (PG91.1304D–05A). Cf. also L. Thunberg, *Microcosm and Mediator: The Theological Anthropology of Maximos the Confessor*, Lund: 1965, 140–52. Thunberg also published a briefer work entitled *Man and the Cosmos: the vision of St. Maximus the Confessor*, New York: St Vladimir's Seminary Press, 1985.

[48] *Apophth.* Poemen 80 (PG65.341C).

[49] 23.3 (976D). Climacus tends to avoid such concepts as eccentricity and madness, instead presenting ways of integration and balance; see for example 27.ii,6 (1108B).

[50] *Mac. Hom.* 15, 32 (145–6). For the notion of the heart in other cultures, see Guillaumont, 'Coeur,' 42 and Spidlik, *Spiritualité*, 105. Cf. also A. Piankoff, *Le 'Coeur' dans les textes égyptiens depuis l'Ancien jusqu'à la fin du Nouvel Empire*, Paris: 1939; and E. Dhorme, *L'emploi métaphorique des noms des parties du corps en hébreu et en akkadien*, Paris: 1923. For the heart in Sufism, see the writings by W. Chittick, *The Sufi Path of Knowledge*, Albany: State University of New York Press, 1996; and *Sufism: A Short Introduction*, Oxford: Oneworld Publications, 2000.

Qualities Peculiar to the Heart

The Guarding Conscience

The heart, as we have seen, must be guarded against the demons: 'Keep your heart with all vigilance' (Prov. 4.23). John does not directly quote this scriptural text, but it underlies his anthropological understanding. Through its sense of grief or joy, the heart acts as a 'safeguard' against danger. It enables one to understand, to discern danger. Being at the center of intelligence or reason, it approximates to what today would be called 'conscience.' Yet John never declares what is 'right' or 'wrong' in any prescriptive sense. Of discernment, for instance, he writes:

> Perhaps, generally speaking, discernment is, and is recognized as, the certain understanding of the divine will on all occasions, in every place and in all matters; and it is only found in those who are *pure in heart* and in body and in mouth.... Discernment is *undefiled conscience* and purity of feeling.[51]

Human conscience is not just whim. It is to be trusted only when it is 'undefiled,' when one acquires 'purity of heart.' Conscience and heart are also closely paralleled in other writers, such as the *Macarian Homilies*:

> The heart has a captain in the mind (*nous*), the conscience, which is ever judging us (Rom. 2.15).[52]

Abba Isaiah speaks still more emphatically about the connection between heart and conscience: 'your conscience speaks with your heart secretly.'[53]

Referring to this internal conversation, or intense concentration, that must be attained in the heart, Abba Arsenius remarks:

---

[51] 26.1 (1013AB). In *Shep.* 96 (1201A) 'heart' is very similar to the modern notion of 'conscience.'

[52] *Mac. Hom.* 15.33 (146). Cf. also 15, 34 (146–7) and 26, 24 (216–17). The terms 'conscience' and 'heart' are closely paralleled in *Apophth.* Poemen 201 (ed. Guy, 30) and Nau 299 (1912, p. 204); Mark the Monk, *Ad Nik.* 6 (PG65.1037AB); Abba Isaiah, *Logos* 4, 8 (14) but without mentioning 'heart;' Theodoret of Cyrus, *De natura hominis* (PG83.932AB) but without mentioning 'conscience;' Isaac the Syrian, *Mystic Treatises* (160); and Greg. Palamas, *Ad Barlaam* 41 (1, p. 249) but without mentioning 'conscience.' The importance of the conscience is clearly stressed in Chrysostom, *Ad Theod. lapsum* 1 (PG47.294); Mark the Monk, *De lege spir.* 69 (PG65.913C), which is taken up later by Symeon the New Theologian: cf. Hausherr, *Vie* 4 (6); *De lege spir.* 187 (928C); Barsanuphius 13 and *Ep.* 2, 187 (504); Diadochus, *Cent.* 23 and 100 (96–8 and 161–3). Cf. also Symeon the New Theologian, *TGP* 3.31 (89), where Symeon speaks of conscience as a mirror, an idea also found in the *Ladder*: cf. 4.71 (712B). Cf. also *TGP* 3.35 (90). Several relevant studies may be cited in this connection: cf. Guillaumont, 'Coeur,' 50; C. A. Pierce, *Conscience in the New Testament*, London: 1955, and especially C. Cavarnos, *Byzantine Thought and Art*, Belmont, MA: 1968, 40–47.

[53] Abba Isaiah, *Logos* 4, 7 (24).

> When one who is living in silent prayer hears the song of a little sparrow,
> that person's heart no longer experiences the same peace.[54]

Concentration allows of no other care but one. Or, as John himself puts it, it is identified with the 'stripping of all attachment and all ties,'[55] taking care of the one thing which alone is necessary (Lk. 10.42). In the desert of Egypt, Abba Alonius observed rather harshly that: 'If a person does not say in one's heart that in the world there is only myself and God, that person will not gain peace.'[56]

What, then, is this concentration, which, according to John, causes one to hate even one's own life, once the heart of life has lost the single desire worth desiring?[57] Concentration is a turning inwards, an 'entropy' or inversion of the heart, a state also called *synnoia* (literally, 'a gathering together of one's mind'), which is nevertheless no self-regarding posture. John calls it ecstatic:[58] it reaches out towards another person in the fulfillment of love. Yet to reach out to God and to others is not primarily an outward but an innately inward action, deriving from within the stillness of the heart. John describes it as 'the inviolable activity of the heart,'[59] eschewing, perhaps neglecting, all other cares, or rather, caring more than ever by surrendering them to God and thereby relieving them of their mundane weight. To relieve is to purify. This is, or can be, a painful process. For the heart is easily susceptible of invasion by unclean, corrupting forces. Like a 'field,'[60] the heart may easily be 'scorched;' and, conversely, it is not easily revived. The heart is, as the *Macarian Homilies* have it, a battlefield for the restoration of the human person.[61]

Hesychia *and Prayer*

Hesychia is an essential feature of the heart's conversation or concentration. The hesychast 'prepares the heart for God' (Ps. 107.2) and discovers God within the heart. Such a person abides with God and 'speaks to God in the heart' (1 Sam. 1.12–13). The body may sleep, but the heart abides in the continual presence of God 'by virtue of an undivided love for heaven.' John writes:

---

[54] *Apophth.* Arsenius 25 (PG65.96AB).

[55] 7.2 (801D).

[56] *Apophth.* Alonius 1 (PG65.133A). Cf. also Isaac the Syrian, *Mystic Treatises* (1–2).

[57] 7.31 (808B).

[58] 7.81 (805A). Isaac the Syrian speaks of the 'blessed madness [ecstasy?], namely the flight of the heart after God.' Cf. *Mystic Treatises* (90).

[59] 27.ii,12 (1109B).

[60] 8.10 (829A). Regarding purity of the heart, cf. Cassian, *Conf.* 1, 4 and 7 (80–81 and 84–5) and Basil, *Reg. Fus. Tract.* 5, 1–3 (PG31.920B–24D).

[61] *Mac. Hom.* 42, 3 (282).

The hesychast is one who says, 'I sleep, but my heart is awake' (S. of S. 5.2).[62]

Barsanuphius carried the image still further:

> Sleep is removed from such a person ... For the fire of the burning heart does not allow anyone to lie down for sleep.[63]

When *hesychia* has reached the depths of the heart, the latter becomes immune to demonic intrusions. Then, *hesychia* is transformed into total 'engagement' with God. The heart in prayer is joined – John's word, *synapto*, is powerful and passionate – with God in personal communion. For the heart and its functions pertain preeminently to the inwardness of the human person, which stands over against all outward, extraneous thinking:

> The beginning of *hesychia* is to throw off all noise as disturbing for the depth [of the heart]. And the end of it is not to fear disturbances, but to remain insensible to them.[64]

This 'attitude' of the heart, its continual 'feeling,' is the act of prayer.[65] To be in God's presence is a permanent way of life. Yet this does not overshadow or threaten the heart. Fear is a painful emotion excited by danger. But fear can become awe, when it is characterized by a particular depth and self-involvement that come from responding to the presence of God. As such, it has all the marks of a conscious but still unworried awareness of being enfolded in the love of God. For John, this fear is turned into faith:

> Divine presence infuses faith, making one an unshakeable pillar.[66]

One can neither comprehend (Eph. 3.18) nor even communicate with God without realizing that God is already present in the heart. For God, to be is to be present, and this presence is perceived by means of a 'direct heart' (cf. Ps. 7.11), 'without any doubting' (cf. Jn 14.1).[67]

According to John, the most destructive experience is uncertainty as to God's presence within the heart. He calls this the fruit of an 'uninformed heart,' 'unfaithfulness,' 'hard-heartedness,' and even – curiously – self-esteem.[68] It is therefore in humility that one recovers a sense of God's

---

[62] 30.7 (1156D).

[63] Barsanuphius 321. Cf. also 519. Isaac the Syrian says that 'the heart will burn and glow as with fire, *night and day*;' cf. *Mystic Treatises* (63 and 372). The fourteenth-century hesychasts also speak at length about the heart. This is examined more closely in the chapter on prayer, bearing in mind the link of the heart with the 'Jesus Prayer.'

[64] 27.3 (1097B).

[65] 28.42 (1136D). Cf. also Diadochus, *Cent.* 97 (159–60).

[66] 27.3 (1097).

[67] 18.4 (937C); 20.3 (945B); 27.ii,34 (113B); 28.1 and 40 (1129AB and 1136C).

[68] 27.ii,8 (1108D).

presence and 'beauty.'[69] 'If you have a heart,' Abba Pambo says quite simply, 'you can be saved.'[70]

Humility

God's presence in the heart is not merely given, 'ready-made.' It is something to be anticipated with labor and awaited in patience. It is eagerly expected in a pregnant moment, the appropriate *kairos*. There is a time for fullness and a time for emptiness. And, the *Ladder* adds, 'there is a time (*kairos*) for hard-heartedness too.' In the words of the *Macarian Homilies*, we must 'await the time when the Lord shall open the closed hearts, and shall pour on us the gift of the Spirit.'[71]

John mentions many ways in which this is fulfilled. However, he repeatedly returns to the subject of humility. Curiously, faith does not lead to self-confidence, but rather to humility. Here, as elsewhere, John echoes Barsanuphius, who carefully identifies watching over one's heart with humility of heart.[72] Climacus asks: 'Who has conquered the body?' And he provides us with the answer: 'The one who has drawn in [literally, 'crushed'] the heart'.[73]

He also adopts other metaphors in order to denote the path of humility, which he calls a 'safe boat' or a 'remedy with which those who have obtained it overcome everything else.'[74] Such metaphors include: 'directness of heart' (Ps. 5.10; Acts 8.21) and 'simplicity of heart' (Eph. 6.5; Col. 3.22), as well as turning to God with all one's heart (Deut. 30.10).[75] John is echoing Abba Isaiah, who writes: 'simplicity and self-effacement purify the heart from evil.'[76] Humility is

---

[69] 25.63 (1004A).

[70] *Apophth.* Pambo 10 (PG65.372A).

[71] *Mac. Hom.* 11, 6 (99–100). The reference to the *Ladder* is found in 26.59 (1032B).

[72] Barsanuphius 278.

[73] 150.80 (901B). Cf. 25.27 (996A); 26.ii,36 (1068A), where Climacus says that it is especially difficult for those 'educated' to be humble; 26.ii,8 (1060B) and 44 (1069B); 26.21 (1020C); 24.9 (984B), where he says that one's humility ought to be like Christ's; 14.17 (868A) and 15.56 (892C). Cassian, *Inst.* 4, 39, 2 (180) closely links *affectus cordis* with *humilitas*, and Mark the Monk, *De lege spir.* 16 (PG65.908B). Symeon the New Theologian, *Cat.* 4 (330) also places great emphasis on humility of heart.

[74] 26.29 (1021C–24B).

[75] 'Directness of heart' is found in 25.59 (1001B) and 26.ii,7 (1060B). 'Simplicity of heart' is found in 15.74 (897D). Similar expressions are found in 15.67 (900AB); 20.3 (945B) and 22.28 (969CD). For 'simplicity of heart,' cf. *Apophth.* Nau 362 (1913, p. 138) and Cassian, *Inst.* 5, 4 1 (194). Evagrius, *De or.* 57 and 85 (PG79.1180A and 1185B) and *Prakt.* 69 (654) speaks of 'simplicity' but without reference to the heart; rather, it is opposed to 'multiplicity' or even distraction in prayer. This is how Isaac the Syrian speaks of 'simplicity;' cf. *Mystic Treatises* (21, 35 and 168). Dorotheus, *Instr.* 6, 74, (276) calls simplicity 'holy.'

[76] *Logos* 6, 2 (43).

further linked with self-surrender, which is also the heart's natural state.[77] Pride, vanity, and ostentation – described as 'poisonous snakes' – are regarded as being alien to and endangering the heart.[78] 'Blasphemy' is the extreme opposite of humility,[79] implying self-deification, which is tantamount to rejection of God or of God's living presence within us. It is the ultimate stage in our alienation from God.

Pride could be subdued by means of one's own effort, but it cannot be defeated except by divine grace. The heart is thus affected in two ways: it is purified by one's action 'in the unceasing fire of the heart.' However, it is purified supremely by God's grace, 'with the oil of God,' which humbles us. Humility is one's needful recognition of personal limitations, a conscious abandonment to God's grace.[80] John also speaks of God's grace as the heavenly 'fire, which visits the heart.'[81] The humble of heart see God (Mt. 5.8) and receive 'heavenly visions.'[82] Humility is the door of the heart to the kingdom of heaven, John believes. It is 'blessed,' for it conquers pride, which only 'darkens the foolish heart' (Rom. 1.21),[83] but also instantly unlocks the inheritance and door of paradise. John's teaching is reminiscent of the Old Testament notion of *kâbôd* that signifies both 'glory' and 'heart.'

Nevertheless, even humility can be deceptive if it is not borne in the face of God's initiative. Throughout this process, it must be understood that the initiative always belongs to God. It is God who first comes to us, before we come to God. 'I was in the prison of my heart, and God came to me,' says the colorful Abba John the Dwarf,[84] interpreting with the license of the desert, Christ's words in the Gospel: 'For I was sick and you visited me; I was in prison and you came to me' (Mt. 25.36).

One final observation here on the matter of humility of heart is called for. The *Ladder* does not promote a sense of humility that is in contrast to a concept of healthy confidence. John shows considerable dislike of mere meekness, deference, or servility. These are, he feels, only substitutes for humility. He even ascribes them to 'sensual,' 'gluttonous' hearts.[85] Indeed, John indicates a 'depth of heart' – a kind of heart-stirring – which is liable to delude one, to conceal the impure state of one's heart, whose true nature is known to God alone. In the passage on hypocrisy, John speaks of:

---

[77] 22.7–8 and 28 (965D and 969CD).

[78] 15.76 (900AB); 20.3 (945B); 22.28 (969CD).

[79] 23.3 (976D); 22.26 (969B).

[80] 7.65 (816A); 23.23 (993C).

[81] 28.47 (1137A).

[82] 25.29 (996AB).

[83] 25.23 (993C), 25.29 (996AB) and 22.26 (969B). Climacus also calls humility 'holy' in 25.22 (993B) and 27 (996A) and 22.28 (969D).

[84] *Apophth.* John the Dwarf 27 (PG65.213B).

[85] 8.20 (823AB); 10.2 (845C) and 25.9 (992B).

> Conceit turned into nature, a foe to humility, a pretense of repentance ...
> hostility to confession, a teacher of willfulness ... a smiling at offenses,
> affected frowning, sham reverence.[86]

This is a false way of living, in estrangement from God's image. In John's own
austere words, it is 'demonic living' and the source of death.[87]

Love

Humility of heart finally leads John to a consideration of love of God and of all
humankind alike:

> If, in the perception of our heart, we consider that our neighbour excels us
> in all things, then the divine mercy is near us.[88]

Compassion toward others is a way of giving and therefore a form of self-
limitation. For this reason, John says, one must never judge others. To think of
others as superior to ourselves and deflate ourselves before them is to bring
God 'nearer to us,' indeed within the heart. On the other hand, John writes: 'if
we have formed the habit of judging, we may be utterly destroyed by this
alone.'[89] Barsanuphius, too, identifies 'having one's heart before God' with
'not speaking anything against any person.'[90] Humility, love, prayer, and
vision of God's light are intimately interlinked, although the link is not clearly
defined by John, except by implication in such laconic statements as:

> Who has crushed the heart? The one who has denied oneself.[91]

In the last analysis, the Scriptures provide the only 'argument' for John's
explanations. Being humble before others, before 'the least of [one's] brethren'
(Mt. 25.45), one is humble before God. A heart that listens humbly to God
listens also to God in others.[92]

The heart, then, is the place of convergence of love for God and of love for
others. Love denies nobody and excludes nobody, even in the case of the most
isolated hermit. Love is indivisible, even if we 'live outwardly with people and
inwardly with God.'[93] Here, John is echoing Barsanuphius, who says that God

---

[86] 24.17 (981C).

[87] 24.17 (981C) and 25.9 (992B).

[88] 25.30 (996B). Cf. also 25.27 (996A) and *Shep.* 96 (1201A). Love is linked with humility of
heart in Ps. Chrysostom, *De caritate* (PG60.775). Other writers link love with purity of heart: cf.
Cassian, *Inst.* 4, 43 (184) and *Conf.* 1, 6–7 (83–5) and Isaac the Syrian, *Mystic Treatises* (168 and
341). For the relation between the heart and love, cf. Spidlík, *Théophane*, 124–42.

[89] 10.16 (848D).

[90] Barsanuphius 836. Cf. also 296 and Dorotheus *Instr.* 4, 54 (236) and 6, 72 (274).

[91] 15.80 (901B).

[92] 26.ii,2 (1057B).

[93] *Shep.* 43 (1185A).

'warms our heart to perfect love, not only towards him but also towards our neighbour.'[94] The indivisibility of love points to its sole source in God: it is a gift of God; or, in Paul's words, 'it is shed abroad in our hearts by the Holy Spirit, which is given to us' (Rom. 5.5). Love is conditioned by humility but at the same time exceeds it. For it embraces God and human beings alike, excluding nothing, except evil, which itself is 'humiliated' by love.[95]

However, as for other ascetic writers, so too for John, neither love (*agape*) nor heart (*kardia*) bear any sentimental connotation.[96] Whether they imply any sentiment at all is a moot point. At any rate, the heart is usually linked with *nous* in an even-sided, corresponding relationship, within which human personality develops and matures. The heart, undoubtedly, is the center of the emotions. However, in the present context, this would unduly limit the concept. When Paul speaks of acquiring the 'heart of Christ' (Eph. 3.17), he is making an ontological, and not a merely psychological, statement, even if the heart does not preclude emotion. The Scriptures do not on the whole treat of the 'heart' as a seat of emotion alone. Indeed, the Greek Fathers do not even have a word equivalent to the English word for 'emotion.' The word *aisthesis* in fact carries the broader meaning of 'sense' or 'perception' in English.

Certain authors use the term 'heart' as a stick with which to challenge the allegedly 'rational' or 'rationalistic' West. By contrast with the East, the West is supposed to have lost its 'heart.'[97] It is not quite clear what kind of conflict between reason and heart is implied here. In fact, emotion, vaguely associated with the heart, has probably gained greater favor in the West than in the East. This is true to some extent of Augustine, as well as in more recent centuries of the cult of 'the heart of Jesus' and of the various forms of stigmatization, especially in the wake of Francis of Assisi.[98] Thomas Aquinas certainly contrasts *cordis affectus* with *intellectus* and *ratio*,[99] but it would be unfair to Aquinas to attribute to him a narrow use of *affectus* in the sense of 'affections' later developed in the West. Similarly, although Aquinas' use of *ratio* is ambiguous, *intellectus* implies the Greek *noesis*, which is certainly not identical with discursive reasoning.

---

[94] Barsanuphius 18. On love of all people, cf. Mark the Monk, *De lege spir.* 26 (PG65.909A); Abba Isaiah, *Logos* 18, 1 (110) and Isaac the Syrian, *Mystic Treatises* (341).

[95] 30.18 (1160BD).

[96] Cf. 7.67 (816B). Only in 7.65 (816A) could one suspect such a meaning, but even here Climacus refers rather to one's warmth and zeal.

[97] Cf. Spidlík, *Spiritualité*, 105.

[98] Cf. J. A. MacCulloch, 'Heart,' *ERE*, 557–8; A. Hamon, 'Coeur,' *DS* 2, 1023–46 and A. Cabassut, ibid., 1047–50. The devotion to the heart of Jesus in Nicholas Cabasilas is an interesting point of comparison with certain Western trends: cf. S. Salaville, 'Le Christocentrisme de Nicolas Cabasilas,' *Échos d'Orient* 35 (1936), 129–67 and 'Nikolas Cabasilas,' *DS* 2, 1–9.

[99] *Summa Theologica* 2–2. 44,5.

The notion of the heart in John Climacus and in other, both earlier and later, writers appears to be characterized by a greater balance or 'sobriety.' At any rate, whether the heart is or is not neglected in the West, it should not be used as an antonym of 'reason.' Certain modern Russian writers have often fallen into this trap. For instance, Theophan the Recluse identifies the terms 'part of the heart' and 'part of the sentiment.'[100] Nevertheless, emotion does not necessarily have any exclusively sentimental connotation. The 'heart' may include, or at least it does not exclude, emotion and it may even serve to support the supremely emotional experience of *stigmata*.[101]

Thus the charge of 'rationalism' leveled against Western theology, at least in sharp contrast to the alleged 'sentimentalism' or 'heartfulness' of Eastern theology,[102] is as tenuous as it is paradoxical. Both tendencies, if contradictory at all, could actually be said to originate in Western thinking, although this would require a special discussion. At any rate, a valid claim can be made for the view that the Eastern ascetical and mystical traditions transcend rationalistic and sentimentalist notions alike, even while embracing the operations of both the intellect and the emotions. It is the human person in its entirety that is entailed in the idea of 'intellect in the heart.'[103]

The Heart as Place of Divine Illumination and Vision

As the meeting-point between God and the human person, the heart is considered the place where the divine light is beheld. Following in the tradition of the 'mystics of light,' Climacus avoids the symbolism of divine darkness. For John, darkness spells sin and ignorance; it signifies the lack of God's incandescent grace, rather than divine transcendence and mystery. Addressing the abbot in the special treatise *To the Shepherd*, John says:

> You have dispelled all manner of darkness and gloom and tempest – I mean
> the thrice-gloomy darkness of ignorance. ... While still in this life, you

---

[100] Cf. Spidlík, *Spiritualité*, 106 where Theophan is quoted. Cf. also Spidlík, *Théophane*, 40f.

[101] Cf. A. Bloom, 'Les Stigmates,' *Messager de l'Exarchat du Patriarchate Russe en Europe Occidentale* 44 (1963), 192–203, where [Metropolitan Antony] Bloom defends the West against the charge of 'psychologism.' Archbishop Basil Krivocheine, ibid., 203–05, by comparison, is more critical of what he believes to be a psychological approach to this phenomenon. Cf. also Ware, *Mark the Hermit*, 356 and 'Transfiguration,' 21, n. 10 where Bishop Kallistos quotes a similar example in Eastern ascetic theology. I have also noticed a passage in Mark the Monk, *Cap. de temp.* 26 (PG65.1065A), although this work is not by Mark but embodies a number of extracts from Macarius and Maximus the Confessor. In this particular passage, it is affirmed that some saints rise to ecstasy, certain others are clothed with light, while others receive this 'vision' in the form of the cross. This reference may or may not imply a connection with *stigmata*.

[102] Cf. for example, Spidlík, *Spiritualité*, p. 335.

[103] Cf. *Mac. Hom.* 15, 20 (139) and Diadochus, *Cent.* 88 (147–8).

perhaps saw future things from behind (cf. Ex. 33.23) – I mean that illumination of knowledge, which will come to pass in the last time.[104]

In John's mind, the light of the age to come is an existent reality, not merely a futuristic figure of speech. There is, however, only an isolated case of personal vision to be found in John.[105] Moreover, the reference in that instance is not to Christ, but in fact to an angel. The emphasis in the *Ladder* is mostly on the experiences of light or on illumination, even if the language in which it is expressed may be metaphorical rather than literal.[106]

Broadly speaking, then, John of the *Ladder* represents the tradition of the 'mystics of light' dominant in the Christian East. He stands alongside Origen (second–third century), Evagrius (fourth century), the *Homilies* attributed to Macarius (fourth–fifth century), Diadochus (fifth century) and the Desert Fathers (fourth–fifth century), a line traced right up to Symeon the New Theologian (tenth–eleventh century) and Gregory Palamas (thirteenth–fourteenth century).[107] While John is far less explicit than all of these, he nevertheless reflects their view that God is revealed as uncreated light, as 'nonmaterial light shining beyond all fire.'[108]

The 'depth of illumination' is found in love, which 'shines in our hearts,' 'a light which shines in a dark place' (2 Cor. 4.6, 2 Pet. 1.19). Love is the 'fiery source' of God's light burning in one's heart.[109] For Climacus, Christ is that very light:

> The Sun, who through the darkness of humility rises on us, ... is the Lord who rides ... into the heart previously in darkness.[110]

The notion of 'the eyes of [one's] understanding being enlightened' (Eph. 1.8) also expresses an idea central with John.[111] The whole human person, including the body, shines if the heart is illumined (Prov. 15.13). Indeed, the *nous*, as the 'eye' of the heart, can see this light when it is clean: 'if your eye is simple, the whole body shall be full of light' (Mt. 6.22).

The divine light is perceived when the *nous* is stable (*ameteoristos*), when it is far from self-loving cares, which should be drowned in the depth of humility. This light is 'unfailing' and is gathered by the ascetic in the heart.[112] For John, this is not merely a mental activity. The attendant struggle is not in word and thought

---

[104] *Shep.* 100 (1204C).

[105] 27.ii,13 (1109C).

[106] Cf. 18.4 (937C); 25.27 (996A); 26.65 (1033B); 26.ii,27 (1065A) and 28.52 (1137C).

[107] Climacus' single, albeit implicit reference to the later Palamite distinction between 'divine essence' and 'divine energies' is related to the sunlight in 25.24 (993D).

[108] 7.12 (804C).

[109] 30.18 (1160BD).

[110] 26.2,44 (1069B).

[111] Cf. 30.11 (1157AB); 26.ii, end verse (1076B) and 7.53 (813B).

[112] 22.22 (969A) and 19 end verse (941D).

alone, but 'in being' and *in actu*. To say, as he does, that 'one receives light in one's heart' is quite unambiguous in this respect. In this passage, John has just been discussing the subject of how to keep 'vigil,' an act of discipline, which specifically involves the body. It may be inferred, at least indirectly, that the light resulting from such 'vigil' is therefore to be experienced by the bodily eyes too.

In accord with biblical sources (cf. Mt. 5.8), John takes it for granted that the heart must be pure in order to see God's light. Purity is a fruit of humility, which, as we have seen, does come about through one's own effort, but is also a gift of God. It further presupposes the confession of sins, which is a 'renewal' of the heart (Ezek. 18.31).[113] John says:

> You will know that you have this holy gift [of humility] within you ... when you experience an abundance of unspeakable light.[114]

In the end, it is God who 'creates a clean heart and who renews the right spirit within' (Ps. 50.10). Yet the confession of sins is what allows the light to enter through the heart. And, conversely, the light that enters the heart further reveals clearly the reality of one's sins:

> As a ray of sun, passing through a crack, lights everything in the house and shows up even the finest dust, so the fear of the Lord entering a person's heart, reveals all one's sins.[115]

The concept of 'fear' here does not imply intimidation. It is a kind of positive awareness of God's presence. It is no cause for one to take alarm, or to turn away, but to go out and face the Lord or to go out and accept the gift of the divine luminous presence. This fear is likened to a ray of sunlight. The Desert Fathers even correlate fear of God with softness of heart. Abba James foreshadows John when he says:

> Just as a lamp lights up a dark room, so the fear of God, when it penetrates the heart of the human being, illuminates that person.[116]

Purity is the heart's natural condition, its authentic state. The 'new heart' (Ezek. 18.31), which one must acquire, is a primordial one. For, when the heart is filled with iniquity, one is no longer human; one is in fact inhuman.[117] The authentic state acquires special meaning in John's 'definition' of the monk: 'A monk is unfailing light ... in the heart'.[118]

---

[113] 26.iii,29 (1088B). For the importance of purity of heart, cf. esp. J.-C. Guy, *Peri Logismon* 20 and *Apophth.* Sarah 5 (PG65.420D).

[114] 25.27 (996A).

[115] 26.iii,29 (1088B).

[116] *Apophth.* James 3 (PG65.232C). Cf. also *Apophth.* Nau 136 (1908, pp. 48–9); Poemen 183 (365D–68A) and Diadochus, *Cent.* 16–17 (92–4).

[117] 15.23 (884BC).

[118] 22.22 (969A).

As has been repeatedly observed, John provides no systematic body of ideas, nor, as will be seen more fully later, does he adhere to the order of any 'eight vices,' like other writers. John's paramount concern is to convey to his readers a personal experience in which humility conquers sin, in which simplicity leads to the way of virtue, and in which, above all, 'purity of heart receives illumination.'[119] The heart must be prepared and purified in order to see Christ. Ultimately, however, it is God who plucks out the heart of stone and grants a heart of flesh (Ezek. 11.19–21). The *First Greek Life* says of Pachomius that: 'he was as one beholding the invisible God through the purity of his heart as in a mirror.'[120] In similar terms, John Climacus writes:

> When the heart is cheerful, the face radiates light, and a person flooded with the love of God reveals in the body, as if in a mirror, the splendour of the soul, a glory like that of Moses when he came face to face with God (cf. Ex. 34.29–35).[121]

Or, as John puts it elsewhere, purity of heart leads to 'illumination,' which is 'an ineffable activity, unknowingly perceived and invisibly seen.'[122] However, unlike darkness mystics such as Philo the Jew (first century), Clement of Alexandria (third century), Gregory of Nyssa (fourth century), and Dionysius the Areopagite (*c.* 500), John lays far less emphasis on the unknowability of God than on the struggle against the passions in order to purify the heart and thereby enable it to reflect God's light. There are no traces in the *Ladder* of the 'mysticism of darkness' that is represented by the above writers. John regards prayer as the experienced and recognizable meeting-point with God, the moment when divine light fills the heart. Some, he says, emerge from prayer 'as if resplendent with light.'[123]

> One who comprehends with feeling of heart that one stands before God ... often becomes suddenly radiant and exultant during prayers.[124]

The entire personality of the monk, and in the end of every Christian, should be in a state of inner and integral harmony. One's heart should be in harmony with one's actions, and one's words with one's thoughts. In the absence of such harmony, one is no longer a genuine image of the living Christ, a king and a priest, an authentic human person.[125] For the human person is not a fragmented being. Rather, the human person is a seeing, willing, knowing and acting being all in one. Yet, in a unique way, the true declaration of one's total

---

[119] 7.53 (813B). Cf. also 26.1 (1013A). On humility of heart, cf. Barsanuphius 256.

[120] Ch. 22 (14, 170). Cf. also *Mac. Hom.* 15, 45 (153–4).

[121] 30.11 (1157B).

[122] 7.53 (813B).

[123] 28.52 (1137C).

[124] 18.4 (937C). Cf. also and Abba Isaiah, *Logos* 16, 2 (88).

[125] 26.18 (1020B).

self is revealed in the heart, which marks a reunion and reintegration within oneself of the opposites, which fallen nature incites to antagonism. What clearly underlies John's pursuit in the spiritual life is a concern, as it were, for 'the heart of the matter.'

The burning bush at the monastery of St Catherine
(Photograph: Elizabeth Williams)

CHAPTER 4

Nous: The Intellect

It is one thing to approach truths by reason;
it is quite another to attain to them by that
intuitive faculty called *nous* by the ancients,
the 'fine point of the soul' by Saint Francis
de Sales, and the 'heart' by Pascal.

(A. J. Festugière, *Contemplation*)

Enlighten the eyes of my intellect within my
heart.

(Eastern Prayer of Thanksgiving)

Introduction

The reality of *nous*, now variously translated as 'mind,' 'reason,' or 'intellect,' manifests itself in diverse phenomena, such as consciousness, perception, memory, believing, types of reasoning, motives, choices and other traits of character. The particular semantics, however, acquire a special significance in the ascetic doctrine of the human person. As will be shown in the discussion that follows, John's view, much like that of his desert predecessors, leads to a necessary distinction between *nous* as discursive reason or intelligence, on the one hand, and, on the other, *nous* as the intellect or the organ of supra-rational, intuitive apprehension of spiritual truth. The former is implied in everyday discourse by the term 'mind,' while the latter relates to the essence of human nature in all the multiplicity of personal existence, beyond any narrowly or, for that matter, any vaguely cerebral phenomena and activities.

In the Septuagint and post-biblical Jewish writings, apart from Philo, the term *nous* is surprisingly infrequent, indefinite and imprecise. However, there is at least one important reference in the book of Isaiah, which reveals that the spiritual intellect should not be equated with discursive reason (Is. 55.9), even though the author does not use the term *nous* but rather *dianoia*, which may include a discursive connotation. Nonetheless, in this particular context, even *dianoia* appears to have a much wider significance. In the New Testament, the term *nous* appears predominantly in Paul's writings. Outside of his epistles, it is only found three times, and there seems to be no direct connection with the philosophical or religious use. The sense, rather, is more popular, similar to our contemporary notion of 'mind.'

In most English translations of classical or, for that matter, patristic texts, the term *nous* is usually rendered as 'mind,' seldom as 'reason,' and only very occasionally as 'intellect,' although there is clearly an implication of intellectual apprehension, sometimes even of intuitive thought. However, closer analysis makes it clear that, in most passages of these ancient writers, *nous* is to be distinguished from mere reasoning and applies to the apprehension of eternal intelligible substances or first principles and, indeed, to the highest divine Mind. Aristotle distinguishes between *dianoia*, which implies discursive or merely syllogistic reason, and *nous*, which signifies an intuitive understanding that perhaps approaches the notion of 'enlightenment' in religious and mystical traditions. In Neoplatonism – even in Porphyry, who adopted an extreme position with regard to the idea of the 'flight from the body' – there is a tendency to consider *nous* and *psyche*, and even the physical universe (*cosmos*) as one reality. The Neoplatonist *nous* is a kind of self-determination of the life that emanates from 'the one,' while the shutting up of oneself in the experiences, desires and concerns of the 'lower nature' is a form of death. There are certainly echoes here of what John Climacus seems to suggest, as will be seen below, but perhaps no more than quite distant echoes.

What is relevant for the semantics of *nous* – at any rate in its philosophical connotation, which originates in Anaxagoras – is that, generally speaking, since the time of Plato (*Phaedo*) and *pace* Aristotle, it is seen as the organ of knowledge. *Nous* is not reducible to the senses, instead springing from a divine element in the soul (*psyche*) that knows the transcendent 'forms' and 'eternal objects,' and thereby reveals its own eternity. This is seen clearly in Plato's threefold distinction between 'opinion' (*doxa*) that rests on sense experience, 'reason' (*dianoia*) that contains mathematical reason, and *nous* that reveals unchanging reality.[1] The distinction between *nous* and *dianoia*, then, is an old one, going back as far as Plato and continuing variously in Aristotle and Plotinus. The latter further distinguishes between *logismos* and *noesis*. *Nous* in Plato and Aristotle ought, in this respect, not to be interpreted simply in terms of reasoning. These philosophers should be seen rather as endowing it with quasi-mystical overtones.[2] Nevertheless, for Aristotle, the emphasis is clearly on knowledge, on epistemology, which carries some rationalistic implications and justifies the use of the term 'intellect' as a translation of *nous*. This usage has been taken over to some extent by modern philosophy, where 'intellect' or 'reason' provides knowledge of certain fundamental concepts, indeed principles, such as substance, unity and cause, which in turn provide its *a priori* features, as distinct from *a posteriori* features derived from empirical experience. Intellect, in this connection, denotes – more passively – the

---

[1] Sometimes Plato presents a fourfold scheme: *eikasia, pistis, dianoia* and *noesis*. Cf. *Republic* 6, 509d–11e.

[2] Cf. *Metaphysics* 12, 1072b and 1047b; *On the Soul* 2, 413a and 3, 431a. Cf. also S. R. L. Clark, *Aristotle's Man*, Oxford: 1975, 182.

acquisition and possession of such knowledge, and – more actively – its exercise and practice in judgement.

In the Greek ascetic Fathers, 'soul' is given a wider and more vague significance than *nous*. The *Macarian Homilies* state 'the soul has many members,' one of which is the *nous*.[3] Patristic literature, overall, considers *nous* to be beyond mere rationality, intellectuality and conceptuality. It is envisaged rather as the 'image of God,' as the focus of personality, as the source of character and intelligence. Despite the fact that *nous* does not signify the intellect in any narrow sense but rather points to something higher than discursive reason, the term 'intellect' probably conveys best the meaning of *nous*, inasmuch as 'intellect' preserves the uniqueness, almost élitism, of that meeting-point within the human person where God is perceived and seen. Such is the rendering of *nous* selected for the purposes of this study.

Philosophical terms are assumed by ascetic writers and used as stones in order to build a bridge between the created and the uncreated: *nous* is one such 'stone.' While in Climacus' contemporary, Isaac the Syrian, it is the heart that is the intermediary between the physical and spiritual realms, in Gregory the Theologian the *nous* performs this function. In creation, says Gregory, God 'bound together in a mystical and ineffable way the earth to the intellect (*nous*) and the intellect to the spirit.'[4] The term *nous*, then, is a customary term borrowed from classical philosophy but endowed with new meaning. Nevertheless, the ascetic literature is not consistent and *nous* may, at times, signify reason and, at other times, a mystical awareness above the level of reason. It seems that today we have neglected somewhat the notion of *nous* as a profound power of spiritual perception, thereby perhaps reducing the human person to a brain with emotions.

In this chapter, the following topics are explored: the relation, as seen by John, of *nous* to other areas of the human person as a whole, which have been treated in the preceding discussion, namely, to the body, to the heart, to the activity of meditating and concentrating on God in prayer, to the ascetic life in general, and to the demons as powers extraneous to, and interfering with, the inherent function of the intellect.

The Intellect and the Human Person

It has been noted already that the word *nous* can mean 'intellect,' in the narrower sense, but always in relation to, or as a component of, the whole

---

[3] *Mac. Hom.* 7, 8 (76).
[4] Greg. Naz., *De moderatione in disputando* 9 (PG36.184C). For the reference to Isaac, cf. *Mystic Treatises* (148).

human person. In Climacus, it usually denotes both. *Nous* signifies the intellect as the superior faculty of the soul uniting human nature in its entirety to God.[5] However, underlying this is the theological mystery of the human person. There is some evidence in John's writings that he identifies *nous* with *prosopon* (person), a word he uses but seldom. John has in view the ultimate dimension of the human person, even when he employs the specific term *dianoia*, which in most other patristic authors bears a specifically mental, reasoning sense. Still, here as elsewhere, John is not at all rigid or even consistent, either in his terminology or in his argumentation. Thus, in one particular passage, *nous* denotes both intellect and person. Climacus speaks of the 'unrestrainable' and 'curious' *nous*, a clear reference to the intellect; but then he also advises:

> Fix your intellect like an anvil to your soul as to the wood of the cross, with blow upon blow of the hammers.[6]

This exhortation points to the human person. We must think of ourselves as 'an anvil nailed to the cross,' as an act of self-knowledge – an act eminently pertaining to the human person – which is a way of knowing the crucified God-Man. One cannot speak of human nature without intimating God. Other terms employed by Climacus as equivalent to *nous* include *ennoia, synnoia* and *logikos nous*, signifying the human person as a rational being, properly speaking.[7] In one passage, *nous* seems to be almost identical with conscience, consciousness, or life itself. This is explained by the fact that, so long as one's *nous* is in good order, one is fully conscious and is certainly alive.[8] It is clear, then, that *nous* is that which corresponds most nearly to the notion of the human person.[9]

In spite of the fact that John is not systematic, rarely does he actually confuse the various notions. Still less does he confuse our fallen condition with the notion of personality or personhood:

> Obedience is *mortification* of the limbs, while the intellect remains *alive*.[10]

Our personal nature is not identical to our fallen nature, which we must continually strive to direct towards God. This subject will emerge in the next section of the present chapter, which is concerned with the body's relationship with *nous*. Here it is necessary simply to draw attention once more to the way in which John marvels at the 'miracle,' at the mystery surrounding the person as

---

[5] Cf. for example 5.5 (765B) and 4.88 (713D). Cf. also John Cassian, *Conf.* 24, 16 (187–8); Abba Isaiah, *Logos* 17, 5 (108) and Maximos, *Amb.* (PG91.1193D).

[6] 4.31 (700B–01B). Cf. also 31.11 (977CD) and 26.iii,2 (1084CD).

[7] For *ennoia*, see 4.88 (713D); 27.2 (1097AB) and 27.ii,6 (1108AB). For *synnoia*, see 7.18 (805A); 11.2 (852AB) and 5.5 (765C). For *logikos nous*, see 26.ii,2 (1057C): *logos* here means 'reason' in the modern sense of discursive thought.

[8] Cf. 5.5 (772C).

[9] John does not use *prosopon* in 26.52 (1029C) but clearly implies it.

[10] 4.3 (680A).

'incorporeal' and yet at the same time contained 'within a body.' The human person has unlimited dimensions, which cannot ever be fully fathomed. Indeed, even when John employs the word 'to define,'[11] he conveys the idea of unsusceptibility to definition. The human person is infinite, while at the same time dwelling in the finite. Also, *nous* as personhood entails more than the notion of nature in that it surpasses what is naturally possible. The human person involves potentialities beyond any mortal individual. Such potentialities, John contends, are realizable by those who live in God. Even *nous* – that is to say, *nous* as a symbol of the human person – is by nature confined. Yet, as John suggests, continuous ascetic struggle leads to the control of all limits by grace:

> If you persevere indefatigably in all this labour, then the one who sets limits
> to the sea of the intellect will visit you too, and during your prayer will say
> to the waves: 'Thus far will you come and no further.' (Job 38.11)[12]

Paradoxically, then, the limitations of the human person are unlimited, divinely self-transcending. They are what they are before God who is truly unlimited (Mt. 19.26; Mk 10.27; and Lk. 18.27). There is, however, no intention to attribute to John an actual identification of *nous* with the person, in the sense of reducing the human person to the intellect. The limitedness and the unlimitedness alike are peculiar to the human person in its noetic capacity as much as in its 'cardiac' capacity. The *nous* contains a breadth analogous to that of the heart.

The Intellect and the Human Body

In a manner characteristic of the earlier ascetic Fathers, John continually stresses the close relationship between intellect (the 'inner form') and body (the 'outer appearance') – in accordance with Paul's words: 'after the inward person' (Rom. 7.22). This relationship is reciprocal, especially in 'beginners,' in whom 'the intellect often conforms to the body.'[13] The key to the noetic struggle lies in continual awareness. Climacus insists that such awareness or vigilance affects also the body. The body is not excluded from the human person; it is not evil in itself, as has already been explained. How can that which 'contains' the human person ever be sinful?[14] Nature, and its

---

[11] 26.52 (1029C).

[12] 28.17 (1132C).

[13] 28.25 (1133B). Cf. also 25.54 (1000D–01A). The relationship is borne out in *Apophth.* Nau 205 (1908, p. 279) and 240 (1909, p. 363); Mark the Monk, *Ad Nic.* (PG65.1040CD) and *De his.* 29 (936A); Diadochus, *Cent.* 79 (137) and Isaac the Syrian, *Mystic Treatises* (319, 345).

[14] 4.3 (680A).

propensities or inclinations, should merely be turned towards God, re-oriented Godward. Climacus says:

> I have seen impure souls raving madly about physical love (*eros*); but making their experience of such love a reason for repentance (*meta-noia*, i.e., a conversion of the *nous*), they transferred the same *eros* to the Lord.[15]

Therefore the *nous* influences, and is influenced by, the body and indeed even by individual parts of the body. For instance, 'visions,' what the eyes behold, are of great importance in the ascetic struggle. So are other external factors, such as food, environment and the like. It is expedient to fast but, at the same time, also to consider one's 'surroundings.'[16] One's whole life, to the smallest elements and details, not limited simply to the body, has a bearing upon the intellect. This entails constant vigilance. Fasting, for example, is of no account in itself; there is no merit or reward attached to it as such. Nevertheless, the ascetic knows that the excess of food causes sensuous smugness and 'fills the intellect with unclean images.' An empty stomach frees the intellect for concentration on God. In the words of Vladimir Lossky, the intellect 'must find its sustenance in God, must live from God.'[17] Worldly cares, which distract us from concentration on God alone, are 'false images' (Ex. 20.4) that displace the 'image of God' (Gen. 1.26–27). The substitution is a betrayal of love for God. It is a form of idolatry, a self-delusion; we think we possess life, but, in fact, are only in possession of dying images.

How then can the body influence the intellect positively? For John, the question acquires special significance in connection with the concept of tears.[18] Love for God is never only noetic, in the sense that it is just 'spiritual.' For it manifests itself in a 'real' and 'physical' form through tears. We weep as we seek God, whom we love. We weep as we recognize what, or rather whom, it is that we have lost. The subject of tears is, however, also treated separately in the next chapter.

To enable the body to affect the intellect in a positive sense, it is often helpful to adopt an outward bodily posture that reflects the inward attitude of prayer. For example, John says, one is able to lift up one's hands and eyes to heaven.[19] The Desert Fathers describe the monk as 'Standing, with arms stretched out in the form of a cross to heaven, calling on God.'[20] The bodily motion is a gesture symbolic of the lifting up of the intellect towards God. Indeed, it is reflected in

---

[15] 5.6 (777A). More will be said about this in the discussion about evil thoughts.

[16] 14.16 (865D–68A) and 7.70 (816C). For the importance of the eyes, cf. *Apophth*. Nau 161 (1908, p. 53), and for the environment, cf. Nau 198 (1908, pp. 277–8).

[17] *Mystical Theology*, 128: Lossky is using the French word 'esprit.'

[18] 26.ii,27 (1060B) and 28.36 (1136B).

[19] 28.25 (1133B).

[20] *Apophth*. Nau 143 (1908, p. 49).

Eastern Orthodox liturgical practice – immediately before to the eucharistic canon – to this day.[21] We reach out with our body, by way of reaching God's grace, which alone can save. Yet no achievement of our own can ever save us. In a sense, the bodily motion signifies not the upward escape of humanity towards God, but the downward assistance of God towards us:

> As we have not yet the strength to resist the demons by firmness of intellect ... raise on high the eyes of your soul ... or, at least, your bodily eyes. Hold your arms motionless in the form of a cross.[22]

And as John wants to protect those who pray in this fashion from any kind of pride, he strongly recommends that they are of course never to do so in public.

Meditation and Concentration

The Vagaries of the Intellect

It is common ground among ascetic writers that, after the Fall, the intellect is 'unrestrainable' or 'restless' and is easily led astray, subject to 'diversion' or 'distraction.' The patristic tradition is well summed up by Gregory of Sinai, who was to play a great role in fourteenth-century hesychasm:

> For, the intellect (*nous*) is not unrestrainable by nature, as if it was ever-moving, but it has appropriated this restlessness through neglect, becoming accustomed to this from the beginning.[23]

The intellect must, therefore, be somehow disciplined. John suggests that one ought to 'practice noetic stillness' (*noera hesychia*). More will be said on *hesychia* when discussing prayer in relation to the intellect, but here it must be stressed that John's concern is not to leave the intellect idle or vacant. No *stasis* is envisaged, nor any suppression of the intellect. One should allow it rather to move freely toward God, to move around within the presence of God, while God is allowed to move freely around within the intellect. It is natural for the intellect to be turned toward God. When God-directed, it fulfills its true entelechy. Restlessness and fragmentation are not natural to the intellect but only results of the Fall. Yet, beyond its instinctive distraction, the intellect also has an inherent impetus toward the divine. John prefers to describe the authentic *katastasis* (or 'state') of the intellect in terms of 'stages' (*stadia*) rather

---

[21] The Armenian liturgy employs the exhortation: 'Lift up your intellects to the Lord.'

[22] 15.76 (900C). Cf. also 25.54 (1000D–01A) and 28.25 (1133B). For a more subtle use, cf. 27.ii,26 (112C) where a possible linking of the Jesus Prayer with breathing is implied. See the chapter below on prayer.

[23] *Chapters* (81).

than 'suspension' (*stasis*). He prefers to speak of progress rather than of immobility.[24] Evil thoughts must be countered by good thoughts. There is no neutrality, only continuity.

To empty the intellect of thoughts suggested by the devil requires their substitution with thoughts filled with God. The intellect is easily sidetracked because it exists 'within a distracted body.'[25] Here, once again, John is thinking of the body in its fallen state. The body moves, sees, feels and suffers. So it is a difficult task for the intellect to sort out or discern good memories, to be preserved and to remain on the straight and narrow path. By virtue of our fallen nature the intellect 'meanders,' and there is nothing sinful in this so long as such 'meandering' is a movement amid good thoughts. However, as we are easily deprived of them, John exhorts us to strive continuously. Vigilance should be unceasing, alertness perpetual: 'Wrestle with your intellect (*ennoia*) unceasingly.'[26]

The intellect is by its very nature forever productive of thoughts. The desert elders recognize that 'one cannot prevent thoughts from arising, but one can resist them.'[27] Mark the Monk observes: 'it is not possible for a logical intellect (*nous logikos*) to remain idle.'[28] To leave the intellect idle, or to expect it to be idle, would be 'proper only to an irrational nature but not to a rational one,' according to John.[29] Anastasius the Sinaite would later write: 'let us *fill* the intellect.'[30] One should not, therefore, suspend or suppress the intellect. Rather, one should control it, by ruling over it as a king. John, however, in fact shows a preference for paternal images as opposed to gubernatorial ones. We may 'rule' over the intellect, but in its turn, 'the rational intellect becomes the father of thought.'[31] One should provide the intellect with good thoughts and channel all thoughts towards God, no thought being evil in itself. The desert wisdom understood this process:

> What condemns us is not that thoughts enter into us but that we use them badly; indeed, through our thoughts we can be shipwrecked, and through our thoughts we can be crowned.[32]

---

[24] 27.ii,6 (1108A) and 26.14 (1017AC).

[25] 4.31 (700B–01B) and 28.16 (1132C).

[26] 4.88 (713D). Cf. also 6.6 (793C).

[27] *Apophth.* Poemen 28 (PG65.329AB).

[28] *De Paen.* 11 (PG65.981B). Seemingly contradictory statements appear in certain writers who suggest a 'denuding' or 'emptying' of the intellect: cf. Ps. Athanasius, *Expos. in Ps.* 45, 11 (PG27.216); *Peri Logismon* 1 (ed. Guy, pp. 171–88); Kallistos/Ignatios, *Cent.* 65 (258). The idea is Evagrian: cf. *De or.* 55 (PG79.1177D), 119 (1193B) and 11 (1169C).

[29] 7.20 (805A). Climacus in fact argues against the intellect being *anennoios*.

[30] *Oratio de sacra synaxi* (PG89.837A).

[31] 7.20 (805A).

[32] *Apophth.* Nau 218 (1909, p. 358).

John, too, believes that we should fight against evil thoughts, which, as a 'worm within the intellect,'[33] eat away at it. We should fight evil thoughts, using the very tactics that the demons themselves employ. Although demons will not actually originate evil thoughts in us, they 'drag down' into the darkness of sin the thoughts we choose to entertain.[34] In this darkness, we should not shut the eyes of our intellect, John says, but instead draw the thoughts out of the darkness into the light, 'drag them' out of the mud. The enterprise has in itself a cleansing effect. This is brought about by investing the intellect with good thoughts (Prov. 2.11), in the same way that the demons infest it with evil ones. Speaking from experience, the desert elders view the monk as being engaged in a 'continual interior occupation; thus, the enemy who approaches this monk from time to time does not find any resting place.'[35] John offers a list of thoughts which the ascetic can foster. Such thoughts include: remembrance of God, or of God's love and kingdom, zeal for the saints, evocation of God's presence or that of the angels, death, awareness of accountability on the last day of judgement, and recollection of hell.[36] These thoughts range from love of God to fear of hell. Not all are equally esteemed as excellent in the spiritual way. Nonetheless, always keen to encourage the weak, John underlines that they are all worthy of praise and able to stimulate the less strong or the beginners. The struggle is a part of being human:

> Do not despond when your intellect is plundered, but take courage and unceasingly recall it. Inviolability is proper only to an angel.[37]

Apophatic and Kataphatic Meditation

The intellect is also restless as a direct result of the Fall. For some of the ascetic Fathers, the thoughts of the intellect must be placed aside. Evagrius clearly speaks of a 'laying aside of all concepts of the intellect (*noemata*).'[38] Here, the emphasis is on the intellect being 'naked,' stripped of all images. This is the apophatic approach applied, beyond any doctrinal formulation, to the practical life of prayer. John, as we have already seen, is undoubtedly influenced by Evagrius, although less so than, for example, his contemporary and theologian, Maximus the Confessor. Nevertheless, even in the *Ladder* one

---

[33] 9.2 (841AB).

[34] 18.3 (937BC) and 15.78 (901AB).

[35] *Apophth.* Nau 241 (1909, p. 363). Regarding this form of indirect warfare, cf. Ps. Chrysostom, *Ep. ad monachos* (PG60.752) and Barsanuphius 91.

[36] 6.17 (796BC). In *Apophth.* Evagrius 1 (PG65.173AC) we find a similarly wide-ranging list of thoughts.

[37] 4.88 (713D).

[38] *De or.* 70 (PG79.1181C).

finds the fundamental Evagrian notion of disembarrassing oneself of all thoughts:

> *Hesychia* is the laying aside of *noemata*, and even the rejection of unreasonable cares.[39]

And elsewhere John exhorts:

> Lay aside cares; strip your intellect (*ennoia*); renounce the world.[40]

The Evagrian allusions in these passages seem explicit but are in fact exceptional and oblique. In the main, John's approach to prayer is kataphatic rather than apophatic, positive rather than negative. The *Ladder* tends to speak of fighting against, and ridding oneself of, evil thoughts by means of good ones. When the monks in the Alexandrian Prison are described as having 'a dumb intellect,' this has no specific Evagrian connotations. It is more akin to an 'illogical soul' – a soul that is perplexed by a consciousness of its sinfulness before God.[41] Yet for John, the soul, which is here tantamount to the intellect, is clearly endowed with 'a perception of the divine.' Therefore, it is far from naked:

> A noetic intellect is certainly wrapped in noetic perception (Phil. 1.9). ...
> Knowing this, one of the wise said: 'And you will attain a perception of the divine' (Prov. 2.5).[42]

Sin is a source of grief; but it can also be a cause for joy. Evil thoughts may depress us; but we should rejoice in them because they testify to our humanity too, a humanity endowed with divine gifts and potentialities. God needs no rational proofs; and each person proves one's humanity in exercising the power of free will, which is the essential mark of one's human 'dignity.'[43] Such proof becomes an affirmation also of God's reality and presence in the world and in the heart, as well as of God's love for us and of human nature. God does not expect our intellect to be unchangeable, immoveable. People are not, and are not called to become, angels. To be human is to dwell in glory as well as in squalor. We can be robbed of the true state of our intellect; but, equally, we can regain it at any time or at all times. We can resist evil thoughts and achieve victory in joy. As such, joy is another essential characteristic of the ascetic way.

Elsewhere, John seems, paradoxically, to avoid inviting 'good thoughts,' such as 'the memory of death,' let alone to command good actions.[44] This is

---

[39] 27.ii,17 (1112A).
[40] 28.28 (1133C). Cf. also 28.44 (1136D).
[41] 5.5 (765B).
[42] 26.17 (1020A).
[43] 1.1 (632A).
[44] 6.6 (793C).

because he does not issue moralistic injunctions against thoughts, words and actions that are considered offensive. The aim of the ascetic is not to be 'good' but to become 'holy.' For this reason, John does not separate moral advice or ethical teaching from the theological doctrine of God and the human person, from the deification of humanity or the 'demonization' and disintegration of human nature. Hence the invocation of death, side by side with a call to recover our humanity by means of a struggle and a re-orientation towards God. As an ascetic firmly rooted in the desert tradition, John Climacus perceives this process taking shape in a sustained practice of the purification of physical and psychological urges, whose limits are established by our mortal condition. 'Memory of death' shows up the limits, yet at the same time eternalizes the perception of our true life and being in God. The *Spiritual Meadow* mentions both of these poles: the monk, it advises, should always try to retain in the intellect (*kata noun*) the memory of both eternal hell and the kingdom of God alike. One should continually keep the intellect in hell, even while not despairing.[45] Death is the source of unbounded reality and, therefore, humility. It is also the source of one's readiness to receive God's grace. Struggle against evil thoughts, the fostering thoughts of love and prayer – even in its 'imageless' state: all these ultimately derive from God's desire to fill our emptiness with divine grace: 'For it is in God's power to establish all things.'[46]

To reject evil thoughts is not a self-regarding activity. We do not merely watch ourselves by 'guarding' the intellect. The implication is far more subtle and discerning. Our thoughts should be purified, but our intellect should be still, 'unwavering.' John makes a clear distinction here, although it is an elusive one. He draws a comparison between East and West:

> The guarding of the thoughts is one thing, and the watching of the intellect is another. As far as the east is from the west (Ps. 102.11), so much higher is the latter from the former; and it is more laborious.[47]

To preserve the purity of thoughts is also a process of self-protection, a way of allowing good thoughts to enter the intellect, which thus serves as a door to the heart and the entire human person. John adopts the word 'unwavering' (*akymantos*), which, on the other hand, implies a continuous being in God's presence. It is a form of inward vigilance, which enables the intellect to be centered or concentrated on God. From meanderer, the intellect becomes a

---

[45] John Moschus, *Pratum Spirituale*, Alexander 142 (PG87.3004C). This teaching was revived in the twentieth century by Silouan of Athos. See Archimandrite Sophrony, *Saint Silouan the Athonite*, Essex, UK: Monastery of St John the Baptist, 1991, 208–13.

[46] 28.16 (1132C). The notion that God alone can establish a wandering mind is taken up especially by the fourteenth-century hesychasts: cf. Greg. of Sinai, *Chapters* (81) and Kallistos/Ignatios, *Cent.* 66 and 70 (261, 265), where the above passage from Climacus is directly and repeatedly quoted.

[47] 27.ii,6 (1108AB).

mediator between the whole person and God. In the end, the intellect is no longer a mere 'door,' nor even simply a 'way.' It is a vehicle of God's life and action. John says:

> Cast off your own wishes and, stripped of them, approach the Lord in your prayer, invoking His will alone. Then you will receive God, who guides the helm of your soul [here, in the sense of intellect] and pilots you to safety.[48]

It is natural for the intellect to be in constant motion. John also contends that it is natural for the intellect to move continually in *one* direction, to concentrate on one thing, or rather one person. It should be nailed to the cross, on which Christ was nailed.[49] He thus clearly distinguishes the level of fallen human nature from that of the *status ante peccatum*. Evil thoughts are fought more effectively when the intellect is concentrated directly on God. Stretching out our hands, as Moses once did, looking up and away from the 'Amalek' of our nature, we look towards God. It has already been noted that the bodily posture itself has a symbolic significance. It is a way of turning the gaze from our faltering, dimming sense to the Lord of light. We are not strong enough for noetic contemplation, and John indicates various bodily actions representing and reminding of this concentration on God, including 'stretching out the hands, beating the breast, sincere raising of the eyes to heaven,' sighing and continual prostrations. It is not always possible to practice these, especially in the presence of others. John's advice is practical enough:

> If possible, go apart for a brief moment. Hide for a while in some secret place. Raise on high *the eyes of your soul* [again, implying the intellect], if you can; but if not, then raise your bodily eyes.[50]

The Vision of the Intellect

As in the above passage, the intellect is often referred to as the 'eye' of the soul or of the human person:

> For as long as the intellect does not shut its eye (literally, 'blink'), we shall not be robbed of our treasure.[51]

---

[48] 28.27 (1133C).

[49] 4.31 (700B–701B). Cf. *Mac. Hom.* 45, 1 (296–7): the *nous* should be 'nailed to the love of Christ.' Many ascetic writers agree that the intellect rises naturally to God: cf. Greg. Nyssa, *De Virg.* 7 (PG46.352BC); Abba Isaiah, *Logos* 2, 1 (5); Thalassius *Cent.* 4, 10 (PG90.1460B) and 1, 24 (1429C), where Thalassius likens the intellect to a chariot moving Godward; cf. also Isaac the Syrian, *Mystic Treatises* (370, not found in the Greek); Niketas Stethatos, *Cent.* 3, 95 (353) and Symeon the New Theologian, *Theol.* 1 (126), where the intellect is likened to a bird.

[50] 15.76 (900AD).

[51] 15.78 (901AB). Cf. also 15.76 (900AD). There is a long history of the notion of the intellect as 'eye': cf. Origen, *De or.* 9, 2 (318, 99); Ps. Basil, *Const. Monast.* 2, 1 (PG31.1340A); Greg. Nyssa, *De*

According to John, the vision of the intellect should be 'unflighty' (*ameteoristos*), forever focused in one direction or on one person. Abba Isaiah of Scetis, in similar fashion, speaks of the demons trying to force the intellect 'to fly off' (*meteoros*).[52] John's comments here are wholly a fruit of his own experience. This may account for his 'lack' of system. It is a matter of personal experience for him that continual vigilance is a condition for contemplating God. In sin, the intellect is not only 'burned' (*pyrōsis*) but also dazzled, 'blinded' (*pērōsis*), in much the same way as the heart is hardened (*pōrōsis*). For God's light burns those of impure vision. On the other hand, we blind ourselves when we choose not to seek the divine light; John suggests that even to blink too frequently is to live in darkness.[53] Without an acuteness of the intellect, the entire human person remains blind, destitute of direction.

Vigilance, then, should be 'continual.' It results in the 'noetic perception' of God's presence.[54] The pure and 'vigilant eye' of the intellect is able to see God. Indeed, purity and simplicity are the natural condition of the intellect. This condition is contrasted with the 'hardened' state (*pōrōsis*), when the intellect is no longer susceptible of the tender action of divine grace. The intellect fails to fulfill its inherent function. John regards this function as a superior faculty, whereby one has the option of entering into communion with God, or refusing to do so. And it is precisely because the potentiality is always there that another representative of the ascetic tradition, Mark the Monk, would insist: '*stay* with your intellect (*dianoia*).'[55]

Virg. 10 (PG46.360C); *Apophth.* Bessarion 11 (PG65.141D); *Mac. Hom.* 1, 2 (1–2); 25, 10 (205) and 7, 8 (76); Barsanuphius 241; Mark the Monk, *De lege spir.* 5 (PG65.905B) and 12 (908A); Maximus, *Myst.* (PG91.673); Cyril of Sythopolis, *Life of Euthymios* 19 (p. 31, 1.25; p.32, 1.3) and *Life of Sabas* 16 (p. 99, 1.5–7). It is a tradition followed by later Fathers: Theoleptos of Philadelphia, *De abscondita operation in Christo* (PG143.392A); Greg. of Sinai, *Chapt.* 23 (34); Kallistos/Ignatios, *Cent.* 70 (265); and Greg. Palamas, *Triads* 1, 3, 21 and 1, 3, 9.

[52] *Logos* 17, 3 (106). Cf. also the use of the word *meteoros* in Basil, *Reg. Fus. Tract.* 201 (PG31.1216C); Greg. Nyssa, *De Virg.* 22 (PG46.404A); Diadochus, *Cent.* 81 (139–40); Cyril of Scythopolis, *Life of John the Hesychast* (p. 202, 1.8–9). Isaac the Syrian has a similar doctrine in *Mystic Treatises* (147).

[53] 26.8 (1016A) and 15.78 (901AB). Here Climacus offers valuable insight into heaven and hell, intimating that, on the last day, God's light will shine on all but will burn those who are not pure since only the purified can behold its brilliance (Mt. 5.8). For those who are pure, there will not be any last day since they behold it even now.

[54] 26.17 (1020AB). This term is similar to the 'perception of the heart' (*kardiaki aisthesis*), which is used elsewhere to refer to the perception of God's presence in one's heart: cf. Diadochus, *Cent.* 14–16 (91–3) and 23 (94–6) and Greg. Palamas, *Triads* 1, 3, 18–21. Diadochus also speaks of *noera aisthesis* in *Cent.* 1, 7, 30, 36, 77, and 79 and 89 (85, 87, 100–101, 105, 135, 137, 149–50), but carefully distinguishes it from any Messalian connotations: cf. *Cent.* 36 (105). *Kardiaki aisthesis* is also found in 7.31 (808B) and 27.2 (1097AB).

[55] *De lege spir.* 164 (PG65.925B): Mark is using *dianoia* in the sense of *nous*.

So long as the light of the 'noetic Sun'[56] shines on the intellect, so long as the intellect is constantly beholding God's presence, so long as the divine Sun does not set (Ps. 103.19–21), then evil thoughts, like wild beasts, cannot enter the mind. And even if they do, they vanish when that Sun's light shines on them. When the living God appears, all idols are smashed (Is. 9.1); when the light shines, all shadows are cast behind the transparent intellect.[57]

Indeed, the intellect is not only illumined but is also redeemed in its unceasing concentration on God. Becoming servants of God alone, we are liberated from the 'captivity' of the intellect as well as from all worldly cares. Only in being divine captives of God do we also receive that freedom which surpasses all captivity. One is enslaved by God but enters rather into 'kinship' with God. Being unfaithful to God, on the other hand, allowing the intellect to be subsumed in worldly cares, is the intellect's way to 'being truly enslaved.' John calls this condition *aphanismos*, disappearance, or utter destruction:

> Prayer disappears when we are captured by useless cares. Prayer is stolen from us when the thoughts of the intellect wander before we realise it.[58]

The loss of communication with the source of life disables one from being truly alive. By contrast, being centered on God is life-giving and makes the intellect 'forever unconquerable,'[59] ever prepared to battle against evil thoughts, not just by means of good thoughts, but directly in and through God's grace.

The intellect is thus impelled to surpass itself and to behold God. To surpass, to 'lift up,' is to move beyond the 'visible creation' or the vanities of this world. This transcendence is a conquest, restoring royal authority to the intellect and 'subjecting all one's feelings to it.'[60] Kinship leads to kingship. More will be said on the regal status of the intellect later. Here it must be stressed that the 'lifting up' is a way of liberating the intellect, and also of 'rendering it holy.' Liberation 'detaches'[61] one from the dejected anxieties of worldly cares, and therefore sanctifies. In comparing the monk to a king, Chrysostom observes: 'A

---

[56] 26.ii,27 (1060B). Diadochus is more explicit in the use of such 'solar' terminology: cf. *Cent.* 6 (87).

[57] 26.ii,44 (1069AB). Regarding the light of the intellect, cf. Evagrius, *Prakt.* 64 (648) and *De or.* 74 (PG79.1184B). Whereas Evagrius is clearly referring to something specific, in Climacus the light seems to be metaphorical. Gregory Palamas speaks of the intellect as transparent in *Antirrheticos* 7, 10, 32 (3, p. 485). Climacus' imagery is taken up by Theoleptus of Philadelphia, *De abscondita operatione in Christo* (PG143.385CD).

[58] 28.24 (1133AB). The language of 'captivity' is to be found in other writers: cf. *Mac. Hom.* 11, 12 (104); Mark the Monk, *Ad Nic.* (PG65.1032D); Abba Isaiah, *Logos* 4, 12 (31): Isaiah's language is strikingly similar to that of Climacus; Thalassius, *Cent.* 3, 41 (PG91.1452C).

[59] 28.49 (1137AB).

[60] 29.2 (1148BC). For the royal function of the intellect, cf. Mark the Monk, *De Bapt.* (PG65.1008B). Cf. also Niketas Stethatos, *Cent.* 1, 85 (293) and Kallistos/Ignatios, *Cent.* 69 (265).

[61] 29.3 (1148C) and the end verse (1152C).

true king is one who preserves the intellect free.'[62] Such liberation and sanctification is a difficult pathway. To watch over one's intellect and indeed to transcend it is an entire 'art' or 'science.' One strives until the intellect can become 'inviolable' (*asyletos*),[63] totally surrendered and entrusted to God. Only then can it never again be snatched from us by the demons. In a sense, it then becomes totally ours, instead of lying at the mercy of the alien power of the demons. It is totally ours by being totally God's. For, in the last resort, God is nearer to us than we are to ourselves. When the 'intellect belongs elsewhere' – John even coins here the wonderful and unique term *allotrionous* – then it is neither God's nor ours.[64]

In the fifteenth step, John speaks of a certain 'flick of the intellect' (*pararripismos noos*), which, so he insists, is a very subtle notion. This marks the first movement of the intellect away from its point of concentration. John, however, humbly admits that he cannot comment on this notion because he does not have the appropriate knowledge; he confesses that he does not possess the faculty of discernment (*diakrisis*) given to other elders.[65] His brief allusions to *pararripismos* may be compared with subtle parallels to the subconscious and similar notions familiar in modern 'depth psychology.'[66] At any rate, John reveals that he is fully aware of the ambiguities in the spiritual life, which necessitate vigilant and acute judgement, as well as profound sensitivity and discernment.

There is no way of concentrating on God, of looking upward toward God, while at the same time subsiding into worldly cares, looking downward or the other way (Rom. 8.8). To look in opposite directions at the same time is to see nothing either properly or clearly. It is a form of duplicity. Abba Isaiah offers the reason for this: 'It is simply impossible for the intellect to care for both'[67] (Mt. 6.25). For John, it is like holding your legs together tightly and simultaneously trying to walk quickly.[68] The intellect is 'pure' (*katharos*) only when it beholds God's grace, which alone can purify it. Total concentration is, in fact, a mutual, personal relationship with God; then, the intellect speaks to God, in prayer, 'face to face,' or rather into God's ear.[69]

---

[62] *Comparatio regis et monachi* 2 (PG47.388).

[63] 27.2 (1097AB). Cf. also Origen, *De or.* 27, 2 (376).

[64] 27.ii, 48 (1116D).

[65] 15.73 (896C–97C) and 27.ii,11 (1109B). For the origin of this notion, cf. Mark the Monk, *Ad Nic.* (PG65.1036B).

[66] Cf. Kornarakis, *Paterika Biomata*, 17–18. The term itself is borrowed from Mark the Monk, as we shall see in the chapter dealing with ascetic struggle.

[67] *Logos* 25, 1 (151–2). See also Ps. Athanasius, *Sermo pro iis qui saeculo renuntiarunt* 1 (PG28.1409A). Cf. also Greg. Nyssa, *De Virg.* 8 (PG46.357A).

[68] 27.ii,19 (1112A).

[69] 27.20 (1100AB).

By turning to God, the intellect, as we have seen, gains light, vigilance and discernment. By seeing God, one discerns what truly *is*, because God illumines all darkness and enables one to know oneself. John speaks of a 'self-understanding' or 'self-knowledge' (*epignosis*). Indeed, to know oneself is to know God. For self-knowledge is a turning inwards, a healthy sense of 'shame' or *en-trope* (literally, a turning inward) before God, which enables us to see ourselves as we are, to become conscious of our limitations in reality and humility. The word *entrope* is very expressive here. John indicates that we acquire self-awareness when we encounter an awareness of God within ourselves. The term *entrope* implies something far more profound than mere 'shamefulness' or 'shyness.' By contrast, when the intellect is not centered on God, one becomes insensible (*analgetos*) and shameless (*anaischyntos*). The intellect hardens (*anaisthesia*) through lack of God's grace. There is a lack of awareness or misapprehension of God's presence (*adiakrisia*). If one does not see God, then one does not see oneself either. In fact, John would not hesitate to say, one does not really see at all (*ablepsia*).[70] Gregory of Sinai's words in the fourteenth century would seem to echo those of John Climacus:

> For it is the same for a person to be dead and insensitive as for that person to be blind in the intellect.[71]

And a very early text, *The Shepherd of Hermas*, sums this up inversely:

> Cling to the Lord and your intellect will perceive everything.[72]

We have spoken of light. This is a gift directly from God. However, there are numerous approximations to and shades of light. Climacus again makes a point to encourage the weakest on their way to illumination. In accordance with Christ's claim in John's Gospel (Jn 14.2: 'in the house of my Father there are many mansions'), John's *Ladder* states that there are 'various lights' and 'many different overshadowings':

> Just as the eyes have various lights in them, so in the soul many different overshadowings of the noetic Sun occur. ... One kind comes through what is contemplated by the bodily eyes, another through the noetic.[73]

The stages towards perfection and even the levels of perfection are many and diverse, presenting the spiritual life with a kaleidoscope of illumination.

---

[70] 26.7 (1013CD).

[71] *Chapt.* 5 (31).

[72] Hermas, *Shepherd*, Mandatum 10, 1. Cf. definition in Hermas, *Shepherd*, Mandatum 4, 2, of repentance (*metanoia*) as a great 'understanding.' Theodoret sees the intellect as a mirror (see Wis. 7.26): cf. *Phil. Hist.* James, 1, 3 (p. 164, 1293D). This notion is also found in Cyril of Scythopolis, *Life of Sabas*, 12 (p. 95, 1.14–17). For Niketas Stethatos, *Cent.* 1, 9 (275), it is through the light of the intellect that one knows God.

[73] 26.ii, 27 (1060B).

The Intellect and the Human Heart

At times, as it has already become evident, John seems to blur distinctions in terminology[74] when he speaks about the intellect and the heart. Yet, more than often, the two are well differentiated. What is perfection, or 'what is dispassion?' John asks; he replies that it could be 'the heaven of the intellect within the heart.'[75] The intellect and the heart, though different, are nevertheless inseparable. The intellect is inside the heart. And there is a harmony as well as a balanced relationship between the two, which accords with the general resistance in the desert tradition to extremes in this regard, whether these are in the form of sentimentalism or intellectualism. There is no separation in John between the 'schools' of the heart and of the intellect; both are drawn together. It should be noted that in Coptic – the language used by most of the monks in Egypt – the same word, 'het,' is employed to designate both the *nous* and the *kardia*.[76] John himself readily interchanges the terms. Nevertheless, in studying the ascetic Fathers in retrospect and identifying himself with their tradition, a later mystic such as Gregory Palamas, who also draws heavily on Gregory of Nyssa, contends that it is basically the same to claim that the intellect is in the heart, or in the head, or for that matter elsewhere.[77] Thus the fourteenth-century hesychast notion concerning the 'descent' of the intellect into the heart is anticipated by John Climacus in the seventh century.

For Mark the Monk, the separation of the intellect from the heart is cause for sin.[78] On the other hand, their harmonious relationship ensures the edification of one's personality in the life of grace. John speaks of the heart of the dispassionate ascetic as containing all of heaven (*ouranos*). God is contained therein, whose throne the heavens are; even the entire universe is contained, whose creator God is. This micro-paradise is guarded by the intellect, constantly vigilant and firmly concentrated on the presence of God within the heart. In this condition, the ascetic no longer fears demons, 'regarding their wiles as mere games.'[79] The intellect guards the heart like 'a dog.' This 'watch-dog' must stand still, guarding the heart. Paradoxically, this stillness or motionlessness (*akinesia*) of the intellect is never idle but forever

---

[74] 30.18 (1060B).

[75] 29.1 (1148B).

[76] Cf. Chitty, *Desert*, 3. See also ed. W. Crum, *A Coptic Dictionary*. Oxford: Clarendon Press, 1939, 642–3.

[77] *Triads* 3, 3, 4; 2, 2, 27 and 29; 1, 2, 3. For the intellect's location inside the heart, cf. *Mac. Hom.* 43, 7 (289) and 15, 20 (139). For the intellect's location within the head, cf. Athanasius, *Ad monachos* 70 (PG25.776CD). The reference to Gregory of Nyssa is from *De opif. hom.* 12 (PG44.156f).

[78] *De Bapt.* (PG65.1016AB).

[79] 29.1 (1148B).

mobile, since movement is the natural condition of the intellect. Yet it is a stillness directed toward heaven, a motion in the presence of God. In his exhortation for motionlessness, John uses the suggestive preposition *pros* (toward), which implies motion:

> When darkness and the night of the passions overtake ... then make your dog [namely, the intellect as watchdog] immovable in night – watching before God (*pros Theon*). And there is nothing improper in calling the intellect a dog, for it drives away the wild beasts.[80]

There, at the entrance, the intellect must confront a variety of beasts – a metaphor for evil thoughts – that arrive in order to distract and darken the intellect. This 'darkening' (*skotasmos*) is also called 'darkness' (*skotia*); it is 'the night of the passions.' According to John, it is only when this dimness is removed that the intellect is 'illumined' and actually 'becomes light,' shining like the sun (Mt. 13.43).

> By ecstasy, ineffably and unspeakably, the intellect is brought to stand before Christ in noetic light.[81]

In its role of guarding the heart, the intellect, as already noted, assumes a royal status and stance. Other writers prefer to adopt the image of the intellect as a charioteer, holding the reigns of the entire human person.[82] The imagery may be traced back to Plato's *Phaedrus*. There, Plato speaks of the intellect as the charioteer, whose chariot is drawn by two horses, *thymos* (the spirited aspect) and *epithymia* (the desirive or appetitive aspect). The implication is that the intellect requires the coordination and cooperation of all of the other dimensions that comprise the human person. John in fact prefers the imagery of the ocean. Possibly raised by the sea, John speaks of God using 'the helm of the soul,' namely the intellect, 'in order to pilot' the ascetic.[83] His is a more biblical language; he refers to the intellect as the heart's priest. Filled with God's presence, the heart becomes a heavenly altar on which the intellect offers 'logical' sacrifices, 'theo-logical' thanksgiving for divine gifts. To underline

---

[80] *Shep.* 9 (1168B). For the intellect guarding the heart, cf. *Mac. Hom.* 15, 20 and 33 (139 and 146); Mark the Monk, *De Bapt.* (PG65.1016D–17A); Diadochus, *Cent.* 64 (124–5) and Nicephorus, *De custodia cordis* (PG147.963B). The image of the 'diamond' is used in Ps. Athanasius, *Life of St. Syncletike* 9 (PG28.1492B), to portray the firmness of the intellect. The same image is found in Climacus' contemporary, Isaac the Syrian, *Mystic Treatises* (359). The image of the 'dog' is used elsewhere to describe the demons (cf. 6.11 [796A]); perhaps this, too, shows that passions are not in themselves evil but must be tamed, mastered and directed in an orderly way towards God.

[81] 26.ii,27 (1065A). See also Greg. Nyssa, *De Virg.* 11 (PG46.365D–68A).

[82] Cf. Greg. Nyssa, *De Virg.* 22 (PG46.404D–05A); Ps. Chrysostom, *Ep. ad monachos* (PG60.751) and *Mac. Hom.* 40, 5 (277).

[83] 28.27 (1133C).

further this royal and the priestly ethos of the human intellect, John plays on the ministerial words 'to oversee' (*episkopein*) or 'to be bishop' (*episkopeusai*):

> For the intellect is a ruler and a high-priest, offering spiritual sacrifices to Christ.[84]

Isaac the Syrian echoes the same imagery when he speaks of 'the intellect's entry behind the curtain of the holy of holies.'[85]

In its 'protective' and 'priestly' roles, the intellect staves off the demons attacking its 'surface.' If they do not penetrate the 'deep waters,' then the disturbance proves lesser, the battle against them easier:

> In those who have already made progress, the demons only ruffle the surface of the intellect. That is why such people soon feel their normal calm.[86]

Here, too, constant vigilance, or the coordination and concentration of every aspect of the intellect (*synnoia*), is required:

> Be concentrated (*synnous*) ... for the demons fear concentration as thieves fear dogs.[87]

The intellect–heart relationship, then, is indicative of the integrated nature of the person. God's presence in the heart gathers and centers the intellect upon itself (*syn-nous*). The intellect thus becomes all eyes, riveting its waking. John has borrowed this from the Egyptian desert:

> Abba Bessarion said: 'The monk ought to be as the Cherubim and the Seraphim: all eye!'[88]

The intellect resembles watching eyes, guarding its 'treasure.' The treasure is God's presence dwelling in the heart. And the object is to bring oneself into the 'treasury,' in the words of the Gospel (Mt. 6.6), where alone God sees us. There is an element of intimacy in this act; it is not an act of isolation. In the same passage, therefore, John guards us 'against displaying ourselves.' The treasure must not be flaunted. God is the only witness. For us, it is simply a case of being there, of being all there, of being all eyes, in the presence of God – in the heart and 'with the intellect.' This is perhaps the more literal translation of the term *synnoia*.

---

[84] 28.52 (1137BC). Cf. also 29.1 (1148B). For the priestly function of the intellect, cf. *Mac. Hom.* 25, 9–10 (204–05); Maximus, *Myst.* (PG91.672D and 681CD) and Thalassius, *Cent.* 3, 55 (PG91.1453B).

[85] *Mystic Treatises* (349).

[86] 26.ii,69 (1073D–1076A).

[87] 7.18 (805A).

[88] *Apophth.* Bessarion 11.

The vision of God in the human intellect and in the heart has the further implication of stressing God's awesome mystery, a reality beyond all knowledge yet known in divine inwardness within us. Symeon the New Theologian was to state later that God is 'well known' within the intellect.[89] Hence the mysteriousness also of the human person in its 'divine' dimension. God is not someone, let alone something, separated from us. The heavenly kingdom and the entire universe are within the vast expanse of the heart. The human person is a microcosm.[90] When we speak of the human person, we are inevitably and invariably speaking of God too. Anthropology and theology share the same language in the ascetic terminology of John Climacus.

For John, the turning of the intellect towards the heart (*en-trope*), towards God's presence within the heart, is also described as 'rapture,' in the wake of Barsanuphius for whom 'God entirely transforms the intellect.'[91] The implication is that it is God who actually does the 'turning.' This is a gift from above and no achievement of ours.[92] The grace of God burns inside the heart as a torch of fire that purifies, and as a light that illumines. One can actually perceive God's fire entering the heart. This 'noetic perception' is, John says, 'both within us, and yet not within us.'[93] John's intention is not merely to speak of the effect of God's grace in an apophatic manner but rather to stress its utterly pervasive, albeit evasive character. God's grace 'plays games' with us. God is mystically revealed and then providentially concealed in order that we may increase in desire and passion and purity.

The Intellect in the Life of the Ascetic

Humility and Meekness

For John, the natural state of the intellect is humility. Like the healthy sense of shame, 'modesty' or meekness renders the heart an 'inviolable treasury.' Humility guards the heart from the demons and from liability 'to be influenced' by them:

---

[89] *Cat.* 24 (40).

[90] Cf. 29.1 (1148B). Cf. also Maximus, *Amb.* (PG91.1285CD and 1248BC); *Cap. de Car.* 4, 44 and 64 (PG90.1057B and 1064A); 3, 44 (1029A) and *Ad Thal.* 56 (581C).

[91] Barsanuphius 173.

[92] 5.5 (764Df.) and 4.31 (700B–01B). Cf. also Diadochus, *Cent.* 28 (99); Isaac the Syrian, *Mystic Treatises* (315); Symeon the New Theologian, *Thanks.* 2 (348); Greg. of Sinai, *Chap.* 118 (53). It is interesting that, in this passage, Climacus uses 'ecstatic' language whereas Origen actually delights in more 'erotic' imagery, portraying the intellect as giving birth: cf. *De or.* 13, 3 (327).

[93] 26.17 (1020A). Cf. 28.51 (1137B).

So the intellect remains unplundered, reposing securely in the casket of modesty, only hearing the knocks and jeers of the thieves, without however being subject to any of their threats.[94]

This differs substantially from the Stoic notion of 'apathy' and from the 'imperturbability' prevailing in certain writers of Stoic tendency, such as Boethius – qualities in the first instance attributed to God, but consequently serving also as a model for the truly religious. It is nearer to early Greek Stoicism[95] – as in Epictetus – that tended to attach greater importance to the human will and purpose. For John, the human person is subject to temptations, but this is not determined by any fatal causality. After all, while still hearing 'knocks and jeers of the thieves,' one may choose either to disregard or else to withstand them.

Humility offers resistance against the demons who attack us, seeking to steal our intellect. To be 'simple'[96] is yet another way of entrenching the intellect. Meekness, or humility, is indeed the opposite of anger (*thymos*), which deranges, darkens and blurs the intellect. Such anger is described as 'the coinhabitant of darkness and ignorance.'[97] In its natural state, as we have seen, *thymos* is actually one of the two horses drawn by the charioteer intellect. For John, however, the intellect should become 'poor,' humble and simple.[98] Unlike Plato, John no longer uses the word *thymos* to describe the intellect that has been purified. It is true that Platonists, Stoics and Christian ascetics alike agree on the indispensable need for purity of the intellect. The difference is that, for the Christian ascetic, the intellect is not divine by nature. It is never a substitute for God, and should, therefore, always remain humble.

The Alexandrian Prison provides an extreme example of the intellect's vocation to humility. We have seen the need for the intellect to be fed with good thoughts. We have also noted the need to concentrate the intellect on the heart and on the presence of God within. But to have achieved this gives no entitlement to merit. In fact, the humble ascetic, having reached this goal, becomes like a 'fool' in Christ. The conclusion is not far-fetched. Ultimately, nothing is achieved of one's own accord. The monk merely brings the intellect before God's throne, presenting it before the divine presence and, to use Origen's imagery, there 'lies noetically prostrated' before God.[99] It is God,

---

[94] 25.5 (989BC). Humility of the intellect is also emphasised in 24.4 (981AB); 24.2 (980D–81A); 26.iii,2 (1084CD); 6.6 (793C); and 4.31 (700B–01B).

[95] For the Stoic view of dispassion, cf. J. M. Rist, *Stoic Philosophy*, Cambridge: Cambridge University Press, 1969, 25, 38, 45, 52, 72–3, and 195. See also J. Bryant, *Moral Codes and Social Structure in Ancient Greece*, Albany: State University of New York Press, 1996.

[96] 23.11 (977CD).

[97] 24.4 (981AB).

[98] Poverty is stressed in 29.3 (1148C).

[99] *De or.* 31, 3 (396).

then, who fills the intellect with good thoughts for meditation; and it is God
who turns the intellect in the right direction. The monk almost appears to
possess no intellect of his own. It is as though the monk were mad or 'depraved
in intellect' on account of having surrendered the intellect entirely to God.
There is nothing left but to weep:

> The monks in the Prison offered to God nothing but a speechless soul and a
> voiceless intellect, filled with darkness and blank despair. ... They had
> already sunk their intellect to the very depths of humility, shedding tears of
> melancholy (*a-thymia*, literally an absence of *thymos*!), which burn like fire.

This fire is the fire of hell. Yet, at the same time, by virtue of God's love, it is
also the fire of God's grace. These 'fools' in Christ stand self-condemned; this is
why Christ will save them. They are deluding neither themselves nor others.
They outrightly exclaim:

> We know very well that, in all fairness, we deserve every punishment and
> torment. Nor are we able to offer any excuse.[100]

The monks in the Alexandrian Prison are neither self-sufficient nor
complacent. They do not consider themselves justified, or even just. They
believe that they deserve only hell. Yet they enter paradise precisely because
of their selfless love, simply because, as John informs us, they loved God and
humanity, never judging anyone. The surrender, therefore, of the intellect
must not be seen superficially in the light of some naive anti-intellectualism
on the part of these ascetics; rather, it is a manifestation of their genuine
humility. In fact, there is a sense in which, through this very surrender of the
intellect, they are in fact emphasizing the supreme significance of the
intellect. For their humility is a genuine act of the intellect. Elsewhere,
Climacus speaks of 'the intellect's proper understanding of its weakness and
limits.'[101]

The Effect of the Demons

John likens the action of the demons to a 'darkening' of the intellect. As
before, the intellect assumes the character of an 'eye.' In order for the intellect
to see clearly the treasure, which it must guard, namely the heart, the demons
must be fought. For they seek to make us lose this treasure. The demonic
method is deceit. Evil thoughts 'darken' the intellect,[102] just as clouds cover
the sun, in an effort to blot out the light of Christ. Evagrius of Pontus states
that every demonic attack has but a single purpose: to render the intellect

---

[100] 5.5 (765C–68A).

[101] 25.3 (988C–89A).

[102] 15.78 (901AB) and 26.ii,14 (1061AC).

dull.[103] Other ascetic writers, including Barsanuphius, are more emphatic in speaking of a 'blindness' that results.[104] Through the demons, the intellect is darkened in two ways, according to John: either by obliterating God's presence, glory and light, or else by making one turn away from God's light. Once deceived and darkened, the soul is destroyed. It grows accustomed to demonic darkness, and can no longer endure the divine light. Yet the destruction is never absolute; and Climacus uses every opportunity to reassure his readers of the abiding mercy of God.

The next strategy of the demons is to present other supposed treasures as substitutes for Christ. These 'treasures' are the various passions, and their appeal may impel surrender. In surrendering, however, we betray the intellect as 'sovereign.' It is a kind of irrational predicament: a darkened intellect leads to irrational, insane deeds, which, John admits, 'only mad people do.'[105] Thalassius provides some explanation of this in his *Centuries*: 'When the intellect is darkened, it sees things and mistakes them for other things.'[106] The only safeguard and remedy, says John, are a source of renewed and enhanced vigilance for the true light.

One way in which the demons frequently assault is by default, namely through a sense of despair or despondency (*akedia*) that 'kills' the intellect[107] by dislodging it from concentration on God; despondency 'enervates' the intellect by deviation of its concentration on God. Loss of trust in God removes God from the center of attention. Humility makes us commend ourselves to the grace and mercy of God. Despondency is withdrawal from God, through which 'prayer is weakened.' Failure to concentrate the intellect on God disables any relationship with God:

> Despondency is a paralysis of the soul, an enervation of the intellect.[108]

When *akedia* pervades the intellect, the latter is sucked up as in 'a whirlpool,'[109] which only draws one further and further down. It overwhelms the intellect, removing it from the sight of God. It is indeed a desperate condition. For to

---

[103] *De or.* 50 (PG79.1177B). Cf. *De or.* 70 (1181C). For this darkening, cf. also *Hist. Monachorum*, 1, John of Lycopolis 23 (17); Thalassius, *Cent.* 2, 88 (PG91.1436B); Symeon the New Theologian, *Cat.* 24 (46) and Greg. Palamas, *Triads*, 1, 3, 9. On demonic deceit, cf. *Peri Logismon* 26 (ed. Guy, 171–81) and Diadochus, *Cent.* 49 (113).

[104] Barsanuphius 256. Cf. also Mark the Monk, *De lege spir.* 103 and 169 (PG 65.917C and 925BC).

[105] 15.78 (901AB).

[106] *Cent.* 1, 86 (PG91.1436AB).

[107] 13.7 (860C). The emphasis on *akedia* in ascetic literature becomes more pronounced after Evagrius: cf. *Prakt.* 28 (564): *Antirrheticos* 7 and 14 (ed. Frankenberg, 523, 525) and *Cent.* 4, 25 (ed. Frankenberg, 379).

[108] 13.1 (857D–60A).

[109] 26.13 (1016D).

behold God is to see oneself as one is, while at the same time enjoying divine beauty, mercy and love.

Nevertheless, despondency too can at times induce greater vigour in the ascetic life. Climacus is rather wary of excessive action becoming a surrogate of true ascetic life, even if the activity is of a positive, beneficent kind.[110] If we do not have *synnoia* – which may also be contrasted with ignorance (*agnoia*) – good deeds may be wrongly motivated. For John, silent prayer is always given priority over loud action. The demons try to dispel prayer by talkativeness (*polylogia*):

> Talkativeness is the dissipation of recollection (*synnoia*), the abolition of guarding the intellect ... and the darkening of prayer.[111]

Despondency, then, leads into a vicious circle that is attended by many other passions. One can be cured of despondency only if one has sufficient 'courage.'[112]

Grace, then, acts in a double way, inspiring love of God and indicating individual unworthiness. Through continual vigilance we may return to the light from the darkness with which the demons enfold us. We may return to self-knowledge in the presence of God, and regain a sense of 'shame for ourselves and our intellect.'[113] This conversion or 'change' (*metastrophe*), however, is itself again an act of God. The 'intellect sees God' when it is turned by God toward God:

> If, through our activity, God arises within us, the enemies will be scattered; and if we draw near to the divine vision, those who hate God will flee from before His face and ours.[114]

This is a pithy summary of the patristic understanding of repentance (*metanoia*), which implies a re-directing of the *nous*, a re-orientation of the entire human person.[115]

Love and Eros

Concentration of the intellect on God is closely linked with humility, as well as with love for others.[116] In the face of God's presence, the intellect is literally

---

[110] 13.1 (857D–60A).

[111] 11.2 (852B).

[112] 13.7 (860C).

[113] 26.8 (1016A).

[114] 26.25 (1021AB).

[115] The opposite of *meta-noia* is called *anoia* (or, lack of intellect, namely total madness!) in Basil, *Sermo de renuntiatione saeculi et de perfectione spirituale* 4 (PG31.636B), Symeon the New Theologian, *Cat.* 15 (226) and Greg. Palamas, *Triads*, 1, 1, 17. The term *aponoia* (namely, being beside one's intellect) is found in Chrysostom, *Hom.* 20 and in *Ep. ad Rom.* 4 (PG60.600).

[116] 24.2 (980D–81A).

'beside itself' – a state amounting to ecstasy. What is implied here is a relationship with God that is also outgoing, a being without being within. The ascetic aims to reach God in a motion of ecstasy, of erotic love.[117] This movement involves the intellect and the heart, that is to say, the total human person. The individual aspects represent a kind of ladder (Ps. 83.6) of ascent and descent. And the totality signifies the function of the human person as a microcosm, which in turn indicates one's reconciliatory role in the world as a mediator.

The inward concentration of the intellect on God should be 'unflighty' (*ameteoristos*) and 'constant' (*adiastatos*).[118] Nevertheless, it is also an act of outward love. There is no individual self-concentration without an outgoing in humility and love; the search is the discovery. It is part of John's apophatic stance that he is able to perceive this irreducible mystery of divine–human relation. The intellect concentrates neither on itself nor on some extraneous object. Like a passionate lover it longs for another. And having found the other, 'it is embraced within with pleasure.' This love is perpetual: whether the lover sleeps or wakes, works or rests, walks or sits, it burns within. At every corner and in every detail, one encounters, sees and speaks to the beloved. Physical *eros* is the only fitting image of divine *eros*. At times, the intellect even enters God's bridal chamber, which is the heart, embracing God frenziedly, everywhere seeing none but God. There is no room for any other concern, for anything that separates the intellect from God.

The Intellect and the Act of Prayer

Love, at one with humility, is also closely linked with prayer. For prayer, too, is an attitude of love, involving a personal relationship. 'The guarding of the intellect' (*phylake noos*) can never be an impersonal act inasmuch as it is intimately related to 'continual prayer.'[119] Prayer is more than an act; it is always an 'art.' Prayer is not mere invocation, 'prayer by mouth alone.'[120] True prayer has not yet been reached when one is uttering words addressed to God. Prayer is much more than lip service. For the *Macarian Homilies*, in prayer:

> The intellect is wholly occupied with the Lord as … a married person is with one's spouse.[121]

---

[117] 26.iii,7 (1060B); 27.20 (1100AB) and 30.18 (1160BD). Cf. also J. Kirchmeyer, 'Extase chez les Pères de l'Église,' *DS* 4 (1961), 2087–113.

[118] 22.22 (969AB).

[119] 27.20 (1100AB); 26.2,3 (1057D–60A); 24.2 (980D–81A) and esp. 6.6 (793C). Continual prayer is the function of the intellect: cf. Maximus, *Lib. Asc.* (PG90.929C) and Barsanuphius 74.

[120] 27.20 (1100AB) and 28.20 (1132D).

[121] *Mac. Hom.* 15, 13 (133–5).

By analogy, Mark the Monk says that sinful thoughts are alien to prayer, resembling 'a flirtation of the intellect.'[122] And for Evagrius, 'if the intellect looks around at the time of prayer, then it is not yet praying as a true monk.'[123]

According to John, the intellect is able to remain centered on God with only a minimum of words. Verbal profusion is liable to have a dispersing effect. A few words, or perhaps simply one word alone (*monologia*),[124] perhaps no more than God's name, will suffice. Prayer is unadulterated concentration on God. In disengaging this concentration, says John, one begins to worship substitutes, 'images, material' or graven.[125] *Polylogia* shatters concentration (*synnoia*). The multiplication of words divaricates, moves away from the 'one thing, which alone is necessary' (Lk. 10.42). A single word may cause the damage:

> By blurting out one careless word, one who has tasted prayer often defiles the intellect.[126]

One cannot be robbed of the intellect by the devil, provided one constantly 'stands before God in prayer.'[127] Barsanuphius speaks of 'having God continually in the intellect.'[128]

For Evagrius, 'prayer is the activity appropriate for the dignity of the intellect.'[129] John, too, speaks of 'noetic activity,' which is unceasing. The monks in the *coenobium* at Alexandria 'achieved another surprising aim. For not even in the refectory did they desist from noetic activity.'[130] For John, there is an 'illumination of the intellect' that occurs through perpetual prayer.[131] Nevertheless, such illumination assumes diverse forms. John always condescends to the weaknesses of his colleagues:

> There are *many activities* for an active intellect. I am referring to meditation on the love of God, on the remembrance of God, on the remembrance of the kingdom, on the remembrance of the zeal of the holy martyrs, on the remembrance of God himself ... on remembrance of the holy and spiritual powers, on remembrance of one's departure, judgement, verdict, and punishment.

---

[122] *De bapt.* (PG65.992B).

[123] *De or.* 43 (PG79.1176C).

[124] 28.9 (1132B). This word points to what later became the fully developed practice of the Jesus Prayer.

[125] 16.12 (982C).

[126] 28.52 (1137B).

[127] 18.4 (937C). Cf. also 11.2 (852B) on *polylogia*.

[128] Barsanuphius 271.

[129] *De or.* 84 (PG79.1185B). Cf. also *Prakt.* 49 (610–12).

[130] 4.18 (685C).

[131] 28.1 (1129B).

Once again, the 'many activities' of the intellect range 'from the sublime' to the ordinary.[132] The essential activity of the intellect is prayer, but this may on occasion be nothing more or less than 'sincerely asking for the prayers of others.'[133]

God may be concealed in order to make the intellect seek the divine presence all the more lovingly. Yet the intellect should never relinquish prayer. To break away from this connection with God is the ultimate sacrilege. For God 'to disappear' may be a measure of mere 'economy.' A single careless word or thought, however, on our part could damage this relationship. Its restoration is only wrought with difficulty and requires much toil. Prayer is 'the mirror of progress, the disclosure of stature.' It is the way to the restoration of our pristine beauty in the image of God's beauty. Prayer not only reaches back to our former glory but it also reaches forward to the last things, to the perception of the nature of heaven and hell, to the last judgement.[134] Nonetheless, in the last resort even the relationship of prayer, 'what is most desired,'[135] depends not on us but solely on the initiative of God's grace.

John places great emphasis on silence (*hesychia*). Silence is the only way of rendering the intellect complete. Words dispel; silence integrates. When the intellect is disturbed, as when there are ripples in a pool of water, one is no longer able to see clearly. The intellect, as we have seen, should be 'unwavering' (*akymantos*), literally without waves.[136] *Hesychia*, however, is more than verbal stillness or wordlessness. Beyond this – and, often, even quite apart from this – it is a way of life,[137] which allows God to be seen in everything that is said and done. Even while speaking, we can concentrate on God. Silence is impeded by anger (*thymos*), a passion against which John militates most strongly. More than all else, anger disturbs the intellect, like the winds tossing the deep seas.[138] It hampers prayer and obscures contemplation. To see God and to see ourselves clearly requires stillness, even as we see things in clear and untroubled waters.

A brief comment must be added here on the relationship between work and prayer, although this will be more thoroughly examined in the specific chapter on prayer. For John, work does not necessarily deflect concentration of the intellect. One may watch the intellect, even while continuing to engage in

---

[132] 6.17 (796A).

[133] 4.22 (689C).

[134] 28.1 (1129AB). Climacus perceives judgement as an act of the revelation of God's glory to all: it sears some, while bringing comfort to others.

[135] 28.51 (1137B).

[136] 27.2,6 (1108AB). Cf. also 4.31 (700B–01B).

[137] Actually John is speaking of a married way of life: *hesychia* is called our 'partner in the yoke of marriage' (*syzygos*) in 11.3 (852B).

[138] 26.iii,22 (1088A).

manual labor. No labor, including any intellectual activity such as reading, will harm the intellect but, on the contrary, may even illuminate it:

> Reading enlightens the intellect considerably, and it helps it concentrate. ... Let what you read lead you to action, for you are a doer (Js 1.22).[139]

Work and prayer, for John as well as for the ascetic tradition in general, cannot be set apart. Prayer (*ora*) is absorbed into work (*labora*); work itself becomes prayer. And prayer becomes 'rapture toward the Lord,'[140] an inward movement towards God. The intellect can be forever brought to focus on God, whatever one happens to be doing:

> If you constantly train your intellect never to wander, then it will be near you even during meals. But if it wanders unrestrained, then it will never stay beside you.[141]

As already observed, the ascetic finally no longer says prayers but actually becomes prayer. The intellect of the monk no longer sees light but is itself transformed into 'unfailing light.'[142] Then, the monk becomes 'a light for all people.'[143] The human person can totally become a burning flame of prayer, as Abba Joseph of Panepho said to Abba Lot:

> You cannot become a monk, unless you become like a single flame of fire![144]

John Cassian transferred this conviction to the West, when he contended that the intellect becomes inflamed, as fervent as fire itself.[145] The ascetic is to acquire 'the *nous* of the Lord' (Rom. 11.34; 1 Cor. 2.6), although Climacus is also careful to stress the struggle required to achieve this:

> The divine Apostle says: 'Who has known the *nous* of the Lord?' And I will say: 'Who has known the intellect of the person who is a hesychast in body and spirit?'[146]

While going through the various stages of life, the human person changes in many ways. Yet every person also always remains the same. It is difficult to state what exactly it is that makes a person one and the same self. For John, as I have tried to show in the foregoing examination of his main anthropological

---

[139] 27.iii,47 (1116C).

[140] 28.20 (1132D). The *orare–laborare* connection is etymologically misleading, but there is a theological parallelism here underlining an interrelation between the two verbs.

[141] 28.22 (1133A).

[142] 22.22 (969A). Cf. also *Mac. Hom.* 1,2 (1–2).

[143] 26.23 (1020D).

[144] *Apophth.* Joseph of Panepho 6 (PG65.229C).

[145] Cassian, *Inst.* 2, 10 (74).

[146] 27.ii,56 (1117B). Cf. also Palladius, *Hist. Laus.* Philoromos 113 (133).

tenets, the essential fact is that, as a person, one is endowed with a body, a heart and an intellect. Each of these stands in a complex and intimate relationship with one other and with God. In fact, the relationship between each of these aspects or spheres of existence is so intimate that they almost flow into one other. This at times makes it difficult even to identify what exactly John Climacus is talking about at any given point, especially where he considers the subtleties of the intellect and the heart. John does, however, establish a certain hierarchy in that relationship, with the *nous* serving as a kind of vertex, perhaps a searchlight, reaching into the heart and watching over it, and through the heart, ruling the body, yet at the same time being infused by the heart and receiving the impressions of the body. The complexity is enhanced by the fact that none of these spheres is constant or static. They depend on each other and, above all, they depend on God's action within them, on our being nothing and everything in the sight of God, on our knowing and unknowing, on the intellect, by way of the heart and body, being illumined and darkened, and on our unceasing focus on God in silent prayer and constant meditation that involves our total being and thereby makes us what we are.

The path to the cave of John Climacus
(Photograph: Elizabeth Williams)

CHAPTER 5

'Joyful Sorrow': The Double Gift of Tears

And so I came to ... this true land of mourners.

(John Climacus, Step 5)

C'est tellement mystérieux le pays des larmes.

(Antoine St Exupéry)

Introduction

There are two basic phenomena underlying John's vision of the human person. First, there is the meeting and interaction between God and humanity which finds its most concrete expression in an ascent through prayer, *ascesis* and self-surrender, to the ultimate transfiguration and deification of the human person. This entails a spiritual drama irreducible to any of the monistic or dualistic conceptions to which abstract, rationalistic thought inexorably tends. The other essential phenomenon, derived from the pristine, divinely created image of humanity and from Christ's divine and human natures, is the integral unity of the human person in its 'noetic' (spiritual, mental, intellectual), 'cardiac' (all-embracing, emotive, sensory) and 'somatic' (bodily, corporeal, physical) manifestations. These are determined by one's relationship with God, with others, and with the environment at large. The matter of tears has a profound bearing on the unity of all these levels, as it affects human nature, and on the interaction of the levels within the human person. Indeed, tears – empirically no more than a reflexively secreted response to a variety of stimuli – are seen as a gift, revealing the kind of intrinsic link, the kinship between the intellect and the body, which has already been examined in the chapter on the heart and elsewhere in the preceding discussion.

The doctrine regarding the 'gift of tears' is by no means unknown in the West, but it seems to have been accorded a higher place in the East, possibly because of the greater emphasis on the heart as a vessel of the Holy Spirit. In this chapter, however, about 'the deep waters of the heart' (Wis. 2.2), emphasis is laid on the Eastern ascetic and mystical tradition, particularly as this is received and represented by John and in which, despite differences of approach, one may discover a fundamental unity of interpretation concerning the significance of tears.

If it is true, as is sometimes said, that this gift has not been given deserved attention by modern theologians,[1] it may be equally if not more true to claim that few subjects have been so little understood, or rather so much misunderstood. In dealing with the subject of tears, we must bear in mind that a mystery is at stake: it is another case of the penetration of the human by the divine. The mystery is peculiar to all ascetical–mystical experience. Despite the above-mentioned fundamental unity, not all 'schools' of thought or spirituality can be said to be uniform in this respect,[2] and indeed even to speak of 'schools' in this regard may itself be debatable. In any case, in the Eastern ascetic literature at least, there are no ordered accounts of the subject of tears. Climacus himself, who devotes a separate chapter to the subject of 'joyful sorrow,' cannot nevertheless be said to provide any coherent statement. In this, as in other respects, no strict categorization applies. In any 'theology of tears,'[3] the only satisfactory category is that of sanctity, which is an all-embracing, catholic, and yet intimately personal phenomenon. The ascetic discovers the 'one thing' that alone is necessary (Lk. 10.42) about this phenomenon; and yet each ascetic pursues this in a particular way. In the last analysis, the only 'school' is the tradition or communion, where all are one and yet each one is unique and unrepeatable.

The gift of tears is native to historical Christianity, distinguishing it from the ascetic or mystical expressions found in other religions. There is an entire tradition in the Christian East concerning tears. It is a line of thought that can be traced to the New Testament, through the Desert Fathers, to John himself who added new dimensions to it, and then through later centuries – with Symeon the New Theologian, who had certainly read the *Ladder*, standing out as one of the greatest witnesses on this matter. As we shall see below, by the fourth century, tears came to play a dominant role. The *Apophthegmata* – Abba Arsenius being the most obvious and notable instance[4] – and the Cappadocians are among the first to emphasize their importance. Other landmarks include Evagrius of Pontus, Abba Isaiah of Scetis, who devotes his entire final discourse to the gift of tears, Diadochus of Photice, the *Macarian*

---

[1] Fr. Lev Gillet, 'Gift of Tears,' 5, and Sister Sylvia Mary, 'Way of Tears,' 431. The fullest treatment of the subject remains that by I. Hausherr, *Penthos*. Cf. also M. Lot-Borodine, 'Don des larmes'; Völker, *Scala Paradisi*, 154–87; Yannaras, *Metaphysike*, 188–202; Ware, *Introduction*, 20–27; Hausherr, *Direction*, 179–80; and G. A. Maloney, *The Mystic of Fire and Light: St. Symeon the New Theologian*, Denville, NJ: Dimension Books, 1975, 129–37.

[2] Sister Sylvia Mary, 'Way of Tears,' 431.

[3] Holl, *Enthusiasmus*, 61, uses this expression but limits its application to Symeon the New Theologian about whom he is writing. H. Biedermann, *Das Menschenbild bei Symeon dem Jüngeren Theologen (949–1022)*, Würzburg: 1949, also deals with tears but largely draws on the article by Lot-Borodine, 'Don des larmes.'

[4] Euthymius sought to emulate Arsenius' tears: cf. Cyril of Scythopolis, *Life of Euthymios* 21 (p. 34, 21–2).

Homilies, Isaac of Nineveh, who was John's contemporary, and, in the West, John Cassian, who was unmistakably influenced by the East in this regard, having spent over ten years in the Egyptian desert; there, he was a disciple of Evagrius, whose doctrine on tears is explicit. The East was not so much the 'cradle'[5] of the practice of tears as the caretaker of a treasure given to Christianity by Jesus: 'Blessed are they that mourn, for they shall be comforted' (Mt. 5.4). In this profound and powerful aspect of the ascetic life, John does not essentially add to the traditional doctrine of tears – even in his emphasis on joyful sorrow – but merely uncovers some of its 'hidden secrets' in a fresh manner.

The present chapter deals with the way of tears, in general, the sanctification of the body through the washing of tears, Climacus' paradoxical notion of 'joyful sorrow,' and the overriding significance of joy in the spiritual life. There will be no attempt to synthesize the theme of tears, but merely to describe some of its key features, first taking as terms of reference the fundamental notions of compunction (*katanyxis*), repentance (*metanoia*) and mourning (*penthos*), and then structuring the discussion of tears around them. However, as will be seen, even these notions are often overlapping and interrelating for John, which makes it all the more difficult to describe them as clearly denoting different or disparate experiences. On the other hand, as will also be seen, some distinction must certainly be drawn, since compunction is not strictly synonymous with *penthos* in name or meaning,[6] while repentance too differs from *penthos*.[7]

The Context of Tears

Compunction (Katanyxis)

A consideration of compunction as viewed by our author is a prerequisite for an understanding of the gift of tears. Compunction or *katanyxis* is not identical with either *penthos* or tears. *Penthos* is a general term describing the precondition of tears, whether as a gift of God or not. According to the *Letters* of Barsanuphius and John:

---

[5] Lot-Borodine, 'Don des larmes,' 65 n. 1.

[6] Hausherr notes that the two terms are 'more or less synonymous:' cf. *Penthos*, 14. George Maloney also blurs the distinction between the two terms in his article '*Penthos* – a Forgotten Necessity,' *Monastic Studies* 7 (1969), 149–59.

[7] 25.7 (989D).

It is not *penthos* that is caused by tears, but tears that come about through *penthos*.[8]

Compunction, on the other hand, is a state producing both *penthos* and tears, and is the cause of joyful sorrow.[9] It is in prayer that *katanyxis* may more easily be identified,[10] because prayer is a relationship with God and acts as a mirror in which we are able to see how we stand before God, a threshold from where we can expect a call from God. There may, however, also be tears accompanying compunction and the order could even be reversed, whereby 'natural' tears precede the state of compunction, which itself is a wider state than tears.[11] John uses aphoristic, apophthegmatic language, and so compunction, *penthos* and the gift of tears often coinhere, although the basic distinction between them remains recognizable.

The Greek word *katanyxis*, from which the English term 'compunction' (based on the Latin *compunctio*) is derived, conveys the notion of a prick or a sting, which has a twofold effect. It is usually a painful but simultaneously a stimulating experience. One has a sudden hurtful sensation and is at the same time urged to move on, to go forward, to advance along a way which opens ahead: such is the way of tears. The term *katanyxis* enjoys a biblical background and connotation. In the Old Testament, its use is similar to the one indicated immediately above, although the Septuagint usually gives it a metaphorical meaning. The word was actually devised by the Seventy, and was then adopted into Christian spiritual language.[12] The word is found twice in the New Testament, although only once does it carry the sense of pricking: the effect of Peter's oration is said to 'prick' the crowd (in Acts 2.37). Romans 11.8 adopts the term in a negative sense, signifying insensitivity or stupor. Régamey insists on the intensity of the prefix *kata*[13] – something lacking in the Latin prefix *com* – which reflects the quality of the tangible stimulating prick. The incisive piercing causes excitement, which is really and consciously experienced by the ascetic. Theodoret of Cyrus observes that the sensation resembles

---

[8] Barsanuphius (Abba John), 285. Ps. Athanasius, *De virg.* 17 (PG28.27C), speaks of the '*penthos* of tears.' Bultmann thinks that *penthein* (*penthos*) is not a theologically significant concept in the New Testament: cf. Friedrich, *TDNT* 6, 43.

[9] 7.11 (804B).

[10] 28.10 (1132B) and 50 (1137B).

[11] Chrysostom links tears with compunction in *De Statuis* 15, 1 and 17, 1 (PG49.153–5 and 171–3). Cf. Lev Gillet, 'Gift of Tears,' 8.

[12] See the *Acta Xanthippae et Polyxenae*, ed. M. R. James, in *Texts and Studies* 2,3 (1893) and Origen, *On the Psalms* (PG12.1145A).

[13] Cf. Lot-Borodine, 'Don des larmes,' 77 n. 3, where the author refers to Guibert, Morin and Régamey. Gregory the Theologian, *Or.* 14, 5 (PG35.864) and *Or.* 43.60 (PG36.573) has a similar understanding of *katanyxis* as a call to advance. Völker, *Scala Paradisi*, 154–87, says little about the significance of compunction.

arrows from above, which sting one by night and day, thereby creating tears.[14] John, too, describes compunction as 'a golden spur (*kentron*) in the soul.'[15]

Compunction, therefore, does not simply involve remorse or regret, but also incitement, a pressing forward, a call to perfection. Its significance is not merely negative but definitely positive. Hausherr rightly observes that the term implies a piercing, a shock, coming from the outside.[16] But this again should not be taken too literally. It would be more correct to say that the actual piercing derives from grace. However, it may either arrive from without, whether directly from God or indirectly through some other person whom we meet or perhaps through a word we hear,[17] or else from within, through the heart, in which case it again originates in God.[18]

The gift of compunction presupposes a 'visitation' from God – 'for the Lord has come uninvited,' says John.[19] It can come about in various ways, precisely because it is the *effect* of God's action, not the divine action itself. According to Mark the Monk, compunction comprises 'a smooth and beneficial breaking of the heart.'[20] True repentance ensues, as will be seen below, only when the grace of God has been accorded. Tears, too, are another effect of compunction: the gift of compunction brings about the gift tears. Hence the title of this chapter: weeping is in fact a 'double gift.'

Moreover, John speaks of a gift that consoles (*parakaloumenous*).[21] The pain (Ps. 30.11) caused by the 'needle' of God's grace[22] results in detachment from the passions, in the removal of the desires of the flesh, and this only causes further pain. Nevertheless, the wound is inflicted by grace and is also, subsequently, soothed by grace. The injury is healed, and both actions proceed

---

[14] *Phil. Hist.*, Publios 5, 7, p. 338 (1356BC). Chrysostom, *De compunctione* 1 (PG47.394), says that sleeplessness is a result of this sting. Cf. also *Hist. Monachorum* 1, John of Lycopolis 37 (p. 23).

[15] 7.2 (801D); although in this passage Climacus uses the more general term *penthos*, which includes compunction, the implicit reference is to the latter. Cassian, too, speaks of a *spina* but the reference there is to the remembrance of one's sins: Cf. *Conf.* 9, 29 (64–5).

[16] *Penthos*, 16.

[17] There are many examples of compunction as a result of hearing something: cf. *Apophth.* Antony 13 (PG65.77D–80A) and 29 (85AB) and Euprepios 7 (172D); Theodoret, *Phil. Hist.*, Palladius, 7, 1 p. 366 (1365A); *Hist. Monachorum* 23, Macarius of Alexandria 4 (131) and 19, Apollonius the Martyr 3 (116); Cyril of Scythopolis, *Life of Sabas* 13 (p. 96, 18); and *Life of Kyriakos* (224, 1). Cassian refers to the various causes of compunction in *Conf.* 9, 26 (62–3). Compunction may also result from seeing someone: cf. Cyril, *Life of Euthymios* 35 (p. 53, 13–14).

[18] Cf. *Apophth.* Hyperechios 8 (PG65.423A).

[19] 7.27 (805D). The notion of compunction as a gift is explicit in Niketas Stethatos, who clearly was influenced by Climacus in this respect, too: cf. *Cent.* 1.24 (278) and 2.46 (309).

[20] *De lege spir.* 15 (PG65.908). Chrysostom says compunction is 'the mother of tears.' Cf. *De compunctione* 1, 7 (PG47.404).

[21] 26.16 (1017D) and 7.33 (808B). *Apophth.* Poemen 39 (PG65.323BC) refers to protection rather than consolation. Cf. also 7.24 (805C).

[22] 7.2 (801D).

from divine grace.[23] The gift, bestowed in the appropriate way by God,[24] issues in the painful realization of one's emptiness, in a movement away from self-sufficiency, in a withdrawal from oneself as being something no less heavy to bear than the cross itself. Yet the emptiness is the prerequisite for the fullness of grace.[25] Any form of pride or self-praise immediately disperses compunction. Climacus says pride 'destroys' compunction.[26] Compunction is properly sustained through the remembrance of death,[27] but there can be no real consolation for the pain outside grace itself, which comes to one 'as cool water,'[28] like a splash of cold water on the face. God's grace in compunction renders the monk 'drunk with a longing for God' (*methystheis katanyxei*). It is a mark of openness, away from masks of 'falsehood.'[29] Tears may not be essential, as some might suggest,[30] but the effort to repent is indispensable.

Apart from remembrance of death as conducive to compunction, the latter is also promoted by fasting, which prepares us for the action of God's grace.[31] The action may never come as compunction, or else we may never know the day or the hour of its coming. Yet, by way of *memento mori*, we must always be ready for it (Mt. 25.13).[32] Moreover, compunction is the prerequisite for any further gift that comes from God, and it assimilates such gifts. The very fact that John describes this needle or 'spur' of compunction as 'golden' shows that it, like all gifts, must come from above, that its value is of divine origin.

Various kinds of compunction are envisaged. Being a precious divine gift, the demons try to steal it from us and deprive us of it by deception. The assault is countered by yet another gift, that of spiritual discernment (*diakrisis*).[33] The 'spur' of compunction can be 'spurious' as well as 'praiseworthy.'[34] Some people may be more easily given to it on account of their peculiar character, for example their greater liability to emotional feeling. Yet, for John, when acquired 'by nature' and 'by inclination,' compunction is not as valuable as the gift that proceeds directly from God. The real criterion is the experience of

---

[23] 7.3 (801D).

[24] 7.61 (813D–16A).

[25] Cf. Basil, *Reg. Brev. Tract.* 16 (PG 31.1092D).

[26] 21.9 (949D); in this passage, Climacus is actually speaking of flattery but this, in turn, causes one's pride to swell. Cf. also 25.10 (992BC) and 7.30 (808D). Loquacity (*polylogia*) can also have the same effect: cf. 11.2 (852B).

[27] 7.30 (808D) and 19.1 (940C).

[28] 7.30 (808D).

[29] 12.8 (856C). Diadochus speaks of spiritual intoxication in *Cent.* 8 (pp. 87–8).

[30] Cf. for example, Greg. Naz., *Or.* 19, 7 (PG 35.1049D–52A).

[31] 14.31 (869B).

[32] Climacus does not in fact quote from Mt. 25.13 but clearly implies it in phrases such as 'the Lord has come uninvited': cf. 7.27 (805D).

[33] 26.2,14 (1061AB).

[34] 7.33 (808B).

pain, the wound that is inflicted. Compunction acquired 'without pain' (*aponos*) is, in John's view, of lesser worth.[35] Anastasius the Sinaite claims that certain people are more liable to tears than others, although he admits that all can receive the gift through humility.[36] Symeon the New Theologian, however, will not accept such a distinction, regarding it as an excuse, even as heresy. For Symeon, anyone can weep who wills.[37]

In contrast to the gift of compunction, painlessness (*analgesia*), which denotes insensitivity to pain, is characteristic of fallen human nature. More about this will be said below. Painlessness is referred to as 'the ignorance of compunction.'[38] Abba Isaiah of Scetis prefers the image of hardness of heart.[39]

As described above, compunction appears as a kind of transitory state. It is a gift opening up and leading to other gifts. Abba Poemen notes: 'the Fathers place compunction at the beginning of every action.'[40] It is, from this point of view, a temporary, almost a momentary, condition. Yet John also allows compunction to exist as a continual state (*katanyxis dienekes*), as a pure, enduring gift of God, not depending on us.[41] There are thus three levels on which compunction operates: as natural inclination; as gift of grace, albeit temporary; and as permanent state, which is the highest gift of grace.

Repentance (metanoia)

The only detectable general definition of repentance offered by John is his statement, somewhat obliquely made, that 'repentance is the cheerful deprivation of every bodily comfort.'[42] He also observes that:

> *Penthos* is the conditioned sorrow of a repentant soul, adding sorrow to sorrow each day, like a woman suffering in childbirth.[43]

Within the comprehensive state of *penthos*, repentance seems to hold an important intermediate position between the initial compunction and the gift of tears. This has already been indicated, and more will be said about it later on. However, repentance is not a mere stage through which the ascetic passes

---

[35] 26.22 (1020CD) and 7.25 (805C).

[36] *Quaestiones* 105 (PG 89.757C–60A).

[37] *Cat.* 4 (p. 318) and 29 (p. 180).

[38] 17.2 (932B). Cf. also 27.ii,8 (1108D).

[39] Cf. *Logos* 14, 3 (80).

[40] *Apophth.* Poemen 69 (PG 65.337CD). Cf. similar comments in *Mac. Hom.* 11, 14 (p. 105) and Symeon the New Theologian, *Cat.* 4 (p. 346).

[41] 26.42 (1028B). Other writers speak of this permanent state: cf. Basil, *Reg. Brev. Tract.* 16 (PG 31.1092D); Cassian, *Inst.* 5, 14, 1 (p. 212); Cyril of Scythopolis, *Life of Sabas,* 13 (p. 96, 27–97, 2); Symeon, *Theol.* 1 (p. 118), where Symeon uses the same words as Climacus: *katanyxis dienekes.*

[42] 7.5 (801D–04A).

[43] 7.60 (813D).

and then leaves behind. Rather it is an attitude that colors one's whole life and for which, at the same time, one must struggle continually. With reference to tears of repentance, John says:

> And with time and patience, the things of which we have spoken are gradually acquired and perfected in us.[44]

Repentance is a way of life. It is not some incident in life, a separate act or stopping-place. It is a continuous pathway, at least in this life, a perennial striving, an all-embracing motion. It is not something done on a particular occasion. God will not ask for miracles and exceptional gifts from us on the last day. God will simply inquire 'whether we have mourned unceasingly.'[45] Such, then, is repentance: never-ending *penthos*. Nevertheless, repentance is at the same time a transforming divine gift, not just a fruit of our own effort or anguish.

There is a close link between repentance and tears. The latter are regarded as the test of genuine repentance. Always keen, however, to encourage every person, John also admits alternative ways for those who are not granted tears.[46] We shall return to these alternatives below. Nevertheless, grief itself is paramount; and it is immeasurable, in proportion to the depth of repentance.[47] Out of grief for their sinfulness – a grief literally able to move rocks! – the ascetics in the Alexandrian Prison cried out to God. The Prison is of parabolic significance here. But it is not a piece of fiction. John is surely describing an actual place of monastic penitential internment in Alexandria, a place of wailing and lamentation. It is a place that John had visited personally, witnessed with his own eyes, and knew at first hand. John realized that the practices in that Prison may have been too fearsome even for the monks at Raithou, the intended recipients of the *Ladder*. Yet he did not expect to repel his readers when giving an account of it.[48] His purpose was for the Prison in Alexandria to be seen as an image of *penthos*, a living icon of repentance, showing that, in a sense, sin is a self-inflicted enslavement – an impasse from which tears are the only way out. The picture is of a savagely prophetic symbol, whose excess is a terrifying reminder of the deathly nature of our afflicted state:

> [Some of them] groaned in their heart, but stifled all sound of their lamentations. Then, sometimes they could control themselves no longer, and would suddenly cry out ... roaring and moaning like lions from their innermost heart to their teeth. ... Their faces were pale and wasted. They

---

[44] 7.22 (805B). Climacus does not explicitly mention repentance in this passage but the context implies it.

[45] 7.73 (816D). Cf. also 5.15 (780A), where tears and repentance are almost identified.

[46] 7.25 (805C) and 48 (809D).

[47] 5.5 (764Df.).

[48] Cf. his own words in 5.7 (777A).

were quite indistinguishable from corpses. Their breasts were livid from blows; and from their frequent beating of the chest, they spat blood. ... When I had seen and heard all this, I nearly despaired of myself, seeing my own indifference and comparing it with their suffering. For what a place of habitation theirs was! All was dark, reeking, filthy and squalid. It was rightly called a Prison and house of convicts. The very sight of the place was sufficient to teach all repentance and *penthos*.[49]

One cannot escape mourning, either in this life or the next. Abba Poemen remarked about another desert elder:

Truly you are blessed, Abba Arsenius, for you wept for yourself in this world! Whoever does not weep for oneself here will weep eternally hereafter; so it is impossible not to weep, either voluntarily or when compelled through suffering.[50]

Gregory the Theologian believed that everyone must weep: he actually identified tears with repentance, even though its ways were many and various, while each person brings before God one's own particular 'virtue.' Still: 'all must shed tears, all must be purified, all must ascend ... .'[51] Several centuries later, Symeon the New Theologian is no less definite:

Remove tears and with them you remove purification; and without purification no one is saved.[52]

The author of the *Ladder* gives no explicit answer to the question as to whether tears are necessary, an essential gift of God to the human person, as later writers such as Symeon the New Theologian would maintain. John tends rather to follow the desert tradition, articulated by Evagrius, who claims: 'only tears truly testify to the fear of God in us.'[53] What John does say clearly is that since *penthos* is a way of knowing oneself[54] and of repenting, one weeps because one has lost one's paradisial identity, or else is homesick for that lost paradise. There is, for John, an intense element of nostalgia in the phenomenon of tears. 'Oh, how they would recall their former attainments!' he exclaims about the monks he observed in the Prison. And he quotes their recollection of the Psalmist's words: 'We remembered the days of old' (Ps. 142.5); and, 'where

---

[49] 5.5 (765B–73B). Similar extremes are found in other ascetic writings: cf. Pachomius, *Vita Prima Graeca* 109 (p. 71, p. 218); *Apophth.* Arsenius 42 (PG65.105D–08B); *Apophth.* Nau 135 (1908, pp. 47–8); Mark the Monk, *Ad Nic.* 11 (PG65.1045D); Cyril of Scythopolis, *Life of Sabas* 62 (pp. 163, 17–18) and *Hist. Monachorum* 1, John of Lycopolis 37 (23).

[50] *Apophth.* Arsenius 41 (PG65.105CD).

[51] *Or.* 19, 7 (PG35.149D–1052A).

[52] *Cat.* 29 (186).

[53] *Letter to Anatolios*, ed. Hausherr, *Traité d'Oraison*, 73. John's opinion in this regard is considered below.

[54] Cf. Ephraim the Syrian (?), *Sermo Asceticus*, vol. 1 (ed. Rome, 1732–46) 254.

are your ancient mercies, Lord, such as you have revealed to our soul in your truth?' (Ps. 88.50–51).[55]

Tears are indeed a mode in which the body contributes to and shares in repentance, just as it shares in the whole ascent of spiritual life, and just as it has shared in our descent and fall. The monks in Syria were called 'mournful ones' (*abila* or *penthikoi*) because they were 'those who wanted to be saved.'[56] For John, a day passed without tears was a day wasted, a day without repentance. Peter the Apostle becomes the 'type' (*typos*) of repentance (Mt. 26.75; Mk 14.72; Lk. 22.62). In contrast to other authors who tend to blur the distinction between tears or *penthos* and repentance, John firmly holds to it:

> Painstaking repentance, *penthos*, cleansed of all impurity, and holy humility in beginners, are as distinct from each other as yeast and flour from bread.[57]

This is not how Symeon the New Theologian addresses his monks in the tenth century:

> For neither is it possible to attain mourning without repentance, nor again tears without mourning, but all these three are interdependent, and one cannot be manifested without the other.[58]

As seen, repentance is not a self-generating act or condition. It is a passing over – or a *pascha* – from death to life and a continual renewal of that life. It consists of a reversal of what has become the normal pattern of development: the movement from life to death. And so it may even be described as 'hell,' although it is more fundamentally perceived as life, as 'resurrection' and renewal of baptismal regeneration.[59] God's initiative requires the ascetic's positive acceptance, but such apparent passivity is in reality highly active. It is a way of perpetually receiving God within, of God being embodied in the ascetic, of divine incarnation through asceticism. To experience repentance is to have tasted God's glory and beauty. It is the mark of our presence before God and of God's presence before us, where we respond to God and in doing so gain salvation and life abundant. It is what St Paul described as 'sorrow working repentance to salvation not to be repented of' (2 Cor. 7.10). For John of the *Ladder*:

---

[55] 5.5 (773CD).

[56] Cf. Hausherr, *Penthos*, 33 and A. Vööbus, *History of Asceticism in the Syrian Orient*, Louvain: 1860, vol. 2, 282. Theodoret of Cyrus says that the monks he met spend their entire life weeping: *Phil. Hist.*, Prol. 7, 136 (1289C). The *Vita Prima* says of Pachomius that he was 'always mournful': cf. 91 (p. 61, 206).

[57] 25.7 (989D). Cf. 5.1 (728D).

[58] *Cat.* 4 (354).

[59] 5.5 (769B), 30 (781A) and 2 (764B).

> Repentance is the daughter of hope and the refusal to despair. ...
> Repentance is reconciliation with the Lord ... and ... a contract with
> God for a second life.[60]

Mourning (penthos)

Etymologically, the word *penthos* shares the same root as the word *pathos*.[61]
Both terms stem from the verb meaning 'to suffer.' Now, suffering may assume
many forms: there is even a righteous suffering, of subsuming suffering in God,
just as one subsumes passion and mourning in God. Similarly, the wounds of
suffering caused by compunction[62] are various, and one of them issues in tears.
Joyful sorrow is the transfiguration of suffering and pain by grace.

Penthos consists in mourning for the loss of God's presence. It is the sadness
and agony of God's absence and an unquenched thirst for God's presence. One
grieves for one's estrangement from God, and one's eyes become 'a source of
tears.'[63] Gregory of Nyssa says that tears are caused by the deprivation of
something desirable. And, for John Chrysostom, tears are a sign of loss; they
are an indication that we have lost our salvation. Theodoret of Cyrus is more
precise about the actual loss, stating that 'it is the passion (*pathos*) for God
which gives rise to these tears.'[64] John sums up:

> *Penthos* according to God is sadness of soul and the disposition of a
> sorrowing heart, which ever madly seeks that for which it thirsts; and when
> it fails in its quest, it painfully pursues it, and follows in its wake grievously
> lamenting.[65]

Climacus rejects all rhetoric and extravagance when speaking of mourning.
He is quite lucid and sober. He rebukes anyone who 'lectures on *penthos* with a
smile on the face.'[66] Mourning is a way of life, and it presupposes a certain
'continual violence' against the fallen nature.[67] *Penthos* leads to self-knowledge,[68] and tears are the only language through which we are able to express

---

[60] 5.2 (764B).

[61] Cf. E. Boisacq, *Dictionnaire étymologique de la langue greque*, 4th edn, Heidelberg: 1950, 766.
The link between *penthos* and *pathos* exists in early Greek usage, as in Pindar, Herodotus and the
tragedians Sophocles, Euripides and Aeschylus.

[62] 7.2 (801D).

[63] 27.ii,36 (1113C). Cf. 26.iii,53 (1089D–92A), 4 (1084D) and 27.ii,39 (113D).

[64] Cf. Greg. Nyss, *De beat. Or.* 3 (PG44.1224A); Chrysostom, *De compunctione* 1, 10
(PG47.409) and Theodoret, *Phil. Hist.*, 30, Domnina 2 (1493AB).

[65] 7.1 (801CD). Cf. also 1.16 (636B) and 16.11 (928B). Modern psychology defines mourning as
a reaction to the loss of a desired person: cf. S. Freud, standard edition of the *Complete
Psychological Works*, vol. 14, New York: 1961, 243.

[66] 17.3 (932BD).

[67] 1.10 (633C) and 16 (636B). Cf. also 20.4 (945B) and 22.22 (969A).

[68] 15.73 (897B).

separation from God, and hence loss of communication with others. Through tears, we learn our true nature and our dispossession. Tears expose our genuine condition.[69] One does not cry when lying, even if John knows that some succeed in shedding false tears. In depicting this loss, certain contemporary ascetic writers have adopted such biblical and liturgical images as Adam sitting opposite paradise in mourning over his bereavement. The *Macarian Homilies* say that one must 'weep one's way back.'[70]

As a concomitant and consummation of repentance, tears are, at the same time, a 'pledge' of our supra-rational condition, the first fruits of infinite joy. As will be shown later, the desire for the *status ante peccatum* and for a return from exile is also an anticipation of the future glory, a beginning of what John calls the 'blessed change and transformation' into the pristine state. John says of Hesychius the Chorebite:

> He was always as if out of his mind, and silently shed warm tears. ... We reverently buried him in the cemetery near the fortress, and after some days we looked for his holy relics, but did not find them.[71]

Pressing on in the same vein, Climacus speaks of tears as the key to a new, yet old country, an inward pilgrimage, an exodus, which is essentially a re-entry. Similarly, for Isaac the Syrian, tears mark a crucial point of transition, the frontier between the present and the future ages, a realm where one anticipates the other. Later, in the tenth century, Symeon the New Theologian assumes the image of the newborn child that weeps on first entering the world, implying that the Christian ascetic weeps at the moment of rebirth into the age to come.[72]

This 'dialectic' of beginning and end, of new and old, is characteristic of John's discourse on *penthos*, as indeed it is of Eastern ascetic thinking generally. Every part of daily life asumes an eschatological dimension, even while paradoxically being a return to the original state of human nature. Everything tends towards and expects the *eschaton* (or, the 'end'), even while being a matter of the here and now – a reversal of the Fall. Tears are produced inasmuch as the monk recognizes individual limitations and humbly awaits God's infinite restoration. To wait is to weep. To wait is to be humble, and therefore to transcend the fallen status.[73] This condition cannot be measured, but the greater the fall, the deeper the mourning and the more certain the

---

[69] 12.3 (856A). Cf. 12.7 (856C).

[70] *Mac. Hom.*15, 17 (137). Cf. also Chrysostom, *De compunctione* 1, 10 (PG47.409). For the image of Adam, see *Kontakion* and *Oikos* of Cheesefare Sunday in *Triodion Katanyktikon* (Rome, 1879), 105. Cf. also the prose-poem by Staretz Silouan in Archimandrite Sophrony, *Wisdom from Mt. Athos*, London: 1974, 47–55.

[71] 6.20 (797A).

[72] Isaac the Syrian, *Mystic Treatises*, 85; Symeon the New Theologian, *Cat.* 29 (184) and 8 (92).

[73] 4.125 (725D) and 5.19 (780B). Cf. also 6.22 (797B) and 1 (793B).

resurrection. John seems to reserve the greatest love, almost to show preference, for the greater sinners. Their thirst for God, he believes, increases in proportion to the experience of their debasement and abasement:

> I saw ... and I was amazed; and I consider those fallen mourners more blessed than those who have not fallen and are not mourning over themselves.[74]

What of the effect of tears on the ascetic's relation to the surrounding culture and environment? Fallen nature is common to all. Tears and repentance, like the Fall and sin, are not individualistic phenomena, but personal events with cosmic implications. All share in the pandemic fall of human nature. Therefore, tears too are shed for all and with all. The sorrow of one person entails the sorrow of the world at large. Weeping for the sins of others, just as the experience of being joyful for others, is part of the hesychast's participatory ascetic discipline. One who has reached this point of perfection will not remain enclosed, but will be ever open and vulnerable to all.[75] Basil the Great says:

> The monk must suffer with (*sympaschein*) those who suffer, and weep with them (*syndakryein*), and mourn (*penthein*) very much for them.[76]

For John, to regard the sins of others as one's own is the shape of true love:

> On hearing that another has fallen into spiritual or bodily misfortune, one suffers and weeps for that person as for oneself.[77]

John clearly identifies *penthos* with the charity and love for which, according to the Gospel (Mt. 25.31–46), Christ will ask us to give an account on the last day.[78] So mourning and love are intimately interconnected. The anonymous editor, who added the short verse at the end of Step 10 ('on slander'), summarily conveyed what Climacus had in mind:

> Tenth ascent. The one who has mastered this, is one who also practices love or *penthos*.[79]

John makes the same point when he speaks of the spiritual elder. He likens the spiritual director to Moses, whom God made to smite the rock in order that water might come out of it and quench the people's thirst.[80] The spiritual guide recognizes one's own fallen nature *pro omnibus* in the vision of divine glory.

---

[74] 5.5 (776B). Cf. also 26.11 (1016B).

[75] 4.40 (705A).

[76] *Quomodo monachum omari oporteat* 1 (PG31.649A). This is the reason why the monk wears black: cf. 7.24 (805C).

[77] 9.11 (841D). Cf. also Barsanuphius 619.

[78] 7.73 (816D).

[79] 849A.

[80] *Shep.* 100 (1204D).

Such a person becomes, as it were, the living water, the source through which divine grace irrigates the entire community and the world. The spiritual guide is the one who represents us before God on Mount Sinai and on Mount Tabor, meeting God face to face on our behalf. Together with such an elder, all mourn, impelled by God's love and goodness, not in fear of punishment. In the Egyptian desert, Antony is said no longer to fear God; for, he now loves God. Yet Antony goes on weeping nonetheless.[81] It is the awareness of God's love and beauty that makes us realize the abyss that separates us from God's gratuitous grace. And it is our total limitation and insufficiency that we place before God in repentance, not just our individual wrongdoings, our sinfulness and not just our transgressions. This complete involvement in the human condition induces the spiritual father to bear the burdens (Gal. 6.2) of every disciple, and induces the ascetic to carry the cross of the world. *Penthos* is the way of life and resurrection for all and in all, as distinct from the way of spiritual self-gratification. The way of tears is a way of love. And the way of love is a way of tears. John's theology of tears is epitomized in Psalm 41 (vv.1–3), which links the soul's longing with tears, as well as in Luke 7 (vv. 44–6), which links the sinful woman's love with tears.

The Way of Tears

The Stages of Tears

In one sense, 'the stages of *penthos*' might be a more accurate description of mourning, as a corollary to repentance, than 'the way of tears.' However, the latter accords more with Climacus' unschematic style of thinking, as reflected in the *Ladder*, and is also more indicative of the concrete anthropological concern peculiar to him. This did not prevent Mme Lot-Borodine, in her general account of the subject of tears, from establishing a fairly rigid system of ascent in the present context – from 'purification' to 'illumination,' and so to 'perfection' or 'union.' Admittedly, John has his own structural logic, but it is not always clear-cut. It does greater justice to this logic to speak of *penthos* in the more fluid terms of aspects or characteristics of the way of tears. Abba Poemen declares the primacy of tears generally:

> Weeping is the way the Scriptures and our Fathers give us, when they said, 'weep!' Truly, there is no other way than this.[82]

---

[81] *Apophth.* Nau 164–5 (1908, pp. 53–4). Cf. also *Apophth.* Poemen 122 (PG65.353B) and Antony 32 (85C).

[82] *Apophth.* Poemen 119 (PG65.353B).

John, too, speaks of various types of tears, which suggest a ongoing way, a continuous process in spiritual life.[83]

There is also the implication of a threefold order of *penthos* (purification – illumination – perfection), which is propounded by Lot-Borodine but for which there is only limited evidence in the *Ladder*. In Step 5, for instance, John contends that *kathartic penthos* results from sins, which 'haunt' one. This may be said to mark a first stage. The second stage is marked by a form of illumination, suggested by an understanding of one's unworthiness of God's grace and one's liability to dishonor (what Climacus calls 'the perfect bearing of indignity'). The third stage – of 'perfection' – cannot be described in words. John warns:

> Let us not be in a hurry to find words to describe this third kind ... for our effort will be in vain.[84]

It can only be experienced. This stage is referred to as *ploutotapeinosis* (or 'wealth of humility'), a term coined by John to express not so much abjectness as God's positive gift of tears. Yet the threefold distinction is neither fundamental nor predominant in John.

The *Ladder* provides greater evidence for a twofold order of *penthos*, indicated by two kinds of tears: tears of fear and of love, the one leading to the other:

> Groanings and sorrows cry to the Lord. Tears shed from fear intercede for us; but tears of all-holy love show us that our prayer has been accepted.[85]

Tears of love have a certain excellence and must be guarded 'like the pupil of the eye.'[86] Yet John is not inflexible even in regard to this simple, evangelical (Jn 4.18 and 1 Cor. 13.13) 'scheme.' Tears of love are a supreme gift, but elsewhere John also admits: 'And it is surprising how much safer the humbler way is, in its season.'[87] As for tears of fear, these express the conscious preparation for an acceptance of God's grace (Ps. 122.2), although in the end the Lord's visitation is a gratuitous gift, which we have not merited by our works. God only seeks our openness to divine love, while the degrees (*to metron*) of *penthos*[88] are as numerous as the degrees of our sinfulness and the degrees of our susceptibility to God's grace. There is also some evidence that, for Climacus, tears are not only a gift of God's loving grace, but also a way of

---

[83] 8.29 (833BC).

[84] Cf. 5.9 (777BC). See also Evagrius, *Prakt.* 27 and 57 (562 and 634); Diadochus, *Cent.* 86–7 (145–7), which refer to tears as a sign of repentance or purification.

[85] 7.9 (804B).

[86] 28.51 (1137B).

[87] 7.76 (816B).

[88] 20.7 (845D).

attracting it, of dragging it down by force; 'tears are able to force God,'[89] he says, or to compel God to love us.

There is, therefore, an initial distinction between tears for beginners (*ta protera*) and those pertaining to the perfect (*ta anothen*),[90] between tears that are bodily (*somatika*) and noetic or spiritual (*noera*) tears, depending on whether they spring 'from the eyes of the body' or 'from the noetic eyes.'[91] There are various kinds of tears, and if their source is in God, they are all precious. However, Climacus also warns:

> Do not trust your fountains of tears before your soul has been perfectly purified.[92]

Furthermore, John speaks of 'external' tears, which seem to be marked by penitence or compunction, and of 'psychic' tears, which nourish the soul. The former are usually dependent on us, while the latter are a gift from God and may be offered on any occasion, since 'every place is convenient for *penthos*.'[93] Thus John distinguishes between tears of fear and tears of love, between tears that depend mainly on us and tears depending solely on God's grace, between external tears and internal ones, and above all, as will be seen below, between tears of sorrow and tears of joy.

Nevertheless, another threefold 'scheme' may be detected in the *Ladder*. There exist tears that are natural (*kata physin*, or sensual), tears that are unnatural or against nature (*para physin*, or sinful), and tears that are above nature or supernatural (*hyper physin*, or spiritual). Genuine tears come from true, sincere mourning, which is called '*penthos* with feeling of heart'[94] – the knowing mirror of the heart of the human person, longing for reunion with God. Tears caused by such mourning may, as we have seen, be either 'internal' or 'external';[95] and the ascetic requires the gift of discernment in order to distinguish whether these are good or evil, spiritual or temporal. There are, after all, many reasons why one weeps. One weeps for one's sins, for one's salvation, for God's love; but one also weeps for flattery, for worldly objects, or from jealousy. John says: 'Let the brethren readily test their intentions in the Lord.'[96]

Ordinary, natural, or bodily tears are not in themselves at fault, but they are fraught with danger. In the ascetic tradition, emotions are deceptive and

---

[89] 5.5 (765A). In 27.iii,6 (1108B), Climacus says that *hesychia* compels God to grant gifts.

[90] *Shep.* 100 (1204D).

[91] 26.ii,27 (1065A).

[92] 7.37 (808C).

[93] 7.14 (804D).

[94] 7.13 (808B). Nowhere does John explicitly employ these terms to distinguish the three types or categories of tears, but they clearly underlie his theology.

[95] 7.14 and 15 (804D).

[96] 26.36 (1025A).

sentiments cannot be trusted, oscillating as they often do between dejection or pessimism and excessive optimism.[97] Their destructiveness,[98] however, is countered not through suppression but through transformation, in which the supernatural is revealed in the natural. The simplicity of the threefold scheme based on 'nature' (*kata physin, para physin, hyper physin*) does not remove the difficulty of differentiating between natural and charismatic tears, which is tantamount to a distinction between nature and grace. John speaks of discernment, not of contraposition. For nature presupposes grace; and grace builds upon nature. *Penthos* may or may not always be a gift, but there is no sharp difference between the given and the innate. John is far removed from the kind of conflict that arose between Pelagius and Augustine, with its far-reaching ascetic and spiritual implications. John's premises, and the terms that he adopts, lie in a different framework of reference. In this, he is at one with the dominant Greek patristic tradition. Accordingly, for John, there can be no sharp contrast between the higher and the lower levels of tears, between sweet and bitter tears, between the joy of illumination and the pain or sorrow attending the way to purification, between the stages leading to the exile and to the return of the Prodigal Son (Lk. 15). If spiritual tears signify the exaltation of sensible experience, then natural tears are 'like blood from the wounds of our soul,' by analogy with Christ's sweat of blood (Lk. 22.44) and therefore lead to spiritual tears.[99] Yet such tears, according to John, are not discarnate, merely inward or imaginary; they are real and sentient:

> It was said of Abba Arsenius that he had a hollow in his chest channeled out by the tears, which fell from his eyes all his life while he sat at his manual work.[100]

Well before John, Evagrius claimed that tears ought to have the characteristic of courage and promise.[101] Defeatist sorrow is overcome through humility and poverty.[102] We would not weep over worldly objects if we possessed none; we would not weep over injustice from others if we

---

[97] Cf. 16.11–12 (928BC) and 18 (928D); 23.7 (977AB) and 26.ii,56 (1072D). Cf. also Mark the Monk, *De his.* 205 (PG65.961).

[98] 3.23 (668AB).

[99] 7.25 (805C). Cf. also Anastasius the Sinaite, *Quaestiones* 8 and 98 (PG89.392AB and 752B), who likens tears to the blood of martyrs.

[100] *Apophth.* 41 (PG65.105CD). For similar examples in the *Ladder*, cf. 5.5 (772A). The Latin collection of *Sayings* explains: 'Whenever Arsenius was doing manual work, he kept a cloth at his chest because of the tears that streamed from his eyes.' See PL73.851–1024.

[101] *Prakt.* 27 (562). Cf. also Ps. Athanasius, *Life of Saint Synkletike* 40 (PG28.151AB); the same words are also found in *Apophth.* Syncletica 27 (Guy, 35). Diadochus' phrase 'God-pleasing sorrow' is identical to Climacus' in 7.27 (805D–08A); cf. *Cent.* 60 (120).

[102] 26.iii,4 (1084D). Chrysostom says that one weeps for one's sins and not for material goods: cf. *Ad Theodorum lapsum* 1, 1 (PG47.277). Gregory Palamas also confirms the importance of poverty in this regard: cf. *Antirrheticus* 7, 11, 34 (3, p. 486).

humbled ourselves before everybody. By the same token, mundane sorrow will bar the way to God by being 'excessive, often making the soul smoky and dark, and drying the stream of tears.'[103]

Finally, it is helpful to consider the role of demons in the way of tears. As noted already, tears essentially comprise a gift. They are a gift that demons seek to snatch from us. Their role is extortionate – the role of thieves.[104] We cannot in fact be deprived of true *penthos* or diverted from its path by the deception of demons.[105] Yet the demons will work through these. They can work tears and produce the kind of spurious sadness, or happiness, for that matter, which moved Climacus to alert his readers:

> Let us watch and see in which season and how they come about. ... For, during temptation, I felt that this wolf was producing incomprehensible joy, tears and consolation in my soul, but I was really being deceived, when I so childishly thought to have fruit from this and not harm.[106]

By nature, we are destined to advance and ascend in spiritual life. Nevertheless, demons divert this course by simulating advance in the form of a fitful movement, a wobbling from side to side, like crabs. One can test the quality of tears by ascertaining whether they are fleeting or fluttering, or perhaps resulting from mere 'sensual softness.' Inconsistency is a danger signal; lastingness is auspicious. One is being tempted by demons when one is caused 'at times to laugh, and at other times to weep for all.'[107] Demons take advantage of tears; only humility, rather than particular ascetic feats, can resist their misappropriation.[108]

Demon use various, even positive, means of simulation, such as presenting God as an image of lenient mercy with the aim of obstructing the way of tears: 'The aim of this dog is to thrust from you your *penthos* and fearless fear.'[109] Having acquired the gift of discernment, however, the monk can transform the gift of tears into a weapon against the very demons who by their manifold wiles try to snatch it away. One who has succeeded in this, John assures us, 'will see the Egyptians sunk in the water of tears.'[110]

---

[103] 26.iii, 9 (1085B).

[104] Cf. for example Abba Isaiah, *Logos* 29, 4 (202).

[105] 27.19 (1100A).

[106] 15.39 (888D). Compare this with the above passage from the *Life of Saint Synkletike*. Cf. also 26.ii,66 (1029A) and 27.19 (1100A) for other examples of passionate or demonic tears.

[107] 26.iii, 11 (1088C).

[108] 8.24 (832D).

[109] 6.11 (796A).

[110] 26.25 (1012A).

Tears and Prayer

Tears are closely linked to prayer; and 'praying alone'[111] is said by John, in one instance at least, even to sustain the experience of spiritual grief. The search for God in prayer should be through mourning.[112] Evagrius says:

> Pray with tears and your request will find hearing. Nothing so pleases the Lord as supplication offered in the midst of tears.[113]

Prayer is said to be at once the cause and the consequence of tears, 'the mother and again the daughter of tears.'[114] Prayer 'contains'[115] our tears – an act whereby we perceive the spiritual condition more clearly and then continue to weep all the more readily.[116] Tears are indeed the highest and fullest form of prayer. In the words of Isaac the Syrian, 'the gift of tears is the accomplishment of prayer.'[117] Prayer should be founded on tears and bathed in them, in the literal sense. 'True prayer,' according to Antony of Egypt, 'is that in which one forgets that one is praying;'[118] and tears are precisely what enable one to forget oneself as praying and simply to long for God, ever present in the tears themselves.

Ascetics weep by being what they are, regardless of their state of perfection. They pray alike *for* tears and *with* tears, which is really another way of saying that prayer begins in *penthos*.[119] The beatitude proclaimed during the Sermon on the Mount: 'Blessed are they that mourn, for they shall be comforted' (Mt. 5.4) comprises both a promise and a behest. Chrysostom says that one should pray for tears, even if one remains deprived of them: one should weep, without despairing of not being able to weep.[120] If tears bespeak a promise, yet they are also proof of hope fulfilled, of sins forgiven.

---

[111] 7.70 (816C). Cf. also 27.ii,6 (1180B); 11.7 (852D) and 5 (852C) where Climacus refers to Peter who, as a result of speaking too much, 'wept bitterly' (Mt. 26.75), intimating that *hesychia* is helpful for tears.

[112] 28.56 (1140A).

[113] *De or.* 6 (PG79.1169A). On praying with tears, cf. also Ps. Athanasius, *De virg.* 16–17 (PG28.272AC); Abba Isaiah, *Logos* 1, 1 (1); 9, 2 (66) and 16, 2 (87); and Isaac the Syrian, *Mystic Treatises* (170).

[114] 28.1 (1192A). For Mark the Monk, prayer causes tears: cf. *Disp. cum quodam causidico* 8 (PG65.1081D).

[115] 11.3 (852B).

[116] 28.10 (1132B). Cf. also 28.50 (1137B).

[117] *Mystic Treatises* (299. Cf. also 302). Cf. Cassian, *Conf.* 9,4 (43).

[118] In Cassian, *Conf.* 9, 31 (66). Cf. also Evagrius, *De or.* 120 (PG79.1193B).

[119] Cf. Evagrius, *De or.* 5–6 (PG79.1168D–69A). Praying for tears is mentioned in Symeon the New Theologian, *Cat.* 4 (360). For monks weeping by being what they are, cf. 7.24 (805C).

[120] *Ad Theodorum lapsum* 1, 19 (PG47.308).

It is said that one ought to pray continually (1 Thess. 5.17), 'just as we carry our own shadow everywhere with us.'[121] In the same way, tears ought to accompany us at all times and flow unceasingly.[122] There is here another side of the intimate link between prayer and *penthos*.[123] Even continual, life-long tears, 'all the night making my bed to swim,' as the Psalmist says (Ps. 6.6), will after all not suffice to wash away our sins:

> He would not have time enough to mourn for himself, even though he were to live an hundred years, and even though he were to see a whole river Jordan of tears streaming from his eyes.[124]

In a similar fashion, Barsanuphius claims that 'there is not enough time for you to mourn and weep for your sins.'[125] *Penthos* is not a series of mournful acts or moments of grief during prayer, but an attitude affecting the whole of life.[126]

There is a persistent interconnection between *penthos* or 'eternal tears' (*aennaon dakryon*), as John describes this phenomenon – or, in Barsanuphius' words, 'inseparable and unceasing tears' (*achoriston kai adialeipton*) – and prayer, however 'paradoxical the achievement may be.'[127] The exhortation from the Desert Fathers to weep unceasingly[128] must be considered in the same light as Paul's command to 'pray unceasingly' (1 Thess. 5.17).

Whether, therefore, one adopts a threefold or else a twofold 'scheme,' tears mark both an initial stage of spiritual ascent and a pervasive attribute of the ascent as a whole. As tears of sorrow, they have an overall cleansing effect, effecting *katharsis*, a washing away of sins (Pss. 50.8; 61; 65.2; 117.1; Mt. 26.75 and 1 Cor. 5.2), and a purification of the human person.

---

[121] *Apophth.* Nau 140 (1098, p. 49).

[122] 28.36 (1136B).

[123] 21.32 (956C). Cf. Evagrius, *De or.* 6 (PG79.1169A) and *Protreptikos* (ed. Frankenberg, 554).

[124] 10.11 (848BC).

[125] Barsanuphius 37.

[126] Cf. 5.5 (764Df.) and 7.37 (816D). See also John Chrysostom, *De compunctione* 1, 1 (PG47.395) and 1, 9 (408).

[127] 4.17 (685C). For Barsanuphius, cf. 461. The notion of continual weeping is common to the Fathers: cf. Chrysostom, *In epist. ad Phil. Hom.*, 3, 4 (PG62.204); Greg. Naz. *Carminum liber, Carmen* 51, verse 12 (PG37.1395): 'Weep, weep, O sinner; it is your only advantage to do so;' Greg. Nyssa, *De vita S. Patris Ephraem Syri* (PG46.829CD), where Gregory describes the continual tears of Ephraim the Syrian. Fr Lev Gillet, 'Gift of Tears,' 8, quotes Evagrius, who says: 'Weep and lament at every hour;' *Apophth.* Euprepios 6 (PG65.172D), Poemen 72 (340BC), Arsenius 41 (105CD); Mark the Monk, *Cap. de temp.* 28 (PG65.1069C), where Mark implies that unceasing tears are the duty of every Christian; Barsanuphius 570: Abba John never communed without tears – this phenomenon can be found later, in Symeon the New Theologian, *Cat.* 4 (314). For continual tears, cf. also Cyril of Scythopolis, *Life of Sabas* 44, pp. 135, 10–11; Isaac the Syrian, *Mystic Treatises* 35, 87, 188, 329, and Symeon the New Theologian, *Cat.* 17 (260) and 31 (228).

[128] Cf. *Epistle* 20, attributed to Abba Antony (Latin translation in PG40.1055–66).

Tears and Baptism

Tears wash away sins external and internal alike, known and unknown, 'seen and perceived,'[129] those committed in body and soul. For, as we have seen, tears are inextricably 'psychosomatic' or 'pneumatosomatic.' This conviction is echoed in Barsanuphius: 'If you want to wash away your filthiness, wash it in tears, for they wash clean every blemish.'[130] According to John, tears wash away all our sins:

> The Fathers have laid down that ... honest tears are a bath (*loutra*).

He plays on the verbs *piptein* (to fall) and *niptein* (to wash). The soul is rendered transparent to God, and God transparent to the soul.[131] This cleansing role of tears may be found in many later writers who were clearly influenced by John. Symeon the New Theologian, writing in the tenth century, says:

> Without water, it is impossible to wash dirty clothing; and without tears, it is still more impossible to wash and cleanse the soul from filth and blemish.[132]

All these statements, in content and form, have an unmistakable baptismal connotation. Indeed, in Step 7, John makes what he himself admits to be a bold assertion:

> Greater than baptism itself is the fountain of tears after baptism, even though it is somewhat daring to say so.[133]

Though John speaks in similar fashion elsewhere, with reference to the 'former love towards humanity and forgiveness of sins,' by comparison with the continual washing away of sins through tears,[134] there is no suggestion of

---

[129] 7.33 (808B).

[130] Barsanuphius 77. Cf. also 257 and 461. On the cleansing power of tears: cf. Ps. Athanasius, *Sermo pro iis qui saeculo renuntiarunt* 10 (PG28.1420A); *Apophth.* Dioscorus 2 (PG65.160D–61A), Poemen 119 (353A) and 122 (353B).

[131] 4.10 (681A) and 26.ii, 49 (1072A). Cf. also Greg Naz., *Or.*, 2 *Apologetica* 7 (PG35.413B–16B).

[132] *Cat.* (348). Cf. also *Cat.* 1, (238); 2, (262); *TGP* 1.77, (62–3); 3.12 and 21 (83, 86). Cf. also Kallistos/Ignatios, *Cent.* 25 (224), where Climacus is quoted and Gregory Palamas, *Tr.* 1, 3, 52. For other references in the *Ladder*, cf. also 26.iii,35 (1088D). Climacus also adopts the image of tears as water quenching the fire of passions: cf. 8.1 (828BC); 7.3 and 7 (801D and 804A). For this image, cf. also Chrysostom, *Hom. in Lazarum* 1,7–8 (PG48.971–74) and *De paenit.* 7, 5 (PG49.334); Cassian, *Inst.* 5, 14, 2 (212) and Kallistos/Ignatios, *Cent.* 81 (276), where Climacus is directly quoted. Other Fathers speak of the fire of tears burning the passions: cf. Symeon the New Theologian, *Cat.* 12 (174) and Niketas Stethatos, *Cent.* 1.23 (278). Another image used in patristic writings is that of tears kindling the divine fire: cf. *Apophth.* Synkletike 1 (PG65.421AB) and Symeon the New Theologian, *Cat.* 4 (350).

[133] 7.8 (804AB). Climacus' source here is Greg. Naz., *Or.* 40, 9 (PG36.369).

[134] 5.5 (7764Df.) and 26.25 (1021AB). Cf. also Greg. Naz., *Or.* 39, 17 (PG36.356).

substituting tears for the sacrament of baptism, let alone of denying repentance and rebirth in baptism in the specific sense. John is perfectly aware of the unique, sacramental status of baptism. This is evident from the passage quoted above. There he states in a deliberately paradoxical form that, on the one hand, tears may be seen to be 'greater' (*meizon*) than baptism, and on the other hand, follow in the wake of baptism; they come 'after' baptism (*meta to baptisma*). The semantic stress is on *meta* rather than on *meizon*. Whatever the importance of tears, they do not replace but simply renew baptism. They do not generate but in fact serve to regenerate baptism. They do not by themselves give us the grace of God but rather bring to our awareness a grace already bestowed in baptism. The power of tears is precisely a rejuvenating one. Tears constitute a kind of continuation of baptism in its cleansing and renewing function, with no implication of any duplication or repetition of baptism proper. Through tears we obtain the grace of God, which is already 'ours' in baptism, by virtue of, as it were, an intimate link between being and becoming. The supremacy and efficacy of the sacrament is never in question by John. Rather, the *Ladder* affirms the need for a conscious receptivity and assumption of divine grace received through baptism. It is this peculiar quality of the baptism of tears, issuing in remission and regeneration,[135] which is of critical importance for John. His commitment to the sacrament itself is never in doubt. The baptism of tears is an illumination, rather than an elimination, of that institutional baptism by water and the Holy Spirit.

Tears as Charisma

It has already been underlined that the way of tears is not something pursued by our own effort. Rather, it comes about spontaneously (*autokinētos*, or rather *eterokinētos*), without any straining. Spiritual tears flow with no contraction of facial muscles; they are a gift from God, not a fruit of human

---

[135] Climacus refers to 'living waters' in 7.42 (809B). Abba Isaac the Syrian comes very close to saying that baptism is lower than tears, but, like Climacus, Isaac attaches the greatest importance to baptism for our life in the Church: cf. *Mystic Treatises* 95, where he sees tears as 'a kind of baptism.' The notion of tears as a baptism is found throughout the patristic tradition: cf. Clem. Alex., *Quis dives salvetur* 42 (ed. *GCS.*, 190); Evagrius, *Protreptikos* (ed. Frankenberg, 555); John Moschus, *Pratum* 176 (PG87.3045BC); Anastasius the Sinaite, *Quaestiones* 98 and 105 (PG89.752B and 757C–60A); Symeon the New Theologian, *TGP.* 1.35 (50) and *Eth.* 10 (266). Symeon even says that tears are more significant than baptism: cf. *TGP.* 1.36 (50) and 3.45 (93). For Gregory Palamas, the notion of tears as a second baptism is explained as *epanaklesis tes theogenesias*: cf. *Triads*, 2, 2, 17. It should be noted that Climacus only once refers to clergy in the *Ladder*, and even this is no more than an allusion and an uncomplimentary one at that: cf. 14.7 (865A). Nevertheless an argument *e silentio* proves nothing, especially since Climacus is addressing his book to monks and thus presupposes a rich liturgical life in the monastery.

effort.[136] John differs in this respect from Evagrius, who says that tears are to be forcibly induced. Even John Cassian, an immediate disciple of Evagrius, believes that tears should not be brought on, although he also states that forced tears are not entirely fruitless.[137] The apparent contradiction between John and Evagrius may be due to the fact that they are speaking of two different kinds of tears. While Evagrius refers to tears of sorrow, John is referring to tears of the Spirit.

Of this gift of tears, Mark the Monk writes: 'Do not be taken in pride when you shed tears in your prayer; for Christ has touched the eyes of your heart.'[138] John says in a similar vein:

> The Lord has come uninvited, and is giving us the sponge of God-loving sorrow and the cool water of devout tears.[139]

The importance of recognizing spiritual tears as a divine gift is illustrated by the thirteenth-century French tale, 'Le chevalier au Barizel,' wherein the knight is supposed to fill up a barrel with water. He travels all over the world in order to do this. Yet the water always somehow passes through the barrel. Seeing that his efforts achieve nothing, the knight weeps; and one teardrop is sufficient to fill the barrel.

As a gift, tears testify to a visitation also from the Holy Spirit. This is preceded by an earlier visitation from that 'Uninvited Guest' who arrives, but later leaves us to mourn – the term *katanyxis* is used here – the divine absence.[140] Christ leaves in order to send the Spirit, which he alone can send for consolation (1 Jn 3.24; Rom. 8.26–27). In this respect, the gift of tears could be seen as another side of the same visitation received in compunction. While no 'gift of God' depends on good works, personal virtues or individual *ascesis*,[141] nevertheless these mark a responsive action on our part. Yet, for Climacus, 'compunction is predominantly a gift of the Lord.'[142] It is primarily

---

[136] 7.27 (805D). Holl, *Enthusiasmus*, 217, says that enthusiasm was a new feature introduced by the hesychasts, but this is a one-sided view since the gift of tears is not merely a result of sentimental enthusiasm, and the Greek Fathers particularly stressed the quality of sobriety (*nepsis*).

[137] *Conf.* 9, 30 (65–6). For Evagrius, cf. *Paraenetikos* (ed. Frankenberg, 560). Isaac the Syrian speaks of tears springing forth 'without compulsion:' cf. *Mystic Treatises* (63, 164, 322, 330). Symeon the New Theologian uses the word 'painlessly:' cf. *TGP* 1.35 (50); *Cat.* 8 (92–4); and 29 (182); and Niketas Stethatos, *Cent.* 1.42 (288–93).

[138] *De lege spir.*12 (PG65.908A).

[139] 7.27 (805D). Cf. also *Shep.* 100 (1204D) and 7.67 (816B). On tears as a gift: cf. Cassian, *Conf.* 9, 28 (63–4); Anastasius the Sinaite, *Quaestiones* 105 (PG89.757C–60A); Symeon the New Theologian, *Cat.* 4 (348) and Gregory Palamas, *Triads*, 3, 2, 2.

[140] 7.27 (805D–08A).

[141] 6.22 (797B). Cf. also Barsanuphius 18.

[142] 7.50 (812A).

'up to God,' and only derivatively up to us. Tears therefore mark a spiritual gift from God to us, but also a mystical offering from us to God.

Since tears are a gift, a *charisma*, we must guard them very closely:

> If you possess the gift of mourning, hold on to it with all your might.[143]

If not guarded 'as the pupil of the eye,'[144] tears may otherwise, as shown, easily be lost to the demons. We must not cease to pray lest the tears, providentially (*oikonomikōs*) given to us, also cease to flow. For we do not know when we shall again receive this grace of water and fire[145] – another allusion to the baptismal meaning of tears. Neither should tears be sought prematurely – as a gift from above, they have their own *kairos*: 'to every thing there is a season, and a time to every purpose under the heaven' (Eccl. 3.1). There is a *kairos* for each divine gift, and the *kairos* is the point at which God acts, while we resist any action but the divine. Waiting for God to act is the surest way of attaining the divine gifts:

> There is a time for tears, and a time for hardness of heart; ... a time for heartfelt sorrow, and a time for spiritual joy.[146]

To await the proper *kairos* requires patience, since the oncoming of tears is gradual: literally, drop by drop.[147]

In perhaps one of the oldest references to tears in Christian ascetic literature, the gift of tears is 'bestowed on a small number who have renounced the world completely.'[148] It is a gift belonging to the spiritually mature or dispassionate, according to Isaac the Syrian.[149] At any rate, as John insists, it is conferred by God on those whom God chooses.[150] As it happens, some may not receive this but be the recipients of certain other gifts, which act as an alternative form of 'inner' weeping.[151] Still others, in their desolation at the absence of tears, find themselves really endowed with them, or with a grace equivalent to them.[152] In the absence of tears, one may at least cast one's mind upon the distance that separates one from God. According to Evagrius, one will then weep all the more fervently.[153]

---

[143] 7.7 (804A). Cf. also Hausherr, *Vie*, 45.

[144] 26.59 (1137B). Cf. also Symeon the New Theologian, *Cat.* 4 (344, 358) and 29 (180, 184).

[145] 28.51 (1137B).

[146] 26.59 (1032B). Cf. also 7.67 (816B).

[147] 8.1 (828BC).

[148] Ps. Athanasius, *De virg.* 17 (PG28.272BC).

[149] Cf. *Mystic Treatises* (86–7).

[150] 7.28 (808A).

[151] This inner weeping is evident in the *Vita Prima* of Pachomius 53 (34–6, 187); *Apophth.* Antony 33 (PG65.85C); Evagrius, *De or.* 42 (PG79.1176B) and Abba Isaiah, *Logos* 25, 24 (178).

[152] 7.25 (805C) and 48 (809D). Cf. also *Apophth.* Nau 142 (1908) 49 and Anastasius the Sinaite, *Oratio de sacra synaxi* (PG89.833A).

[153] *De or.* 78 (PG79.1184C). Cf. Hausherr, *Penthos*, 33.

Nevertheless, John is always a realist. Unlike Symeon the New Theologian, who places greater emphasis on tears as being essential, John does recognize that, in reality, people differ greatly in character, and that some are likely to be more prone to tears than others:

> For I have seen small teardrops shed with difficulty like drops of blood; and I have also seen fountains of tears poured out without difficulty. And I judged those labourers more by their toil than by their tears; and I think that God does also.[154]

John's intention always is to stress that it was 'God who, out of love for humanity, gave us tears.'[155]

God gives and God takes away: the giving, the taking away, and even the withholding are all part of the same gift of tears. Nilus says that we must be thankful to God when we are deprived of this, provided God deprives us and gives it to someone else, for 'we are all members of one another (1 Cor. 12.20). ... If you but quicken your longing for tears in the face of God, you will be cleansed from your sins.' In the perspective of sharing, even being deprived of a gift that is granted to another is another way of receiving.[156] Deprivation can be a token of restitution:

> As soon as a baby begins to recognize its father, it is all filled with joy. But if the father goes away for a time on business (*oikonomikōs*) and then comes home again, the child becomes full of joy and sorrow – joy at seeing the beloved, and sorrow at being deprived for so long of that fair beauty.[157]

On the other hand, the loss of the gift of tears may also be the result of our own making. It may, for instance, be a consequence of the passion of pride:

> Tears often lead frivolous people to pride, and that is why they are not given to some. And such people, seeking tears in vain, consider themselves unfortunate, and condemn themselves to sighing, lamentation, sorrow of soul, deep grief and utter dismay. All of these, though profitably regarded by them as nothing, can safely take the place of tears.[158]

Though an invaluable gift, tears, according to Climacus, are not to be considered an end in themselves or as sufficient to themselves. They are only a 'way,' perhaps not even the only or absolutely necessary one. Tears are not even listed in the second alphabet that pertains to those who have reached perfection.[159] God does not require tears. It is we who need them as assistance,

---

[154] 7.25 (805C).

[155] 7.8 (804B). Cf. also 7.15 (804D) and 53–4 (813BC); 4.82 (713C); 5.16 (780A) and 15.73 (897BC).

[156] *Ep.* 3, 257 (PG79.512A–13B); in all probability this letter belongs to Nilus.

[157] 7.57 (813C). Cf. also Diadochus, *Cent.* 87 (146–7).

[158] 7.48 (809D).

[159] 26.14 (1017BC).

as a source of purification or delight or joy or illumination. The ultimate goal is the transcending joy and light experienced by Adam in paradise before the Fall.[160] In any case, the emphasis in John is never on the tears themselves, but on the disposition that makes one able to receive them, on humility, repentance and sorrow at one's real state. Great care must be taken not to turn the antidote to passions into another passion. Evagrius learned this truth from the Egyptian desert:

> Do not transform the defense against passions into a passion itself, so that you do not further anger Him who has bestowed the gift; many who weep for their sins, forgetting the purpose of tears, lost their senses and became mad.[161]

The Glory of the Body

Tears are a way in which God's grace affects the body. They serve to sanctify or to spiritualize the body and its senses:

> Those who aim at ascending with the body to heaven, indeed need violence and constant suffering ... and chastity through *penthos*.[162]

Isaac the Syrian regards tears as the preeminent manifestation of the participation of the body in spiritual life; they comprise 'a manifest sign of the real apperception.' And Symeon the New Theologian identifies tears with the 'sanctification' of the entire human person.[163] Tears, we have seen, are a direct expression of *penthos*, a commencement and a sign of spiritual transfiguration. The argument is as follows: if, even in our present state, human eyes shed physical tears, why should they not shed spiritual tears when, together with the rest of our body, they are transformed by grace? In fact, to speak of spiritual tears is not a device for rendering them immaterial. What is envisaged is something quite tangible, very real, not something disembodied or airy. Spiritual tears actually flow and moisten the cheeks, as John believes: 'May the interior joy of the heart break out onto the face'

---

[160] 7.45–46 (809C).

[161] *De or.* 8 (PG79.1169AB): in this passage Evagrius emphasizes that tears are a gift and a means towards an end different from themselves, towards a 'purpose.'

[162] 1.16 (636B). For the spiritualization of the senses, cf. Lot-Borodine, 'Don des larmes,' 99 n. 1, 100 and 102 n. 1. Cf. also K. Rahner, 'Le début d'une doctrine des cinq sens spirituels chez Origène,' *RAM* 13 (1932), 113–45. For this notion in the ascetic tradition, cf. Evagrius, *De or.* 29 (PG79.1173A); *Cent.* 2, 68 and 3, 40 (ed. Frankenberg, 176f and 216f.); Cassian, *Inst.* 10, 4 (390) and 11, 18 (444); Greg. Nyssa, *In Cant. Cant.* 1 (PG44.780C) and *Mac. Hom.* 2, 2 (14–15) and 4 (17–18); 4, 7 (32) and 11 (35–6) and 8, 6 (83).

[163] *Cat.* 28 (154). For Isaac, cf. *Mystic Treatises* (35).

(Prov. 15.13).[164] This quotation from Proverbs is cited by John and is echoed by his contemporary, Isaac the Syrian:

> For a joyful heart renders the body beautiful. These tears moisten the whole face ... and joy is diffused over the face.[165]

In a way, tears resemble Evagrius' 'small resurrection.' They are part of John's vision of 'resurrection before the resurrection.' It may, then, be said that tears in fact play the greatest role in the human effort toward the transfiguration of the body. For they 'wash,' cleanse and elevate the whole body. A polluted or a purified body is a polluted or purified person as a whole; in John's view, this is always a truly wonderful 'miracle.' As pollution is an opening to death (*prooimion thanatou*), so the sharing of the body in the *penthos* of repentance is an opening to the resurrection (*prooimion anastaseos*). The miracle is that the clay itself cleanses the clay.[166]

The body does not merely relate to or affect the person, but through tears becomes that very person in its entirety – an indication perhaps of the extreme, ultimate and only possible form of 'materialism' underlying the ascetic experience and John's own conception of human nature. Yet, for John, the heart, too, is of central importance, as we have already seen, and this is renewed with clarity in his theological anthropology of tears. For it is not only a person's eyes that weep when one is granted God's gift of tears, but the heart is also in pain, as opposed to feeling painlessness. The whole human person is in grief.[167] The pierced heart issues in blood and tears, just as Christ's side brought forth blood and water (Jn 19.34). Likewise, the whole person is 'sublimated,'[168] although 'sublimation' here must be understood to imply a change or movement from the *para physin* to the *kata* or *hyper physin*. We have not yet reached the eschatological paradise. However, it is anticipated in the here and now.

We have seen how the theology of tears expresses an aspect of deifying grace. Spiritual life allows of great freedom, and there are many and various ways of arriving at *penthos*. The latter is linked with all kinds of *ascesis*, whether fasting, remembrance of death, or others:

---

[164] 7.42 (805B) and 46 (809C). That tears are real is stressed in Pachomius *Vita Prima* 85 (57–8, 204) and Isaac the Syrian, *Mystic Treatises* (95, 322, 330).

[165] *Mystic Treatises* (165). For Climacus, cf. 30.11 (1157AB).

[166] 14.24 (868C).

[167] 6.14 (796B).

[168] Cf. Lot-Borodine, 'Don des larmes,' 101.

> Satiety of the stomach dries the tear-springs, but the stomach when dried produces these waters.[169]

Strangely, the association of *penthos* with tears makes dryness too a cause for tears. Ultimately, complete desiccation in humility brings down God's grace to imbue the heart. We must die in order to live (Mk 10.11).

There is, as we have seen, some ambiguity as to whether tears, through which the body is sanctified, mark the perfect state of holiness or else indicate a continuous process, which never ends. Indeed some, having reached the supreme stage – Hesychius the Chorebite and the monk Menas are cases in point[170] – no longer need tears.[171] However, so long as the spiritual ascent is a matter involving humanity as a whole, and 'the whole of creation groans and travails in pain together' (Rom. 8.22), the ascetic will continue to weep for the world as well as for personal sins. If the ascetic is already purified, then any tears for others are part of the ascetic's responsibility for their sins and a participation in their transfiguration. The responsibility and the participation are as much gifts as the tears themselves. In a somewhat ambivalent piece in the *Letters* of Barsanuphius and John, we read:

> The Fathers have made it clear to the younger ones that no one ought to leave his own dead in order to go and mourn for another. For, it is the perfect that are able to suffer with their neighbour; but for the younger ones to do so is a deceit of the demons.[172]

John stresses the all-embracing psychosomatic significance of even a single drop of tears:

> Never cease, even for a moment, to purge and cleanse defiled souls, and especially defiled bodies, so that you may boldly procure wreaths of victory from the good Judge of the contest, not only for the souls of your brethren, but also for the souls of others.[173]

---

[169] 14.16 (868A).

[170] 6.20 (796D–97B) and 4.29 (697B–700A). Cf. 29.2 (1148BC). Cf. also Athanasius, *Vita Ant.* 45 (PG26.908C) and 67 (940); Antony mourned daily, yet his face is said to have 'had a surprising grace ... never troubled, and his soul was calm.'

[171] 7.46 (809C).

[172] Barsanuphius 341. Cf. also Pachomius, *Vita Prima* 62 (42, 192).

[173] *Shep.* 72 (1193B). Cf. also *Shep.* 78 (1193CD). On the notion of weeping for the sins of others, cf. Clem. Alex., *Quis dives salvetur* 35 and 41 (ed. *GCS*, 183, 187); Ps. Athanasius, *Life of St. Synkletike* 40 (PG28.1512AB); Basil, *Reg. Brev. Tract.* 31 (PG31.1104B); Greg. Nyssa, *De or. dom.* 5 (PG44.184–85); *Apophth.* Pambo 4 (PG65.369B); Mark the Monk, *De paen.* 11 and 12 (PG65.981AC); Theodoret of Cyrus, *Phil. Hist.*, Julian Sabas 2, 8, p. 214 (1313B); and Symeon the New Theologian, *Cat.* 28 (150).

Charmolype – **Joy and Sorrow**

Charopoion Penthos – *Joyful Sorrow*

John's most original contribution to the theology of tears must surely be the way that he identifies the sorrow of *penthos* with joy or happiness. The technical terms that he uses to describe this state of joyful sorrow – *charopoion penthos* and *charmolype* – are also found for the first time in his writings. John devotes an entire chapter/step to this subject, and this has also proved the most influential part of the *Ladder*.[174]

The bitterness of tears is sweetened through repentance. Tears of fear develop into tears of love.[175] The phenomenon requires closer examination. The monk remembers death, and this memory is painful. Yet the monk does so not only on account of personal sins but also from love of God, from a longing for the kingdom that was once ours but now is lost.[176] The monastery, or the cell, therefore becomes a tomb before the terminal tomb, a grave before the final grave. Yet, at the same time, these are seen to be heaven on earth. Similarly, the monastic garment represents not a funeral robe but a 'wedding garment,' a sign of spiritual joy rather than of sorrow, since it is for joy and not for sorrow that God has created us.[177] One who mourns continually in a way that is pleasing to God 'does not cease to feast daily.' Each day is transformed into a feast, as the monk grieves at the condition of his stricken state. At the same time, however, the grief marks a step forward – or backward – towards unfallen nature, and this becomes a source of joy. In our sorrow, there is expectation. We await the visitation of God's grace. The sorrow is imbued with eschatological hope, which is tasted even now. But the joy springs from sorrow:

> Eternal *penthos* awaits the person who does not cease to feast daily.[178]

Penthos carries an element of the 'beautiful.' Climacus coins another term in this regard: *kallipenthos*. Humanity 'is to blame' for having lost this 'harmony' of joy and sorrow, the intertwining tears and happiness contained in 'the beauty of *penthos*,' which Climacus spells out also in another descriptive phrase: *kallos penthous*. The idea marks Climacus' dialectical approach. He

---

[174] Just as the section on the Prison in Step 5 (764D–77A) proved to be the most 'terrifying' to readers, so also – apart from references to the 'Jesus Prayer' which are examined in the chapter concerning prayer – the seventh step proved the most positively influential. The theme is taken up by Symeon the New Theologian: cf. *Cat.* 2 (260); 26 (74); *Theol.* 1 (118); *Eth.* 3 (438) and *TGP* 3, 8 and 9 (82). Cf. also *Cat.* 22 (372) and Niketas Stethatos, *Cent.* 1, 69 (289).

[175] 7.28 (808A). Cf. also Lev Gillet, 'Gift of Tears,' 10 and Evagrius, *Prakt.* 57 (632).

[176] 1.10 (633C).

[177] 4.93 (716B) and 82 (713B); 7.41 (809A) and 45–6 (809C). Isaac the Syrian refers to the cell as 'the place of mourning:' cf. *Mystic Treatises* (121, 169).

[178] 7.38 (808D).

believes that to destroy this harmony in tension is to be imprisoned in *penthos*, with nothing left but 'to sigh.'[179] The true life of repentance is a balance of perdition and resurrection,[180] of death and life, of despair and hope in 'reconciliation with the Lord,'[181] of grief derived from a desire for God.[182] It is the case of a crucified heart containing Gethsemane and Tabor. *Ploutotapei-nosis*,[183] another term that John has coined in order to describe 'the riches of humility,' accurately describes joyful sorrow, the weeping that is mingled – almost identified – with joy.[184] It is a simultaneous experience of Holy Friday and Easter Sunday: 'dying, and behold we live ... sorrowful, yet always rejoicing' (2 Cor. 6.9–10). This coinherence of joy and sadness goes back once again to Christ's beatitude: 'Blessed are they that mourn, for they shall be comforted' (Mt. 5.4), and to Christ's own ascension in which he left the disciples, but promised always to be with them (Jn 14.12, Mt. 28.20). One weeps like a child who, as quoted above, is:

> Filled with joy and sorrow – joy at seeing the beloved, and sorrow at being deprived for so long of that fair beauty.[185]

John is far more erudite and masterful. He is able to condense the whole patristic teaching on tears in his doctrine on *charmolype*. Other writers have alluded to this concept of joyful sorrow,[186] but John explicitly develops it for the first time, both coining the term and drawing his ascetic conclusions from Christ's beatitude, in which beatific 'comfort' is eschatologically anticipated in the here and now.

---

[179] 7.39 (808D) and 28 (808A).

[180] 5.5 (769B) and 30 (718A).

[181] 5.2 (764BC).

[182] 5.5 (776D).

[183] 5.9 (777BC).

[184] Cf. 7.61 (816A). Cf. also Isaac the Syrian, *Mystic Treatises* (85).

[185] 7.57 (813C). Cf. also 7.35 (813B).

[186] Beck tries to make Climacus seem less knowledgeable: cf. Beck, *Kirche*, 451. Many other writers have alluded to the doctrine of joyful sorrow. For example, Antony's face is joyful, though he always weeps: cf. Athanasius, *Vita Ant.* 67 (PG26.940); also Abba Ammon, *Letters* 28, in Halkin's *Sancti Pachomii Vitae Graecae*, 115, where Ammon says that the Lord changes our mourning into joy; Chrysostom, *In epist. ad Phil. Hom.* 14 (PG62.281AD). 'This joy is not opposed to that sorrow; it is born of that sorrow,' and *In Epist. ad Col. Hom.* 12, 3 (PG62.384); Greg. Naz., *Or.* 16, 14 (PG35.952B): 'Let us sow in tears, in order to reap exultation.' (Ps. Chrysostom, *De paenitentia* [PG60.768], where the words are similar to those of Greg. Naz. above); Evagrius, *De or.* 153 (PG79.1200BC), 5–6 (1068D–69A) and 78 (1184C); Cassian, *Conf.* 9, 28 (63–4), speaks of tears which give joy; Nilus, *Epist.* 1, 220 (PG79.164AB); Diadochus, *Cent.* 100 (161–3): 'tears of love:' tears of enjoyment, sweetness and refreshment; Theodoret of Cyrus, *Phil. Hist.*, Peter, 9, 14 p. 432 (1388B); Abba Isaiah, *Logos* 16, 3 (90): 'for sorrow according to God is joy;' Ephraim the Syrian (?), *Sermo Asceticus*, Rome: 1732–46, vol. 1, 60: 'A face washed with tears is an imperishable beauty.'

Penthos is described as 'blessed and full of grace' and as 'blessed, joyful sorrow.' On the other hand, compunction, a preliminary and preparatory gift, is called 'holy.' For *penthos* is not merely a vexation at our fallen state but a positive motion towards God, a foretaste of what we were and are to be, a beginning of the process toward *katharsis* in order to render human nature as God originally intended it to be.[187] In this process, remembrance of death is considered as the first stage of joyful sorrow. We begin with fear, pass through 'fearlessness' and end up in 'unceasing joy.' In the words of Abba Isaac the Syrian: 'let joy be kindled in your mind at the recollection of death.'[188] The recollection of death, therefore, is not identical with mere dread of death. What is at stake is the recognition that no moment in our lives can ever be relived. Each moment, then, and each encounter should be experienced in their fullness, involving life and death. Remembrance of death, according to John, is a life-giving remembrance, a way of life[189] characteristic of Christian piety, which transcends self-sufficient religious norms.

The fruition of the 'holy flower of love' and the change from 'painful' to 'painless tears' occurs 'miraculously.'[190] It is a gift from above. Joyful sorrow is supernatural, a gratuitous gift from God, having no source in human passions. The joyful sorrow is astonishing for John himself:

> I am amazed at how that which is called *penthos* and grief should contain joy and gladness interwoven within it, like honey in the comb.[191]

Spiritual Joy

There is an underlying optimism in John, consisting in his belief that human nature was created by God for joy and not for sorrow, for laughter and not for tears: 'Rejoice in the Lord always; and again I say, Rejoice' (Phil. 4.4). In Step seven, John says:

> My friends, God, does not ask or desire that one should mourn from sorrow of heart, but rather that, out of love for Him, one should rejoice with spiritual laughter.[192]

Ascetic writers are normally wary of laughter (Eccl. 7.8). However, there are as many kinds of laughter or joy as there are of tears. Laughter may be the result

---

[187] 7.11 (804BC).

[188] *Mystic Treatises* (31). For John, cf. 7.54 (813BC).

[189] 4.43 (705B) and 7.41 (809A).

[190] 7.53–54 (813BC). Cf. also Symeon the New Theologian, *Cat.* 4 (320, 324 and 342).

[191] 7.50 (812A).

[192] 7.454 (809C).

of pride,[193] or sinful pleasure,[194] of insensitivity.[195] Nevertheless, spiritual laughter is a special case.[196] Worldly laughter 'disperses' (*dialyei*, literally 'dissolves') *penthos*.[197] Such laughter and joy must be subdued and repelled.[198] Here, too, the gift of discernment comes into its own. We are required to ask:

> Which of the demons make us sad, and which make us cheerful?[199]

Joy is various,[200] just as sorrow and tears are various. Even prayer may not help to sort out what is what, with the demons lurking to deceive us.[201] The gift of discernment is always like a sure guide in a spiritual maze.

Worldly laughter is to spiritual laughter as drunkenness from spirits is to spiritual drunkenness.[202] John says that the only 'person' one should laugh *at* is the devil.[203] Genuine joy is always combined with humility; the 'wedding garment'[204] of the monk is a 'garment of joy and humility.'[205] For John, spiritual joy[206] is a *katastasis* (literally, a 'state') filled with love, a condition excluding any 'dark night of the soul' and devoid of any sadness. He even remarks:

> Remove sin and the tear of sorrow is superfluous for your eyes. What is the use of a bandage when there is no wound?[207]

This may be at variance with some of his other statements on tears, but it is consistent with his conception of the highest level of spiritual joy.

---

[193] 21.7 (949D); 26.29 (1021C–246B); 28.21 (1133A) and 3.42 (672A). Patristic texts usually speak of laughter negatively: cf. Ps. Athanasius, *Sermo pro iis qui saeculo renuntiarunt* 4 (PG28.1412D); Basil, *Reg. Brev. Tract.* 31 (PG 31.1104B); Pachomius, *Vita Prima* 104 (p. 68, p. 214; *Apophth.* John the Dwarf 9 (PG65.205D–08A) and Nau 139 (1908, p. 49); Pambo 13 (372B) says that it can be good; Diadochus, *Cent.* 33 (102–04); Evagrius, *Ep. de virg.* (ed. Frankenberg, 563 and 565); Abba Isaiah, *Logos* 5, 5 (40) and 28, 1 (194); Barsanuphius 570; and John Moschus, *Pratum*, John 187 (3065AB).

[194] 7.17 (805A); 14.32 (869BD) and 26.2, 41 (1068CD).

[195] 17.3 (932BD) and 5 (933BD).

[196] 7.10 (804B).

[197] 7.7 (804A). Cf. also 12.1 (853D) and 3–4 (856AB).

[198] 7.40 (809A).

[199] 26.ii,66 (1073CD).

[200] 26.iii, 30 (1088C).

[201] 28.21 (1132D–33A) and 18.3 (937BC).

[202] 7.16 (804D).

[203] 14.10 (865C).

[204] 7.41 (809A).

[205] 28.52 (1137C).

[206] 7.41 (809A) and 45 (809C). Cf. similar words in Greg. Palamas, *Antirrheticus* 7, 11, 34 (3, p. 486).

[207] 7.46 (809C). Isidore of Pelusium contends that angels, at any rate, do not weep: cf. *Epist.* 319 (PG79.368AB).

Sadness gives way to joy, when all tears are wiped away by the hand of the one who sends the Comforter in order 'that [our] joy may be made full' (Jn 16.24 and 20). Just as there is a *kairos* for all things, including those 'above' the sun (Eccl. 3.1), there is also 'a time to weep and a time to laugh' (Eccl. 3.4). There is joy in arriving and joy in being on the way.[208] However, joy is complete only *in patria*, in paradise. There is a conjunction between joy (*chara*) and grace (*charis*), which share the same source – etymologically, theologically and spiritually alike.

As with so much else in John, his account of the gift of tears is a testimony, not a treatise. It is a homily perhaps, but not a doctrinal discourse with a fixed set of axioms and rules. Yet John shows an extraordinarily subtle insight into that 'mysterious land of tears,' into the variousness of weeping, its status and significance in the spiritual life. In the *Apophthegmata Patrum*, Abba Isaac says of Abba Poemen that when the latter was once asked what he was thinking about, he responded that his mind was with the Virgin Mary standing beneath the cross; Poemen only wished that he too could weep like her.[209] For John also, life is a continual standing beneath the cross, a continual weeping. However, the tears are not tears of despair. Their source and object is the light of the resurrection shining beneath the cross, or ahead of it, and transforming sorrow into joy.

---

[208] 7.46 (809C). Cf. Diadochus, *Cent.* 60 (120). It is also the view of Isaac the Syrian that tears are transitory: cf. *Mystic Treatises*, 29, 86.

[209] *Apophth.* Poemen 144 (PG65.357B).

The cave hermitage of John Climacus
(Photograph: Elizabeth Williams)

CHAPTER 6

Ascesis: The Ascetic Struggle of the Monk

> One virtue stands out above all the others:
> the constant striving upwards, the wrestling
> with oneself.
>
> (Goethe)

> The secret of grace is that it never comes
> too late.
>
> (François Mauriac)

Human Nature

Levels of Existence

There is no such thing as an atomized human being. People may do this and that, but we reach no understanding of them from a recital of their ostensible actions. People may harbor a collection of ideas, but even a flood of abstract principles presents no more than an ornamental intellectual confusion, providing no contact with the inward sources of our life, and often only keeping just one step ahead of the impotence of our dislocated designs and actions. It is, therefore, particularly important to stress at this point what has emerged throughout the preceding account. John Climacus, together with earlier ascetic mystics, interprets human faculties, for good and evil, indeed all attitudes and practices, in relation to the total structure of the human person. This chapter approaches the same subject from a number of angles, now considered in its active, more 'militant' perspective – the perspective of the ascetic struggle of the monk. More particularly, it examines John's view of human nature, and its relation to and interaction with divine grace. This implies a consideration of the impact of alien forces in the shape of demons, and the way of regaining wholeness in confrontation with them. The ascetic will be seen to be a 'passionate' being, ridden with passions and freed from them, in discernment, sensibility and contest. Eventually, the struggle of human nature will be illumined by its subsumption in divine passion (*eros*).

'Nature' (*physis*) cannot be separated from the total structure of the human person. Vague in many passages where it is used by John, this term reflects the recovery of one's true self, oriented towards God, who makes life holy and who is its ground and goal of existence. However, there are levels or dimensions in human nature. John's *Ladder* distinguishes two such levels: the unfallen nature of the human person created in the image of God, and the fallen or sinful nature. The distinction between the two marks a fundamental Christian dichotomy. Yet it is a dichotomy not between nature and grace, but between two levels within human nature. One's perpetual struggle is a search for the state of glory properly belonging to human nature:

> I long for the immortal beauty, which you gave me before this clay.[1]

Following the tradition of the *Life of Antony*, which advises the ascetic to be preserved in accordance with God's creation and intention,[2] the *Ladder* exhorts the ascetic to seek that 'pure nature of the soul, as it was created.'[3] The conviction is that one has undergone 'a change in nature' and a 'distortion in behavior,'[4] though not a catastrophe. Terminologically, 'nature' (*physis*) is somewhat ambivalent in John, signifying mostly unfallen nature, though on occasion also denoting fallen nature.[5] Nonetheless, this does not affect the substance of the matter.

The evil within us is not natural, but it can become something like second nature to us.[6] It is this nature which the monk faces and fights with force; Climacus speaks of 'the continual violence of nature.'[7] The aim of the effort is to expel this second nature from the intellect,[8] to reject it; Climacus speaks of 'the supernatural denial of nature.'[9] Ultimately, the purpose is to overcome it:

> The person who has conquered the body has conquered nature; and the person who has conquered nature has certainly risen above nature.[10]

In connection with the latter expression, when John is being more precise, he makes a twofold distinction, between *para physin* (fallen nature) and *kata physin* (unfallen nature). Sometimes, however, as in the passage just quoted, he

---

[1] 29.15 (1149D).

[2] Athanasius, *Life of Antony* 20 (PG26.873B); note also the use of *kata physin* in ch. 14 (864B–65B): the ascetic struggle does not repress but in fact restores *physis*.

[3] 24.15 (981C).

[4] 21.2 (949A).

[5] Cf., for example, 15.83 (901C); 14.8 (865A) and 26.22 (1020CD).

[6] 24.7 (981C) and 26.iii,17 (10885D). Cf. also Greg. Nyssa, *De virginitate* 9 (PG46.357B); Evagrius, *Prakt.* 70 (656); Nilus, *Epist.* 2, 239 (PG79.321CD); *Mac. Hom.* 4,8 (22–32); Diadochus, *Cent.* 3 (86) and especially 83 (143); *Hist Monachorum,* 1, John of Lycopolis 48 (29); Dorotheus, *Instr.* 2, 36 (200); Thalassius, *Cent.* 3,7 (PG91.1448D) and Symeon the New Theologian, *Cat.* 2 (270).

[7] 1.10 (633C). Cf. also 14.31 (869A); 15.23 (884C); *Hist. Monachorum* 20, Dioscorus 3 (119); and *Mystic Treatises* (93).

[8] 7.4 (801D).

[9] 15.2 (880C) and 11.1 (633C).

[10] 15.70 (896C) and 1.11 (633C).

implies a threefold distinction (*para kata* and *hyper physin*, or 'above nature'), although one should not read any basic inconsistency into this.

It is against their fallen nature that the ascetics in the Alexandrian Prison fought so ruthlessly. The battle was fought as a fight against death, which is 'unnatural.'[11] 'Although we all sin of our own volition, no one in reality actively chooses to sin against God.'[12] We were created good by God, and our nature is neither evil in itself 'nor responsible' for the evil in the world.[13] This is not to say that it is neutral, but rather that it is in essence good. Such is the basic Greek patristic view of *physis*, with which Climacus is in basic accord:

> Sin, or passion, was not originally planted in nature; for, God is not the creator of passions.[14]

There are many natural virtues, as we shall see below, but no natural vices. In fact, sin is often un-hypostasized, rather than en-hypostasized, in ascetic literature.[15] Other writers, such as Clement of Alexandria, distinguish 'passion' from 'nature,'[16] while the *History of the Monastics* describes passions as 'alien or superfluous.'[17] Sin alone is contrary to human nature (*para physin*). For Abba Isaiah of Scetis and Dorotheus of Gaza, the *para physin* state is tantamount to disease or sickness.[18] However, it is we who have averted from God those inclinations, which were by nature good[19] and marred the condition of our unfallen nature. Barsanuphius observes in one passage that the devil is actually even the cause of this marring.[20] Hence we seek our former state of natural 'relation' with God, and we must do so in a manner described by John as 'insatiable.'[21]

---

[11] 6.3 and 4 (793BC).

[12] 10.5 (845D).

[13] 29.7 (1149A). Cf. also Athanasius, *Life of Antony* 20 and 34 (PG26.873A and 893B).

[14] 26.41 (1028A). Similar expressions may be found in earlier writers, and especially in Cassian, *Conf.* 9, 6 (314), and, later, in Symeon the New Theologian, *Cat.* 4 (322).

[15] Cf. *Mac. Hom.* 16, 1 (157–8) and Dorotheus, *Instr.* 10, 106 (340–42) and 11, 116 (362).

[16] *Paedagogus* 2, 10 (ed. *GCS*, 209). Cf. also Barsanuphius 246. On Clement, see D. Hunter, 'The Language of Desire: Clement of Alexandria's Transformation of Ascetic Discourse,' *Semeia* 57 (1992), 95–111.

[17] Macarius of Alexandria 23 (only in Rufinus' additions in PL21.453). Cf. also *Mac. Hom.* 15, 13 (128–9).

[18] Abba Isaiah, *Logos* 25, 23 (117) and Dorotheus, *Instr.* 10, 106 (342). See also Mark the Monk, *De his.* 83 (PG65.941CD). Cf. also Abba Isaiah, *Logos* 8 (53); and 18 (112); and Abba Isaac the Syrian, *Mystic Treatises* (251).

[19] 26.ii,41 (1068C). Cf. also Abba Isaiah, *Logos* 2 (4) and Greg. Palamas, *Triads*, 3, 2, 19.

[20] Barsanuphius 192.

[21] 26.ii,19 (1064A).

The Need for Grace

Although John appears to emphasize the human element in ascetic life,[22] by constantly addressing the practical discipline of the monk, nonetheless a careful study of the *Ladder* reveals the priority and importance that he attaches to divine initiative. If fallen nature is to be overcome at all, this is in the last resort due to God:

> Where the supernatural God dwells, much that is supernatural happens.[23]

One cannot conquer fallen nature on one's own.[24] That condition calls for God's grace; consequently, one is always 'indebted' to it.[25] What the monk is called to do is to lay down his natural weakness humbly before Christ, in recognition of his own nothingness and in request of God's grace.[26] Whatever we have is not ours, but always received from others, whether directly from God or indirectly from other people's prayers:[27]

> It is shameful to be proud of the adornments that are not your own, but utter madness to fancy that one deserves God's gifts.[28]

John is far removed from any form of Pelagianism, let alone of reliance on an egocentric self. God does not act as a *deus ex machina*. God acts 'in synergy' with humanity. John actually speaks of *synergeia* in two passages, closely adhering to the earlier Palestinian tradition of Barsanuphius and Dorotheus.[29] The ascetic does not repudiate human nature, which provides the only premise and final promise for either salvation or damnation. Human nature is the ground where grace or sin alike abide and abound. Yet 'nature,' too, is not simply given like a finished product. It is a moving ground in the process of

---

[22] John continully speaks of a fight with which the ascetic must put up [cf. 4.1, 2 (677D) and 111 (720AD); 116 (852CD); 14.19 (868AB); 26.33 (1024D); 15.28 (885C); 21.4 (949B); 22.17 (968C); 26.59 (1032BC) and 26.iii, 28 (1088B)], causing much sweat [cf. 26.26 (1021B)] and toil [cf. 26.27 (1021B)].

[23] 26.3 (1013B).

[24] 15.4 (881A).

[25] 22.15 (968B). What John calls *hreōstēs*, Mark the Monk calls *opheiletēs*, adhering more closely to the language of the New Testament (Gal. 5.3); cf. *De lege spir.* 32 (PG65.909B) and *De his.* (929C).

[26] 15.22 (884B).

[27] 15.76 (900B).

[28] 22.15 (968B).

[29] Cf. 14.19 (868B), where the word is found in its verbal form (*synergei*); 15.76 (900B), where Climacus quotes Paul in 1 Cor. 4.7. Cf. also Barsanuphius 215 and 213 and Dorotheus, *Epist.* 1 (112) and *Epist.* 6, 191 (510). For the notion of 'synergy,' cf. Athanasius, *Vita Ant.* 5 and 19 (PG26.849A and 827A); Mark the Monk, *Ad. Nic.* 6–7 and 13 (PG65.1037B, 1040D and 1049BD). Also see, 'A Monk of the Eastern Church,' *Orthodox Spirituality*, London: 1945, 23.

continuous self-transcendence and restoration, always engaged in interaction with God's grace.

Virtues

The question of virtues is immediately related to that of nature and grace, inasmuch as virtues are considered as either part of the endowment of nature, of being human, or else arising as special gifts of God. For John they are, characteristically, both. In any case, it is alien to him to have recourse to *a priori* rules of conduct. He lays stress on virtue, but only and always in the light of particular circumstances. The practice of virtue will, for instance, depend – in the monastic context – on whether one pursues the cenobitic, semi-cenobitic, or fully eremetic life,[30] as well as on whether one lives in a monastic community at all or in the secular world. *Ascesis* by those living in the world comes worse off in the *Ladder*. Their struggle is said to be diminished because of their many cares.[31] As a result, their virtue is not so well tried or tested. For John, the authentic measure or tone for asceticism is provided by monastic life: 'The monastic life is a light for all people.'[32]

As regards virtues, there is a certain hierarchy or 'order' envisaged.[33] Some are shown to be supernatural; others are seen as part of the natural state. This depends on the source of activation, rather than on moral substance. For example, some virtues are attained on one's own initiative, although, even then, it is the saints who exemplify them for us. Prayer was taught to both Antony and Pachomius by the angels, while only God can teach us love.[34] In the end, everything is imparted by God. The *Ladder*, however, contains a fairly clear distinction between 'natural' and 'acquired' virtues. While both are divine gifts and must be acknowledged as such, the latter, according to John, are spiritually, if not also morally, superior.[35] Moreover, there are people whose fallen nature positively resists virtue.[36] Nevertheless, all these distinctions are, in the final analysis, secondary. They do not require or imply any conventional classification or enumeration. They interact or overlap like 'a chain,' or rather like 'the colours of a rainbow.'[37] Or, to adopt the imagery of the *Ladder* itself,

---

[30] 20.1 (945B).

[31] 2.9 (656B).

[32] 26.23 (1020D).

[33] 24.1 (980C).

[34] 26.42 (1028B) and 26.ii,28 (1065AB). Cf. also Pachomius, *Vita Prima* 23 (14, 170).

[35] 24.8 (984AB).

[36] 26.22 (1020CD).

[37] 25.7 (989D). Evagrius, *De or.* 1 (PG79.1068BC) and *Mac. Hom.* 40.1 (275–6) also speak of the interdependence of virtues. Kallistos/Ignatios, *Cent.* 11 (204) use the word 'robe' (*alourgis*), the threads of which are the virtues.

they are like rungs, together, and one after the other, leading to heaven, in contrast to passions, which weigh down like the chains of Peter.[38]

Virtues reveal one's natural condition:

> There are in us many natural virtues from God ... so then it follows that the virtues are not far from nature.[39]

Here again, John is in agreement with the established Palestinian view on the matter.[40] Through virtues, one reaches God.[41] There is no suggestion of mere conformity of behavior with the principles of morality. Rather, virtues resemble a *topos*, the 'place' that holds and where one beholds God, the 'Burning Bush' that conceals God, the 'Mount Sinai' where one contemplates the divine presence. This condition may be reached even while undergoing many adversities, just as the harassed Moses returned to Egypt having encountered God in the Burning Bush. John continues to be sensitive to human weakness. He is compassionate toward the sinner. A twentieth-century hermit, Paisios (d. 1994), who had lived near the cave where John himself had lived, referred to the Alexandrian Prison as a real place of wretchedness. He once told me:

> Saint John of the *Ladder* must have seen the ascetics in that Prison as a symbol of fallen humanity, of his *own* fallen humanity primarily. I am certain that he would have tried to smuggle some bread and water to those wretched ascetics. If for no other reason, he would have done so because they persevered, in spite of their weakness.

John Climacus only looked for continual striving. He is austere in his expectations. Yet he is neither hard nor unsparing. He supports others against external and internal enemies, not least from forces which, in the shape of demons or passions, threaten virtue in its vulnerability.

According to John, the demons resemble pirates intent on storming, plundering, and running off with any virtues we may have or have acquired.[42] The demons will try to take possession of what is not even our own property. After all, we do not own virtue; it belongs to God. They aim to deceive us in every possible way and will often pretend that what is vicious is in effect virtuous.[43] Still, demons are not to be considered scapegoats. They are not omnipotent; they cannot deprive us of the freedom to choose. Moreover, one is

---

[38] 9.1 (841A) and 28.12 (1132B).

[39] 26.41 and especially 42 (1028AB).

[40] Dorotheus, *Instr.* 1,1 (146–8); 11, 122 (374) and 12, 134 (396); Barsanuphius 245 and 762; and Abba Isaiah, *Logos* 2, 1–2 (4–6).

[41] 5.25 (780C) and 7.43 (809B).

[42] 26.13 (1061D).

[43] 12.7 (856C). Cf. also Evagrius, *De or.* 95 (PG79.1188CD).

exposed not only to demons in the spiritual life, avid to attack virtue, but also to wicked people in real life.[44]

The ambivalent nature of virtues, the existence of different or even conflicting manifestations of them, is shown in that, paradoxically, virtue may appear in persons who are victims of passions. In the end, however, genuine virtue is bound to reveal itself:

> As the sun makes gold glitter, so virtue makes manifest the person who possesses it (cf. Mt. 5:14).[45]

'Glitter,' for John, is not showiness or blatancy or self-righteousness or sanctimoniousness, even if he admits that 'we should always perform every virtue ... with great feeling.'[46] Self-righteousness or vainglory,[47] on the contrary, is a supremely divisive and, therefore, demonic claim of ultimacy for oneself. Humility is, once more, the only virtue which is not usurpable.[48] Through humility, one is able resolutely to 'wage war' against every demonic assault.[49]

By nature, it is in fact easier for us to acquire virtue than to yield to passions, although it may appear to be a more difficult task.[50] Yet even a passion can lead to an understanding of just how passionately its corresponding virtue is to be sought.[51] We shall return to this theme. Climacus knows, then, that we can learn from 'the shrewdness of the children of this world' (Lk. 16:8). John himself is rather 'shrewd.' He is aware that we must often choose, in any given circumstance, between alternative virtues or even alternative passions. His realistic advice is that one should choose the highest virtue or the weakest passion.[52] Choice is inevitable; when imitating others we should choose only their virtues, 'like a person who knows how to pick good grapes.'[53]

Though we may be dragged downward by the enemies of virtue, our aim is to become and remain one with virtue.[54] We are to dress with virtue, wearing it as our own nature, in accordance with the original design for humanity. This

---

[44] 26.ii,17 (1061D).

[45] 26.iii,21 (1064B) and 15.43 (889A).

[46] 28.42 (1136D). This is also emphasized in *Apophth.* Poemen 207 (ed. Guy, 31).

[47] 21.3 (949B), 26 (953C) and 29 (956AB).

[48] 25.16 (993A).

[49] 25.63 (1001D–04A). Cf. also *Apophth.* Macarius of Egypt 11 (PG65.268BC).

[50] 26.ii, 18 (1061D–64A). Cf. also 26.41 (1028B) and 26.ii,41 (1068CD), and a similar statement in Athanasius, *Life of Antony* (PG26.973AC).

[51] 16.31 (1024B). Cf. *Apophth.* Pambo 4 (PG65.369B), where Pambo weeps because he is not as concerned to please God spiritually as a prostitute is to please people sensually.

[52] 26.43 (1028BC).

[53] 10.17 (848D). Cf. similar teaching in *Apophth.* Poemen 130 (PG65.353D–56A).

[54] 22.22 (969A).

union is not merely 'spiritual;' it excludes nothing. It includes the body. Indeed, there is no virtue without the body:

> If I strike [the body] down, I have nothing with which to obtain virtues.[55]

The acquisition of virtues, in the same way as the control of the passions, is not an act accomplished in a moment.[56] It results from a long ascetic process and is itself a part of the ongoing process. The ascetic requires 'patience,' endurance. John confesses: 'Such a laborer needs patience more so than food.'[57] Barsanuphius agrees: 'This is the work of the monk: to endure wars and resist with courageous heart.'[58] To speak of virtue as a 'result' of ascetic practice is, however, misleading. Strictly speaking, the opposite obtains. John says: 'the beginning of labors is virtue.'[59] Virtue, then, is both beginning and continuation – an unending beginning. One can never attain all the virtues. Even when one has achieved every virtue, one is still far from God:

> Though you may have climbed the whole ladder of virtues, pray for forgiveness of sins.[60]

In any case, just as in perfection, God is never possessed. To acquire virtues is not to possess them. Later, in the tenth century, Symeon the New Theologian would echo John: 'Even if the soul appears to be adorned with all virtues, it has not participated of the fire.'[61] God remains forever elusive, though not distant from the true seeker.

The elusiveness implies an idea of unending yet culminating expansion. It is a case of never-ending perfection:

> All creatures have received from the creator their order of being and their beginning, and some their consummation too. But the end of virtue is endless.[62]

Barsanuphius even uses the verbal form of *epektasis*:

> For as much as one progresses (*epekteinetai*), one does not stop. Instead, one always sees oneself as lacking and as continuing to make progress.[63]

---

[55] 15.83 (901D). See also Ps. Athanasius, *Life of Saint Synkletike* 19 and 100 (PG28.1496C and 1549B).

[56] 26.iii,47 (1089C).

[57] 27.ii,38 (1113C) and 4.3 (700B–01B).

[58] Barsanuphius 258.

[59] 26.iii,55 (1092B).

[60] 28.12 (1132B) and 25.23 (993C).

[61] *Cat.* 33 (248). Cf. also Evagrius, *De or.* 56 (PG79.1177D–80A).

[62] 26.ii,37 (1068A).

[63] Barsanuphius 410.

This idea is frequently found in Greek patristic literature, and originates in a rejection of virtue as an end in itself. According to the *Macarian Homilies*, virtues are merely 'milestones and waymarks' leading to heaven.[64]

'Many are the paths of piety and destruction,'[65] writes John. There exist, not just one, but many ways of salvation. Indeed, each person constitutes a unique – though not an independent – way leading either to or else away from salvation. John refrains, then, from giving any one-way prescription or suggesting a moral formula. He prefers to address particular cases, so long as they provide an avenue for the restoration of human nature and illumination by divine grace.

Demons

Evil Spirits

The importance of the demonological theme in John's ascetic spirituality may be gaged from the account of his anthropology in the preceding chapters. At times, demons seem to dominate the stage. Still, John never succumbed to any obsession with demonology of the kind which characterized the second- and third-century Gnosticism and which was responsible for the erection of a vast and complex system of demonic hierarchies. Certainly, as we have already seen, John reflects an intense experience of demonic influence, which brings about splits and conflicts within human nature and impels us to struggle against its divisive claims. To split, to divert, to shift, to disrupt is its essential procedure. Yet the struggle is basically *within* human nature. Nonetheless, John's demonological language is at times highly objectified, pointing, as will be seen, to real agents rather than to imaginary shadows.

Demons are spirits (*pneumata*)[66] or noetic beings (*noeroi*).[67] They are evil;[68] and their main function is to darken one's intellect.[69] Being spirits, they are more difficult to deal with than people.[70] They are 'haters of good,'[71] and it is

---

[64] *Mac. Hom.* 27, 23 (230). For the notion of *epektasis* in other early ascetic writers, cf. Evagrius, *Prakt.* 87 (678); Mark the Monk, *De lege spir.* 29 (PG65.909A) and *Disp. cum quodam causidico* 3 (1073D); Diadochus, *Cent.* 89 (149–50) and Abba Zosimas, *Alloquia* 2 (PG78.1684B).

[65] 26.77 (1036B). Cf. also similar doctrine in Greg. Naz., *De moderatione in disputando* 33 (PG36.212AB), who uses almost the same words; Mark the Monk, *De lege spir.* 196 (PG65.929A) and *Disp. cum quodam causidico* 13 (1089D).

[66] 3.40 (672A).

[67] 15.25 (885A).

[68] 7.71 (816C).

[69] Cf. 26.7 (1013D).

[70] 21.14 (952A).

[71] 4.99 (716D). Cf. also Paulos Evergetinos, *Synagoge* 1, 30 (265).

they and our consent to them, not we or others, that cause evil. They sow the seed of sin within us[72] and 'force us to sin.'[73] Yet they cannot predict the consequences of their sowing. They cannot know the future[74] or even perceive our innermost thoughts – except, as the *Macarian Homilies* imply, by virtue of the fact that they have been with us for so long.[75] God 'knows' that they cause sinful thoughts and that, at times, they may act even without our consent.[76] Their main characteristic, as we shall see below, is judging, or discriminating against others[77] – etymologically, *diaballein* (the root verb for *diabolos* or devil) means to slander, to throw over, to separate, to divide. In fact, people become 'diabolical' by acting in this fashion.[78] It seems that people, too, can become demonized and thus act against themselves as well as against others.[79] Indeed, in the tradition of the Egyptian desert, it is generally accepted that demons approach us in a form corresponding to our own inward state. Satan admits to Antony of Egypt in conversation:

> It is not I who trouble [the monks]. It is they who trouble themselves.[80]

Before examining some of the ways in which demons tempt us, one must note that such expressions as 'demon of despondency'[81] and 'demon of fornication'[82] indicate primarily *the aim* of the demonic assaults rather than any distinction between the spirits as such. It is only in this sense that each demon may be said to have a particular function or role to fulfill.[83]

Demons in the Desert

Whatever the predominance of demons in John Climacus, other ascetic sources, for instance the *Life of Antony*, reflect an even greater preoccupation with them. John approaches Evagrius, who regards 'demon' (*daimon*) and 'thought' (*logismos*) as almost interchangeable. Even in Evagrius, however, the former overrides the latter. Climacus tends to follow the Palestinian tradition

---

[72] 10.5 (845D).

[73] 10.13 (848C).

[74] 3.41 (672A). Cf. also Athanasius, *Life of Antony* 31 (PG26.889BC).

[75] *Mac. Hom.* 26, 9 (209).

[76] 23.4 (976D), 8 (997B) and 11 (997C).

[77] 4.16 (685AB).

[78] 8.20 (832A).

[79] 27.13 (1097D).

[80] Athanasius, *Life of Antony* 41 (PG26.904AB) and 42 (905A). John Climacus himself makes this point in 22.25 (969B) and 26.15 (1017C).

[81] 13.5 (860B).

[82] 15.20 (884A). In Evagrius, 'demons' are interchangeable with 'passions:' cf. *De octo vitiosis cogitationibus* (PG40.1272–6) and *Prakt.* 58 (636–8).

[83] 15.25 (885A).

in this regard. Like Barsanuphius, he is concerned not with apparitions but with the inward ascetic struggle. The demons are present, but they do not stand out. John's attention is drawn to the almost frightening inner scale and power of demonic activity, as well as to its vertiginous possibilities. He elaborates an intricate and subtle strategy to defend and immunize the violated human person. The demons are not mere figments enlisted to act as scapegoats, to impersonate warring elements with a psyche divided against itself. Nor are they, as some would have us believe,[84] purely psychological, that is, mere subjective states as in a phantasmagorian tale. They are represented as real forces, but functionally rather than in terms of monsters reminiscent of classical or medieval mythology.

It would be wrong to contend that texts such as the *Life of Saint Antony*, which to some extent 'over-dramatize' the demonic element, are simplistic in comparison with the more sophisticated St Paul or Isaac the Syrian. Both kinds of literature underline the extrinsic, alien, though not necessarily external, character of evil. The *Life of Antony* and the *History of the Monastics* liken demons to large dragons (cf. Rev. 12.3–9) or serpents. Dorotheus of Gaza not only calls the devil 'an enemy' but also describes him as *antikeimenos*[85] – quite literally, the one who 'stands in opposition' to us. In John, demons appear as hybrid, intrusive, but basically alien forces attempting to coerce people into acting against their true nature and to prevent them from attaining their higher spiritual aspirations. The same point is emphasized by Symeon the New Theologian, who says that the demons 'continually stand opposite us, facing us, even if they cannot be seen by us.'[86]

This extraneousness is a critical measure of the pristine, divinely created perfection of human nature. The most unnatural, indeed sub-human aspect, of human nature is deprivation of freedom and, in the end, death, as distinct from innate, punishable corruption, requiring human justification. Human beings as such are free agents, not separated from grace against their will. Yet they can be, and are being, assailed *from without* by demonic forces. This is the early Christian ascetic answer to Messalianism.[87] In this perspective, spiritual struggle for the ascetic is not a matter of the contortions of human nature. It is a confrontation with an enemy from without, who prevents us from living

---

[84] Cf. J. Stoffels, 'Die Angriffe der Dämonen auf den Einsiedler Antonios,' in *Theologie und Glaube* 2, 1910, 721–32 and 809–30, esp. 732. On rationalizing the influence of the demonic, cf. the study by C. Stewart, *Demons and the Devil: Moral Imagination in Modern Greek Culture*, Princeton, NJ: Princeton University Press, 1991, esp. 116–34. In particular reference to the Byzantine understanding of the demonic, cf. R. Greenfield, *Traditions of Belief in Late Byzantine Demonology*, Amsterdam: A. M. Hakkert, 1988.

[85] *Instr.* 2, 27 (188).

[86] *Cat.* 3 (308).

[87] Further on Messalianism, see C. Stewart, *Working the Earth of the Heart: the Messalian controversy in history, texts and language to AD 431*, Oxford: Clarendon Press, 1991.

according to our true, integrated nature in communion with and illumined by divine grace.

Snares of the Demons

The guiles adopted by the demons in order to tempt us are innumerable.[88] The assaults come from all sides in a most harrowing fashion.[89] Abba Isaiah and Barsanuphius agree that the demons never rest from assaulting us.[90] John, in similar terms, refers to the devil as having 'ten thousand heads.'[91] He exclaims in astonishment: 'I have been amazed at the diversity of evil.'[92] And elsewhere:

> 'My hair and my flesh quivered,' said Eliphaz (Job 4.15) when describing the malice of the demon.[93]

The struggle against demons is complicated and made more difficult because they can actually cause good.[94] So deceitful are they, that it is possible to conceive good thoughts, which are in reality demonic.[95] One may receive intimations of purity, which are in effect impure. The demons can feign virtues;[96] they can even be so transformed as to appear as spiritual beings (2 Cor. 11.14) and saintly people.[97] They endeavour to 'gain territory' in the soul by assuming the form of angels or martyrs, even by ostensibly offering us 'gifts.'[98] This is why the struggle against them requires the gift of discernment,[99] a fruit of the perfect,[100] of those who are experienced in the unseen warfare. However, although demons may appear as virtues, this is 'hypocrisy' on their part. After all, their aim is at all times 'the destruction of

---

[88] 15.52–3 (889D–92A), 55 (892B) and 67 (896A); 4.50 (708AB); 7.69 (816C); 8.24 (832CD); 13.5 (860BC); 26.ii, 14 (1061A) and 66 (1073CD).

[89] 21.27 (953CD).

[90] Abba Isaiah, *Logos* 21, 7 (127) and 23, 1 (142); Barsanuphius 196. Cf. also Symeon the New Theologian, *Cat.* 7 (72).

[91] 161.1 (924C).

[92] 4.86 (713D).

[93] 20.7 (945D). Cf. also Athanasius, *Life of Antony* 22 (PG26.876B); *Apophth.* Macarius 6 (PG65.264D–65A) and Theodore of Pherme 8 (189A); Mark the Monk, *De lege spir.* 167 (PG65.925B), 173 (925C) and *Ad Nic.* 11 (1048B) and Abba Isaiah, *Logos* 29, 8 (206).

[94] 26.ii,70 (1076A); 19.13 (940D). Cf. *Hist. Monachorum* 1, John of Lycopolis 32–4 (20–21) says that they can cause 'sympathy.'

[95] 26.ii,39 (1068BC); 8.24 (832CD).

[96] 26.56 (1029D–32A); 12.7 (856C).

[97] 3.42 (672A).

[98] 22.19 (968CD). For demons as angels, cf. also Evagrius, *De or.* 95 (PG79.1188CD) and *Apophth.* Nau 224 (1909, pp. 359–60), 310–12 (1912, p. 206).

[99] 26.ii,14 (1061B).

[100] 26.ii,17 (1076A); 3.42 (672A).

the soul.'[101] Even if one demon seems to contradict another,[102] in effect they are paving the way for each other and working mutually for the same destructive purpose.[103] The strategy of their fight is so well planned that they may also give the semblance of collaborating with our fellow human beings.[104]

At times, the ways in which the evil spirits will tempt us seem quite absurd. They play 'games' with us,[105] enacting a kind of mad *divertissement*. In the *First Greek Life of Pachomius*, the demons actually try to make Pachomius laugh.[106] According to the *Ladder*, their 'purpose' is to steal time from our prayer.[107] They seek to divert us from turning or looking towards God, to pilfer our thoughts.[108] The demons' methods vary according to the person against they are fighting. Their ways against a monk may differ from those applied to someone living in the world. Even within the monastic lifestyle, demons will discriminate in their manner of assault upon a hermit or a cenobite.[109]

This is perhaps a good reason why monks should not be judgemental of others. Judging others is in fact one of the demons' own favorite devices. If they cannot persuade a person to fall into sin, they will try to ensnare that person into passing judgement on others who have done so.[110] If that snare is kept off, they will try to inject a dose of vainglory, especially during contact with others. Their aim is to maintain conversation with us. This is qualified by an aside, typical of John, to the effect that:

> Perhaps it is better for you to be sprinkled with a few drops of vainglory, if only you can become a channel of profit for many.[111]

Another trick is flattery, which is said to be particularly perilous.[112] As with those judging others, one who flatters is 'a minister to the demons,' leading others into numerous passions.[113]

Pride, too, is described as 'a denial of God, an invention of the demons.' Elsewhere, it is defined as follows:

---

[101] 15.12 (881D) and 78 (901AB).

[102] 26.57 (1032A).

[103] 27.ii,15 (1109D).

[104] 21.16 (952B).

[105] 21.16 (1100A); 29.1 (1148); 14.7 (865A) and 7.49 (809D).

[106] *Vita Prima* 17–19 (11–13, 167–79). Cf. also Anonymous, *Peri Logismon* 3.

[107] 28.39 and 42 (1135CD).

[108] 4.80 (713B).

[109] 26.15 (1017C).

[110] 10.13 (848C).

[111] 12.4 (856B).

[112] 21.27 (953D); 4.86 (713D).

[113] 21.9 (949D). Demons often flatter us: cf. 26.6 (1013C).

[Pride is] the denial of God's assistance, the extolling of one's own exertions, demonic in character.[114]

John sums up the relationship between pride and demons:

A proud monk has no need of a demon; he has become a demon and an enemy unto himself![115]

Also, those who try to enforce their opinion on other people, whether rightly or wrongly, are said to possess 'the sickness of the devil.'[116] The demons are, of course, wicked. John describes wickedness as 'a demonic way of life,' 'a science, or rather a demonic deformity.'[117] A wicked person is 'a namesake and companion of the devil' or 'food for the demons.'[118]

Furthermore, since the body greatly affects the passions of the soul,[119] the demons want us to submit to carnal sin.[120] This will keep us steeped in mud, and enable them all the more to assail us. Curiously, one final variant of demonic subterfuge can even be piety:

One who had experience of this craftiness told me that the demon [of sensuality] very often hid himself completely ... and would suggest to the monk extreme piety.[121]

Though the reference here as elsewhere is to personal 'experience,'[122] it is not clear what is at stake,[123] unless it be stark hypocrisy, which, as is known, is the compliment vice pays to virtue.[124]

Struggling against Demons

No sin is attributed to the mere fact of being attacked by the demons. Indeed, we are called 'blessed' if we endure their attacks. What is considered wrong is to give cause to the demons for tempting us, whether through 'carelessness' or pride.[125] Just as there are a number of ways in which demons wage war against us, so there are many ways of defending ourselves against and confronting

---

[114] 21.1–2 (965BC). Cf. also Basil, *Sermo de renuntiatione saeculi* 10 (PG31.648B) and Evagrius, *Prakt.* 14 (532–4).

[115] 22.25 (969B).

[116] 4.41 (705A).

[117] 24.17 (981C) and 19 (981B).

[118] 24.18 (981D) and 21 (948A).

[119] See, for example, 7.49 (809D).

[120] 15.32 (888B).

[121] 15.64 (893C). Cf. similar words in Abba Isaiah, *Logos* 16, 8–9 (97) and Isaac the Syrian, *Mystic Treatises* (182).

[122] Cf. also 25.12 (992).

[123] 26.40 (1025C).

[124] 8.11 (829C); 15.12 (881CD).

[125] 26.4 (1013B).

them, at times using their own tactics. John describes a wise elder, who, 'by divine inspiration, contrived to conquer the guile of the spirits by a pious ruse.'[126] The aim is not merely 'to wrestle' with them (*palaiein*), not merely to engage in combat, but to take the initiative in driving them away, to open fire and 'declare war' on them (*polemein*).[127] Symeon the New Theologian's explanation is particularly pointed in this regard:

> It is one thing to resist and fight one's enemies and another thing to completely defeat and subdue them, putting them to death; for the first belongs to athletes and those brave in *askesis*, but the second belongs rather to the dispassionate and perfect.[128]

The battle against the demons is an entire science. Abba Arsenius refers to the 'alphabet' of this science. It must be learned by experience, starting from a young age. For, as John admits, 'to see an elderly person going to a children's school is a great disgrace.'[129] If we have been trained well enough in this science, we will be able to mock the demons.[130] At any rate, we should be just as brazen and ruthless in our counterattack as those who attack us. To neglect the fight is to be 'shallow.' It is to remain on the surface and be turned into 'tools of the demons.'[131] The demons do not strike at random; in their shrewdness, they aim directly at our weak spots. That is precisely where the battle must be given.[132] We should parry 'where we are fought,' 'deftly taking the demons by surprise,'[133] a matter which demands discernment.[134]

It is natural to turn one's very passions against the demons;[135] the monk is aroused in order to enter the wilderness and fight the demons dwelling there.[136] The notion of the wilderness, the desert as a dwelling-place of demons, is commonplace in ascetic literature, going back to Leviticus 16.22. The retreat into the desert is not a negative gesture, a form of escapism, but a positive counteraction against demonic forces in their 'outer darkness' (cf. Mt. 8.12). The demons attempt in every way to drive the monk 'back into the city.'[137] Of

---

[126] 25.23 (993C). Cf. also *Apophth.* Theodore of Enaton 2 (PG65.196C–97A).

[127] 26.ii,24 (1064B).

[128] *TGP* 1.97 (69).

[129] 26.14 (1017A) and 48 (1029AB). For Arsenius, cf. *Apophth.* Arsenius 6 (PG65.89A).

[130] 14.10 (865C); 25.23 (993C).

[131] 26.ii,17 (1061D).

[132] 15.42 (889A). Cf. also Basil, *Reg. Fus. Tract.* 75 (PG31.1136A) and *Apophth.* Matoes 4 (PG65.289D).

[133] 25.12 (992C). Cf. Isaac the Syrian, *Mystic Treatises* (192).

[134] 15.62 (893B).

[135] 26.ii,41 (1068C).

[136] 15.60 (893A) and 7.71 (816C). Cf. also Athanasius, *Life of Antony* 13 (PG26.861C) and 41 (904AB); Palladius, *Hist. Laus.* 19 (ed. Butler, 50) and Cyril of Scythopolis, *Life of Sabas* 2,7 (110, 27–111, 2). On the significance of the desert, see B. Lane, *The Solace of Fierce Landscapes.*

[137] 15.60 (893A); 7.71 (816C) and 21.16 (925B).

course, both the desert and the city lie especially within. And so, in that very confrontation, there lies the promise of encountering God. It is a promise given in the tormenting trial of strength between good and evil. This is a struggle in which God participates[138] and in which, as John says, the demons try 'to dash [their victim's] foot against the stone' (Ps. 91.11 and Mt. 4.6).[139] In the end, the monk turns into a martyr and 'confessor.'[140]

While there are no recipes or patent stimulants for pursuing the spiritual warfare, there are ways for sustaining it. The *Macarian Homilies*, for instance, speak of prayer, which 'burns the demons like fire melting wax.'[141] And John sees the monk standing 'with feeling of heart before God in prayer; then, none of the ... demons can make sport of him.'[142] Above all, the demons are disabled by humility, which can turn even demons into angels.[143] John steers away from the question as to whether the demons might actually be saved, a matter that Gregory of Nyssa seriously considered.[144] But then, in the *Ladder*, Climacus is overwhelmingly concerned with *human* salvation.

One thing that demons cannot withstand or falsify is humility.[145] In other respects, they not only threaten us during a conflict of opposing forces, but they even have a way of, as it were, participating distortedly in the holy and virtuous. They involve themselves intimately in our very struggle. One may, through *ascesis*, wear down the body in order to prevent the demons from settling comfortably in it.[146] Yet they will then try to take advantage of the struggle itself. The struggle, therefore, must not remain self-contained or self-sufficient. It must neither occur in isolation from one's total commitment to God nor exceed one's limited strength.[147] Sense of proportion, ingenuity and 'logic' should always be exercised. On reaching dispassion, one may outfool the demons. One may, as we shall see, have no passions at all, while at the same

---

[138] Cf. *Apophth.* Moses 1 (PG65.281BC). Cf. also Athanasius, *Life of Antony* (PG 6.904B–05C); Ps. Athanasius, *Doctrina ad monachos* (PG28.1425A) and *Mac. Hom.* 3, 6 (24–5).

[139] 5.5 (776C).

[140] 4.25 (696A). For the monk–martyr theme, cf. also 4.6 (680BC) and 37 (704D). Cf. also M. Viller, 'Martyre et perfection,' *RAM* 6 (1925), 2–25; A. Phytrakis, '*Martyrion kai monachikos vios,*' *Theologia* 19 (Athens, 1941–48), 301–29; and especially E. Malone, *The Monk and the Martyr. The Monk as Successor of the Martyr*, Washington: 1950.

[141] *Mac. Hom.* 43, 3 (268–87). Climacus himself states that he can offer no recipes: cf. 26.ii,55 (1072CD).

[142] 18.4 and 3 (937BC).

[143] 25.60 (1001BC) and 43 (997D–1001A). Cf. also *Apophth.* Theodora 6 (PG65.204AB) and Nau 298 (1912, p. 204).

[144] *Or. Cat.* 26 (PG45.68A–69C).

[145] 25.16 (993A). Cf. 23.3 (976D); 22.19 (968CD) and 22 (969AB).

[146] 26.iii,8 (1085B).

[147] 26.ii,8 (1060BC). Cf. also Ps. Athanasius *De virg.* 8 (PG28.261AB); Evagrius, *Prakt.* 40 (592); *Apophth.* Poemen 129 (PG65.353D); Pachomius *Vita Prima* 126 (80, 228) and Abba Isaiah, *Logos* 4, 4 (19).

time pretending to be entirely subject to them. The struggle is an extraordinarily multiform, versatile and intricate process. It provides no security at any point of its stages and persists uninterrupted to the end of this life.[148]

Indirect Warfare

In describing the struggle against the demons, Barsanuphius is ingenious and resourceful:

> Do not argue with them; for, this is what they want and they will never stop.[149]

John's advice is likewise to fight demons indirectly, disregarding them and doing the exact opposite of what they intimate.[150] This is achieved by feeding one's mind with good thoughts each time that they sow evil ones.[151] This does not contrast with Evagrius' exhortation 'to stand there firmly' and not 'to flee or to shun such conflicts.'[152] John is referring to the manner of outflanking the demons while actually facing their battle. It could prove suicidal to attempt to fight them directly,[153] or even to attempt 'to overthrow them with refutations and pleadings.'[154] Our attitude towards them should be one of 'mindfulness of evil.'

> Have remembrance of wrongs and spite against the demons.[155]

One must direct one's energy elsewhere, namely toward practicing the virtues, while at the same time being firmly conscious of the facing enemy. All of these strategic propositions: that one should not be involved with the demons but rather mind one's own business,[156] that one should fight them positively yet indirectly,[157] and that one should not underestimate the force of the demons,[158] are variously emphasized in the *Sayings of the Desert Fathers*.

---

[148] 4.80 (713B). Cf. also *Apophth.* Abraham 1 (PG65.129D–32B); Antony 4 (77A); Nau 226 (1909, pp. 369–70) and *Vita Prima* of Pachomius, 22 (14, 169).

[149] Barsanuphius 91.

[150] 7.49 (812A) and 14.10 (865C).

[151] 4.8 (680D). Cf. also *Apophth.* Evagrius 1 (PG65.173AC) and Nau 241 (1909, p. 363) and Isaac the Syrian, *Mystic Treatises* (61).

[152] *Prakt.* 28 (564).

[153] 4.30 (700B). Cf. also Mark the Monk, *De lege spir.* 109 (PG65.917D).

[154] 16.20 (884A). Cf. also Barsanuphius 558.

[155] 9.8 (814C). Cf. also 3.40 (672A).

[156] Cf. *Apophth.* Poemen 20 (PG65.328A).

[157] Cf. *Apophth.* Poemen 111 (349C) and Serapion 3 (416CD).

[158] Cf. *Apophth.* Syncletica 18 (428A).

Positive View of Demons

Without temptation, the monk could never attempt to reach perfection. This leads John to admit that one should thank the Lord for the trials that one undergoes.[159] Abba Antony said: 'Whoever has not experienced temptation cannot enter the kingdom of heaven.' And he repeated it with conviction: 'Without temptations, no one can be saved.'[160] Temptations thereby acquire a positive quality. They become occasions for gratitude. Origen early stated:

Let us give thanks for the goods revealed to us through temptations.[161]

And, much later, Symeon the New Theologian asserted:

Learn to love temptations as if they are to be the cause of all good for you.[162]

Demons have no power by themselves. They do what they do because God allows them to do so. In this sense,[163] they are to be seen as instruments, used by God for our salvation. Ultimately, they are a cause of our crowns: the more there are of them, the more abundant the crowns.[164] Without sorrow, there can be no salvation: without our demons, we would lose our angels too. Thus the monks in the Alexandrian Prison, in a mood of well-nigh self-torture, even pray for further temptation and affliction:

And some prayed to become possessed by devils; others begged the Lord that they might fall into epilepsy; some wished to lose their eyes and present a pitiful spectacle; others, to become paralyzed.[165]

Everything, to the cruelest snare of the devil, transforms into a providential part of God's final design:

---

[159] 4.25 (696A).

[160] *Apophth.* Antony 5 (PG65.77A). Cf. also John the Dwarf 13 (208BC); Athanasius, *Life of Saint Antony* 56 (PG26.952A); Mark the Monk, *De his.* 8 (PG65.932A); Abba Zosimas, *Alloquia* 9 (PG78.1692B; Cyril of Scythopolis, *Life of Theodosios* (239, 24–5); John Moschos, *Pratum* 14 (2861C) and Abba Isaac the Syrian, *Mystic Treatises* (50 and 188).

[161] *De or.* 29, 17 (391, 160–61).

[162] *Cat.* 2 (242).

[163] 26.ii,44 (1069AB).

[164] 26.ii,42 (1069A) and 14 (1061AB). It is also implied in 22.10 (968A). Anastasius the Sinaite speaks of demons as 'ministers' (*leitourgoi*) of God; cf. *Quaestiones* 31 (PG89.568D); and Isaac the Syrian says that a merciful heart prays for demons, too: cf. *Mystic Treatises* (507–08). In 28.3 (1192C), Climacus says that those who throw us out of the king's palace are his 'servants' and 'ministers' (*leitourgoi*). These could be the angels but they could also be the demons, who 'bind us' and 'exile us from God's face.'

[165] 5.5 (776A). Cf. also Athanasius, *Life of Antony* 22 (PG26.876A), where it is stated that demons were originally created good.

Wonderful sight – a demon curing a demon. Yet perhaps this is the work not of demons but of divine providence.[166]

Passions

Classification of Passions

Until the beginning of the twentieth century, it was generally assumed that the first attempt in Christian ascetic literature to classify passions or, more specifically, to define them as being eight in number, belonged to Evagrius of Pontus. Scholars further attributed the origin of the procedure to Stoic philosophy.[167] This, however, is only partially correct. The origins of the Evagrian scheme in fact go back to Origen, some one hundred and fifty years earlier – though Origen does not as clearly refer to the passions as being eight in number, neither less nor more. Moreover, the original evidence in the Christian context goes back to the New Testament – though certainly the New Testament nowhere adopts a precise classification in the way that Evagrius does. Admittedly, Origen was not consistent in his view of the matter; nor did he adhere to any strict ordering of the passions. Moreover, there were other contemporaneous attempts in ascetic circles to classify vices.[168] However, Evagrius is most probably responsible for the systematic ordering that has come down to us. There is no doubt that John's view, in this regard, is largely influenced by Evagrius.[169]

It is not at first sight clear how to relate John's list of fourteen passions to the usual list of the eight passions or 'evil thoughts' found in Evagrius:

	Climacus	**Evagrius**
Step:	8. anger	4. anger
	9. malice	
	10. slander	
	11. loquacity	
	12. falsehood	

---

[166] 9.6 (841B). Cf. also Chrysostom, *Ad Stagirium ascetam a daemonio vexatum* 1,4 (PG47.433).

[167] Cf. Hausherr, 'Huit péchés,' 164–75. One passage in the *Ladder* may, in fact, recall two Stoic vices, namely *koiliomania* and *oxycholia*: cf. 4.118 (725B).

[168] Cf. *Life of Saint Synkletike*, especially ch. 22–70 (PG28.1500B–28C). While the *Life* was always widely read in the East, but the list of 'thoughts' (*logismoi*) was not generally accepted.

[169] Cf. for example, Ps. Nilus, *De malignis cogitationibus* (PG79.1200D–33A) and Evagrius, *De octo vitiosis cogitationibus* (PG40.1272A–76B). Völker proves this: cf. *Scala Paradisi*, esp. 69–153, where Völker offers a detailed study of the eight passions.

13. despondency	5. despondency
14. gluttony	1. gluttony
15. lust	2. lust
16. avarice	3. avarice
17. insensitivity	
18. sleep	
20. fear	
21. vainglory	6. vainglory
22. pride[170]	7. pride
	8. dejection[171]

Despite correspondences and contrasts, the two lists are apparently quite different. Nevertheless, this is largely because John normally implies a link between the dependent passions and the primary seven passions:

The unholy vices … by their nature beget (and stifle) one another.[172]

In fact, his intention in using any list at all is primarily to illustrate this interdependence.[173]

Climacus' list, therefore, in Steps 8 to 23, is almost the same as Evagrius' in both content and order. The only exception is that 'dejection' is not included and the two vices 'anger' and 'despondency' are moved closer to the top of the list. In this way, John is placing the passions of the soul's incensive aspect before those of the appetitive. The resulting comparative order would read something like this:

Climacus   **Evagrius**

anger   anger

---

[170] See titles of Steps 8–23, omitting Step 19. Elsewhere Climacus speaks of twelve passions [cf. 22.6 (965CD)], but he is quoting Mark the Monk [cf. *De lege spir.* 136 (PG65.921C)]: read 'twelve' for 'eleven.'

[171] For Evagrius' list, cf. *De octo vit. cogit.* 1 (PG40.1272A) and *Prakt.* 6 (506–08). It is from Evagrius that Cassian formed his list of eight primary vices: *gastrimargia, fornicatio, filargyria (avaritia), ira, tristitia, acedia, cenodoxia,* and *superbia* [cf. *Inst.* 5, 1 (190)]. The only difference is that *ira* and *tristitia* are in reverse order from that of Evagrius. Cf. also *Conf.* 5, 2–3 and 25 (190 and 215–16), where Cassian claims they are mentioned in the Scriptures, too.

[172] 9.1 (841A).

[173] 22.6 (965CD), 8 (965D) and 9.1 (840D–41A). Thus: anger (Step 8) leads to malice (Step 9) [9.1 and 2 (841A)]; malice (9) leads to slander (10) [10.1 (849B)]; slander (10) leads to loquacity (11) [11.1 (852A)]; loquacity (11) leads to (i) falsehood (12) [12.1 (853D)]; and (ii) despondency (13) [13.1 (857D)]; despondency (13) leads to lust (15) [27.ii,15 (1109D)]; gluttony (14) leads to (i) lust (15) and (ii) insensitivity (17) [14.32 (869D) and 16.24 (929B)]; insensitivity (or 'unbelief') (17) and vainglory (21) lead to fear (20) [20.1 (945B)]; vainglory (21) leads to pride (22) [21.1 and 2 (949AB)]; pride (22) leads to blasphemy (23) [23.1 (976B)].

despondency	despondency
gluttony	gluttony
lust	lust
avarice	avarice
	[dejection]
vainglory	vainglory
pride	pride

The fact that Evagrius calls passions 'evil thoughts' derives from the Gospels, where sins are said to originate in thoughts (cf. Mt. 15.19). John's differentiation between 'pride' and 'vainglory' may indicate that he did not attach too much importance to classifications in general. More especially, it shows that he was not influenced deeply by the list of seven passions as formulated by Gregory the Great, although the latter was not the first to unite 'pride' and 'vainglory' under the one category, even if John thought that he was.[174] In any case, John himself does not refer to Gregory the *Dialogos* but rather to Gregory the *Theologos*. However, such an error may be due to the fact that his treatment of classification is avowed second-hand, attributed by him to 'other monks' whom he describes as 'men most holy, dispassionate,' and 'blessed.'[175]

The order in the Evagrian list also has an intrinsic logic, in accordance with a graduated development of spiritual life:

(a) the beginner's stage is marked by the cruder and more materialistic passions, namely gluttony, lust and avarice;
(b) the middle stage is identified by more inward passions, namely dejection, anger and despondency;
(c) the advanced, or contemplative, stage is recognized by the more subtle and 'spiritual' vices of vainglory and pride.

There is, however, no such equivalent order in the *Ladder*, where the choice seems more random. Evagrius' pattern reflects the threefold division of the soul into the appetitive (*epithymitikon*), incensive (*thymikon*) and intelligent (*logikon*) parts, a division also adopted by Climacus in one passage.[176] Yet,

---

[174] Cf. Hausherr, 'Huit péchés,' 174–5. Cf. also 21.1 (949A), and Ware, *Introduction*, 64 n. 246. Gregory the Great's list is found in his *Moralia* 31, 87 (PL76.621); his 'seven deadly sins' are especially familiar and formative in the Middle Ages. On the connection between Gregory the Great and the monastery on Mt Sinai, recorded in Anastasius (ed. Nau), *Récits* no. xxxix, cf. also, Chitty, *Desert*, 170.

[175] 26.29 (1021CD).

[176] Cf. *Shep.* 15 (1172D): this is only an isolated instance. In a second list by Climacus, given in the text above, we have already seen how Climacus places the *thymikon* before the *epithymitikon*.

characteristically, Climacus generally prefers not to follow any definite scheme. For him, sin is in the end unclassifiable since, by its very nature, it is disordered, formless, amorphous:

> And these dispassionate people kindly instructed me saying: 'The irrational passions have no order or reason, but they have every sort of disorder and chaos.'[177]

He is clearly familiar with the Evagrian scheme of the eight passions.[178] Like Evagrius, he sometimes distinguishes between the principal three and the last five, which spring from the first.[179] On one occasion, he even expresses a preference for the sevenfold pattern – allegedly derived from Gregory the Theologian, at least according to John – which juxtaposes vainglory and pride:

> And so, they say that there are eight primary and capital thoughts of evil.
> But Gregory the Theologian and other teachers have spelled out that there
> are seven; and I am strongly inclined to agree with them. For which person,
> who has conquered vainglory, possesses pride within?[180]

Still, in practice John differs from the Gregorian pattern and treats 'vainglory' and 'pride' separately, in two distinct steps, even if the two are interdependent.[181] The Evagrian 'dejection' (*lype*) is also commonly omitted from the list, perhaps because it is considered, as with Gregory, to be identical with 'despondency' (*akedia*), but it is not altogether ignored.[182] Similarly, John

---

Such a threefold division, however, while frequent in an author like Maximus the Confessor – who was more deeply influenced by Evagrius – is not common in the *Ladder*. It was first formulated by Plato in his *Republic* 4, 434d–41c and was used widely by the Fathers: cf. for example, Evagrius, *Prakt.* 86 (676) and 89 (680–88), who says that he borrowed it from Greg. Naz.: cf. *Poems* 2, i. 47 (PG37:1381A–84A). Nevertheless, Evagrius does not actually say where in Gregory the Theologian he found it, and it may have originated in oral teaching. The vices are explicitly linked with the three aspects of the soul in Cassian, *Conf.* 24, 15 (186–7), who gives a list of eighteen vices in all, including all eight of the Evagrian list. Couilleau conflates Climacus' and Cassian's lists, but, although the argument is sound, the correspondence is by no means exact; cf. 'Saint Jean Climaque,' *DS* 8, 377.

[177] 28.29 (1021CD) and 40 (1025C).

[178] 26.29 (1021CD); 13.8 (860C) and 16.24 (929B).

[179] 16.24 (929BC); 26.29 (1021CD) and 2 (1013AB). For a different distinction, cf. 27.ii,9 (1109A).

[180] 21.1 (948D–49A).

[181] Cf. Steps 21 and 22 (948D–72B). Although it is true that Climacus deals very briefly with 'vainglory,' yet the reason for this does not lie in the fact that he believes it to be identical with 'pride,' but because it does not lend itself to easy analysis: cf. 21.1 (948D–49A). The similarity in number, then, between Climacus' and Gregory's list on occasions is by no means enough to prove any direct influence.

[182] Cf. 27.ii,22 (1112C), where it is included.

disregards Gregory's 'envy' and, in contrast with Gregory, substitutes 'pride' for it.[183]

One might conclude that, although John draws upon earlier authorities for his classification of the passions, he does not adhere strictly to any single source, showing once again the way in which he is able to combine tradition and personal insight in the *Ladder*.

Stages of Temptation Leading to Passion

Knowledge of the passions is gained either through experiencing them personally as a sinner or else through the gift of discernment.[184] We cannot conquer them 'immediately,' says John, but only gradually. It entails a struggle of a lifetime[185] – a continual struggle against 'a sea of thoughts.'[186]

The *Ladder* contains various descriptions of the stages followed by the vices, but, as always, John's account lacks any accurate system.[187] This lack does not invalidate his understanding of the matter. Rather, it serves to illustrate that there is no set course in which the demons tempt us. Although John, at least superficially, seems to be stricter than the more systematic Evagrius, he is in fact more lenient about the limitations, the weaknesses, as well as the unpredictabilities of human nature.[188] Neither does he insist on any clear distinction between cause and effect in regard to passions:

> Some say that it is from thoughts that passions invade the body. Others affirm that it is from bodily senses that evil thoughts are born.[189]

Elsewhere, however, John offers a kind of structural order in the process of spiritual warfare:

1 assault
2 converse
3 consent
4 captivity

---

[183] Cf. 29.7–13 (1149AB): here, Climacus only differs from the Evagrian scheme in his omission of 'dejection' and in his inversion of the positions for 'despondency' and 'anger;' hence the precedence given to 'despondency.'

[184] 27.1 (1096CD).

[185] 20.7 (945C) and 26.iii,47 (1089C).

[186] 14.32 (869A).

[187] Some fundamental patterns are found in 26.66 (1033B) and 15.83 (901C–04B). The clearest pattern is in 15.73 (896C–97C), which will be discussed in detail below.

[188] Cf. 14.8 (865C).

[189] 15.74 (987C) and 75 (897D). For similar notions, cf. Evagrius, *Prakt.* 37 (584); Mark the Monk, *De lege spir.* 81 (PG65.928B); Thalassius, *Cent.* 3,5 (PG91.144BC) and Greg. of Sinai, *Chapt.* 74 (41).

5 struggle
6 passion.[190]

These are technical terms in early ascetic theology, and they require closer examination.

Assault (prosbolē)

This marks the first stage. It signifies the initial presence within us of some alien impulse intervening into consciousness from outside by the will of the adversary.[191] John defines it as:

> A simple conception, or an image of something encountered for the first time, which has entered the heart.[192]

Abba Poemen said:

> You cannot prevent thoughts from arising, but you can resist them.[193]

Sinful thoughts, though unnatural, are unavoidable.[194] They are sown in the heart by the demons.[195] They should be checked and driven away immediately[196] (cf. 2 Cor. 10.5), whether they seem important or not.[197] Abba Silvanus explained how he attained sanctity:

> I have never let a thought that would bring the anger of God upon me enter my heart.[198]

---

[190] 15.73 (897C–97A). A similar, though not as clear, pattern is found in 27.ii,8 (1108C–09A).

[191] Cf. Athanasius, *Life of Antony* 23 (PG26.877A); Ps. Athanasius, *De virg.* 23 (PG28.280A) and *Vita Sanctae Synkleticae* 88; *Apophth.* Nau 184 (1908, pp. 271–2); Cassian, *Conf.* 7, 16 (259–60), and *Inst.* 4, 9 (132). Cf. also Lossky, *Mystical Theology*, 130.

[192] 15.73 (896D). Cf. Evagrius, *De or.* 55–6 (PG79.1177D–80A), where Evagrius speaks of *psila noemata*. Mark the Monk differs from Climacus in that his 'assault' is not an 'image' but is defined as *aneidolon kinema kardias* ('an imageless motion of the heart'): cf. *De lege spir.* 141 (PG65.921D).

[193] *Apophth.* Poemen 28 (PG65.329AB). Cf. also *Apophth.* Nau 184 (1908, pp. 271–2) and Anonymous, *Peri Logismon* 18.

[194] 25.21 (993B), 32 (996B) and 51 (1000C); 4.27 (696D–97A) and 80 (713B); 7.20 (805A); 10.5 (845D) and 18.3 (937BC).

[195] 21.16 (952B); 15.82 (901C); 10.5 (845D); 4.44 (705BC); 23.4 (976D); 26.75 (1036A) and 55 (1029D). Cf. *Apophth.* Poemen 21 (PG65.328A) and 93 (344C–45A).

[196] 12.4 (864D) and 15.4 (881A). Cf. *Apophth.* Sisoes 22 (PG65.400C) and later, Symeon the New Theologian, *Cat.* 3 (301).

[197] 25.53 (1000D); 1.32 (637D); 26.69 (1033C); *Shep.* 60 (1189CD); 26.ii,46 (1069C) and 5.14 (780A).

[198] *Apophth.* Silvanus 6 (PG65.409D). Cf. also Cyril of Scythopolis, *Life of Euthymios*, 6 (14, 16–17).

Coming from the devil and imposed upon us from outside, assault is not equivalent to sinful action. It is 'guiltless' (*anamartetos*),[199] since only the surface of the heart is affected.[200] Nevertheless, although evil thoughts are inspired by the demons, it is essential to set a clear line of demarcation between the assault and the thought (*logismos*), for which we are clearly responsible, if we give assent. One should take hold of and question each *logismos*.[201] If one can cut off the temptation at this stage, from the very start, one could be entirely rid of it:

> Therefore, one who regards the first assault dispassionately cuts off at a single blow all the rest, which follow.[202]

Converse (synduasmos)

John distinguishes this from 'assault' and clearly stresses the moral responsibility involved at this stage. He does, however, admit that it is not as serious as 'consent.' It is a flirting familiarity or conversation, an entertaining of the thought with feelings of passion or even dispassion, but it nonetheless stops short of collusion. The distinction between 'converse' and the next stage of 'consent' is somewhat similar to that made by John on one occasion between error (*sphallō*) and fall (*piptō*).[203] Nevertheless, 'converse' does not even imply the gravity of error. The *nous* is subject to evil thoughts, which will try to drag it into familiarity because, after the Fall, it is 'like a dog sniffing around the meat, or loving the filth.'[204] Yet this 'friendship' should be cut short. Abba Poemen says:

> Take care not to speak; but if you do speak, cut the conversation short.[205]

Consent (synkatabasis)

This stage indicates a further and crucial step on the path to evil. No longer does one merely harbor temptation as a possibility, whether remote or proximate. Now one definitely gives approval and sanction to temptation. In Stoic sources, this denotes the assent that the mind gives to its perceptions. Yet

---

[199] 15.73 (897A).

[200] 26.ii,69 (1073D–76A).

[201] Cf. 14.32 (869Bf). At the end of each step, Climacus poses questions to the passion he has dealt with.

[202] 15.73 (897A).

[203] 15.40 (889A). 'Converse' is a dangerous state, almost tantamount to sin, in Symeon the New Theologian, *Cat.* 2 (256) and 5 (378).

[204] 1.17 (636B).

[205] *Apophth.* Poemen 34 (PG65.332AB). Barsanuphius actually adopts the word 'to cut:' cf. 432.

while the Stoics employed the word in an epistemological sense, for John the implications are moral. Consent signifies an act of turning towards the evil thought. It actually initiates sin, depending on one's condition in spiritual life.[206] Elsewhere, John almost identifies consent with sin when he speaks of its opposite, namely purity, as 'the thought that gives no consent' (*asynkatabetos logismos*).[207] Evagrius writes:

> The sin that a monk has particularly to watch out for is that of giving mental consent to some forbidden pleasure.[208]

Captivity (aichmalōsia)

This is one of the final, 'concluding' stages. The point here is that, because of past voluntary 'consent,' one's free will is now impaired and undermined. The result is that one is now *forced* to consent involuntarily. Climacus calls this 'a forcible and involuntary rape of the heart.' The heart is 'carried away,'[209] though not irrevocably. For there is still a further stage, during which we continue to struggle. Some passions, however, commence at this stage, leading straight into captivity.[210]

Struggle (palē)

In this stage of 'struggle,' one falls prey to the demons only through one's free will (cf. Prov. 11.15). This, too, however, depends on one's inclination and spiritual condition. It can become 'an occasion of either crowns or of punishments.'[211] Indeed, as the *Sayings of the Desert Fathers* state:

> Through our thoughts we can be shipwrecked, and through our thoughts we can be crowned.[212]

---

[206] 15.73 (897A).

[207] 15.4 (881A).

[208] *Prakt.* 75 (662). There exists an extensive ascetic literature that refers to 'consent:' cf. *Apophth.* Isidore the Priest 3 (PG65.236B); Nau 169 (1908, p. 55) and 360 (1913, p. 137); *Mac. Hom.* 15, 28 (143); *Hist. Monachorum* 1, John of Lycopolis 34–5 (21–2); Mark the Monk, *De lege spir.* 142 (PG65.921D–24A); Barsanuphius 258 and 432; and Cyril of Scythopolis, *Life of Euthymios* 24, (37, 1–3).

[209] 15.73 (896D).

[210] Cf. for example, 14.32 (869D). For 'captivity,' see also *Hist. Monachorum* 1, John of Lycopolis 54 (31); Abba Zosimas, *Alloquia* (PG78.189B); Dorotheus, *Instr.* 16, 172 (470). Diadochus, *Cent.* 82 (140–42), who clearly distinguishes 'captivity' from the next step of 'struggle.'

[211] 15.73 (897A).

[212] *Apophth.* Nau 218 (1909, p. 358).

Passion (pathos)

Pathos is the ultimate fall from which one is rescued in repentance, or for which one is punished:

> But passion is unequivocally condemned in every case, and demands either corresponding repentance or future punishment.[213]

Although *pathos* is not an act of sin, a specific 'fall,' it is a state resulting from many specific acts of consent and falls.

For Aristotle – and with Theodoret in his wake – passions have an ethically neutral character, since they appear apart from our will.[214] By contrast, the Stoic philosophers – and to a certain degree, Clement of Alexandria and Gregory of Nyssa – saw passions as intrinsically evil, as excessive and 'illogical' drives. This accounts for the need to eliminate them.[215] In the New Testament, the notion of *pathos* occurs only in Paul's writings, where it is virtually identified with sinful desire (cf. Rom. 1.26, Col. 3.5 and 1 Thess. 4.5).[216]

It is important to analyse this concept of *pathos* because the meaning attached to it – whether Aristotelian or Stoic – will influence the consequent understanding of dispassion. For instance, if passion is sinful, then dispassion must have a merely negative connotation. If passion is not in essence sinful, then dispassion, too, acquires a more positive significance, implying the purification of passion rather than its elimination.

Passions, for John, are urges that are misdirected[217] (cf. Ps. 37.10). They are not evil in themselves since, as has been noted, they may even be used to fight other passions. This is why the passionate are to be encouraged.

All the dispassionate have progressed from passion to dispassion.[218]

---

[213] 15.73 (897B).

[214] Cf. *Nic. Eth.* 2, 4, 1105b–06a.

[215] Cf. Yannaras, *Metaphysike*, 130f, where Yannaras gives an historical account of the term *pathos* in classical philosophy and theology. For an example in Clement of Alexandria, cf. *Paedag.* 1, 9 (ed. *GCS*, 134). Nevertheless to view *pathos* as evil in itself is not the case in most Fathers, even in Evagrius: cf. John Eudes Bamberger, *The Praktikos*, Spencer, MA: Cistercian Publications, 1970, 19 n. 29.

[216] *TDNT* 5, 928.

[217] 26.ii,41 (1068CD); 26.41 (1028AB); 3.19 (665CD); 8.17 (829CD); 7.16 (816C) and 15.58 (892CD). Greg. Palamas, like Climacus, prefers to speak of the 'transferral' or 'transformation' (*metathesis*) of *pathos* rather than of its mortification (*nekrōsis*): cf. *Triads* 2, 19 and 3, 3, 15. See also K. Ware, 'The Way of the Ascetics: Negative or Affirmative?,' in Wimbush and Valantasis, *Asceticism*, 3–15.

[218] 28.30 (1133D). Cf. Greg. Nyssa, *De virg.* 9 (PG46.360B); Symeon the New Theologian, *TGP* 1.78 (63).

Furthermore, passions are closely linked with virtues, 'just as the so-called bindweed twines around a cypress tree.'[219] For this reason, we should merely redirect our inclinations towards God, or rather allow God to enter within us and direct our life.[220] Yet passions are not to be seen as existing on some separate, neutral ground. Passions are admittedly 'blind' drives, but they are that only in the sense of being disoriented. As is usual with him, Climacus has here, too, no consistent view.[221] However, this must be assessed in a context peculiar to him and in the light of his spiritual experience.

Without mentioning Mark the Monk by name, John's process of temptation and evaluation of *pathos* reproduces virtually *in toto* what Mark proposes. Two of the terms/stages – 'captivity' and 'struggle' – are taken directly from Evagrius.[222] Otherwise, however, John closely follows Mark. He also adopts and further elaborates Mark's somewhat cryptic term *pararripismos*.[223] The point here is that even seemingly unnoticed, unrecognized (*agnōstōs*) movements may lead to sin. Thus it is possible for a person to commit fornication in the heart as a result of a mere glance (Mt. 5.28), or a touch of the hand, or by hearing a song, 'without even harbouring any notion or thought.' Yet Climacus is aware of the 'subtlety' of this condition.[224] The *Ladder* further employs two other terms belonging to Marcan terminology – *protonoia*[225] and *prolepsis*[226] – which makes plain his debt to his predecessor.

Struggle Against the Passions

John reassures his readers that, even after one has fallen into sin, one can still attain purity.[227] In fact, he personally prefers those who fall and subsequently weep:

---

[219] 26.ii,46 (1069C).

[220] Cf. 28.43 (1136D) and 26.70 (1033C).

[221] 26.41 (1028A). Cf. also 15.73 (897B). Note here that *pathos* is definitely condemned as sinful.

[222] Although both terms are also found in Mark the Monk, they do not have a specific technical sense. Therefore, part of this analysis also goes back to Evagrius: cf. Hausherr, 'L'erreur,' esp. 234–5. Cf. also Ware, *Mark the Hermit*, 299.

[223] *Ad. Nic.* 7 (PG65.1040B). Other patterns are found in *Mac. Hom.* 15.50 (155–6) and Greg. of Sinai, *Chapt.* 3 (63). In Ps. Athanasius, *Syntagma ad quemdam politicum* (PG28.1397D–400B), we find a pattern similar to that of Climacus: 'assault,' 'converse,' 'passion,' 'struggle,' 'consent' and '*energia*.' Nevertheless, this work is not Athanasian, but a *florilegium* of patristic ideas. Cf. Ps. John Damascene, *De octo spiritibus nequitiae* (PG95.85–97) [= Ps. Ephraim, *Opera* (Rome, 1746), 3, 423–35]. Philotheus of Sinai later takes up four of Climacus' stages: 'assault,' 'converse,' 'captivity' and 'passion,' but also speaks of 'struggle:' cf. *Chapters* 34–6 (285).

[224] 15.73 (897B).

[225] 26.76 (1036A). Cf. also, much later, Theoleptus of Philadelphia, *De abscondita operatione in Christo* (PG143.397AB).

[226] 4.68 (712A); 17.2 (932B); 26.7 (1013D), 28 (1021B) and 65 (1033B); 26.i,6 (1085A). Cf. Mark the Monk, *De lege spir.* 140 (PG65.921D).

[227] 15.66 (893D).

'I saw them, Father, and I was amazed; and I consider those fallen mourners more blessed than those who have not fallen and are not mourning over themselves; because as a result of their fall, they have risen by a sure resurrection.'[228]

Abba Sarmatas agrees:

I prefer a sinful person who knows that one has sinned and repents, to a person who has not sinned and considers oneself to be righteous.[229]

The Fall, for John, is a merely an opportunity for life-giving *penthos* and for true resurrection.

Diakrisis – discernment

Discernment occupies an important place in the thought of John Climacus. The individual chapter devoted to it (Step 26) is one of the longest in the *Ladder*. The notion of *diakrisis* is most significant in the ascetic tradition,[230] which distinguishes four major and varying senses:

(i)   discrimination – between two courses of action (Heb. 5.14);
(ii) insight into the thoughts of others;[231]
(iii) discernment of spirits (Lk. 9.55; 1 Cor. 12.10), which is by far the most frequently employed sense;[232] and
(iv) discretion.[233]

Climacus himself offers some form of sequence in Step 4 on obedience:

From *obedience* comes humility ... from *humility* comes discernment ... from *discernment* comes clairvoyance, and from *clairvoyance* comes *foreknowledge*.[234]

---

[228] 5.5 (776B).

[229] *Apophth.* Sarmatas 1 (PG65.413B).

[230] The importance of *diakrisis* is clearly seen in *Apophth.* Antony 7 (PG65.77AB); Cassian, *Conf.* 1, 23 (107–08) and 2, 4, pp. 115–16; Paulos Evergetinos, *Synagoge* 3, 31 (372) and Barsanuphius 173 and 60.

[231] 27.i,49 (116D). Cf. also Barsanuphius 572 and Greg. Palamas, *Triads*, 3, 1, 40.

[232] For this, there is an extensive ascetic tradition: cf. Athanasius, *Life of Antony* 22 (PG26.876B), 38 (900A), 44 (908A) and 88 (965B); Evagrius, *De or.* 95 (PG79.1188CD); *Apophth.* Poemen 52 (PG65.333CD); *Hist. Monachorum* 15, Pityrion 2–3 (111); Mark the Monk, *De lege spir.* 78 (PG65.913D–16A); Diadochus, *Cent.* 31 (101); Barsanuphius 98; Isaac the Syrian, *Mystic Treatises* (188); Symeon the New Theologian, *Cat.* 18 (292) and Niketas Stethatos, *Cent.* 1.13 (276).

[233] Cf. *Apophth.* Antony 8 (PG65.77B) and John the Dwarf 7 (205BC).

[234] 4.105 (717B).

Much has already been said about the gift of discernment. At this point, it has to be examined with special reference to the stages of spiritual warfare. Discernment is above all a gift (1 Cor. 12.10) of seeing, whereby the ascetic receives 'eyes to [fore]see'[235] and to see within. Its primary sense is that of insight, rather than foresight, although the two are connected. For John, the gift of discernment is a fruit of humility.[236] Lowering oneself before all creation,[237] the monastic is raised up by God (Lk. 14.11 and 18.14) to a point from which one can *see* the mysteries in an unspoken way (2 Cor. 12.2). The monastic becomes the prominent seer. Spiritual sight is thereupon transformed and illumined,[238] whereas normal sight is short and darkened[239] (cf. 2 Pet. 1.9). Such a person can perceive demonic deceits, and is therefore enabled even to see through others (*diorasis*)[240] and to foretell events (*pro-orasis*),[241] using the 'eye of the soul,' the *nous*.[242] For Diadochus, discernment is 'light,' and Barsanuphius observes: 'this is given by God as a guide for the monk.' John goes still further and claims that the monk has become the light whereby others can see[243] the will of God.[244] Yet it is up to us to provide the spiritual antennae capable of receiving the signal of the charismatic saint.[245]

'You shall seek wisdom among evil people, and you shall not find it' (Prov. 14.6).[246] Discernment presupposes many things[247] absent in a passionate person, who suffers from 'lack of vision.'[248] In the first place, a discerning person distinguishes between the sin committed and the sinner: the sin is condemned, but the sinner is loved.[249] Discernment is essential for

---

[235] *Shep.* 21 (1177A).

[236] 4.105 (717B).

[237] Cf. John the Sabbaite in 4.113 (724AB).

[238] 26.ii, end verse (1076B). Cf. also *Mac. Hom.* 4, 1 (25–7) and 6, 13 (65–6).

[239] 26.iii,38 (1088D).

[240] 27.ii,49 (116D). Cf. also Barsanuphius 572.

[241] *Shep.* 21 (1177A). A holy ascetic will often foretell his own death: cf. Athanasius, *Life of Antony* 89 (PG26.968A); Cyril of Scythopolis, *Life of Euthymios* 21 (34, 27–8) and *Life of Theodosios* (241, 4–6).

[242] 26.72 (1033C). Cf. also *Mac. Hom.* 1, 2 (1–2).

[243] 5.5 (772C). Cf. also 27.ii,30 (1113A). References are to Diadochus, *Cent.* 6 (87) and Barsanuphius 173.

[244] 27.ii,32 (113AB).

[245] 27.ii,49 (1116D).

[246] 15.75 (897D).

[247] 16.6 (924D); 24.2 (980D); 25, end verse (1004B) and 27.ii,6 (1108B). Cf. also Ps. Athanasius, *Sermo pro iis qui saeculo renuntiarunt* 6 (PG28.1416AB).

[248] 26.7 (1013D).

[249] 10.5 (845D). Cf. also Ps. Athanasius, *Life of Saint Syncletike* 64 (PG28.1525A) and the same words in *Apophth.* Syncletica 13 (PG65.425BC); Greg. Naz. *Or.* 1,4 (PG35.397B); Barsanuphius 453; Dorotheus, *Instr.* 16, 171 (466–8); John Moschus, *Pratum* 140 (3004B) and Isaac the Syrian, *Mystic Treatises* (239).

distinguishing between good and evil,[250] for ensuring that virtue is free from vice – not an unlikely blend in the mind of John.[251] One who has discernment will 'wisely' avoid the snares of the devil.[252] Yet discernment is unteachable. It is a gift, even if an acquired gift at times.[253] It is a pledge of wisdom, though it cannot be dispensed like a multipurpose medicine. One must personally know 'for whom, and in what manner, and when all these measures are to be applied'[254] in order to be able 'to examine and prescribe medicines which are suitable.'[255] In this way we learn when, how and to what extent to fight the passions.[256] Indeed, we recognize whether we should fight them at all, since indirect warfare or even flight from the scene of battle is at times more proper and prudent.

Discernment may also mean allowing God the time to act (Ps. 118.126), not rushing things before their right or ripe moment. We should not attempt too much too soon, presuming that we can climb the ladder of perfection in one leap.[257] This had earlier been stressed by Barsanuphius:

> We ought not to put our foot on the first step of the ladder, and immediately expect to set foot on the top rung.[258]

For John, 'there is a time for all things' (Eccl. 3.1),[259] and what seems lower on the scale may actually be higher when done at the proper time.[260] It is a duty of the spiritual elder to assist in discerning and seizing the 'proper time' (*kairos*) of each monk.[261] The demons, according to Gregory of Nyssa, attempt to steal this *kairos* from us.[262] However, as Anastasius of Sinai observes, we must hold onto it fast.[263]

To achieve discernment, one must have passed beyond the preliminary stage of spiritual life (cf. Heb. 5.14), or at least be in the intermediary stage.[264] Over and above this, it is the Holy Spirit who is always the Giver:

---

[250] *Shep.* 14 (1169C). Cf. also Greg. Nyssa, *De virg.* 11 (PG46.364D); *Apophth.* Syncletica 17 (PG65.428A); Cassian, *Inst.* 11, 4 (430) and Isaac the Syrian, *Mystic Treatises* (212).

[251] 26.37 (1025BC) and 27.ii,46 (1116C).

[252] 14.5 (864D) and 9 (865BC); 15.75 (897D).

[253] 8.30 (833CD).

[254] *Shep.* 29 (1180AB). Cf. also Evagrius, *Prakt.* 40 (592).

[255] *Shep.* 32 (1181C) and 55 (1189A).

[256] 26.ii,65 (1073C).

[257] 14.8 (865B); 4.30 (700AB).

[258] Barsanuphius 85. Cf. also Isidore of Pelusium, *Epist.* 1, 258 (PG78.337B).

[259] 26.59 (1032B) and 38 (1025C). The notion of *kairos* is also found in Evagrius, *Prakt.* 15 (536–8) and Cyril of Scythopolis, *Life of Euthymios* 4 (12, 21–5).

[260] 7.76 (816B).

[261] *Shep.* 54–5 (0089A).

[262] *De proposito secundum deum* (PG46.301A).

[263] *Oratio de sacra synaxi* (PG89.828B).

[264] 26.14 (1017B).

> Wisdom is given by God. ... For it is not for everyone to decide quickly
> and precisely on such fine points.[265]

The aim of this consideration is not to establish any spiritual élitism. Rather, it
is to stress that *diakrisis* is a divine gift at whatever stage in the spiritual
struggle it comes into force.

Apatheia – Dispassion

Preliminary Note on Insensitivity (Anaisthesia)

As has been pointed out already, *pathos* carries a double sense, both negative
and positive. Hence, also, *apatheia* may signify the elimination of passions as
well as their transformation into *eros*. Yet, even when *pathos* is understood
negatively, 'dispassion' is not normally identical with 'insensitivity,' nor does it
signify an absence of temptation.

The term *anaisthesia* (or, insensitivity) usually has a negative connotation in
the *Ladder*, often coupled with such terms as 'hardness,' 'forgetfulness of the
above,' 'despondency,' 'lack of soberness and discernment,' and 'hard-
heartedness.'[266] The entire seventeenth step is devoted to this concept of
insensitivity, and describes it as 'hard,' 'sharp-edged,' 'raging,' and 'foolish.'[267]
Nevertheless, in certain instances, it appears that a more positive meaning
prevails:

> Truly blessed is the one who has acquired perfect insensibility to every body
> and colour and beauty.[268]

On one occasion John even identifies the concept of insensitivity with the
content of dispassion:

> I am completely insensitive to everything of this kind, because I am wholly
> united with God, and always will be.[269]

Anaisthesia is approved by Evagrius, who speaks of it as 'absence of any sense
perception' rather than as 'insensitivity.'[270]

---

[265] *Shep.* 19 (1177A) and 26.ii,1 (1057A). Cf. also Cassian, *Inst.* 5, 32, 2 (232) and Barsanuphius
265.

[266] 4.83 (713C); 13.10 (860D–61A); 26.7 (1013CD) and 29 (1021C–24B) and 27.ii,8 (1108C–09A).

[267] Cf. especially 17.5 (933B). Cf. also Philo, *Vita Moysis* 1, 49.

[268] 15.5 (881A).

[269] 29.14 (1149C).

[270] *De or.* 120 (PG79.1193B). Cf. also Cassian, *Conf.* 9, 31 (66).

Nature and Gift of Dispassion (Apatheia)

In the *Ladder*, dispassion is not treated as the final stage of the ascetic process. Nor is it considered an end in itself or the ultimate stage in the spiritual life. There exist various stages beyond dispassion, which must be continually 'perfected' in the virtues. It could be seen as the beginning of the end; but even a beginning may fail. God too sometimes providentially allows failure, which will eventually lead to greater humility.[271] And within dispassion itself there are different grades:

> There is a dispassionate person, and there is one who is more dispassionate than the dispassionate.[272]

Perfection is never static. It is a continuing process:

> So this is the perfect, but still unfinished, perfection of the perfect.[273]

Gregory of Nyssa expresses the same idea, and may well provide John's source on this concept:

> One is always being perfected, never reaching the end of perfection.[274]

Dispassion, in its negative significance, is linked to 'purification' and the 'washing away of sin.'[275] It is aided by other ascetic efforts such as fasting, but also *penthos*.[276] For it is the entire human person, to the most hidden parts of the subconscious, that must be cleansed.[277] It is a pursuit of reaching the natural condition of the human person, that in which one was created, and in which dispassion approximates purity (*agneia*). This implies, negatively speaking, 'the mortification of the body'[278]:

> Purity is worthy of such great and high praise that certain of the Fathers ventured to call it dispassion.[279]

Cassian, too, renders dispassion as *puritas cordis*,[280] not, I imagine, because of any difficulty in translating the term. Rather, this is the meaning of the term learned by Cassian in the desert of Egypt. Elsewhere Climacus remarks:

---

[271] 15.53 (892A).

[272] 29.4 (1148D). Climacus merely hints at a notion which Maximus the Confessor develops more fully: cf. *Cap. de car.* 4, 53–4 (PG90.1060BC).

[273] 29.3 (1148C).

[274] *De perfectione* (PG46.285CD).

[275] 7.35 (808C) and 51 (813A).

[276] 7.51 (813A); 14.31 (869AB) and end verse (872B).

[277] 15.9 (881B).

[278] 15.4 (881A).

[279] 15.65 (893CD) and 15.2–3 (880D–81A).

[280] Cf. *Inst.* 4, 43 (184); later, Symeon the New Theologian also links it with purity: cf. *Cat.* 18 (294).

> Purity too is called dispassion; and rightly so, for it is the harbinger of the general resurrection and of the incorruption of the corruptible.[281]

It is this eschatological prospect of dispassion that gives it a uniquely Christian meaning, distinct from the earlier Stoic idea.[282]

The negative element of dispassion involves cleansing of sins. However, dispassion ultimately entails a negation of the negation. For it aims at incorruption: it is positive, then, even in its negativity. Nowhere does dispassion imply immunity from temptation or impeccability, or as John puts it:

> It is the property of angels not to fall. ... And it is the property of human beings to fall.[283]

In agreement with the established ascetic tradition, John views temptation as a perpetual reality and cause of injury in this life. In Mark the Monk's words: 'Do not say that the dispassionate person cannot be upset.'[284] Diadochus reflects the same experience:

> Dispassion is not the fact that one is not fought against by the demons ... but rather the state of remaining unwarred whilst being fought against by them.[285]

Having lost all that he possessed, Job – a model for ascetic writers through the centuries – remained 'undisturbed.'[286] Yet he was certainly neither invulnerable nor insensitive. He did not lose his faith and love for God, even at the limit. Indeed, it was these very virtues that helped him to endure and embrace his tribulations.

The negative sense of dispassion is not unfamiliar in the *Ladder*, even to the point of regarding all things as lifeless,[287] but this is definitely not the dominant notion. Usually dispassion implies a different way of looking at the world, a different attitude to beauty. The monk who glorified God on seeing a beautiful naked woman is a case in point; it is regarded as 'an extraordinarily supreme degree of purity.'[288] Dispassion, according to John, is certainly not

---

[281] 29.4 (1148D) and 1–2 (1148BC).

[282] Nevertheless, even in the Stoic sense, dispassion is not totally negative: cf. Rist, *Stoic Philosophy*, esp. 25, 38, 45, 52, 73, 195.

[283] 4.27 (696D).

[284] *De his.* 123 (PG65.948D). Völker also finds many parallels between Climacus and Maximus on the subject of dispassion: cf. *Scala Paradisi*, 247–54.

[285] *Cent.* 98 (160). Cf. also Maximus the Confessor, *Cap. de car.* 1, 36 (PG90.968AB); Thalassius, *Cent.* 1, 40 (PG91.1432B); and *Mystic Treatises* (345). For the patristic view of dispassion, cf. L. Thunberg, *Microcosm and Mediator: the Theological Anthropology of Maximos the Confessor*, Lund: 1965, 316–17.

[286] 16.21 (929A).

[287] 15.3 (880D–81A) and 29.8 (1149A).

[288] 15.58 (892CD).

indifference, some cold neutrality or impeccability. It is the characteristic quality of a person 'adorned in virtues'[289] like 'a bride,' as Abba Isaiah observed.[290] This positive side prevails (*apathous apathesteros*) over the negative one (*apathēs*). Dispassion is not apathy, but the absence of *pathos*; it implies not immunity from sin, but plenitude of virtue.[291]

Dispassion is a godlike gift. A person is dispassionate, according to the measure in which he/she is like unto God or 'assimilated' to God and wholly united with God.[292] Through dispassion, the heart is cleansed and God can, unhindered, enter 'our house.'[293] This gives dispassion an extending, impelling significance. It is, as has been noticed already, not a static condition but a continual progress in God, who provides many rooms in the heavenly house (Jn 14.2).[294] The dispassionate is:

> The one who keeps one's soul before the face of the Lord, ever reaching out
> to the Lord even beyond one's strength.[295]

In this personal relationship with God, dispassion does not leave one alone in any self-regarding posture, implied at least by some interpreters of the Stoic use of the term.[296] As will be seen below, John links dispassion with the divine love, which is alien to the Stoics, even though they were very conscious of their bonds with humankind and saw each person as a world citizen, obliged to play an active role in public affairs. Curiously enough, however, this went hand in hand with an essentially private ethic of apathy and strength of mind for the separate individual.

Consequent on this direct relationship with God, John sees dispassion as closely (indeed, very intimately: *nymphikōs*) linked with humility: 'An abundance of humility is the daughter of dispassion.'[297] Humility is the effect of, and the quickest way to, dispassion.[298] The dispassionate monastic is at all times conscious of the limited self and, at the same time, aware of the action of God's grace. The higher the degree of dispassion, the deeper the humility.[299]

---

[289] 29.1 (1148B) and 15.3 (880D–81A).

[290] *Logos* 25, 20 (174). Cf. also in *Ladder* 25.10 (992BC).

[291] 29.4 (1148D) and 25.10 (992BC). Diadochus speaks of 'the fire of dispassion,' thus referring to dispassion as 'passionate,' active: cf. *Cent.* 17 (93–4).

[292] Title of Step 29 (1149A); *Shep.* 100 (1201C) and 29.14 (1149C) and 5 (1148D–49A). Climacus himself does not normally use *theosis* language.

[293] 26.iii,55 (1092C) and 26.14 (1017C).

[294] 29.16 (1149D); 7.35 (808C) and 29.4 (1149D). Cf. also *Mac. Hom.* 8, 6 (83) and Mark the Monk, *Cap. de temp.* 27 (PG65.1068C).

[295] 29.2 (1148B).

[296] Cf. Yannaras, *Metaphysike*, 178.

[297] 26.iii,55 (1092C) and 25.10 (992BC). Cf. also Cassian, *Inst.* 112, 33, 1 (500) and Niketas Stethatos, *Cent.* 1.45 (283); 2.38 (307) and 3.76 (347).

[298] 25.35 (997A); 4.65 (709D) and 15.35 (889D–92A).

[299] Cf. 25.34 (996C–97A), 45 (1000A) and especially 4.19 (688B).

The proud person can never attain dispassion, though that person may be deceived into thinking that he/she has in fact attained it. Death, however, will ultimately tear away the mask of dispassion.[300] The relation between humility and dispassion is so intimate that the dispassionate are likened to the phenomenon of the 'fools' for Christ, to whom John in fact refers, at least implicitly, in one instance.[301] 'Fools' for Christ embody utter simplicity. They are not 'primitive,' but they are pristine, living in the image of Adam.[302] It is only in humility and obedience that dispassion proves lasting. Yet dispassion assumes a variety of forms, depending on circumstances. Dispassion in *hesychia*, for instance, may differ from that found in the world, outside a monastery.[303] Isaac the Syrian is more restrictive here. For him, 'dispassion and purity cannot be acquired without solitude.'[304] John may imply that a dispassionate state is actually easier to achieve in the monastic way of life, but this is nowhere explicitly stated. Still, he is addressing himself mainly to monks.

The demons, unflagging as they are, do not cease their warfare against the dispassionate monk. Indeed, they harass the monk all the more. One of their most common subterfuges is to let the monk believe that he has reached dispassion or, even, to let him actually reach this state.[305] Those who have attained dispassion must, therefore, fight still more relentlessly in order to preserve it. To succeed, they should make use of all manner of tricks against the demons, such as pretending to be subject to some passion so as to conceal dispassion.[306] Symeon the New Theologian may well have had the *Ladder* in mind when he said:

> One who pretends to be passionate when one is in fact dispassionate, acts for the salvation and benefit of many; such a person behaves just like the old Father, [and] is praiseworthy and blessed.[307]

In any case, those who have reached dispassion know the dangers to which they are exposed. They may often even plead with God that they might be given back their passions. This would provide them with something tangible to fight against. It is not that they cannot endure God's grace,[308] but, in

---

[300] 22.27 (969BC).

[301] 25.40 (997BC). On 'fools' for Christ, see J. Saward, *Perfect Fools: Folly for Christ's sake in Catholic and Orthodox Spirituality*, Oxford: Oxford University Press, 1980, and D. Krueger, *Symeon the Holy Fool: Leontius' Life and the Late Antique City*, Berkeley: University of California Press, 1996.

[302] 24.7 (984A) and 26.40 (1025C–28A).

[303] 15.34 (888BC).

[304] *Mystic Treatises* (349).

[305] 26.40 (1025C–28A).

[306] 26.ii,25 (1064BC).

[307] *Cat.* 8 (86).

[308] 26.16 (1017D) and 15.17 (884A).

dispassion, they run the risk of not being sufficiently aware of its necessity, or else of taking it for granted.[309] This idea reflects a widespread ascetic view, which goes back to the epistle of James:

> Count it all joy, my brethren, when you meet various trials. ... Blessed is the one who endures trial, for such a person has stood the test and will receive the crown of life, which are promised to those who love God. (1.2,12)

Only a dispassionate person, who is both simple and humble, will recognize that this state is a divine gift:

> God is the bestower and champion of all dispassion, by which God translates to heaven those still sojourning upon earth.[310]

The attainment of 'most extreme dispassion' does not issue from more ascetic effort and mortification of the body.[311] Its deepest source is always the grace of God. However, it does require much time, patience and desire on our part.[312] As regards dispassion, Barsanuphius says: 'This is a gift of God: God bestows it on the person who wants it.'[313] And according to the *Macarian Homilies*: 'To talk of dispassion and of perfection is easy; but, in experience, for it to be brought to perfection is the lot of the few.'[314] Indeed, dispassion has its pitfalls, although Climacus says that all must struggle for it continually.[315] In one instance, John even substitutes the word 'salvation' for 'dispassion.'[316] Generally, however, he views dispassion as a *condition* for salvation.

'There is,' as Climacus states in a number of contexts, 'a *kairos* for all things' in the spiritual life. For the dispassionate, there is the '*kairos* of passion;' and for sinners, there is the '*kairos* of dispassion.'[317] Dispassion fits the occasion. Abba Isaiah claims that only God knows the *kairos* of each person. We must simply be patient.[318] Also, in John's view, dispassion is directly related to the struggle with passions:

---

[309] Cf. *Apophth.* John the Dwarf 13 (PG65.208BC) and the example often attributed to Ephraim the Syrian in the *Ladder*, 29.5 (1148D). For Ephraim, cf. also Peter Damascene, *On the seven bodily acts* (66), where Peter refers to Climacus.

[310] *Shep.* 100 (1201D) and 26.47 (1092A). For dispassion as a gift, cf. Mark the Monk, *De lege spir.* 193 (PG65.928D); *Mac. Hom.* 9, 7 (86–7) and 31, 6 (250–51); Barsanuphius 182; Dorotheus, *Instr.* 1, 5 (152–4), 11 (162–4), 20 (176–8) and 10, 108 (346–8); Thalassius, *Cent.* 1, 40 (PG91.1432B); Symeon the New Theologian, *Cat.* 18 (294) and Niketas Stethatos, *Cent.* 1.57 (286).

[311] 21.25 (953B).

[312] 26.iii,49 (1089C).

[313] Barsanuphius 72.

[314] *Mac. Hom.* 17, 11 (173).

[315] 26.38 (1025C) and 54 (1029D).

[316] 28.28 (1133C); 26.54 (1029D).

[317] 26.38 (1032B).

[318] *Logos* 21, 8 (130).

> For all the dispassionate have progressed from passion to dispassion. ...
> And thus a passionate undertaking becomes for them a cause for
> dispassion.[319]

Addressing himself to concrete circumstances, and always bearing in mind
human frailty, John Climacus disapproves of aiming too high, beyond
endurance (Ps. 130.1), in the spiritual struggle. He always gives preference to
praxis over *theoria*, to humility, obedience and discernment even over
dispassion. Accordingly, Steps 25, 4 and 26 are much longer in terms of
content than Step 29.

The true nature of dispassion emerges in Climacus' identification of it with
love. The two, he says, 'are only distinguished in name,'[320] constituting the
positive and negative sides of the same reality. In the words of Abba Isaiah of
Scetis:

> Blessed is the soul that has reached such love; for it is indeed
> dispassionate.[321]

Eros

John's Imagery

There are many ways in which one could describe the spiritual life, aim and
struggle of an ascetic. Dispassion is one; 'passion,' paradoxically, is another.
Climacus delights in the imagery of erotic love and fire. The two images are
closely connected. 'Love,' he tells us, 'is a source of fire,' and he commands a
love which he has personally experienced:

> And now you have ravished my soul. I cannot contain your flame. So I will
> go forward praising you.[322]

---

[319] 28.30 (1133D) and *Shep.* 41 (1184CD).

[320] 30.4 (1156B) and 7.35 (808C). This is found in other writers too: cf. Evagrius, *Prakt.* Prologue
(492), 81 (670) and 100 (710); *De or.* 52 (PG79.1177C): Climacus is almost certainly drawing here
directly on Evagrius. Cf. also Cassian, *Conf.* 16 (222–47); *Apophth.* Evagrius 6 (PG65.176A);
Diadochus, *Cent.* 17 (93–4); Abba Isaiah, *Logos*, 26, 1 (181) and *Logoi* 16 (85–101) and 24 (150);
Maximus, *Cap. de car.* 1, 2 (PG90.961AB), 81 (997CD) and 4, 91 (1069CD); Maximus, too, is
clearly influenced by Evagrius. See also Greg. of Sinai, *Chapt.* 5 (64) and Greg. Palamas, *Triads*, 2,
2, 20.

[321] *Logos*, 21, 9 (131).

[322] 30.18 (1160B) and 1 (1156A). Love is described as fire in Cassian, *Inst.* 5, 18, 1 (220); especially
Diadochus, *Cent.* 14 (91), 16 (92–3) and 74 (132–3) and Symeon the New Theologian, *Cat.* 19 (318)
and *TGP* 1.7 (42). Völker finds parallels between Climacus and Maximus the Confessor on the
theme of love: cf. *Scala Paradisi*, 255 ff.

It is appropriate, then, that John should also speak of *eros* in the way of sexual union (*synousia*).[323] For there is a holy passion or blessed madness (*makaria mania*) in love.[324] To acquire virtue, for one thing, is not a mere addiction to the human person. It is integral, and at one with the human person, as if in wedlock.[325] Fire is, for Climacus, the most adequate image for expressing one's passionate love of God. It conveys both the warmth of love and its luminous impress on life, the burning desire enshrined in it and its unquenchable quality, the searing or consuming effect it has on human passions and the power it has to test us, like silver or gold in fire, the swiftness with which it may both spread and be extinguished. The 'thirst' and the 'yearning' of our love for God continually 'burn' and 'consume' us.[326]

Divine Eros *and Worldly Love*

John uses imagery taken from daily life and applies it to ascetic spirituality. In the search for virtues, John wants us to act as jealous husbands towards their wives. We are told that love of God is far greater or far stronger than the love of a mother for her child, which is her own flesh.[327] John is impelled to adopt erotic imagery. *Eros* is not merely an icon, a symbol or figure of speech. Above all, it is an energy, a way, a prototype, a specific mode of existence. John's words are *typos* and *hypodeigma*:

> As an example of the fear of the Lord, let us take the fear that we feel in the presence of rulers and wild beasts; and as an example (*hypodeigma*) of desire for God, let carnal love serve as a model (*typos*) for you. There is nothing against taking (*poieisthai ēmas*) examples of the virtues from what is contrary (*enantiōn*).[328]

The phrase *poieisthai ēmas* shows that carnal love is not good in itself but must be 'made' good, as will be seen below. The word *enantiōn* further shows clearly that, for John, there is a *contrast* as well as an *analogy* between carnal and divine love. With this qualification, the *Ladder* speaks the vivifying language of lovers:

---

[323] 28.1 (1129A).

[324] 30.1 (1156A). Cf. also Isaac the Syrian, *Mystic Treatises* (263) and Symeon the New Theologian, *Eth.* 4 (74).

[325] 25.10 (992B) and 22 (993B).

[326] 30.9 (1157A) and especially 27.ii,2 (1105BC). This burning thirst is also found in *Mac. Hom.* 9, 9 (87–8); Diadochus, *Cent.* 8 (87–8); Isaac the Syrian, *Mystic Treatises* (24) and Greg. of Sinai, *Chapt.* 59 (39).

[327] 30.5 (1156C) and 11 (1157AC). Cf. also Dorotheus, *Sayings* 14 (528) and Symeon the New Theologian, *Eth.* 4 (72).

[328] 26.31 (1024BC). Cf. also Yannaras, *Metaphysike*, 149–66, although Yannaras does not sufficiently emphasize the qualification (made below) of *poieisthai ēmas* and *enantiōn*.

> Blessed is he who has obtained such love and yearning for God as a mad lover has for his beloved.[329]

Human, including physical, bodily *eros*, does not exclude but includes a divine spark. John approves of people whose worldly love many Christians eagerly, but quite incongruously, condemn. John says of these:

> They have transferred the same love to the Lord, and spurred themselves insatiably on to the love of God.[330]

Worldly love can be readily redirected (*metaphora*) towards God. It is Climacus' firm conviction that 'if anyone is willing, it is possible and easy to graft a wild olive tree onto a good one.'[331] The *Macarian Homilies* say: 'the soul is accepted not because of what it has done, but because of what it has despised.'[332] Because the prostitute in the Gospel account 'loved much' (Lk. 7.37–48), John claims that she could 'easily expel love by love.'[333] Consequently, even corporeal, that is, worldly or allegedly corrupt love, must not be condemned out of hand or even censured. It, too, may be transfigured into spiritual love. One love can retrieve another, just as spiritual fire can quench the material fire of passions.[334] The unloving person, who is not consumed with desire, will be diminished in the fervour of the search for God.

Nevertheless, John does not advocate carnal love as such. When seen as an end in itself, without Christ as its sacred dimension, it becomes something unnatural, even 'inhuman' and insane. Without God, love is not even fully human. The natural cannot subsist without the supernatural. Abba Serapion describes monks as those who 'anticipate the things of the future through desire.'[335] John intensifies this desire; he calls it 'violence.' For John, monks are 'those who do violence' against the unnatural state, being 'desirers' of the heavenly kingdom, of the natural 'relationship' with God, whom they seek 'insatiably.'[336] The ascetic sets out on the long road of spiritual struggle with a view to attaining love. And, as an insane lover and suitor, the ascetic makes divine love a personal pursuit and endeavor. Driven by a desire for God, the ascetic leaves behind all mundane cares:

---

[329] 30.5 (1156C). Cf. also Anastasius the Sinaite, *Quaestiones* 135 (PG89.788D).

[330] 5.6 (777A). Abba Poemen also speaks of a 'transformation' in *Apophth.* Poemen 123 (PG65.353B). Cf. also Greg. Nyssa, *De virg.* 5 (PG46.348D).

[331] 15.66 (893D).

[332] *Mac Hom.* 37, 9 (269).

[333] 5.6 (777A).

[334] 15.2 (880D) and 5.6 (777A).

[335] *Ep. ad mon.* 7 (PG40.932D).

[336] 26.ii,19 (1064A) and especially 15.23 (884BC). Cf. also Diadochus, *Cent.* 91 (152–3). Such 'violence' is also stressed in Basil, *Sermo de renuntiatione saeculi, et de perfectione spirituale* 9 (PG31.645D); Abba Isaiah, *Logos* 5 (34–5) and Isaac the Syrian, *Mystic Treatises* (187).

> Exile (*xeniteia*) means ... constant determination to love God, abundance of *eros*.[337]

John knows that a single vivid experience of *eros* in all its intensity will advance one much further in the spiritual life, will be more effective than the most arduous struggle against the passions and the severest ascetic exercise. By the same token, moreover, it is this erotic desire for the beloved person of Christ that alone accounts for the otherwise unaccountable and seemingly senseless or even eccentric ascetic feats.[338]

The virtues themselves are described not only as women or kinswomen, but as qualities of lovers[339] (cf. S. of S. 1.3–4). They seduce one *on the way* to one's ultimate love; therefore, it would be wrong to cling to them as ends in themselves. Both virtues and passions have a feminine gender in the Greek. Climacus stresses 'remembrance of God' (*mneme Theou*); the word 'remembrance' has the same root as the word 'bride' (*mnester*). In the desert experience, one is to remember God with passionate desire – just as a lover recalls a bride – and not simply in rational recollection. By the same token, sin is regarded as an act of unfaithfulness, of adultery. John's contemporary, Isaac the Syrian, writes: 'The world is a whore and by the desire of its beauty, it attracts those who seek it so that they may love it.'[340]

Divine Love as Passionate

Eros, passionate in its desire (cf. Dan. 9.23 and Wis. of Sol. 8.2), throws light on the notion of the aberrant (cf. Is. 5.4; Jer. 2.21) or sinful passions. As we have already seen, these are not to be suppressed or blotted out, but transposed, moulded, educated, put on their correct and natural course. In the monastic context, passions are dealt with differently. They are transcended by the conquest of greater and nobler passions. The monk turns all passion towards God (cf. Prov. 4.27) and submits every loving effort at the feet of his Lord:

> I have seen hesychasts who insatiably nourished their flaming desire for God through stillness, generating fire by fire, *eros* by *eros*, desire by desire.[341]

It is in this erotic context – *eros* as 'complete union with God, now and always' – that dispassion may be properly understood.[342] The monk who has reached

---

[337] 3.1 (664B) and especially 18 (1160BD).

[338] 26.iii,8 (1085D) and 5.5 (764D).

[339] *Shep.* 100 (1205B).

[340] *Mystic Treatises* (153).

[341] 27.14 (1097–00A).

[342] 27.14 (1149C).

dispassion continually longs to behold the Lord's countenance (Ps. 41.3) and can almost no longer endure the force of personal desire for God. The *Macarian Homilies* refer to such a monk as being 'overcome with heavenly longing.'[343] But, for John, it is God who moves the monk, who dwells and is active within the ascetic. God is the 'tenant' (*enoikos*), as well as the passion, of such a person. It is no longer the monk who lives, but Christ lives in him (Gal. 2.20).[344] Thus:

> The body has been rendered pure and incorruptible by the flame of purity, which has extinguished the flame [of passion.][345]

Already in Evagrius, prayer is seen as a way of increasing one's desire for God.[346] Yet, for John, the erotic connection between God and humanity is the essence of prayer:

> Prayer by reason of its nature, is the converse (*synousia*) and union (*enōsis*) of humanity with God.[347]

The erotic terminology is apparent; the sexual overtones are explicit in the Greek. John's ascetic thought reaches the depth of mystical poetry. The monk says:

> What have I in heaven? Nothing. And what have I desired on earth beside you? Nothing. Nothing but to cling continually (*proskollasthai*) to you in prayer without distraction. ... For what higher good is there than to cling to the Lord and persevere in unceasing union (*enōsei*) with him?[348]

Love, being a personal relationship, inevitably entails the self – a personal insatiability and unending desire. All sinful passions end in sin, are self-defeating, as though preordained to miscarry by an act of God's loving providence. Nonetheless, authentic passion – for God – can have no end and is never fully satisfied. Or, even while being satisfied 'insatiably,' it seeks to outdo and exceed itself, 'generating fire by fire, love (*eros*) by love (*eros*), desire by desire.'[349] Like fire, which 'in the measure that it wells up, so it inflames the

---

[343] *Mac. Hom.* 4, 15 (30–31).

[344] 29.15 (1149CD).

[345] 30.11 (1157B).

[346] *De or.* 118 (PG79.1193AB).

[347] 28.1 (1129A) and 25.27 (996A). Cf. also Greg. Nyssa, *Life of Moses* 2 (PG44.401C).

[348] 28.28 (1133C) and 33 (1136A). Cf. also Athanasius, *Life of Antony* 91 (PG26.972A); Mark the Monk, *De his.* 89 (PG65.944AB) and Cyril of Scythopolis, *Life of Euthymios* 6 (14, 13–15).

[349] 28.14 (110A). Cf. also *Mac. Hom.* 15, 37 (149) and 25, 3 (200–201), and Symeon the New Theologian, *Cat.* 23 (24). Symeon uses language reminiscent of the *Ladder*: cf. *Cat.* 20 (346) where Symeon uses the words 'desire by desire ... and *eros* by *eros*,' and *Cat.* 17 (256), where Symeon says 'fire by fire ... flame by flame ... ascent by ascent ... light by light.' There appears to be a direct influence of Climacus on Symeon here.

thirsty person,'[350] the desire of the monk has no limits. So such monks turn, perhaps self-defeatingly, into angels:

> They are never weary of pursuing their divine maker. ... They will never cease to advance in love ... until they become angels.[351]

This can only be understood in the eschatological sense (Mt. 22.30; Lk. 20.30) of continual love. It is not a superficial version of angelism. It is a mania for the extreme.

Divine Love as Gift and Joy

As with all else in the spiritual life, erotic love, 'the abundance of *eros*,' which we may have for God, is not of our making but a response to God's call (cf. 1 Thess. 4.9), a consequence of God's alluring grace (cf. Jer. 31.3), of being stung by Cupid's arrow [*tō velei trōtheis*] (cf. S. of S. 2.5). The *Macarian Homilies* also speak of a person being 'wounded with the passionate affection for the divine Spirit.'[352] 'Cling, then, without hesitation to Christ who has loved us,' says Barsanuphius.[353] For John, too, our love of God is but an image of God's ravishing love for us. We are for God 'a longed-for dwelling place'[354] (cf. Heb. 3.6 and Ps. 45.11), in spite of our unfaithfulness (2 Tim. 2.13). To respond to God is like accepting a divine nuptual union. If we cannot do this faithfully, we must then try to find a place beside the divine bridal chamber or at least within the courtyard of the divine palace.[355] More daringly, Symeon the New Theologian describes the relationship with God as sexual 'intercourse,' as 'union in sleeping with Christ,' though it always resembles the love of a pauper for a princess.[356]

Being an act of divine grace, *eros* evokes an attitude of eager expectation, of waiting upon the Holy Spirit, of appeal, of imprecation. This expressed in John's rhetorical question:

---

[350] 30.18 (1160B).

[351] 27.26 (1101AB). The danger of angelism is more evident in Evagrius, cf. *De or.* 113 (PG79.1192D), who is clearly influenced by his Origenistic background. For angelism, cf. J. C. Didier, 'Angélisme ou perspectives eschatologiques?' in *Mélanges de science religieuse* (1954), 31–48. Cf. also P. Suso Frank Ofm, *Angelikos Vios*, Münster: 1964. For the way in which the ascetics avoid angelism, cf. the story of John the Dwarf in *Apophth.* John the Dwarf 2 (PG65.204C–05A).

[352] *Mac. Hom.* 4.16 (38–9). The references to the *Ladder* are from 15.2 (880D) and 30.7 (1156D). Other monastic literature also speaks of this wound of love: cf. Greg. Nyssa, *In Cant. Cant.* 4 (PG46.852A–53A); *Mac. Hom.* 5, 6 (50–59) and 9, 9 (87–8); Symeon the New Theologian, *Cat.* 17 (258).

[353] Barsanuphius 20.

[354] 15.2 (880D) and 30.7 (1156D).

[355] 29.17 (1152A).

[356] Cf. *Eth.* 15 (446), 6 (128) and 4 (70).

Can there can be any greater good than being glued in union with the Lord
and unceasingly waiting on (*proskarterein*) this union?[357]

The word *proskarterein* here denotes an ardent expectation, a desirous waiting
for the grace of God. Divine grace may at times seem to abandon us (cf. Jn 16.5–
7), in order either to induce a spirit of humility[358] or to wound the heart with
penthos. Thus, one must persevere, in tears and pain (cf. 2 Cor. 7.7), 'ever madly
seeking ... and following' God.[359] Yet one is never quiescent in one's desire for
God. *Eros* does not stop in its course and 'allows no respite to the person
wounded by its blessed madness.'[360] So, wounded by love for God, John says
that his 'heart stays awake in the abundance of love (*eros*).'[361] The experience is
of continual 'loss' and 'recovery' of the one sought for. It is the taste of Christ's
presence even in absence. At any rate, love is nothing in the abstract. It is nothing
if not love of another, existing person.[362] As a person burning with love, the
monk never abandons the image of the lover, never lets go of, and unceasingly
speaks to, the divine other, whether in waking or sleeping. 'The abundance of
eros' is great indeed;[363] 'as it is with bodily things, so it is with the bodiless!'[364]

As a source of inspiration, *eros* bears a transfiguring effect. It even makes us
'cheerful, glad, and carefree.'[365] It is a distinctly Christian quality of asceticism
that the experience of divine love makes for joy and lightness. John observes
that God's love can 'eat away a person,' but this in no way implies some
miserable posture or sad countenance. There is always such nagging pain in the
never-ending search for God and in the searing effect of God's grace.
Nevertheless, as John concludes:

> When the whole person is, in a manner, commingled with the love of God,
> then *even the outward appearance in the body*, as in a kind of mirror, shows
> the splendour of the soul. That is how the God-seer Moses was glorified.[366]

Love embraces anguish and joy, dejection and ecstasy. It is a virtue containing
everything and rising above everything.[367] This, in a way, well sums up all that
can be said about the virtues as adumbrated by John, in his conception of the
total person engaged in the variegated, checkered struggle of spiritual life.

---

[357] 28.33 (1136A) and 19.1 (940CD).

[358] 4.50 (708B). Cf. also Diadochus, *Cent.* 69 (120) and 87 (146–7).

[359] 7.1 (801CD).

[360] 30.1 (1156A). Symeon the New Theologian uses very similar words in *Cat.* 2 (247).

[361] 30.7 (1156D).

[362] Cf. 7.57 (813C).

[363] 30.7 (1156D) and 3.1 (664B). Cf. also Theodoret, *Phil. Hist.*, Julian Sabas, 2 (198).

[364] 30.6 (1156D) and 7.57 (813C).

[365] 30.10 (1157A).

[366] 30.11 (1157B) and 12 (1157C). Climacus knows that demons can cause an illusion of joy,
which spreads darkness: cf. 26.ii,14 (1061B).

[367] 30.18 (1160BD). Cf. also Ps. Athanasius, *Life of Saint Synkletike* 22 (PG28.1500C).

The monastery church in Pharan
(Photograph: Elizabeth Williams)

CHAPTER 7

The Ascetic at Prayer

Be still, and know that I am God.
(Psalm 45)

The greatest revelation is stillness.
(Eastern proverb)

Prayer as Dialogue

Prayer reveals the true dimensions of the association between God and the world, of the true and total nature of the ascetic in regard to self-involvement and commitment to God. Accordingly, this chapter will deal, in the first place, with John's understanding of prayer as divine–human dialogue, with the eschatological implications of prayer, and with those forces which act as a rupture in this association. There follows a discussion of prayer as an 'introverted' and an 'extroverted' act, and, finally, an examination of certain specific aspects of prayer related to and focused on the 'Jesus Prayer.'

John speaks of prayer as the touchstone of the monk's spirituality. It is 'the disclosure of stature, an indication of one's condition … a sign of glory.'

> Your prayer will show you what condition you are in. Theologians say that prayer is the mirror of the monk.[1]

The explicit reference to monks in this connection should be seen as having a kind of archetypal significance. John knows that praying is not a monastic privilege, even if it is preeminently what monks are designed to do. Prayer constitutes the fundamental form of relating to God as a personal reality, and as such has universal meaning.

Prayer, Climacus is convinced, must be personally lived. One must 'touch' it or be 'touched' by it.[2] It cannot be experienced in the way that objects are experienced, by means of some detached, exterior perception. Prayer does not even exist by itself. It exists only as the activity of a praying person, or as the human person in prayer. And silence (*hesychia*), too, presupposes a person already leading a life of obedience and *ascesis*. It can never be thought of in

---

[1] 28.1 and 38 (1129B and 1136C). For prayer as a mirror, cf. Ps. Chrysostom, *De patientia* (PG63.941), and similar definitions in Igumen Chariton, *The Art of Prayer*, London: Faber, 1966, 51.

[2] 27.ii,21 (1112AB).

abstraction, isolated from the praying ascetic.[3] Both prayer and *hesychia* are relationship words.

Prayer, therefore, is a dialogue of the human person face to face with, or in the presence of (*parastēnai*), and speaking to (*syllalēsai*) Christ, the king, who speaks to human beings as royal subjects. John asks:

> How can you truly hold converse with the one whom you have not seen?

> One who has not yet known God is unfit for *hesychia*.[4]

The praying person does not soliloquize but is conversant with God (S. of S. 2.16 and Wis. of Sol. 8.3). Hence *hesychia* signifies an attitude of listening to the one of whom we are wholly conscious from within. The 'wing' of prayer is faith in God.[5] And prayer is also a test, a 'demonstration' or 'proof' of this faith, an act of self-verification.[6]

There is, quite clearly, a mutual and immediate relationship between God and the hesychast, who is 'informed' directly from God.[7] So strong is this personal relationship that it may be seen not only as a distant dialogue, but as a dialogue within the person at prayer. In this sense, *hesychia* is pregnant silence, not mere muteness. It is a stillness within which lies the divine Word itself. The grace of God descends into the ascetic's heart and lifts it to heaven.[8] Or, perhaps more accurately, it is Christ who prays within the human heart:

> One who possesses the Lord will no longer express one's object in prayer.
> For then, within, the Spirit intercedes for that person, with sighs too deep
> for words (cf. Mt. 10.20 and Rom. 8.26).[9]

The attitude of the person praying is one of attentive listening (Eccl. 12.13), of expectancy. It is a way of continual waiting upon Christ quietly. Abba Isaiah, too, speaks of 'waiting upon God with all one's heart and with all one's

---

[3] Cf. 27.26 (1100D) and 26.42 (1028B).

[4] 28.19 (1032D) and 27.ii,20 (111A). Cf. especially 28.3 and 4 (1029CD). The *parastēnai–syllalēsai* notion is found in Origen, *De or.* 8, 2 (317, 97). Climacus' imagery and words are taken up almost verbatim by Symeon the New Theologian in *Eth.* 15 (446).

[5] 27.ii,32 (1113B) and 28.29 (1133CD). The link between faith and prayer is also found in Ps. Athanasius, *On Virginity* 10 (PG28.264A); John Moschus, *Pratum* 188 (PG87.3065B–68A); Isaac the Syrian, *Mystic Treatises* (254) and Greg. of Sinai, *Chapt.* 103 (48).

[6] 28.1 (1129B) and 26.ii,2 (1057B). Cf. also Mark the Monk, *De his.* 109 (PG65.945BC).

[7] 27.ii,32 (1113AB). Prayer needs no intermediaries: cf. *Apophth.* Ammonas 7 (PG65.121A); Pambo 7 (369C); Evagrius, *De or.* 3 (PG79.1168CD) and Isaac the Syrian, *Mystic Treatises* (135–6).

[8] 28.47 (1137A). Abba Isaiah says that silence is 'both hidden and revealed:' cf. *Logos* 5, 1 (34).

[9] 28.34 (1136D). Cf. also Origen, *De or.* 10, 2 (320, 99); *Mac. Hom.* 12, 17 (117–19); 19, 8 (187) and 37, 9 (269); Isaac the Syrian, *Mystic Treatises* (174); Symeon the New Theologian, *Thanks.* 2 (348). Evagrius, however, warns against trying to see Christ in prayer: cf. *De or.* 115 (PG79.1192D–93A).

might.'[10] To wait upon Christ is to love Christ. And, for John, prayer is a measure of that love:

> The work of prayer exposes lovers of God.[11]

The same notion of waiting and its understanding as love of God are both found in Mark the Monk: 'Prayer without distraction is a sign of love of God for the one who persists in prayer.'[12] A praying person is one who stands before God in faith and hope, but also in humility, without overbearing and petulance:

> That person stands in prayer without boldness (*parrhēsia*) but with praiseworthy audacity (*anaideia*), as one who is shattered, steadying oneself with the staff of hope.[13]

To stand before God is itself an act of audacity, but a 'praiseworthy audacity' conjoined with humility. God, in turn, will respond. Yet there is no uniformity as regards the manner in which God chooses to do so. For, it may be either directly (Is. 58.9) or else indirectly through other people.[14] Further, this does not impair the dialogical character of the relation. For, while speaking from person to person, God does not speak or respond to an isolated individual but through and in everybody and everything, as well as directly. Not all prayer is from the beginning direct. There are preliminary stages. In fact, there is a certain shift in perspective in John's treatment of prayer. Sometimes, he has in mind the final goal; at other times he is referring to the first steps, the starting point. Nevertheless, God's response will surely come in its own due time, in God's time (*kairos*), unpredictably:

> So let us not be deceived by proud zeal, and seek prematurely what will come in its own good time; that is, we should not seek in winter what comes in summer, or at seed time what comes at harvest; because there is a time to sow labours, and a time to reap the unspeakable gifts of grace. Otherwise, we shall not receive even in season what is proper to that season.[15]

Prediction is imposition – an act of pride (*hybris*) on our part, to presume God's answer in our time.[16] The order in the spiritual life cannot be reversed. It is God who takes the initiative; it is God who 'anticipates' us (*prokatalamvanei*)

---

[10] *Logos* 8, 13 (57). Cf. also *Logos* 17, 3 (105); Kallistos/Ignatios, *Cent.* 53 (252) and Palamas, *Antirrheticus* 5.6.21 (vol. 3, p. 301). *Mac. Hom.* 2, 3 (15–17) emphasizes continual expectancy.

[11] 19.5 (941A) and 18.7 (937D).

[12] *De his.* 90 (PG65.944B).

[13] 25.37 (997A). For the positive significance of *parrhēsia*, cf. S. B. Marrow, '*Parrhēsia* and the New Testament,' *The Catholic Biblical Quarterly* 44, 3 (July 1982), 431–46.

[14] 28.53 (1137D).

[15] 26.59 (1032C).

[16] 26.38 (1025C) and 21.34 (956CD).

and, paradoxically, responds first so that 'prayer itself,' to use Rudolph Bultmann's words, 'is already its own answer.'[17] To presume priority for oneself in prayer, according to John, is a temptation of vainglory. It is to be overcome by greater and more genuine prayer,[18] in contrast with 'untimely' (*akairos*) prayer, which is inexpedient and therefore wasteful.[19]

Just as the relation between God and the ascetic surpasses privacy, so too does prayer. It is, in an important sense, a corporate act, which is shown in the experience of standing together with others in prayer.[20] When praying, one prays not only for oneself but for all and with all (1 Tim. 2.1). One's 'I' is identified with the 'we' of humankind. And if one is debarred from this experience by the divisive action of demons, one can only again resist by turning to prayer with others and to psalmody, even if for John psalmody is less powerful – an extensive rather than intensive form of prayer. For his distinction between prayer and psalmody, John draws on the existing tradition:

> In chanting with many, it is impossible to pray with the wordless prayer of the Spirit. However, your intellect should be engaged in contemplation of the words being chanted or read, or you should say some definite prayer while you are waiting for the alternate verse to be chanted.[21]

Diadochus suggests the use of psalmody when prayer is not practically possible.[22] Barsanuphius, too, recommends it although he admits its drawbacks.[23]

The togetherness of prayer is borne out for John by the sense of tenderness and contrition due to the guardian angel's presence in prayer.[24] The idea of the angel being with us in prayer is an old one.[25] Far from undermining the reality and immediacy of the dialogue, it serves to underline its true character. The *Macarian Homilies* note that 'those who pray in silence edify everybody

---

[17] Cf. his exegesis of 1 Jn in 5.15 in *Theology of the New Testament*, trans. K. Grobel (London, 1955), 2, 87. Cf. also 21.34 (956CD).

[18] 21.32 (956C) and 26.ii,59 (1073A).

[19] 21.32 (956C), 22.13 (968A) and 21.34 (956CD).

[20] 18.5 (937C). See the *agraphon* saying of Jesus: 'Where there is only one person all alone, there I shall be likewise,' quoted in A. Louf, *The Message of Monastic Spirituality*, trans. L. Stevens, New York: 1964, 107. Cf. also Evagrius, *De or*. 124 (PG79.1193C).

[21] 18.5 (937CD). Cf. Evagrius, *Prakt*. 69 (654) and *De or*. 82–5 (PG79.1185A–C); *Apophth*. Evagrius 3 (PG65.173D); Thalassius, *Cent*. 1. 30 (PG91.1429D) and 2, 92 (1441D). For the influence of Evagrius on Climacus on the subject of prayer, cf. Völker, *Scala Paradisi*, 230–46.

[22] *Cent*. 73 (132).

[23] Barsanuphius 429 and 447. Cf. also Isaac the Syrian, *Mystic Treatises* (94, 146) and Greg. of Sinai, *Chapt*. 99 (48).

[24] 20.11 (948A) and 28.10 (1132B).

[25] Cf. especially Evagrius, *De or*. 81 (PG79.1185A), 30 (1173B) and 115 (1192D–93A) and Symeon the New Theologian, *Cat*. 11 (162). See also Isaac the Syrian, *Mystic Treatises* (23).

everywhere.'[26] The cosmic significance of prayer, its formative and transformative force in the world, bears important implications not least for the understanding of the nature of monasticism. The love of God is not exclusive but all-inclusive. It is immanent in the love for others, and there cannot be love only for one or the other.[27] As the Gospel has it, to say that we love God when we do not love our neighbor is to prove ourselves liars (1 Jn 4.20). John Climacus says, the converse also holds true:

> If you say that you love, then pray secretly.[28]

John also cautions that much care is needed when praying for particular individuals.[29] Nevertheless, there is a mutual interdependence linking all human persons, and we can be saved by praying for others.[30] One receives a hundredfold of what one offers to others. The monk, by praying, is above all being 'merciful.'[31] Climacus is certainly alluding to the beatitude: 'Blessed are the merciful, for they shall obtain mercy' (Mt. 5.7). The monk, whether physically close to society or not, becomes love incarnate. Mark the Monk likens the monastic to:

> An ambassador of God, who out of great love for God, begins to pray for the world, that Adam – the entire world – may be saved; and burning with love, the monk wishes that all may be saved.[32]

John pursues the matter further, by linking the love of God and of others with that of oneself – as a way of purifying and illuminating one's own person. Without 'purity,' prayer is 'disdained.'[33]

The ascetic in prayer becomes 'an unshakable pillar,'[34] in whom all find stability and protection. In agreement with other ascetic writers, John claims that prayer must be regarded as 'a wall,'[35] which supports the foundations of the whole world. He says, in the wake of Barsanuphius, that the monk prays for the entire world – even for those who are indifferent to their salvation and for those who are his enemies.[36] Prayer mirrors the prayer of a spiritual elder viewed as 'a protection' for all people and for all circumstances.[37] The spiritual

---

[26] *Mac. Hom.* 6, 3 (65–6).

[27] 9.11 (841CD); 10.3 (845CD); 9.2 and 9 (841A and C).

[28] 10.3 (845D). Cf. also Abba Isaiah, *Logos* 16, 6 (94).

[29] 28.56 (1140A).

[30] 28.40 (1136C).

[31] 28.46 (1137A).

[32] *Cap. de temp.* 27 (PG65.1068CD).

[33] 15.23 (884C).

[34] 18.4 (937C).

[35] 4.10 (681A). Cf. similar words in Isaac the Syrian, *Mystic Treatises* (71).

[36] *Shep.* 64 (1192A), 100 (1205A) and 24.2 (980D). Cf. also Barsanuphius 127.

[37] 4.2 (677D). Cf. 20.6 (945C).

elder resembles Moses, who lifted up his hands in order that his people might conquer Amelek.[38] The monk, too, lifts up his hands for the whole creation, as Abba Arsenius once did.[39] Though the monk owns nothing, yet in effect he rules over all and everything:

> A monk without possessions is a lord of the world.[40]

John tells the monk to halt when a word in prayer induces a sense of contrition and tenderness. As mentioned above, this marks the coming of one's angel to join in prayer.[41] A single word may contain the whole world within itself. One who has attained to pure prayer is called 'a saviour of people'[42] because true prayer 'by reason of its action upholds the world and brings about reconciliation with God.'[43]

Prayer, being a compelling personal relationship of love with God,[44] allows of no objectification. God, in John's ascetic theology, is not an idol or an object of idolatry.[45] In prayer, we should not fashion any images or icons, which the imagination may fantasize. In fact, one should try to exclude these altogether. For we seek the Giver, not the gifts; we want to know God through direct personal experience, not by substitutes.[46]

> Prayer is converse and union of the human with God.[47]

To cease praying is to create a gulf between oneself and God. It is to destroy this direct and intimate union.[48] Barsanuphius says that, in *hesychia*, the soul 'forever clings to the Lord.'[49] And, in fact, for John, there can be no greater joy than to experience 'the beauty of prayer':

> What is higher than unceasing union with God?[50]

---

[38] *Shep.* 100 (1204BC). The action of lifting up one's hands in prayer is implicit in Origen, *De or.* 31, 2 (396, 164) and explicit already in Ps. Athanasius, *Ad Castorem, Ep.* 1 (PG28.852A).

[39] Cf. *Apophth.* Arsenius 30 (PG65.97C).

[40] 16.12 (928C).

[41] 28.10 (1132B). Nicetas Stethatos, *Cent.* 2,73 (316–17) and Kallistos/Ignatios, *Cent.* 25 (225) advise one to stop when the *nous* is seized.

[42] See the second 'alphabet' for the 'perfect' in 26.14 (1017C). Cf. also Serapion, *Ep. ad monachos* 3 (PG40.929AB), 4 (929BD) and 11 (937BC).

[43] 28.1 (1129A). Cf. Barsanuphius 110, 173 and 569.

[44] Cf. 25.27 (997A) and 27.ii,6 (1060B).

[45] 21.6 (949C).

[46] 28.44 (1136D–37A).

[47] 28.1 (1129A). Cf. similar words in Niketas Stethatos, *Cent.* 2.64 (14) and Greg. Palamas, *Triads*, 2, 3, 13.

[48] 27.ii,27 (1112C).

[49] Barsanuphius 2.

[50] 28.33 (1136A). Cf. also 27.ii,21 (1112AB) and 28.28 (1133C). Cf. Evagrius, *De or.* 34 (PG79.1173D) and echoes of Climacus in Symeon the New Theologian, *TGP* 1.28 (47–8).

The personal reality of the union is of the kind, which impels John to resort once more to the image of love between two lovers. Knowing is loving; just as loving is knowing:

> If the face of the loved one clearly and completely changes us ... what will the face of the Lord not do when the Lord's presence is felt invisibly?[51]

The *Macarian Homilies* describe pure prayer as the state wherein the person 'is wholly occupied with the Lord as ... a married person is with one's spouse.'[52] It is only in the context of this loving union through prayer that one could ever claim to have attained the knowledge of God in one's heart, which is a treasure of richness (Mt. 6.21; Lk. 12.34). Prayer is 'the wealth of monastics, the treasure of hesychasts.'[53] There is no danger of fusion between the persons in prayer. We have already seen that John also describes prayer as dialogue; there is always a person face to face with *another* person.

'First of all pray to be purified from your passions,' says Evagrius.[54] This is succinctly re-stated by Abba Isaiah of Scetis, when he claims that 'to be pure is to pray to God' or even that 'purity itself prays to God.'[55] It is a precondition of being in the presence of God. John does not speak of prayer as a first stage in spiritual life. Rather, he places the theme of prayer in the middle stage, between the two alphabets of the beginners and the perfect, perhaps envisaging it more as a pervasive activity. For prayer, however, to be entirely pure the praying person must reach the final stage, and be ranked among the 'perfect.'[56] Here, John differs from writers such as Mark the Monk, who regards prayer as 'an activity for the beginners, as well as for those in the middle and final stages.'[57] Nevertheless, perhaps different senses of prayer are here involved. For obviously, in a sense, beginners also pray. Prayer is not something that merely happens at a particular point. It presupposes a life already integrated in the ascetic life of the community. There is an entire 'preliminary task' to be fulfilled before prayer attains its pure or guileless state. John is clear on this:

> It is naturally impossible for one who does not know the alphabet to study books.[58]

---

[51] 30.10 (1157A).

[52] *Mac. Hom.* 15, 13 (133–5). Cf. also 10, 4 (95–6) and Evagrius, *De or.* 118 (PG79.1193A).

[53] 28.1 (1129B).

[54] *De or.* 37 and 4 (PG79.1176A and 1168D).

[55] *Logos* 22, 8 (140) and 26.1 (181).

[56] 26.14 (1017B).

[57] *De paenitentia* 11 (PG65.981B).

[58] 27.ii,12 (1109B).

One requires humility,[59] purity of soul[60] and freedom from passions. In the absence of such humility and freedom, one stands shamefacedly in God's presence.[61] The loving union in prayer implies a cleansing from impurities and various passions. If sin is an act of unfaithfulness, and the sinner a prostitute, then sinning and prostitution demean love and put the human person to shame before the divine loved one. Possessed of passions, one is not only disabled for praying purely;[62] but prayer itself becomes false, a piece of 'false piety.'[63] To pray 'unworthily'[64] is to turn away from God; it is to belie the dialogue with the one who initiates it.[65] It is a form of supreme haughtiness. We are called upon to present ourselves denuded to God, albeit armed with appropriate 'weapons and clothing, suitable for those who stand before the King,'[66] ready to reject anything in the way of receiving God. This is why John knows that 'a non-possessive person is pure during prayer' (cf. Ps. 73.21).[67]

Prayer as the Last Judgement Anticipated

> One who has experienced the beauty of prayer will shun crowds like a wild ass.[68]

To experience prayer and taste of its beauty is to be prepared to abandon all other things in approaching it, naked of all other cares. Such nakedness is not only a result of, but also a prerequisite for, God's visitation in prayer. One must be stripped of all sin. Paradoxically, the laying aside of the sinful will is identified with the assuming of the 'royal dress' mentioned above. And one must approach God in a state of nakedness, free from the covering of the flesh.[69] The 'less' clothing we wear in the presence of the divine king – standing in the royal presence bare and undisguised – the closer our relationship with God.[70] John almost identifies prayer with the pristine, unspoiled, unencumbered glory of the body when he notes that it should 'cleave to the bosom of our soul.'[71] The *Macarian Homilies* claim that through prayer one is made

---

[59] 28.11 (1132A).

[60] 30.10 (1157A).

[61] 9.2 and 9 (841A and C).

[62] 16.7 (924D).

[63] 17.5 (933C). Cf. also Origen, *De or.* 3, 2 (304, p. 87).

[64] 26.38 (1025C).

[65] 28.54 (1137D–40A).

[66] 28.3 and 4 (1129CD).

[67] 16.12 (928C).

[68] 27.ii,21 (1112AB).

[69] Cf. 15.76 (900AD); 16.7 (924D); 26.ii,2–4 (1057B–60A) and 27.26 (1100D–01A).

[70] 19.1 (940BC).

[71] 14.30 (869BC).

greater than Adam. The human person is deified.[72] Regarding prayer in this sense of looking beyond creation to the creator, of assuming and passing beyond one's original state, John writes:

> Prayer is nothing other than estrangement from the world, visible and invisible.[73]

Repentance is clearly not only a presupposition for prayer but preeminently a result of one's praying relationship with God. It is an effect of God's 'invisible visitation' in prayer.[74] In the fourth step, the monks first 'breathe' God, and only then turn to fight their passions.[75] For repentance is not so much a looking down with distaste at one's sinful self, in a self-regarding way. Rather, it is the beholding with love of God's heavenly splendour. Prayer itself, coinhering with the glory of God, is ultimately 'comfort to the souls ... and healing to the wounds.'[76] The monks look up to heaven, from there alone seeking God's mercy.[77] Prayer is an act of self-denial in love, of repentance and of God's loving response in the forgiveness of our sins. God's mercy is divine love poured out in action. A close examination of the two terms, prayer and repentance, will reveal that the latter leads to the former in a continuing succession:

> It is rather in my repentance that a fire of prayer will be kindled consuming that which is material (cf. Ps. 38.4).[78]

Yet, besides constituting 'forgiveness of sins,' prayer is also regarded by John – indeed in the very same passages that link it with repentance – as 'the door of paradise and its delight.'[79] It is the way of salvation, realized here and now. We can, admittedly, only enter paradise when God has judged our sins on the last day. Nonetheless, John preempts, as it were, the last day and indicates another dimension of the judgement, which has a bearing on the idea of heaven and hell. At each moment of our life, he would say, we are either being saved or condemned. Each moment, John argues, is or should be an anticipation of death. In fact, in one of his rare theological formulations, prayer and remembrance of death are identified as correlative aspects of an individual reality:

---

[72] *Mac. Hom.* 26, 1 (205–06). Cf. also Evagrius, *De or.* 84 (PG79.1185B) and *Prakt.* 49 (610–12).

[73] 28.28 (1133C). The same notion is also found in *Mac. Hom.* 8, 1 (76–7).

[74] 30.10 (1157A). A similar 'visitation' is envisaged in Evagrius, *De or.* 62 (PG79.1180C).

[75] 4.19 (688C).

[76] 28.2 (1192C) and 25.27 (996A).

[77] 5.5 (765A).

[78] 5.29 (780D). Prayer and repentance are linked in Mark the Monk, *De lege spir.* 95 (PG65.917A).

[79] 14.31 (869B) and 28.1 (1129B).

> Some say that prayer is better than the remembrance of death, but I praise two natures in one person.[80]

Isaac the Syrian observes that 'love of solitude is the constant expectation of death.'[81] Hence we stand in prayer as if at the last judgement, with a sense of awe, instead of speaking to God unmindfully and impassively. Abba Isaiah of Scetis writes that 'one who is in *hesychia* ought to have the fear of personal encounter with God anticipating one's every breath.'[82] John is still more precise:

> During prayer and supplication, stand with trembling like a convict standing before a judge, so that, both by your outward appearance as well as by your inner disposition, you may extinguish the wrath of the just judgement; for God will not despise a widow soul standing before him burdened with sorrow and wearying the weariless one (Lk. 18.1–8).[83]

Symeon the New Theologian uses similar language: 'Stand in prayer as one who is condemned … as if the Lord is present in body.'[84] If we are judged favorably by God in this life through prayer, we will also be saved on the last day. The prospect of heaven or hell depends on our inmost relationship with God:

> For one who truly prays, prayer is the court, the judgement hall and the tribunal of the Lord before the judgement to come.[85]

However, as already noted, John normally prefers medical imagery to the terminology of the law-court and the judgement hall. In the end, prayer is an act of healing; and words of prayer are not so much pleas to a judge as cries to a physician who is ready to operate on us.[86]

Dialogue with God, union with Christ, salvation – these implications of prayer inevitably attract the demons, who mobilize their forces to disturb or obstruct our prayer, to sow confusion,[87] and if possible to divert us completely from praying.[88] They adopt every strategy of intrusion into prayer at its very inception, in order to thwart it when one has already begun to pray,[89] and to

---

[80] 28.48 (1137A).

[81] *Mystic Treatises* (310).

[82] *Logos* 26, 1 (106).

[83] 7.13 (804CD).

[84] *Cat.* 30 (206) and 22 (370). Cf. also Niketas Stethatos, *Cent.* 2. 78 (317–18) and Gregory Palamas, *Triads*, 2, 2, 15.

[85] 28.1 (1129B).

[86] 26.7 (1132A).

[87] 26.ii,14 (1061A); 28.24 (1133AB) and 42 (1136D); 4.101 (717A); 12.4 (856AB) and 13.1 (860A). Cf. also Evagrius, *De or.* 10 (PG79.1169BC).

[88] 19.9 (941AB); 14.10 (865C); 28.58 (1140AB) and 5.11 (777D).

[89] 18.3 (937BC) and 19.4 (941A). Cf. *Apophth.* Theodora 3 (PG65.201BD).

haunt one after completing prayer.[90] More often than not, they begin to tempt one as one begins to pray and to insinuate themselves when one no longer prays.[91] For their aim is to interrupt or disrupt the dialogue with God: to convince one, for example, that one cannot be saved, which leads to despair.[92] We must in turn mock them,[93] by contending that we *were* being saved before their arrival, until they retreat. The dialogue must at all costs be resumed. One must press on with the course of communication and never abandon hope of hearing God's voice. 'The praying person abstains from hopelessness,' as Mark the Monk says.[94]

The rapacious temptations of the devil will continue to assail one, 'in order to dissolve the fixity of one's purpose,' as Evagrius says.[95] In John's words, 'those thieves aim at stealing from us one hour after another.'[96] For Evagrius:

> Every war fought between us and the impure spirits is engaged in for no other cause than that of spiritual prayer. This is an activity that is intolerable to them; for, they find it so hostile and oppressive.[97]

One's aim is to retaliate indirectly, to 'turn away from them,' not to head directly for them.[98] Prayer is highly effective in achieving this. It is like a weapon,[99] if a weapon of evasion. Nevertheless, the notion of a weapon suggests confrontation. Its use should be immediate[100] against the demons, who 'will flee as from fire when scourged by prayer.'[101] Although *qua* judgement, it can also be directed against us, prayer is primarily a weapon in our own hands, to be aimed at demons and passions.[102] Indeed, judgement, too, is in our hands since it 'depends' on us. 'The kingdom of heaven is at hand' (Mt. 3.2).

Like the desert theoreticians Evagrius and Cassian, John of the *Ladder* distinguishes different types of prayer. However, unlike them, he offers no

---

[90] 19.12 (941C).

[91] 23.6 (976D–77A).

[92] 23.7 (977A).

[93] Cf. 14.10 (865C).

[94] *De his.* 24 (PG65.933C).

[95] *De or.* 9 (PG79.1169B).

[96] 28.39 (1136C).

[97] *De or.* 49 (PG79.1177AB).

[98] 15.79 (901B).

[99] 20.6 (945C); 15.76 and 77 (900A–01A); 18.3 (937BC); 13.10 (860D–61A); 26.3,3 (1084D); 27.21 (1100B) and 18.4 (937C).

[100] 26.75 (1036A) and 26.2,1 (1057A). On prayer as a weapon, cf. *Apophth.* Elias 7 (PG65.184D–85A); Mark the Monk, *De his.* 135 (PG65.949D); Diadochus, *Cent.* 33 (102–04), although Diadochus refers to 'remembrance of God;' Niketas Stethatos, *Cent.* 1, 94 (295–6) and Greg. of Sinai, *Chapt.* 113 and 114 (51).

[101] 28.61 (1140C). Cf. also *Mac. Hom.* 23, 2 (195–6).

[102] 17.3 (932CD) and 27.ii, end verse (1117B).

systematic classification of its many forms, which include psalmody, reading, manual work and even thinking of or contemplating spiritual themes.[103] Although he prefers prayer in the night to other forms of prayer,[104] which are nevertheless not regarded as alternatives, he appreciates differences of human character and makes allowances for preferences and weakness.[105] John seems to agree with Mark the Monk that 'there are many ways of praying and each differs from the other. There is, furthermore, no way of praying that is harmful.'[106] For the author of the *Ladder*, some people speak to God erect, 'face to face,' others by kneeling before God, and still others by crying out to God from among the crowd. Yet God listens to them all.[107] Even if 'rapture in the Lord,' being ecstatic, is the highest form of prayer,[108] other forms are also acknowledged:

> God accepts and values the offerings of each, according to their intention and power.[109]

Prayer – Inward and Outward

As we have seen, prayer is a divine–human dialogue. By its nature, then, it is a way of counteracting the experience of alienation. However, the path to union with God is also a path of re-establishing unity within, in the midst of divisive forces that threaten us on the twofold path of integration. There is obviously something 'intellectual' – in the sense of 'noetic' about the phenomenon of prayer – but it is not an activity that in any way undermines the wholeness of the human person. On the contrary, it is placed by John at the center of one's total life as a person. It involves not only the intellect, but also the body and the soul.[110] This is what John means when saying that 'the heart is united with prayer.'[111] That is to say, it is the heart, the intellect, and the body that are at

---

[103] 19.1 (940C). For Evagrius, cf. *De or.*, esp. 85 (PG79.1185BC) and for Cassian, cf. *Conf.* 8 and 15 (48–9, 51–3).

[104] 27.ii, 47 (1116).

[105] 28.60 (1140B).

[106] *De lege spir.* 19 (PG65.908C). Cf. also *Ladder* 26.51 (1029BC); Mark the Monk, *Disp. cum quodam causidico* 5 (PG65.1077A) and Isaac the Syrian, *Mystic Treatises* (113).

[107] 27.20 (1100AB). For similar words, cf. Theoleptus of Philadelphia, *De abscondita operatione in Christo* (PG143.393B).

[108] 28.20 (1132D).

[109] 19.1 (940D).

[110] 28.59 (1140B). Cf. also Origen, *De or.* 2, 4 (301–02, 85); *Mac. Hom.* 13, 1 (119); 15, 13 (133–5); 27, 18 (228); Mark the Monk, *Disp. cum quodam causidico* 4 (PG65.1076B); Isaac the Syrian, *Mystic Treatises* (98); Theoleptus of Philadelphia, *De abscondita operatione in Christo* (PG143.389BC and 393A) and Greg. of Sinai, *Chapters*, 80.

[111] 26.iii,24.

prayer, or simply the heart, the intellect, the body at one with God. Even bodily forms of prayer are necessary manifestations, although they may make us susceptible of ostentation and pride. John warns against making a spectacle of prayer in the presence of others.[112] While Barsanuphius is indifferent to physical postures,[113] other ascetic writers stress the role of the body in prayer (cf. 1 Tim. 2.8). John writes:

> For those who have not yet obtained true prayer of the heart, violence in bodily prayer is a great help. I mean stretching out the hands, beating the breast, sincere raising of the eyes to heaven, deep sighing, frequent prostrations.[114]

The role of the body is affirmed, but it must be sanctified. Prayer that is merely bodily, externalized, lacking inward candor, is an abomination.[115] In fact, one can see in John indications of the later idea of the hesychasts regarding the unity of the heart and intellect in prayer. For it is also a cause of the intellect's unity with prayer. John speaks of 'noetic work'[116] or 'noetic *hesychia*,'[117] which must be unceasing.[118] Such prayer is so deeply embedded in us as to make John describe it as an act of the heart.[119]

John offers what he regards as a fundamental sequence of prayer:

1   thanksgiving,
2   confession, and
3   petition.

We do not begin by confessing sins but by gazing outward and upward to the beauty of God. Thereby, we recognize our own unseemliness without despair and repent in hope:

> Before all else, let us list sincere *thanksgiving* first on the scroll of our prayer. On the second line, we should put *confession* and heartfelt contrition of soul. Then let us present our *petition* to the king of all. This is the best way of prayer, as it was shown to one of the brethren by an angel of the Lord.[120]

---

[112] 28.25 (1133B). Cf. also Ps. Athanasius, *On Virginity* 10 (PG26.261D); *Apophth.* Tithoes 1 (PG65.428B); Cassian, *Conf.* 9, 35 (70–72) and especially Barsanuphius 74.

[113] Barsanuphius 509.

[114] 15.76 (900C). See also Evagrius, *De or.* 110 (PG79.1192B); Abba Isaiah, *Logos* 3 (12); Isaac the Syrian, *Mystic Treatises* (367); Greg. of Sinai, *Chapters*, 80. Abba Isaiah and Gregory of Sinai even offer a 'method' of bodily postures.

[115] 28.52 (1137C).

[116] 19.7 (941A) and 4.18 (685C).

[117] 4.31 (700C).

[118] 4.18 (685C); 28.35 and 36 (1136AB).

[119] 27.ii,12 (1109B) and 15.76 (900C).

[120] 28.6 (1132A).

John himself admits that this sequence is 'shown' or revealed. Indeed, it is not without precedent in the ascetic tradition. Evagrius of Pontus and Abba Isaiah of Scetis seem to allow for a certain introductory period in prayer, while the *History of Monastics* and Barsanuphius emphasize thanksgiving as the beginning of prayer.[121]

The character of prayer also depends on the situation in which it is practiced. Not all kinds of prayer are suited to all circumstances.[122] Nevertheless, no place precludes prayer, and even the most heinous or impure one can serve as one's temple.

> In an unclean place, I prayed to drive away unclean thoughts in order to be cleansed of impurity.[123]

According to Barsanuphius, 'one ought to pray in all places.'[124] For Evagrius, 'place (or: *topos*) for prayer' is a technical term closely connected to the phrase 'place (or: *topos*) of God.' Both refer to the awareness of God's presence and are derived from the Septuagint account of the appearance of God to Moses and to the elders on Mount Sinai (cf. Ex. 24.10–11).[125] It provides the context for the phrase found in the *Sayings of the Desert Fathers* that 'in the place where God was, there Antony would be.'[126]

Two matters often misunderstood, in early ascetic texts, call for brief examination here with reference to the *Ladder*. The first concerns the question as to whether it is more important in the minds and lives of the monastics to pray for other people than to support them socially or practically. There is no clear answer to this in John. Prayer for him is alike love for Christ and love for those who reflect Christ. The ability to discern whether, in any given case, prayer as serving others (*diakonia*) is more important than prayer as silence (*hesychia*), requires much vigilance and careful discernment, since either one or the other may prove a snare of the demons.[127] Though John usually emphasizes the practical side of the spiritual life in preference to the theoretical,[128] in certain

---

[121] Evagrius, *Prakt.* 42 (596); Abba Isaiah, *Logos* 4, 7 (24); *Hist. Monachorum*, Prol. 8 (27); Barsanuphius 142 (97).

[122] 27.ii,29 (1112CD) and 7.70 (816C).

[123] 15.77 (901A).

[124] Barsanuphius 441 and 709.

[125] For *topos proseuhēs*, cf. *De or.* 56 (PG79.1177D–80A), 71 (1181CD), 102 (1189BC) and 152 (1200B). For *topos Theou*, cf. *De or.* 57 (PG79.1180A). Macarius speaks of Jerusalem or Sion in preference to Sinai as being the place of God: cf. *Mac. Hom.* 4, 12 (36–7). Mystical or allegorical speculation as to how God might rightly be named 'place' dates back at least to Philo: cf. for example, *De Somniis*, 1, 62–4; cf. also J. A. Montgomery, 'The "Place" as an Appellation of Deity,' *Journal of Biblical Literature* 24 (1905), 17–26.

[126] *Apophth.* Antony 28 (PG65.84D–85A).

[127] 4.95 (716C) and 75 (712D).

[128] Cf., for example, 13.10 (860D) and 19.9 (941AB).

passages he is on his guard, suspecting that the demons can cause prayer to weaken, while encouraging us to devote our energies to *diakonia*:

A soul weak in prayer [is] often like iron in service.[129]

John does claim that 'love is greater than prayer.'[130] Yet he also identifies love for God and for one's neighbor with the act of prayer,[131] namely with the act of service *par excellence*. In certain cases, it is even legitimate to upset people 'so as not to lose that which is greater,' although in this passage John is referring to prayer being 'greater.'[132] To quote Isaac the Syrian, 'the person who has experienced the quiet of the cell does not avoid meetings out of despise for one's fellow, but because of the fruits gathered from solitude ... For love comes from prayer; and prayer comes from a solitary way of life.'[133] It is, therefore, a grave thing to intrude on someone's *hesychia*, to interrupt one's prayer,[134] or to expect of that person to serve us in a more 'material' or 'tangible' way. Climacus again explicitly states:

A servant of the Lord (*diakonon*) is one who in body stands before people but in intellect (*nous*) is knocking at the gate of heaven with prayer.[135]

It seems, then, that no answer in the abstract can be given to the first question. One must act appropriately in a given situation:

If there is a time (*kairos*) for everything under heaven ... then there is a time for unceasing prayer and a time for sincere service (*diakonia*).[136]

Unceasing prayer is not continual prayer. It is prayer in its *kairos*. And *diakonia* outside of its *kairos* is deception.

The second, and related, question is the seeming conflict between prayer and work. The *Ladder* quite clearly describes prayer as work:

Prayer is ... a work (*ergon*) of the angels ... an unending activity (*ergasia*).[137]

---

[129] 13.1 (860A) and 4 (860AB).

[130] 26.34 (1028B). Cf. also Origen, *De or.* 10, 1 (344, 121) and Niketas Stethatos, *Cent.* 2, 76 (317).

[131] Cf. 26.ii,25. Cf. also Evagrius, *Prakt.* 91 (692–4) and Mark the Monk, *De lege spir.* 115 (PG65.920B).

[132] 27.ii,29. Cf. also Mark the Monk, *Disp. cum quodam causidico* 6 (PG65.1077D).

[133] *Mystic Treatises* (206, 295).

[134] 28.50 (1137B).

[135] 4.102 (717A). On prayer and service, cf. G. Gould, *The Desert Fathers on Monastic Community*, 167–82.

[136] 26.59 (1023BC) and 19.9 (941AB).

[137] 28.1 (1129BC). Cf. also Origen, *De or.* 12, 2 (324, 104); *Apophth.* Apollo 2 (PG65.133C–36B); Palladius, *Hist. Laus.*, Paul of Pherme 23 (62–3); Anastasius Sinaite, *Quaestiones* 93 (PG89.732B).

There is no case for speaking of prayer *and* work.[138] The fact that prayer is an act belonging to the 'noetic powers' of angels – Barsanuphius prefers to describe it as 'an inner activity'[139] – does not mean it differs from work but merely that work is given a new dimension, just as the fact that the monk is called 'an earthly type of angel'[140] in no way detracts from but fulfills the monk's humanity. Prayer is alike a way of acting and a way of making one's action effective.[141] The ascetic writers are convinced that prayer is not a form of 'idleness.'[142]

In regard to the above two questions, one point is constantly stressed throughout John's discussion of prayer, namely the certainty that, through it, one is transformed into fire, light and joy.[143] To use Origen's words, 'we would call the entire life of a saint one great unbroken prayer.'[144] The ascetic aims to pass beyond the various acts of prayer in order to become a fiery torch of prayer, a living prayer.

Prayer, however, is not an end in itself. As noted, it is a means towards the end of union with God and with others. It is love in humility.[145] The ascetic does not love God in order to pray. Rather, it is through prayer that the ascetic loves God. One does not enter the desert or a monastic community to pray, but to love. One seeks no experience outside the personal experience of God's love. For John, prayer is only one of the presuppositions of *hesychia*,[146] which is life centered on the love of God. The distinction is reminiscent of Diadochus' distinction between prayer and theology.[147] This indicates movement, progression, even within the state of prayer. John actually speaks of progress

---

[138] 27.26 (1101A). Cf. also Evagrius, *De or.* 113 and 39 (PG79.1192D and 1176A); *Apophth.* Macarius of Alexandria (PG65.305A) and Niketas Stethatos, *Cent.* 2, 47 (309).

[139] Barsanuphius 214.

[140] 27.15 (1100A).

[141] 27.ii,45 (1116BC).

[142] Isaac the Syrian, *Mystic Treatises* (114, 300, 328), although Isaac also speaks of work as an impediment to prayer (cf. 40); Symeon the New Theologian, *TGP* 1.95 (68) and Kallistos/Ignatios, *Cent.* 28 (227).

[143] 30.10 (1157A); 28.52 (1137C) and 18.4 (937C). On becoming fire in prayer, cf. *Apophth.* Arsenius 27 (PG65.96BC), Zacchariah 2 (180A), Isaiah 4 (181AB), Silvanus 12 (412C), Tithoes 1 (428B); Barsanuphius 1; John Moschus, *Pratum* 69 (PG87.2921BC); 104 (2961BC); 123 (2985B); Symeon the New Theologian, *TGP* 3.21 (86); 1.68 (59); *Cat.* 23 (26) and 22 (378). For 'light' imagery, cf. Ps. Athanasius, *Sermo pro iis qui saeculo renuntiarunt* 2 (PG28.1409B); *Apophth.* Hilarion 1 (PG65.241C); *Mac. Hom.* 47, 6 (306); Abba Isaiah, *Logos* 4, 1 (15) and 16, 2 (88), where Isaiah uses the same words as Ps. Athanasius; John Moschus, *Pratum* 51 (PG87.2908A); Thalassius, *Cent.* 1.11 (PG91.1429A) and 81 (1436A). For joy, cf. *Apophth.* Benjamin 4 (PG65.145A).

[144] *De or.* 12, 2 (325, 104).

[145] 26.43 (1028B) and 25.33 (996C).

[146] 27.ii,12 (1109B). Cf. also Greg. of Sinai, *Chapt.* 5 (64).

[147] *Cent.* 68 (128–9).

being made.[148] He observes that, although, externally, there may be only one stage in prayer at a given time, yet internally there are many stages. One can pray to God even as one speaks to a friend. Or, one may intercede with God for the sins of others. Or, again, one may ask to be forgiven for one's own sins.[149]

John insists that prayer should be 'continual,'[150] even when one has reached the very top of the ladder of perfection.

> Although you may have climbed the whole ladder of virtues, pray for forgiveness of sins.[151]

In any case, prayer is to be pervasive. It is identified with 'remembrance of God.' It is continual[152] (1 Thess. 5.17), even while asleep (cf. Ps. 74.61), although sleep may be an 'unjust spouse' inducing detachment from prayer.[153]

Prayer is described as 'the queen of virtues,'[154] as a virtue 'above nature.'[155] It is essentially a gift, taught us by others or even by God personally.[156] It is only in this latter sense that John says that it can be learned 'scientifically.'[157] Yet ultimately God bestows this gift from above. In effect, it is caught, not taught, even though an effort is required on our side:

> Acquire all courage, and you will have God for your teacher in prayer.
>
> Prayer has a teacher all its own, God, who teaches us knowledge (cf. Mt. 18.20) and grants prayer to the one who prays.[158]

---

[148] 28.35 (1136AB).

[149] 28.5 (1129D).

[150] 28.35 (1136AB), 26 (1133B) and 22 (1133A).

[151] 28.12 (1132B).

[152] 28.36 (1136B). The link between 'remembrance of God' and prayer is found in Origen, *De or.* 8, 2 (317, 98); Diadochus, *Cent.* 3 (86), 27 (98–9), 32 (102), 33 (102–04), 81 (139–40), 96 (158–9), 97 (159–60) and 100 (161–3); Barsanuphius 249; Dorotheus, *Life* 10 (138) and Isaac the Syrian, *Mystic Treatises* (6, 237). All the ascetis writers refer to continual prayer: cf. Serapion, *Ep. ad monachos* 3 (PG40.928D–29A); Origen, *De or.* 22, 5 (349, 125); Athanasius, *Life of Antony* 3 (PG26.845A) and 55 (921B–25A); Abba Isaiah, *Logos* 1, 1 (1); Barsanuphius 441 (221) and 709 (322); Dorotheus, *Life* 3 (126) and Isaac the Syrian, *Mystic Treatises* (62, 89).

[153] 19.8 (941A). For prayer even during sleep, cf. Diadochus, *Cent.* 61 (120–21) and Isaac the Syrian, *Mystic Treatises* (176) also quoted in Kallistos/Ignatios, *Cent.* 90 (284). Other writers say one ought to fight sleep: cf. Clem Alex., *Paedag.* 2, 9 (205–07), and spend at least half the night in prayer: cf. Abba Isaiah, *Logos* 4, 4 (20).

[154] 28.2 (1129B). Cf. also Greg. Nyssa, *De proposito secundum deum* (PG46.301D); *Mac. Hom.* 40, 2 (276) and *Epistola* (PG34.432C) for precisely the same words as in the *Ladder*. Mark the Monk, *Disp. cum quoodam causidico* 8 (PG65.1081D).

[155] 26.42–43 (1028B).

[156] 26.42 (1028B).

[157] 27.20 (1100B) and 26 (1101A).

[158] 28.62–3 (1140C), 17 (1132C) and 32 (1133A). Cf. the same words in Evagrius, *De or.* 58 (PG79.1180AB). Also see *Mac. Hom.* 19, 8 (187) and 33, 2 (258–9) and Barsanuphius 182. For

Thus prayer is nothing more than an offering back to God of the very gift received from above.[159] When the grace of God visits us in prayer, we should not let go of it, because we do not know when it will come again.[160] Naturally, John is realistic enough to recognize the difficulty of holding on to this gift:

> The common run of people are wont to find [it] quite alien to themselves.[161]

The Jesus Prayer

True prayer is endowed with simplicity, in contrast to loquacity or verbosity, which John depreciates (Lk. 18.10 and Mt. 6.7):

> Do not try to be verbose (*polylogein*), when you pray, lest your mind be distracted in searching for words. One word of the publican propitiated God, and one cry of faith saved the thief. Loquacity (*polylogia*) in prayer often distracts the intellect (*nous*) and leads to fantasy, whereas brevity (*monologia*) makes for concentration.[162]

True prayer is 'loss of *polylogia*,'[163] which is, in fact, 'the darkening of prayer.'[164] Silence, on the other hand, gives rise to prayer (cf. Job 33.33; Eccl. 12.13): 'Intelligent silence is the mother of prayer.'[165]

Nevertheless, it is inevitable that we should use words in prayer, at least at the earlier stages of spiritual life. John urges:

> Try to lift up, or rather to enclose your thought within the words of your prayer.[166]

---

prayer as a gift, cf. Evagrius, *De or.* 69 (PG79.1181C) and 87 (1185C); *Mac. Hom*.17, 5 (169); 26, 21 (215) and 31, 4 (249); Isaac the Syrian, *Mystic Treatises* (116); and Greg. Palamas, *Triads* 2, 1, 31; 2, 4 and 2, 1, 31.

[159] 28.41 (1137C).

[160] 28.51 (1137B).

[161] 27.2, 6 (1108B). In prayer, there is need of violence: cf. Evagrius, *De or.* 30 (PG79.1173B); *Apophth*. Agathon 9 (PG65.112B); *Mac. Hom.* 19, 3 (119–20); and Abba Isaiah, *Logos* 5, 3 (36).

[162] 28.9 (1132B). Cf. also similar words in Symeon the New Theologian, *Eth.* 11 (342) and *Cat.* 41 (162).

[163] 27.ii,6 (1180A).

[164] 11.2 (852B) and 14.31 (869AB). On *polylogia*, cf. also Evagrius, *De or.* 151 (PG79.1200B); Diadochus, *Cent.* 70 (130) and Abba Isaiah, *Logos* 11, 1 (72).

[165] 11.3 and 4 (852BC). Silence, *hesychia*, is both greatly prized and praised in the desert: cf. Athanasius, *On Virginity* 22 (PG28.277C) and *Sermo exhortatorius* 2 (PG28.1112C); *Apophth*. Arsenius 2 (PG65.88C) and 40 (105BC); Agathon 1 (108D–09B) and 15 (113B); Palladius, *Hist. Laus.*, Macarius of Alexandria 19–20 (51–4); Diadochus, *Cent.* 11 (89); Abba Isaiah, *Logos* 16, 4 (92); Barsanuphius 554 (263–4); Cyril of Scythopolis, *Life of Euthymios* 15 (24, 22–3); Isaac the Syrian, *Mystic Treatises* (232); Niketas Stethatos, *Cent.* 1. 26 (278–9) and Kallistos/Ignatios, *Cent.* 16 (215).

[166] 28.16 (1132C). The monks in the Alexandrian Prison say nothing in their prayers: cf. 5.5 (765B).

For this purpose, he recommends the use of short, simple prayers, sometimes a verse from the Psalms:

> Cry to the one who has the strength to save, not with cleverly-spun phrases but in humble words, preferably making this your prelude: 'Have mercy on me, for I am weak.' (Ps. 6.3)[167]

Elsewhere John proposes a series of different scriptural texts to be used by the monk. Yet he leaves one free to choose, since 'not all the loaves of heavenly bread have the same appearance.'[168] It is clear that several forms of prayer are envisaged. However, there is one type of simple prayer, to which particular importance is attached. This is the invocation or remembrance of the Name of Jesus.

Short prayers are mentioned already in the *Sayings of the Desert Fathers*: 'Abba Poemen said that Abba Paphnutius ... had recourse to short prayers.'[169] And, although Nilus lays a certain emphasis on the invocation of the Name of Jesus, it is still peripheral in spiritual practice. It is only with Diadochus of Photice that this acquires an important and even central role, which was to influence later authors. Diadochus mentions the invocation of the Lord Jesus' Name,[170] while Barsanuphius and John continue the same tradition, speaking of short prayers with particular reference to the Name of Jesus and to unceasing prayer. One passage is fairly explicit about this: 'Pray ... saying the words "Lord Jesus Christ have mercy on me".'[171] Dorotheus of Gaza combines the traditions of Diadochus and Barsanuphius alike.[172] He is followed by the Sinaite writers: John of the *Ladder*, Hesychius and Philotheus. The fully developed technique of the Jesus Prayer does not emerge until the fourteenth century when the hesychasts try to establish its Apostolic source and its theological justification.[173]

The *Ladder* does not deal with the matter explicitly. Nonetheless, there are three passages where the Jesus Prayer is mentioned and which greatly influenced subsequent authors. There is a possible fourth reference where John speaks of 'the prayer of Jesus,'[174] but more probably this implies the Lord's Prayer.

---

[167] 15.76 (900CD); 18.3 (937D) and 28.4 (1129D).

[168] 27.ii, 42 (1116A).

[169] Cf. *Apophth.* Poemen 190 (ed. Guy, 30). Cf. also *Apophth.* Elias 7 (PG65.184D–85A), Macarius 19 (269C) and *Apophth.* Nau 184 (1908, 271–2); Cassian, *Conf.* 9, 36 (72–3). For the Egyptian practice, cf. L. Regnault, 'La prière continuelle "monologistos" dans la littérature apophtegmatique,' *Irénikon* 47 (1974), 467–93.

[170] Cf. *Cent.* 31 (101), 59 (113), 61 (114), 88 (147–8) and 97 (159–60).

[171] Barsanuphius 446. On short prayers, cf. 39 and 93. On the Name, cf. 304. On unceasing prayer, cf. 225.

[172] *Life* 10 (138).

[173] Cf. Greg of Sinai, *Chapters* (80); Kallistos/Ignatios, *Cent.* 50 (249–51), 21 (222) and 25 (224).

[174] 9.1 (841C).

(i) Let the remembrance of death and the Prayer of Jesus, being of single phrase (*monologistos Iēsou euchē*), go to sleep with you and get up with you.[175]

The context here is the assault of demons at the time of sleep. The author proposes remembrance of death and the Prayer of Jesus as ways of fighting them. The expression *Iēsou euchē* is probably used for the first time by John. He is also the first to describe it as *monologistos*, concise. The term literally means, 'consisting of a single phrase.' And it is adopted and adapted from Mark the Monk, who uses it to qualify, not prayer but hope.[176] There is no evidence in John of any precise form of words that corresponds to the Jesus Prayer. Nevertheless, it would be wrong to claim that, in this passage, Climacus is simply recommending verbal brevity, as in the case of some other prayers that he mentions.[177] One should not read too much into Climacus' advice. However, it is probable that he envisages the Name of Jesus as a source of power and an essential part of the prayer, whose sources must be traced to the New Testament (1 Cor. 12.13; 1 Jn 4.2; Mt. 16.16 and 1 Cor. 14.19).

Previous ascetic authors show that the Name of Jesus was usually not employed alone but was followed by other invocations. Abba Elias, in the *Sayings of the Desert Fathers*, employs the phrase, 'Jesus, save me;' and Barsanuphius uses a similar phrase: 'Jesus, help me.' Both these authors use 'Jesus' without 'Lord,' but Diadochus of Photice adopts the phrase 'Lord Jesus.' Later hesychasts will stress that only the perfect are able to invoke the Name of Jesus alone.[178] The standard form of the Jesus Prayer is first found in *The Life of Abba Philemon*, a text about a monk in Egypt. While this document is difficult to date, it is perhaps more or less contemporary with the *Ladder*.[179] The words, it seems, were not yet crystallized and John may have preferred to allow a free choice here.

---

[175] 15.51 (889CD). This passage is quoted by Kallistos/Ignatios, *Cent.* 24 (224) and 74 (274) and Greg. Palamas, *Triads* 1, 3, 2.

[176] *De lege. spir.* 10 (PG65.905C) and *De his.* 140 (952). But in Mark, presumably, *monologistos* means, not 'of a single phrase' but 'unwavering.'

[177] Cf. 15.76 (900D) and 27.ii,42 (1116A).

[178] *Apophth.* Elias 7 (PG65.184D–85A); Barsanuphius 39, 126, 225, 268, 448 and 659; Diadochus, *Cent.* 59 (113), 61 (114), 31 (101), 88 (174–8) and 97 (159–60); the hesychastic text is from Kallistos/Ignatios, *Cent.* 50 (250). Cf. also Dorotheus, *Life* 10 (138). Yannaras may be reading too much into Climacus' words when he claims that the Jesus Prayer, as developed by the fourteenth-century hesychasts, is found clearly developed in the *Ladder*: cf. *Metaphysike*, 231.

[179] For the words, 'Lord Jesus Christ, Son of God, have mercy on me,' cf. *Life of Abba Philemon* in *Philokalia* 2 (244). On the importance of this text, cf. B. Krivochéine, 'Date du texte traditionnel de la "Priére de Jésus",' *Messager de l'Exarchat du Patriarche russe en Europe occidentale* 7–8 (1951), 55–9.

(ii) As you go on your way, arm yourself with prayer. When you reach the place, stretch out your hands. Flog your enemies with the Name of Jesus (*onomati Iēsou*), for there is no stronger weapon in heaven or on earth.[180]

The context of this second quotation concerns the use of the Name of Jesus Christ as a weapon against childish fear. There is specific reference to the power of the Name of Jesus (cf. Mt. 16.17–18; Jn 14.13; 16.23 and 26; Acts 4.12 and Phil. 2.10) and to its invocation as a weapon against the demons, as is also apparent in the previous passage. The word 'weapon' suggests an 'aggressive' attitude towards the fallen nature and a real desire for glorification. In this passage, a particular bodily posture is also envisaged and encouraged.

(iii) Let the remembrance of Jesus (*Iēsou mnēmē*) be united with your breath, and then you will know the value of stillness.[181]

Here, John is being more general. He speaks only of 'remembrance,' not specifically of a 'prayer' or the 'Name,' as in the above two passages. The context refers instead to the notion of 'the laying aside of thoughts.' The Jesus Prayer is a way of laying aside one's thoughts and of attaining to imageless prayer. The Name 'Jesus' itself ceases to be a thought or mere meditation, and becomes more a sense of Christ's presence. The implication is more vague and diffuse, in the sense of remembering Jesus continually. Moreover, the reference to breathing may be seen as an indication of the uninterrupted use of prayer.[182] Curiously, many later authors give the phrase a far more specific meaning, believing that a physical technique is implied. There is, however, no clear and unambiguous mention of such a technique, at least in the Greek tradition, until the late thirteenth and early fourteenth centuries. What concerns John here is that the monk should pray without ceasing:

Stillness is unceasing (*adiastatos*) worship and waiting upon God.[183]

Adiastatos signifies that there is no stopping, no *stasis*. And breathing, similarly, implies that prayer is a continual movement towards and progression in God. Any concentration upon the Name of Jesus is an attempt to gather up one's dispersed thoughts with a view to focusing them upon a single object, or rather subject, with a single purpose.

---

[180] 20.6 (945C). Quoted by Greg. of Sinai, *Chapters* (81) and Kallistos/Ignatios, *Cent.* 49 (249). Emphasis on the Name is also found in other writers: cf. for example Ps. Chrysostom, *Ep. ad monachos* (PG60.752–53); Diadochus, *Cent.* 31 (101); Abba Isaiah, *Logos* 23, 7 (148); Barsanuphius 103, 417, 424, 427 and 430; Niketas Stethatos, *Cent.* 1.97 (296–7). On the importance of the Name, cf. Ware, 'The Power of the Name.'

[181] 27.ii,26 (1112C). Quoted by Kallistos/Ignatios, *Cent.* 22 (223).

[182] Cf. also 4.19 (688C).

[183] 27.ii,25 (1112C).

The notion of imageless prayer is already emphasized in Evagrius, who also recommends the use of short formulas.[184] This rejection of images is not in itself a negative movement, but rather an acceptance and veneration of a greater and more 'objective' reality. Nevertheless, Evagrius does not state explicitly how imageless prayer is attained, nor does he recommend any particular form of words.

These appear to be technical matters. But they do not obscure – indeed they serve to emphasize – the fact that the incessantly repeated call, whether in the form 'Lord have mercy' or 'Lord Jesus Christ, have mercy on me,' or any other short entreaty, reflects the basic understanding, which Climacus expresses, of prayer as a person-to-person relationship in its significance for the relational aspect of the ascetic. It does not even need to be articulated in logical word structure and sentences: 'We do not know how to pray as we ought, but the Spirit intercedes for us with sighs too deep for words' (Rom. 8.26). And this lies also at the basis of John's theory and practice of prayer.

---

[184] *De or.* 98 (PG79.1189A) and 151 (1200B). For this Evagrian notion, see Chapter 4 above.

Conclusion: Popularity, Manuscripts and Editions

The Reading of the *Ladder*

With the exception of the Scriptures and the liturgical books of the Christian Church, no other writing in Eastern Christendom has been studied, copied and translated to the same extent as *The Ladder of Divine Ascent* of St John Climacus. The *Ladder* is a text that has greatly influenced and shaped not only the Eastern Orthodox world, and especially its monastic tradition, but the entire Christian world. It is still, therefore, more surprising that there are relatively few scholarly monographs dealing with this remarkable document, while, at least in the English language, nothing has emerged over the last two decades since certain fundamental portions of this book were presented as a doctoral dissertation at the University of Oxford.

The respect for the author of the *Ladder* is evident from the unusual prominence that he enjoys in the Orthodox ecclesiastical year. Besides the annual commemoration on 30 March during the calendar of fixed feasts, the fourth Sunday during Lent, together with most of the liturgical texts of that day, is also dedicated to him. This marks him out as the ascetic author *par excellence*, whose writings provide a standard and model for the whole Church.

Even today, the *Ladder* is appointed to be read aloud in churches or in the refectory, as well as privately in the cells of Orthodox monasteries, each year during Lent.[1] The origins of this practice cannot be precisely traced. There is no doubt, however, that it began from the time of the author's life. After all, abbot John of Raithou requested the *Ladder* specifically for the spiritual benefit of the monks of his monastery. It would not be too difficult to imagine the monks of Raithou listening to the reading of the *Ladder* during their Lenten mealtimes. As pointed out in Chapter 1, the text is intended for cenobites. Therefore, in fact, many older monks will have listened to or read it perhaps as many as fifty or sixty times during their lifetime. Nevertheless, the popularity of the *Ladder* is also to be seen among laypersons throughout the centuries.[2] To this day, it has proved the favorite reading of countless Orthodox people in Greece, Bulgaria, Serbia, Russia and elsewhere. The

---

[1] *Triodion Katanyktikon*, ed. M. I. Saliveros (Athens, n.d.), 75 and 78. Cf. also H. Brockhaus, *Die Kunst in den Athos-Klöstern*, Leipzig: 1924, 82f.

[2] Cf. Ware, *Introduction*, 66–8, and *Introduction*, ed. Holy Transfiguration Monastery, xxvii–xxviii.

striking symbol of the ladder, which binds together the entire book, the author's combination of monastic shrewdness and refreshing humor, his skill in drawing so many themes into a single, traditional, yet original synthesis, and above all the unequaled depth of his spiritual insight: these are at least some of the aspects of the *Ladder* which must have caught the attention and imagination of innumerable readers over the years.

There is no equivalent of the *Ladder* in the West, but its popularity may be compared with that of the *Imitation of Christ*. Nonetheless, the two books differ greatly in character. The wide diffusion of the *Ladder* is further attested by the numerous surviving manuscripts, often both well maintained and elaborately illustrated, even including commentaries, such as in the edition of Rader reprinted in Migne (*Patrologia Graeca*, vol. 88). In Dr Martin's book, thirty-nine illuminated Greek manuscripts alone are dealt with. The Sinaite monastery of St Catherine, of which John himself was for a while the abbot, has in its possession at least fifteen manuscripts, one of which dates back to the ninth century (Mt Sinai 421). Moreover, many monasteries of Mount Athos also possess several such manuscripts, some of them very ornate.[3]

Unfortunately, no critical edition exists as yet and the *editio princeps*, still in use, belongs to the Jesuit scholar Mattheus Raderus (Paris, 1633), who used eight manuscripts as his chief sources.[4] Seven of these are at present in the *Bayerische Staatsbibliothek* in Munich. The eighth was loaned to him by Andreas Schott of Antwerp. The text is sufficiently faithfully transmitted, the textual variations between manuscripts being very few. Therefore, it was found to be reasonably accurate and satisfactory for the purposes of this study. Rader's edition, however, is by no means critical, at least in the modern sense.

The best edition is the more recent one published in Constantinople in 1883 by the monk Sophronios of the Athonite monastery of the Great Lavra. This has an apparently edifying intention rather than a critical one.[5] Yet L. Petit pronounces it as 'supérieure sous certains rapports à celle de Raderus–Migne.'[6] It was Sophronios who also introduced the numbering of paragraphs for the reader's convenience, as he himself observes in his prologue.

The Rader edition has been republished by P. Trevisan in 1941 at Turin in two volumes of the series *Corona Patrum Salesiana* 8–9, while more recently the edition of Sophronios was republished by 'Astir' in Athens (1970).

---

[3] I had the opportunity of studying one of the fourteenth-century manuscripts, with impressive miniatures and illuminations, at the monastery of Stavronikita; cf. Ms. 915, f. 50. An account of the existing manuscripts of the *Ladder* is found in Bogdanovic, *Jean Climaque*, 25–7.

[4] Cf. PG88.621–22. The treatise *To the Shepherd* was earlier published by Rader, Augsburg: 1606.

[5] Cf. Martin, *Illustration*, 6.

[6] 'Saint Jean Climaque,' *DTC* 8, 693.

Influence and Translations

The influence of John of the *Ladder* on later spiritual writers has been at once extensive and impressive. On Mt Sinai itself, his teaching on prayer and *hesychia* was developed by Hesychius (?seventh–eighth century), who makes Climacus' scattered allusions to the Jesus Prayer his dominant theme,[7] and later by Philotheus (?ninth–tenth century). Anastasius (*c.* 700), another Sinaite, and Theodore the Studite (759–826) were also influenced by Climacus.[8] Although, surprisingly, the *Ladder* is nowhere cited in the vast eleventh-century anthology of writings, stories and sayings entitled *Synagoge* by its compiler Paulos Evergetinos, it was certainly read and valued by Symeon the New Theologian and probably also by Symeon's disciple and biographer, Niketas Stethatos. Symeon was particularly helped by Step 13, on despondency. Indeed, the *Ladder*'s influence is especially evident in Symeon's teaching on the gift of tears and on the role of the spiritual father. Although the *Ladder* is only cited twice in his *Catechetical Orations*,[9] it is known that Symeon hardly ever makes explicit reference to other writers.

Peter of Damascus (twelfth century) quotes Climacus at least thirteen times, and the fourteenth-century hesychasts clearly draw heavily upon the *Ladder*. There are thirteen citations from the *Ladder* in Gregory of Sinai – far more than from any other author – and Gregory places Climacus' name first in his list of writers approved for monastic reading.[10] In the *Triads in Defense of the Holy Hesychasts* of Gregory Palamas, the *Ladder* is quoted some twenty-five times. Although in this work Palamas does not usually refer to the author of the *Ladder* by name, in his other writings Climacus is referred to at least as many times, frequently even by name. Kallistos and Ignatios Xanthopoulos quote the *Ladder* more than thirty times in their *Century*. These fourteenth-century writers chiefly refer to Step 27 on *hesychia*, to John's statements on the invocation of the Name of Jesus, and to Step 28 on prayer.

The influence is by no means small also in the West, where the *Ladder* enjoyed popularity in various monastic orders, especially among Franciscans, Benedictines, Cistercians, the monks of Chartreuse, who wrote many commentaries on it, and to a lesser degree among Jesuits.[11] In France, the

---

[7] Cf. Völker, *Scala Paradisi*, 291–314, where Völker makes a good comparison between Climacus and Hesychius.

[8] Cf. Couilleau, 'Saint Jean Climaque,' *DTC* 8, 386. Cf. also Bogdanovic, *Jean Climaque*, 159–61.

[9] *Cat.* 4 (358) and 30 (204). Cf. also Hausherr, *Vie*, 12, and *La Méthode*, 121.

[10] *De quietudine et duobus orationis modis* 11 (PG150.1324CD). Gregory's list is: John Climacus, Isaac the Syrian, Maximus Confessor, Symeon the New Theologian, Niketas Stethatos, Hesychius and Philotheus. On the influence of Climacus on the fourteenth-century hesychasts, cf. Hausherr, *La Méthode*, 131; and Meyendorff, *Palamas*, 18, 141–3.

[11] Cf. Couilleau, 'Saint Jean Climaque,' *DTC* 8, 387–8, and Viller, *Spiritualité*, 92.

Jansenists took a liking to Climacus, together with a number of other ascetic authors.

The commentaries or collections of *scholia* written on the *Ladder* are numerous. Three in particular should be mentioned here, two Eastern and one Western. Elias, metropolitan of Crete between the years 1120 and 1130, was the first to write a commentary in any systematic form, and many manuscripts exist of his work.[12] Another commentary was written in the East by Nikephoros Kallistos Xanthopoulos (d. 1333),[13] and in the West by Dionysius the Carthusian during the fifteenth century.[14]

Before the end of the seventh century, indeed very soon after John's death, the *Ladder* was translated into Syriac. In fact, one of the oldest manuscripts in any language is a Syriac codex in the British Museum (Add. Ms 14593), written in Edessa and bearing the date 817.[15] Several manuscripts existed among Melchite circles by the ninth century. Climacus' book was also translated into other Eastern languages: into Arabic and Georgian[16] before the tenth century, and into Romanian by the early seventeenth century.[17] Russian, Serbian and Bulgarian translations saw the light as a result of Slavonic influence in the Orthodox world. Its effect on the fifteenth-century Russian monastic revival can be seen in the leaders alike of the Non-Possessors, Nil of Sora, as well as of the Possessors, Joseph of Volokalamsk.[18] The Serbian despot George Brankovic commissioned a new translation of John's book. And, in the correspondence of Tsar Ivan IV, often called 'the Terrible,' next to the Bible, the *Ladder* is the book most often quoted.[19]

---

[12] Cf. Codex 2101. f. 88 of Esphigmenou monastery on Mount Athos. Cf. also V. Laurent, 'Le synodicon de Sybrite et les métropolites de Crète aux X–XIII siècles,' *Echos d'Orient* 32 (Paris, 1933), 385–412, and S. Salaville, 'Elie de Crète,' *DTC* 4, 2331–3.

[13] Cf. Politis, 'Agnostos Ergo,' 69–83. Cf. the edition published in Preveza, 2002; (see Bibliography).

[14] Cf. *Introduction* (ed. Paraclete), 12. Dionysius the Carthusian also produced a full translation of the *Ladder*.

[15] Cf. W. Wright, *Catalogue of Syriac Manuscripts in the British Museum acquired since the Year 1838*, Part 2, London: 1870–72, 590f; A. Smith Lewis, *Codex Climaci Rescriptus*, Cambridge: 1909, xi; and A. Baumstark, *Geschichte der Syrischen Literatur*, Bonn: 1922, 165–6.

[16] Cf. the fragmentary translation by the tenth-century monk Euthymios, printed in *Analecta Ballandiana* 49 (1931).

[17] Cf. M. Heppell, 'Some Slavonic Manuscripts of the "*Scala Paradisi*",' *Byzantinoslavica* 18, 2 (1957), 233–70. Cf. also Heppell, *Introduction*, 27–9; N. Corneanu, 'Contributions des traducteurs roumains à la diffusion de l'Echelle de saint Jean Climaque,' *Studia Patristica* 8 (Berlin, 1966), 340–55, and C. Kern, *Les traductions russes des textes patristiques*, Chêvetogne: 1957.

[18] Cf. Meyendorff, *Byzantium and the Rise of Russia*, Cambridge: 1981, esp. 124, 131, 239, 260. Cf. also Bogdanovic, *Jean Climaque*, 172–82, Couilleau, 'Saint Jean Climaque,' *DTC* 8, 387; F. von Lilienfeld, 'Der athonitische Hesychasmus des 14 und 15 Jahrhunderts im Lichte der zeitgenössischen russischen Quellen,' *Jahrbücher für die Geschichte Osteuropas* 6 (1958), 439 and 443f, and Krumbacher, *Geschichte*, 144.

[19] Heppell, *Introduction*, 28, 33; *Introduction*, ed. Holy Transfiguration Monastery, xxvii–xxviii.

There are several modern Greek translations which have either been published or which exist in manuscripts, such as those belonging to the sixteenth or seventeenth century and found in the Athonite monasteries of Koutloumousiou, Stavroniketa and Dionysiou. The published editions are four. These include, first, that by the erudite author Maximos Margounios, whose translation appeared in Venice in 1590; second, the one by the Cretan priest–monk Athanasios Varouchas (in two editions: Venice 1690 and 1693); and, third, that by the Cretan Archimandrite Jeremiah of Sinai, although this last edition mingles the text with the *scholia*. More recently, a translation by Archimandrite Ignatios (Pouloupatis), subsequently reprinted several times, is based on various manuscripts and contains an introduction and indices (Athens, 1978, first edition). Monk Georgios (Makedos) also published a translation, with a helpful introduction and notes, in Athens (Mt Sinai Publications, 2000).

In the West, a Latin translation appeared at least as early as the eleventh century, although this was fragmentary. Another, more complete, though clumsy, version was produced in the thirteenth or early fourteenth century by the Franciscan 'spiritual' of the Strict Observance, Angelus Clarenus,[20] who also familiarized the West with the works of Basil the Great and Macarius of Egypt. A later edition was published in Venice in 1518.

The first Italian translation was made in 1474 by Gentile da Foligno, a disciple of Angelus Clarenus. The *Ladder* also appeared in Portuguese in the fourteenth century – although this translation has been lost – in Spanish by Juan de Estrada in 1504 at Toledo, in French by R. Gaultier in 1603, and in German by F. Handwercher in 1834. Furthermore, among the first books printed in America was a Spanish edition of the *Ladder*, published in Mexico in the sixteenth century under the title *Escala Espiritual de San Juan Climaco*.[21]

The first English translation was by a Cistercian monk as late as 1858. Characterized as 'chiefly appertaining to solitaries,'[22] Step 27 on *hesychia* was to a great extent abridged in this edition, which is often more a paraphrase than an exact rendering. A second English translation appeared in 1959, based on both Greek and Slavonic manuscripts, and is far more accurate and complete than the first.[23] This was reissued by the Holy Transfiguration Monastery in

---

[20] J. Gribomont, '*La Scala Paradisi*, Jean de Raithou et Ange Clareno,' *Studia Monastica* 2 (1960), 345–58; A. Siegmund, *Die Ueberlieferung der griechischen christlichen Literatur in der lateinischen Kirche bis zum 12 Jahrhundert*, München–Pasing: 1949, 179–80.

[21] H. R. Wagner, *Nueva bibliografia mexicana del singlo XVI* (Mexico), 5–8.

[22] Father Robert, Monk of Mount Saint Bernard's Abbey, *The Holy Ladder of Perfection by Which We May Ascend to Heaven*, Leicestershire: 1858, esp. 392.

[23] Archimandrite Lazarus (Moore), *The Ladder of Divine Ascent*, London: 1959. For Heppell's introduction, cf. 13–35. A fresh translation of the treatise *To the Shepherd* may also be found in J. Chryssavgis, *Soul Mending*, 176–93.

Brookline, MA (1978, second [and revised] edition: 1991; third edition: 2001), and included the brief work, *To the Shepherd*, which was omitted in the first two editions of Fr Robert and Fr Lazarus, but which omitted the introduction by Dr M. Heppell included in Fr Lazarus' version. There has also been a third rendering in the series *The Classics of Western Spirituality* (New York, 1982) with indices, including an introduction by Bishop Kallistos (Ware).[24]

'This is a ladder that we must each ascend for ourselves,' writes Bishop Kallistos Ware.[25] John himself ascended the divine ladder and, in fact, had no need to write. He wrote as an act of sharing. Fr Georges Florovsky observes that 'the level of the *Ladder* is very simple: it is defined by the logic of the heart rather than by the logic of the intellect.'[26] Climacus himself, however, defines areas difficult, if not impossible, to describe. Scholars want to discover his sources and his influences. It has been the purpose of this study to place John within his literary context of the Egyptian desert and the monastic regions of Palestine. Yet that which Climacus received from his predecessors he made his own, and this he has transmitted to his successors in the Byzantine world and to his readers through the centuries, namely the personal encounter with Christ at each step of the ladder. For Christ is at the beginning of the journey, Christ is the goal, and Christ, again, is the way (Jn 14.6).

John became known for concepts and terms that he coins and bequeaths in relation to the way of tears and silence. However, John became influential because he speaks out about an experience of eternity relevant to all times. He speaks, through the reader's experience, of his own experience. He is compassionate and free, but at the same time his experience is a judgement. His compassion and his judgement are closely linked with, and stem from, his ability to love. He has undergone the difficulties that his readers will face in ascending the ladder. He began from the very bottom; this is why, for him, illumination is to be found not in ecstasy but in *ascesis*. Herein perhaps lies the role of an ascetic who does not run away from society in order to become distanced from it, but rather in order to bridge the gap between humanity and divinity, by virtue of divine grace. The monastic does not seek experiences or visions of light, not even continual prayer or deification, but merely humbly and lovingly seeks life for and in God. He writes on his tombstone, not on pieces of paper to be buried in libraries. To live for God is to die for God; and Climacus is writing precisely from this act of living-and-dying.

---

[24] Translated by C. Luibheid and N. Russell. For Ware's introduction, cf. 1–70.

[25] Introduction, 68.

[26] Cf. *The Byzantine Fathers (5th–8th Century)*, re-edited by Gregg International, UK: 1972, 179 (in Russian).

Bibliography

This bibliography is divided into two sections: (i) primary sources, and (ii) contemporary sources. The second section likewise contains two parts: (a) bibliography on John Climacus, and (b) general bibliography.

Patristic Sources

Agapetus, *Expositio capitum admonitorium, PG*86: 1164–85.
Ammonius, *The Forty Martyrs of the Sinai Desert*, translated from the Syriac by A. S. Lewis, in *Horae Semiticae* IX, Cambridge: 1912
Anastasius, *Narratives*, in F. Nau, 'Le texte grec des récits du moine Anastase sur les saints pères du Sinai,' in *Oriens Christianus* II (1902), 58–89 and III (1903), 56–90.
Anastasius the Sinaite, *Quaestiones, PG*89: 312–824.
*Apophegmata Patrum, PG*65: 76–440. Latin translations in *Vitae Patrum, PL*73–74. Anonymous supplement to the alphabetical collection, ed. F. Nau, *Revue de l'Orient chrétien* (1905, 1907–13); cf. also *Patrologia Orientalis*, vol. VIII, (Paris, 1912) 164–83. English trans. Benedicta Ward, *The Sayings of the Desert Fathers: The Alphabetical Collection*, Oxford: Mowbrays, 1975, and *The Wisdom of the Desert Fathers: Apophthegmata Patrum, The Anonymous Series*, vol. 48, Oxford: Fairacres Publication, 1975; for the Latin collection, cf. B. Ward, *The Desert Fathers: Sayings of the Early Christian Monks*, London: Penguin Books, 2003.
    L. Regnault, *Les sentences des pères du désert. Nouveau Recueil*, Abbaye Saint-Pierre-de-Solesmes: 1970, and *Troisième Recueil* (1976), which contains much additional material.
    Anonymous, 'On Evil Thoughts (*Peri Logismōn Ponērōn*)' in J.-C. Guy, 'Un dialogue monastique inédit. *Peri Logismōn*,' *RAM* 33 (1957), 171–88; Coptic collection in M. Chaîne, 'Le manuscrit de la version copte en dialecte sahidique des "Apophthegmata Patrum,"' *Bibliothèque d'études coptes*, vol. VI, Cairo: 1960; 'The Story of Thais,' *Annales du Musée Guimet* XXX, 51.
Athanasius, *Vita Antonii, PG*26: 837–976.
Pseudo-Athanasius, *De virginitate, PG*28: 252–82.
———, *Doctrina ad Antiochum ducem, PG*28: 589–98.
———, *Vitae monasticae institutio, PG*28: 845–50.
———, *Sermo exhortatorius, PG*28: 1107–14.
———, *Syntagma ad quemdam politicum, PG*28: 1395–140.
———, *Sermo pro iis qui saeculo renuntiarunt, PG*28: 1409–20.

————, *Doctrina ad monachos, PG*28: 1421–26.

————, *Vita Sanctae Syncleticae, PG*28: 1488–557.

Barsanuphius and John, *Answers*, ed. Nikodemus of the Holy Mountain and S. N. Schoinas, Volos: 1960. Cf. also critical ed. of Greek text (1–124 only) by D. J. Chitty, *Patrologia Orientalis* XXXI, 3, Paris: 1966. French transl. by L. Regnault, P. Lemaire and B. Outtier, *Barsanuphe et Jean de Gaza Correspondance, recueil complet*, Sable-sur-Sarthe: 1972, which sometimes corrects the Greek edition of Schoinas. Critical edition by L. Regnault, F. Neyt and P. de Angelis-Noah, in *Sources Chrétiennes*, vol. 426–27 and 251–22, Paris: Cerf, 1997–2002. Full English translation by J. Chryssavgis (forthcoming). A selection is available in J. Chryssavgis, *Letters from the Desert*, New York: St Vladimir's Seminary Press, 2003.

Basil the Great, *Homilia dicta tempore famis et siccitatis, PG*31: 304–28.

————, *Ad adolescentes de legendis libris gentilium, PG*31: 563–90.

————, *Praevia institutio ascetica, PG*31: 620–25.

————, *Sermo de renuntiatione saeculi, et de perfectione spirituale, PG*31: 625–48.

————, *De ascetica disciplina, PG*31: 648–52.

————, *De judicio Dei, PG*31: 653–76.

————, *De fide, PG*31: 676–92.

————, *Initium moralium, PG*31: 700–869.

————, *Sermo asceticus, PG*31: 869–81.

————, *Regulae fusius tractatae, PG*31: 889–1052.

————, *Regulae brevius tractatae, PG*31: 1080–305.

————, *Epistola I, 2, PG*32: 224–33.

————, *Epistola 207, Ad clericos Neocaesarienses, PG*32: 760–65.

Clement of Alexandria, *Paedagogus, Liber I, II, III, PG*8: 247–376, 377–553, 553–684. Cf. also O. Stählin (ed.), *Die Griechischen Christlichen Schriftsteller der Ersten Jahrhunderte*, Berlin: 1972.

*Stromateis, Libri I–IV, PG*8: 685–1381 and 'Libri V–VIII,' *PG*9: 9–601. Cf. also O. Stählin (ed.), *Die Griechischen Christlichen Schriftsteller der Ersten Jahrhunderte*, 2 vols, Berlin: 1960 and 1970.

*Quis dives salvetur, PG*9: 604–52. Cf. also O. Stählin (ed.), *Die Griechischen Christlichen Schriftsteller der Ersten Jahrhunderte*, Berlin: 1970.

*Protrepticus, PG*8: 49–245. Cf. also O. Stählin (ed.), *Die Griechischen Christlichen Schriftsteller der Ersten Jahrhunderte*, Berlin: 1972.

Clement of Rome, *Ep. I and II, Ad Corinthios, PG*1: 201–328, 329–48. K. Bihlmeyer, *Die Apostolischen Väter*, Tübingen: 1956, 35–70 and 70–81.

Cyril of Scythopolis, *Works*, ed. E. Schwarz, *Texte und Untersuchungen* 49. 2, Leipzig: 1939; French translation by A. J. Festugière, *Les Moines d'Orient*, III/1, 2, Paris: 1962.

Diadochus of Photice, *Works*, ed. E. Places, *Sources Chrétiennes*, no. 5 bis, Paris: Cerf, 1965.

Dorotheus of Gaza, *Works PG*88: 1613–1841; ed. Regnault and J. de Préville, *Sources Chrétiennes*, no. 92, Paris: Cerf, 1963.

Etheria, *Itinerarium Aetheriae*, in *Sources Chrétiennes* 21, Paris: Cerf, 1948.

Evagrius, *Praktikos, PG*40: 1220–52. Also in *Sources Chrétiennes*, ed. A. Guillaumont, no. 171, Paris: Cerf, 1971.

————, *Rerum monacalium rationes, PG*40: 1252–64.

————, *Capitula* XXXIII, *PG*40: 1264–68.

————, *Spirituales sententiae, PG*40: 1268–69.

————, *Ad Eulogium, PG*79: 1093–140; among the works attributed to Nilus.

————, *De octo spiritibus malitiae, PG*79: 1145–64.

————, *De oratione, PG*79: 1165–2000.

————, *De diversis malignis cogitationibus, PG*79: 1200–33.

————, *Institutio ad monachos, PG*79: 1236–40.

————, *Sententiae, PG*79: 1240–49.

————, *Capita paraenetica, PG*79: 1249–64.

————, *Ep. VIII*; among the works of Basil, *PG*32: 245–68.

————, *Centuries*, ed. A. Guillaumont, *Patrologia Orientalis*, vol. XXVIII, 1, Paris: 1958.

————, *Antirrheticus, Gnosticus, Protrepticus, Paraeneticus* and *Letters*, ed. W. Frankenberg, *Evagrius Ponticus*, Berlin: 1912.

————, *Speculum monachorum* and *Speculum virginum*, ed. H. Gressman, *TU* 39, Leipzig: 1913, 143–65.

Evergetinos, Paulos, *Synagoge*, Athens: 1957.

Gregory of Nazianzus, *Oratio VI (De Pace I), PG*35: 721–52.

————, *Oratio XXII (De Pace II), PG*35: 1132–52.

————, *Oratio XXIII (De Pace III), PG*35: 1152–68.

————, *Oratio XIV (De pauperum amore), PG*35: 857–909.

————, *Oratio XVI (In patrem tacentem . . .), PG*35: 933–64.

————, *Oratio XIX (De suis sermonibus . . .), PG*35: 1044–64.

————, *Oratio XX (De dogmate et constitutione episcoporum), PG*35: 1065–80.

————, *Oratio XXVI (In laudem Heronis Philosophi), PG*35: 1228–52.

————, *Orationes XXVII–XXXI (Theologicae I–V), PG*36: 12–25; 25–72; 73–104; 104–33; 133–72.

————, *Oratio XXXII (De moderatione in disputando), PG*36: 173–212.

————, *Oratio XXXII (In sancta Lumina), PG*36: 336–60.

————, *Oratio XLIII (Funebris oratio in laudem Basilii Magni), PG*36: 493–605.

————, *Oratio XLV (In sanctum Pascha), PG*36: 624–64.

————, *Ad Hellenium, PG*37: 1451–77 in *Carminum Liber, PG*37: 397–1600.

Gregory of Nyssa, *De hominis opificio, PG*44: 124–256.

————, *De vita Moysis, PG*44: 297–430; Vol. 7.

————, *Commentary in Canticum Canticorum, PG*44: 755–1120; Vol. 6.

————, *De beatitudinibus*, *PG*44: 1193–302. Cf. ed. J. H. Sprawley, *The Catechetical Oration of Gregory of Nyssa*, Cambridge: 1903; *Oratio catechetica*, *PG*45: 9–105.

————, *De anima et resurrectione*, *PG*46: 12–160.

————, *Quid nomen professione Christianorum*, *PG*46: 237–49; Vol. 8/1, 129–42.

————, *De perfectione*, *PG*46: 252–85; Vol. 8/1, 173–214.

————, *De proposito secundum deum*, *PG*46: 288–305.

————, *Adversus eos qui castigationes aegre ferunt*, *PG*46: 308–16.

————, *De virginitate*, *PG*46: 317–416; Vol. 8/1, 247–343.

————, *De mortuis*, *PG*46: 497–537; Vol. 9, 28–68.

————, *De vita S. Patris Ephraem Syri*, *PG*46: 820–49. The volume and page number in brackets refer to the edition of Gregory's works by W. Jaeger, Leiden: 1960–67.

Gregory Palamas, *Triads in defence of the Holy Hesychasts*, ed. J. Meyendorff, *Spicilegium Sacrum Lovaniense*, 30–31, 2 vols, Louvain: 1959. Cf. also *Works*, ed. P. Christou, 3 vols, Thessalonika: 1962, 1966, 1970.

Gregory of Sinai, *Chapters, Philokalia*, IV, 31–88 *PG*150: 1240–346.

Hermas, *The Shepherd*, *PG*2: 891–1012; ed. M. Whittaker, *Die Apostolischen Väter, Die Griechischen Christlichen Schriftsteller der Ersten Jahrhunderte*, Berlin: 1967.

Hesychius, *De temperantia et virtute centuriae 1–2*, *PG*93: 1479–544. References to *On Watchfulness and Holiness*, in *Philokalia I*, 141–73.

Historia Monachorum In Aegypto, Greek text, ed. A. J. Festugière, *Subsidia Hagiographica* 34, Brussels: 1961. Second edition with more notes in *Subsidia Hagiographica* 53, Brussels: 1971.

Latin translation by Rufinus, *PL*21: 391–462; English translation in N. Russell, *The Lives of the Desert Fathers*, Oxford: Mowbrays, 1981, which includes additions of Rufinus' Latin text and of the Syriac text.

Ignatius of Antioch, *Epistola ad Smyrnaeos*, *PG*5: 707–18. ed. K. Bihlmeyer, 105–10.

Isaac the Syrian, *Mystic Treatises by Isaac of Nineveh*, translated from Bedjan's Syriac text by A. J. Wensinck, Amsterdam: 1923. Page references herein are to the Wemsinck edition. Greek translation, ed. Nicephoros Theotokis, Athens: 1895. For a more recent English translation, see *The Ascetical Homilies of St. Isaac the Syrian*, Boston, MA: Holy Transfiguration Monastery, 1984.

Isaiah of Scetis, *Logoi*, ed. Augoustinos, Jerusalem: 1911. French trans. by L. Regnault, Bellefontaine: 1976, based on a study of the manuscripts. English translation by J. Chryssavgis and P. R. Penkett, *Abba Isaiah of Scetis: Ascetic Discourses*, in *Cistercian Studies Series* (Kalamazoo, MI, Cistercian Publications, 2002).

Isidore of Pelusium, *Epistolae 1, 319 Dorotheo Presbytero*, *PG*78: 368.

————, *Epistolae IV, 101 Martyrio Presbytero, PG*78: 1165–69.

John Cassian, *Collationes*, ed. E. Pichery, *Sources Chrétiennes* 42, 54, 64; 3 vols, Paris: 1955–59.

————, *Institutiones*, ed. J.-C. Guy, *Sources Chrétiennes* 109, Paris: 1965.

————, *De octo vitiosis cogitationibus, PG*79: 1436–72.

John Chrysostom, *Ad Theodorum lapsum I and II, PG*47: 277–308, 309–16.

————, *Adversus oppugnatores vitae monasticae, PG*47: 319–86.

————, *Comparatio regis et monachi, PG*47: 387–92.

————, *De compunctione I and II, PG*47: 393–410, 411–22.

————, *Ad Stagirium ascetam I–III, PG*47: 423–48, 447–72, 471–94.

————, *De anathemate, PG*48: 945–52.

————, *De statuis, PG*49: 15–222.

————, *Non esse ad gratiam concionandum, PG*50: 653–62.

————, *De non evulgandi fratrum peccatis, PG*51: 353–64.

————, *Non esse desperandum, PG*51: 363–72.

————, *Quod nemo laedatur nisi a seipso liber, PG*52: 459–80.

————, *Ad eos qui scandalizati sunt, PG*52: 479–528.

————, *De perfecta caritate, PG*56: 279–90.

————, *In Joannem Homilia LXXXIII, PG*59: 447–56.

————, *Dicta postquam reliquiae martyrum ...*, *PG*63: 467–72.

————, (Spuria): *Sermo catecheticus in Sanctum Pascha, PG*59: 721–24.

————, Pseudo-Chrysostom, *Ascetam facetiis uti non debere, PG*48: 1055–60.

————, *De jejunio et eleemosyna, PG*48: 1059–62.

————, *Epistola Theodori lapsi ad Chrysostomum, PG*48: 1063–66.

————, *Christi discipulum benignum esse debere, PG*48: 1069–72.

————, *De fugienda simulata specie, PG*48: 1073–76.

————, *De salute animi, PG*60: 735–78.

————, *Contra virginum corruptores, PG*60: 741–44.

————, *Epistola ad monachos, PG*60: 751–56.

————, *De non judicando Proximo, PG*60: 763–66.

————, *De paenitentia, PG*60: 765–68.

————, *De caritate, PG*60: 773–76.

————, *De patientia et consummatione saeculi, PG*63: 937–42.

————, *Hom. de virtute animi, PG*64: 473–80.

John Moschus, *Pratum Spirituale, PG*87, 3: 2852–3112. French translation in *Sources Chrétiennes*, Paris: Cerf, 1946. English translation by J. Wortley, *The Spiritual Meadow*, Kalamazoo, MI: Cistercian Publications, 1992.

Macarius, *Homilies*, ed. H. Dörries, E. Klostermann and M. Kroeger, *Die 50 geistlichen Homilien des Makarios*, Berlin: 1964.

————, *The Great Letter*, ed. W. Jaeger, *Two Rediscovered Works of Ancient Christian Literature: Gregory of Nyssa and Macarius*, Leiden: 1954, 233–301.

————, Makarios/Symeon Metaphrastes, *PG*34: 821–968.

————, E. Klostermann and H. Berthold, *Neue Homilien des Makarius/ Symeon: Aus Typus III*, TU 72, Berlin: 1961

————, H. Berthold, *Makarios/Symeon. Reden und Briefe, Die Griechischen Christlichen Schriftsteller der Ersten Jahrhunderte*, 2 vols, Berlin: 1973.

Mark the Monk, *Works*, *PG*65: 905–1140.

————, *Adversus Nestorianos*, in J. Kunze, *Marcus Eremita Ein Neuer Zeuge für das Altkirchliche Taufbekenntnis*, Leipzig: 1895, 6–30.

Maximus the Confessor, *Quaestiones ad Thalassium*, *PG*90: 1–65, 243–786.

————, *Expositio orationis Dominicae*, *PG*90: 871–910.

————, *Centuriae de caritate*, *PG*90: 960–1080. Critical edition by A. Ceresa-Gastaldo, 'Massimo confessore. Capitoli sulla carità,' *Verba Seniorum* 3, Rome: 1963.

————, *Capita theologica et oeconomica*, *PG*90: 1084–173.

————, *Capita quinquies centena*, *PG*90: 1177–392.

————, *Mystagogia*, *PG*91: 657–718.

————, *Ambiguorum liber*, *PG*91: 1031–418.

Niketas Stethatos, *First Century (Kephalaia Praktika)*, *Philokalia III*, 273–97, *PG*120: 851–900.

————, *Second Century (Kephalaia Physika)*, *Philokalia III*, 298–325, *PG*120: 900–952.

————, *Third Century (Kephalaia gnostika)*, *Philokalia III*, 326–55, *PG*120: 953–1010.

————, *Life of Symeon*, ed. I. Hausherr, *Un grand mystique Byzantin. Vie de Syméon le Nouveau Théologien par Nicetas Stethatos, Orientalia Christiana* 12 no. 45, Rome: 1928.

————, *Works and Letters*, ed. J. Darrouzès, *Sources Chrétiennes*, 81, Paris: Cerf, 1961.

Nilus of Ancyra, *Epistolae*, *PG*79: 81–581.

————, *Liber de monastica exercitatione*, *PG*79: 720–809.

————, *De voluntaria paupertate*, *PG*79: 968–1060.

————, *De monachorum praestantia*, *PG*79: 1061–93.

Origen, *Ad martyrium*, ed. P. Koetschau, *Die Griechischen Christlichen Schriftsteller der Ersten Jahrhunderte*, vol. 1, Leipzig: 1899, 3–47.

————, *Contra Celsum*, ed. P. Koetschau, *Die Griechischen Christlichen Schriftsteller der Ersten Jahrhundert*, vols 1 and 2, Leipzig: 1899.

————, *De oratione*, ed. P. Koetschau, *Die Griechischen Christlichen Schriftsteller der Ersten Jahrhundert*, vol. 2, Leipzig: 1899, 297–403.

————, *De principiis*, ed. P. Koetschau, *Die Griechischen Christlichen Schriftsteller der Ersten Jahrhundert*, vol. 5, Leipzig: 1913.

Pachomius, *Sancti Pachomii Vitae Graecae*, ed. F. Halkin *Subsidia Hagiographica* 19, Brussels: 1932.

————, *Pachomiana Latina*, ed. A. Boon, Louvain: 1932. French translation in *Les Moines d'Orient* IV, 2, ed. A. J. Festugière, Paris: 1965. English transl.

by Armand Veilleux, *Pachomian Koinonia*, Kalamazoo, MI: *Cistercian Studies Series* 45–46, 1980–81.

Palladius, *Lausiac History*, ed. C. Butler, *Texts and Studies* VI, 2 vols, Cambridge: 1898–1904.

Peter of Damascus, *Biblion, Philokalia*, III, 5–168.

The Philokalia: the complete text, ed. G. Palmer, P. Sherrard and K. Ware, 5 vols, London: Faber and Faber, 1979f. References to Greek text, Athens: 1957–63.

Philotheus of Sinai, *On the guard of the heart, Philokalia*, II, 274–86.

————, *Capita 1–40 de sobrietate vitae, PG*162: 1169.

Serapion, Bishop of Thmuis, *Epistola ad monachos, PG*40: 925–42.

Symeon the New Theologian, *Catechetical Orations 1–5*, ed. B. Krivochéine and J. Paramelle, *Sources Chrétiennes*, 96, Paris: Cerf, 1963.

————, *Catechetical Orations 6–22, Sources Chrétiennes*, 104, Paris: Cerf, 1964.

————, *Catechetical Orations 23–24*, and *Thanksgivings, Sources Chrétiennes*, 113, Paris: Cerf, 1965.

————, *Chapters*, ed. J. Darrouzès, *Sources Chrétiennes*, 51, Paris: Cerf, 1957.

————, *Theological and Ethical Treatises*, ed. J. Darrouzès, *Sources Chrétiennes*, 122 and 129, 2 vols, Paris: Cerf, 1966–67.

————, *Hymns, I–XV*, ed. J. Koder and J. Paramelle, *Sources Chrétiennes*, 156, Paris: Cerf, 1969.

————, *Hymns, XVI–XL*, ed. J. Koder and L. Neyrand, *Sources Chrétiennes*, 174, Paris: Cerf, 1971.

————, *Hymns, XLI–LVIII*, ed. J. Koder, J. Paramelle and L. Neyrand, *Sources Chrétiennes*, 196, Paris: Cerf, 1973.

Testamenta XII Patriarcharum, ed. R. H. Charles, *The Apocrypha and Pseudepigrapha of the Old Testament*, Vol. 2, Oxford: 1969, 296–360.

Thalassius, *Centuriae de caritate, PG*91: 1428–69.

Theodore of Studium, *Testamentum, PG*99: 1813–24.

Theodoret of Cyrrhus, *Philotheos Historia*, ed. P. Canivet and A. Leroy-Molinghen, *Sources Chrétiennes*, 234 and 257, Paris: Cerf, 1977–79.

Theoleptus of Philadelphia, *De abscondita operatione in Christo, PG*143: 381–404. Cf. also *Philokalia*, IV, 4–15.

Xanthopouloi, Kallistos and Ignatios, *Century, Philokalia*, IV, 197–295. *PG*147: 636–812.

Xanthopoulos, Nikephoros Kallistos, *Brief Exegesis on the Ladder of St John* (in Greek, Preveza: Holy Monastery of Nikopolis Publications, 2002).

Zosimas, *Alloquia, PG*78: 1679–702. English translation by J. Chryssavgis, *In the Heart of the Desert*, Bloomington, IN: World Wisdom Books, 2003.

Service Books

Triodion Katanyktikon, ed. Rome: 1879, *Services for the Fourth Sunday of the Great Fast* (Lent), 423–31.
Menaia, ed. Rome: 1898, *Services for 30 March*, Vol. 4, 213–24.

Contemporary Sources

Bibliography on John Climacus

Acta Sanctorum (30 March), Vol. 3, Anvers: 1668, 834–37.
Altaner, B., *Patrologie. Leben, Schriften und Lehre der Kirchenväter*, Freiburg: 1951, 468.
Ball, H., *Byzantinisches Christentum*, Zürich: 1958^2, esp. 9–62.
Bardenhewer, O., *Geschichte der altkirchlichen Literatur*, Vol. 4, Freiburg: 1913–32, 79–82.
Barsotti, D., 'L'amore di Dio in S. Giovanni Climaco,' *Rivista di vita spirituale* 8 (1954), 179–85.
Beck, H. G., *Kirche und Theologische Literatur im Byzantinischen Reich*, Munich: 1959, esp. 353 and 451–52.
Benesevic, V., 'Sur la date de la mosaïque de la Transfiguration au Mont Sinaï,' *Byzantion* 1 (1924), 145–72.
Bogdanovic, D., *Jean Climaaue dans la littérature byzantin, et la littérature serbe ancienne*, Institut d'Etudes Byzantines, Monographies, Fascicule 11, Belgrade: 1968. (In Serbo-Croat, with summary in French on pp. 215–25.)
Bontschew, A., *Die Asketik und Mystik des Johannes Klimakos*, Marburg: 1945 (unpublished thesis).
Chitty, D. J., *The Desert a City. An Introduction to the Study of Egyptian and Palestinian Monasticism under the Christian Empire*, Oxford: Mowbrays, 1966, esp. 168–78.
Christou, P., 'Ioannes o Sinaites,' *TEE* (in Greek: Athens, 1965), 1211–13.
Colugna, A., 'La escala espiritual de san Juan Climaco,' *Vida sobrenatural* 31, Salamanca: 1936, 269–77.
Corneanu, N., 'Contributions des traducteurs roumains à la diffusion de "l'Echelle" de saint Jean Climaque,' *Studia Patristica* 8, Berlin: Peeters, 1966, 340–55.
———, (ed.), *Scara Raiului: precedata de viata pe scurt a lui Ioan Scolasticul*, Timisoara: 1994. Translation of and introduction to the *Ladder*.
Couilleau, G., 'Saint Jean Climaque,' *DS* 8 (Paris, 1974), 369–89.
Dahari, U., *Monastic Settlements in South Sinai in the Byzantine Period: the archaeological remains* (Jerusalem: Israel Antiquities Authority, 2000).

Delahaye, H., *Synaxarium Ecclesiae Constantinopolitanae*, Brussels: 1902, 571–74.

Deseille, P. in French transl., 'L'Echelle sainte,' *Spiritualité Orientale* 24, Bellefontaine: 1978, esp. Introduction, 7–15.

Devreesse, R., 'Le christianisme dans le Péninsule Sinaïtique, des origins à l'arrivée des Musulmans,' *Revue Biblique* 49 (April, 1940), 205–23.

Elert, W., 'Theodor von Pharan und Theodor von Raithu,' *Theologische Literaturzeitung* 76 (1951), 67–76.

Fountoulis, J., 'O Aghios Ioannes tes Klimakos, Didaskalos tes Proseuches,' *Leitourgika Themata 4* (in Greek: Thessalonika, 1979), 75–89.

Georgoulis, K., 'Ioannes tes Klimakos,' *Enkyklopaidikon Lexikon Heliou* 7 (in Greek: Athens, 1949), 702–04.

Gribomont, J., 'La Scala Paradisi, Jean de Raithou et Ange Clareno,' *Studia Monastica* 2 (Barcelona, 1960), 345–58.

Hausherr, I., '*Penthos*. La doctrine de la componction dans l'Orient chrétien,' *Orientalia Christiana Analecta* 132 (Rome, 1924), 137–73.

———, 'Noms du Christ et voies d'oraison,' *Orientalia Christiana Analecta* 157 (Rome, 1960), 248–53.

———, 'La théologie du monachisme chez saint Jean Climaque,' *Théologie de la vie monastique*, Paris: 1961, 385–410. Also in *Etudes de Spiritualité Orientale*, Rome: 1969, 361–86.

Heppell, M., Introduction to the English translation by Archimandrite Lazarus (Moore), *The Ladder of Divine Ascent*, London: 1959, 13–33.

Hofmann, G., 'Der Hl. Johannes Klimax bei Photius,' *Orientalia Christiana Periodica* 7 (Rome, 1941), 461–79.

Kornarakis. J., 'E Krise tautotetos kata ton Osion Ioannen ton Sinaiten,' *Koinonia* 1–4 (in Greek: Athens, 1979), 40–67.

Krumbacher, K., *Geschichte der Byzantinischen Litteratur von Justinian bis zum Ende des oströmischen Reiches* (527–1453), Munich: 1897, 143–44.

Lane, B., *The Solace of Fierce Landscapes: exploring desert and mountain spirituality*, Oxford: Oxford University Press, 1998.

Lot-Borodine, M., 'Le mystère du "don des larmes" dans l'Orient chrétien,' *La Vie Spirituelle* 48 (Paris, 1936), 65–110. Reprinted in O. Clément and others, *La douloureuse joie, Spiritualité orientale* 14, Bellefontaine: 1974, 131–95.

Mack, J., *Ascending the Heights: A Layman's Guide to* The Ladder of Divine Ascent, Ben Lomond, CA: Conciliar Press, 1999.

Maloney, G. A., '*Penthos* – A Forgotten Necessity,' *Monastic Studies* 7 (New York, 1969), 149–59.

Martin, J. R., *The Illustration of the Heavenly Ladder of John Climacus, Studies in Manuscript Illumination* 5, Princeton: Princeton University Press, 1954.

Merton, T., 'L'Echelle qui mène à Dieu,' *Contacts* 21 (Paris, 1969), 128–38.

Miquel, P., 'Saint Jean Climaque,' *Supplément à la lettre de Ligugé* 178 (July 1976).

Morey, C. R., 'Two Miniatures from a Manuscript of St. John Climacus, and their Relation to Klimax Iconography,' *Studies in East Christian and Roman Art* (New York, 1918), 1–30.

Mouratides, K., 'E Theologia tes Klimakos tou Agious Ioannou,' *Praktika Synaxeos Theologon* (in Greek: Athens, 1974), 1–18. Also *Koinonia* 2 (Athens, 1974), 62f.

Nau, F., 'Note sur la date de la mort de Saint Jean Climaque,' *Byzantinische Zeitschrift* 11 (Leipzig, 1902), 35–37.

———, 'Le texte grec des récits du moine Anastase sur les saints Pères du Sinai,' *Oriens Christianus* 2 (Leipzig, 1902), 58–89.

———, 'Les récits inédits du moine Anastase,' *Revue de l'Institut catholique de Paris* 7 (Paris, 1902), 1–26 and 110–51.

Pargoire, J., 'Un prétendu document sur St. Jean Climaque,' *Échos d'Orient* 8 (Paris, 1905), 372–73.

Paschos, P. B., *Eros Orthodoxias* (in Greek: Athens, 1973), 261–66.

Peterson, E., 'Scholia,' *Theologische Literatur-Zeitung* 55 (Leipzig, 1930), 257; *Byzantinisch–Neugriechische Jahrbücher* 9, Berlin: 1932–33, 45–51; *Zeitschrift für Katholische Theologie* 57, Innsbruck: 1933, 277; *Theologische Revue* 32 (Münster, 1933), 242.

Petit, L., 'Saint Jean Climaque,' *Dictionnaire de Théologie Catholique* 8 (Paris, 1924), 690–93.

Phokilidis, I., 'Ioannes o tes Klimakos,' *Ekklesiastikos Faros Alexandreias* (in Greek: Alexandria, 1920), 432–64.

Pitsilkas, A. B., *E Adialeipte Proseuche sten Didaskalia tou Agiou Ioannou tes Klimakos* (in Greek: Thessalonika, 1981).

Politis, L., 'Agnosto ergo tou Nikephorou Kallistou Xanthopoulou: Exegese ston Ioanne tes Klimakos,' *Kleronomia* 3,1 (in Greek: Thessalonika, 1981), 69–83.

Popa, Ioasaf, 'Invatatura ascetica a Spintului Joan Scaracul,' *Studii Teologice* 10 (Bucharest, 1958), 253–69.

Pouloupatis, I., 'Ioannou tou Sinaitou Plakes Pneumatikai ē Klimax,' *Paradose* 12–14 (in Greek: Athens, 1989), 127–36.

Rabois-Bousquet, S. and Salaville, S., 'Saint Jean Climaque: sa vie et son oeuvre,' *Échos d'Orient* 22 (Paris, 1923), 440–54.

Sakkos, S., *Peri Anastaseōn Sinaitōn* (in Greek: Thessalonika, 1964), esp. 179–85.

Saudreau, A., 'Doctrine spirituelle de Saint Jean Climaque,' *La Vie Spirituelle* 9 (Paris, 1924), 353–70.

Schuster, I., 'La dottrina spirituale di S. Benedetto e la Scala di perfezione di S. Giovanni il Climaco,' *La Scuola Cattolica* 72 (1944), 161–76.

Skrobucha, H., *Sinai*, transl. by G. Hunt, London: 1966, 19–47.

Sophrony, Archim, 'De la nécessité des trois renoncements chez St. Cassien le Romain et St. Jean Climaque,' *Studia Patristica 5: Texte und Untersuchungen* 80 (Berlin, 1962), 393–400.

Sumner, M. O., 'St. John Climacus. The Psychology of the Desert Fathers,' *The Guild of Pastoral Psychology, Guild Lecture* no. 63, London: 1950.

Tatakis, V. N., *Themata Christianikes kai Byzantines Philosophias* (in Greek: Athens, 1952), 76–81.

Tikkanen, J. J., 'Eine illustrierte Klimaxhandschrift in der Vaticanischen Bibliothek,' *Acta Soc. Scient. Fennicae* 19, 2 (Helsingfors, 1893).

Vedernikov, A., 'Der heilige Johannes Klimakos als Lehrer des Gebetes,' *Stimme der Orthodoxie* 4 (Berlin, 1964), 43–49; and 5 (1964) 46–52.

Viller, M. and Rahner, K., *Aszese und Mystik in der Väterzeit*, Freibourg-en-Brisgau: 1939, 155–64.

Vlassis, D., 'L'action de l'ange sur l'homme dans l'oeuvre de Saint Jean Climaque,' unpublished thesis for the 'Licence en théologie orthodoxe,' Paris: 1981.

Völker, W., *Scala Paradisi. Eine Studie zu Johannes Climacus und zugleich eine Vorstudie zu Symeon dem Neuen Theologen*, Wiesbaden: 1968.

Ware, K., Introduction to the English translation of John Climacus, 'The Ladder of Divine Ascent,' *Classics of Western Spirituality*, New York: Paulist Press, 1982, 1–70.

Yannaras, C., 'Eros divin et éros humain selon St. Jean Climaque,' *Contacts* 21 (Paris, 1969), 190–204.

———, *La métaphysique du corps. Etude sur saint Jean Climaque*. Thèse inedited, Paris: Bibliothèque la Sorbonne, 1970. Greek: *E Metaphysike tou Somatos. Spoude ston Ioanne tes Klimakos*, Athens: 1971. References are to the Greek version.

General Bibliography

Adnes, P., 'Jésus (Prière à),' *DS* 8 (Paris, 1974), cols 1126–50.

Aries, P. and Bejin, A. (eds), *Western Sexuality. Practice and Precept in Past and Present Times*, English transl.: Oxford, 1985.

Bardy, G., 'Discernement des esprits. Chez les pères,' *DS* 3 (Paris, 1957), cols 1247–54.

Baynes, N. H., 'St. Antony and the Demons,' *Journal of Egyptian Archaeology* 40 (1954), 7–10.

Behr-Sigel, E., 'La prière de Jésus ou le mystère de la spiritualité monastique orthodoxe,' *Dieu Vivant* 8 (Paris, 1947), 69–94.

Bettencourt, E. T., 'L'idéal religieux de Saint Antoine et son actualité,' *Studia Anselmiana* 38 (Rome, 1956), 45–65.

Binns, J., *Ascetics and Ambassadors of Christ: The Monasteries of Palestine 314–631*, Oxford: Clarendon Press, 1994.

Bobrinskoy, B., 'L'histoire du monachisme orthodoxe après le VIe siècle,' *Contacts* 12 (Paris, 1960), 81–88.

Bois, J., 'Les hésychastes avant le XIVe siècle,' *Échos d'Orient* 5 (Paris, 1901), 1–11.

Bousset, W., *Apophthegmata. Studien zur Geschichte des ältesten Mönchtums*, Tübingen: 1923.

Bouyer, L., *La vie de S.Antoine. Essai sur la spiritualité du monachisme primitif*, S. Wandrille: 1950.

———, *Le sens de la vie monastique*, Brépols: 1951.

———, *La Spiritualité du Nouveau Testament et des Pères*, Paris: 1960.

Bremond, A., 'Le Moine et le Stoïcien. Le Stoïcisme et la Philosophie du Désert,' *Revue d'Ascétique et de Mystique* 8 (Toulouse, 1927), 26–40.

Brock, S. and Harvey, S. (eds), *Holy Women of the Syriac Orient*, Berkeley: University of California Press, 1988.

Brown, P., *The Body and Society: Men, Women and Sexual Renunciation in Early Christianity*, New York: Columbia University Press, 1990.

Bultmann, R., *Theology of the New Testament*, Vol. I, London: 1974.

Bunge, G., *Akèdia: la doctrine spirituelle d'Evagre le Pontique sur l'acèdie*, Bégrolles-en-Mauges: Abbaye de Bellefontaine, 1991.

Burton-Christie, D., *The Word in the Desert: Scripture and the Quest for Holiness in Early Christian Monasticism*, Oxford: Oxford University Press, 1993.

Bynum, C. W., *Holy Feast and Holy Fast: the religious significance of food to medieval women*, Berkeley: University of California Press, 1987.

Camelot, Th., 'Ascèse et mortification dans le Nouveau Testament,' *L'Ascèse chrétienne et l'homme contemporain* (Paris, 1951), 13–30.

Chollet, A., 'Discernement des esprits,' *DTC* 4 (Paris, 1911), cols 1375–415.

Chryssavgis, J., *Soul Mending: the art of spiritual direction*, Brookline, MA: Holy Cross Orthodox Press, 2000.

Clarke, E. A., *Ascetic Piety and Women's Faith. Essays on Late Ancient Christianity*, Lewiston: Edwin Mellen Press, 1986.

Clément, O., 'A Note on Prayer in Eastern Christianity,' *Cistercian Studies* 9, 2–3 (Bourlers, 1974), 185–91.

Coakley, S., *Religion and the Body*, Cambridge: Cambridge University Press, 1997.

Colliander, T., *The Way of the Ascetics*, New York: St Vladimir's Seminary Press, 1985.

Couilleau, G., 'Le coeur et la cellule,' *La Vie Spirituelle* 3 (Paris, 1980), 384–92.

Dahl, M. E., *The Resurrection of the Body*, London: 1962.

Daniélou, J., 'Les démons de l'air dans la vie d'Antoine,' *Antonius Magnus Eremita, 356–1956. Studia ad Antiquum Monachismum Spectantia*, cura B. Steidle, Rome: *Studia Anselmiana* vol. 38, 1956, 136–47.

Elm, S., *'Virgins of God:' The Making of Asceticism in Late Antiquity*, Oxford: Clarendon Press, 1994.

Festugière, A. J., *Contemplation et vie contemplative selon Platon*, Paris: 1967.

Foucault, M., *The Use of Pleasure. The History of Sexuality*, 3 vols, New York: Pantheon Books, 1985.

Fytrakis, A., *'Tais ton Dakryon Roais' ... o Klauthmos ton Monachon* (in Greek: Athens, 1946).

Gillet, L., 'The Gift of Tears,' *Sobornost* 12 (London, 1937), 5–10.

Gomez, A., *'Compunctio lacrymarum.* Doctrina de la compunción en el monacato latino de los siglos IV–VI,' *Collectanea Ordinis Cisterciencium Reformatorum* 23 (Rome, 1961), 232–53.

Gouillard, J., *Petite Philocalie de la prière du Coeur*, Paris: 1968², esp. introduction.

Gould, G., *The Desert Fathers on Monastic Community*, Oxford: Clarendon Press, 1993.

Guillaumont, A., 'Les sens des noms du coeur dans l'antiquité,' *Le Coeur: Études carmélitaines* 29 (Bruges, 1950), 41–81.

———, 'Le "coeur" chez les spirituels grecs à l'époque ancienne,' *DS* 2 (Paris, 1952), cols 2281–88.

Guillaumont, A. and C., 'Démon. Dans la plus ancienne littérature monastique,' *DS* 3 (Paris, 1957), cols 189–212.

———, 'Évagre le Pontique,' *DS* 4 (Paris, 1961), cols 1731–44.

Guillaumont, A., 'Les "Kephalaia Gnostica" d'Évagre le Pontique et l'histoire de l'origénisme chez les grecs et chez les syriens,' *Patristica Sorboniensia* 5 (Paris, 1962).

———, 'Une inscription copte sur la "Prière de Jésus",' in *Orientalia Christiana Periodica* 34 (Rome, 1968), 310–25.

———, 'The Jesus Prayer among the Monks of Egypt,' *Eastern Churches Review* 6 (1974), 66–71.

———, Collected articles in *Aux origines du monachisme chrétien, Spiritualité Orientale* 30: Bellefontaine, 1979.

Guy, J. C., 'Un dialogue monastique inédit. *Peri Logismon*,' *RAM* 33 (1957), 171–88.

Hausherr, I. *La méthode d'oraison hésychaste, Orientalia Christiana* 9, 2, Rome: 1927.

———, 'L'origine de la théorie orientale des huit péchés capitaux,' *Orientalia Christiana Periodica* 30, Rome: 1933, 164–75.

———, 'Le Traité de l'Oraison d'Évagre le Pontique,' *RAM* 15 (Toulouse, 1934), 34–93 and 113–70. Revised edition in *Les leçons d'un contemplatif. Le Traité de l'Oraison d'Évagre le Pontique*, Paris: 1960.

———, 'Les grands courants de la spiritualité orientale,' *Orientalia Christiana Periodica* 1 (Rome, 1935), 114–38.

——, 'L'erreur fondamentale et la logique du Messalianisme,' *Orientalia Christiana Periodica* 1 (Rome, 1935), 328–60.

——, *Direction spirituelle en Orient autrefois, Orientalia Christiana Analecta* 144 (Rome, 1955). English translation by Cistercian Publications: Kalamazoo, MI, 1990.

——, 'Le moine et l'amitié,' *Message des moines à notre temps* (Paris, 1958), 207–20.

——, 'L'hésychasme. Étude de spiritualite,' *Hésychasme et Prière: Orientalia Christiana Analecta* 176, Rome: 1966, 163–237.

Holl, K., *Enthusiasmus und Bussgewalt beim Griechischen Mönchtum. Eine Studie zu Symeon dem Neuen Theologen*, Leipzig: 1898.

Jugie, M., 'Les origines de la méthode d'oraison des hésychastes,' *Échos d'Orient* 30 (Paris, 1931), 179–85.

Kirchmeyer, J., 'Hésychius le Sinaite et ses *Centuries*,' in *Le Millénaire du Mont Athos 963–1963*, Vol. 1, Chevetogne: 1963, 319–29.

Kornarakis, J., *Paterika Viomata tes Endekates Horas* (in Greek: Thessalonika, 1971).

Lacarrière, J., *The God-Possessed*, London: 1963.

Larchet, J., *Thérapeutique des maladies spirituelles. Une introduction à la tradition ascétique de l'Eglise Orthodoxe*, 3rd edn, Paris: Cerf, 1997.

Leloir, L., 'Le diable chez les Pères du Désert et dans les écrits du Moyen-Âge,' in M. Schmidt, ed., *Typus, Symbol, Allegorie bei den östlichen Vätern und ihren Parallelen im Mittelalter*, Regensburg: 1982, 218–37.

Lienhard, J. T., '"Discernment of Spirits" in the Early Church,' *Studia Patristica* 17 (Berlin, 1982), 519–22.

Lossky, V., *The Vision of God*, London: 1963.

——, *The Mystical Theology of the Eastern Church*, London: 1957.

Lot-Borodine, M., 'La doctrine de la déification dans l'église grecque jusqu'au XIe siècle,' *Revue de l'Histoire des religions* 105 (Paris, 1932), 5–43, 106 (1932), 525–74, 107 (1933), 8–55.

Mangenot, E., 'Démon,' *DTC* 4 (Paris, 1939), 321–22.

Marty, F., 'Le discernement des esprits dans le *Peri Archon* d'Origène,' *RAM* 34 (Toulouse, 1958), 147–64 and 253–74.

Marx, M. J., 'Incessant prayer in the *Vita Antonii*,' *Studia Anselmiana* 38 (Rome, 1956), 65–107.

McGinn, B., Meyendorff, J. and Leclerq, J. (eds), *Christian Spirituality: Origins to the Twelfth Century*, New York: Crossroads, 1985.

Meredith, A., 'Asceticism – Christian and Greek,' in *Journal of Theological Studies* 27 (1976), 313–32.

Meyendorff, J., *A Study of Gregory Palamas*, London: 1964. See also (fuller) French edition: *Introduction à l'étude de Grégoire Palamas*, Paris: 1959.

Nellas, P., *Zoon Theoumenon. Prooptikes gia mian Orthodoxe katanoese tou anthropou* (in Greek: Athens, 1979). English transl. *Deification in Christ*, Crestwood, NY: St Vladimir's Seminary Press, 1987.

Neyt, F., 'Précisions sur le vocabulaire de Barsanuphe et de Jean de Gaza,' *Studia Patristica* 8 (Berlin, 1975), 247–53.

Papadopoulos, S., 'Provlemata tou archaiou monachismou,' *Kleronomia* 2,1 (in Greek: Thessalonika, 1970), 149–99.

Peterson, R. M., 'The Gift of Discerning Spirits in the *Vita Antonii*,' *Studia Patristica* 17 (Berlin, 1982), 523–27.

Rahner, K., 'Le début d'une doctrine des cinq sens spirituels chez Origene,' *RAM* 13 (Toulouse, 1932), 113–45.

Regnault, L., 'La prière continuelle "monologistos" dans la littérature apophthegmatique,' *Irénikon* 47 (Chevetogne, 1974), 467–93.

Resch, P., *La doctrine ascétique des premiers maîtres égyptiens du quatrième siècle*, Paris: 1931.

Robinson, J. A. T., *The Body. A Study in Pauline Theology*, London: 1952. Reprinted by Xpress Reprints: London, 1993.

Rousse, J., 'Ascèse et pénitence,' *La Vie Spirituelle* 6 (Paris, 1974), 890–904.

Rousseau, P., *Ascetics, Authority and the Church in the Age of Jerome and Cassian*, Oxford: Oxford University Press, 1978.

———, *Pachomius: The Making of a Community in Fourth Century Egypt*, Berkeley: University of California Press, 1985.

Sheils, W. J. (ed.), *Monks, Hermits, and the Ascetic Tradition*, Padstow: T. J. Press, 1985.

Spanneut, M., *Le stoïcisme des Pères de l'Église de Clément de Rome à Clément d'Alexandrie*, Paris: 1957.

Spidlík, T., *La Doctrine Spirituelle de Théophane le Reclus. Le Coeur et l'Esprit*, Rome: 1965.

———, *La Spiritualité de l'Orient Chrétien*, Rome: 1978. English translation: *The Spirituality of the Christian East*, Kalamazoo, MI: Cistercian Publications, 1985.

Steidle, B., 'Die Tränen, ein mystisches Problem im alten Mönchtum,' *Benediktinische Monatsschrift* 20 (Beuron, 1938), 181–87.

Stoffels, J., 'Die Angriffe der Dämonen auf den Einsiedler Antonius,' *Theologie und Glaube* 2 (1910), 721–32 and 809–30.

Sylvia Mary, Sister, 'St. Symeon the New Theologian and the Way of Tears,' *Studia Patristica* 10 (Berlin, 1970), 431–35.

Touraille, J., 'L'hésychasme ou l'attention théologique,' *La Vie Spirituelle* 6 (Paris, 1975), 812–24.

Tresmontant, C., *Essai sur la Pensée Hébraïque*, Paris: 1953.

Von Lilienfeld, F., '"Anthropos Pneumatikos"–"Pater Pneumatophoros": Neues Testament und Apophthegmata Patrum,' *Studia Patristica* 5 (Berlin, 1962), 382–92.

Von Severus, E., 'Meditation und Aktion,' *Schöpfegeist und Neuschöpfung* (Limburg/Lahn, 1957), 91–100.

Veselinovits, A., *Barsanuphius the Great, John the Prophet and Dorotheus the Abba* (in Greek: Athens, 1939).

Veyne, P. (ed.), *A History of Private Life: From Pagan Rome to Byzantium*, Cambridge, MA: Harvard University Press, 1987.

Viller, M., 'La spiritualité des premiers siècles chrétiens,' *Bibliothèque catholique des Sciences religieuses*, Paris: 1930. (Cited under a different edition in specialist bibliography on Klimakos.)

Wallace-Hadrill, D. S., *The Greek Patristic View of Nature*, Manchester: 1968.

Ware, K. T., *The Ascetic Writings of Mark the Hermit*, Oxford: 1965. Dissertation submitted for the Degree of Doctor of Philosophy. Faculty of Theology.

——, 'The Transfiguration of the Body,' in A. M. Allchin, ed., *Sacrament and Image*, London: The Fellowship of St Alban and St Sergius, 1967, 17–32.

——, 'Tradition and Personal Experience in Later Byzantine Theology,' *Eastern Churches Review* 3 (1970), 131–41.

——, 'The Jesus Prayer in St Gregory of Sinai,' *Eastern Churches Review* 4 (1972), 3–22.

——, *The Power of the Name. The Jesus Prayer in Orthodox Spirituality*, Oxford: Fairacres Press, 1974.

——, 'The Monk and the Married Christian,' *Eastern Churches Review* 6 (1974), 72–83.

——, 'The Spiritual Father in Orthodox Christianity,' *Cross Currents* 24 (West Nyack, NY, 1974), 296–313 (–20). See his *The Inner Kingdom: Collected Works*, Vol. 1, New York: St Vladimir's Seminary Press, 2000, 127–54.

——, 'Silence in Prayer: the Meaning of *Hesychia*,' in B. Pennington, ed., *One Yet Two: Cistercian Studies Series* 29 (Kalamazoo, MI, 1976), 22–47. See his *Collected Works*, Vol. 1, 89–110.

Wimbush, V. L. (ed.), *Ascetic Behavior in Greco-Roman Antiquity: a sourcebook*, Minneapolis, MN: Fortress Press, 1990.

Wimbush, V. and Valantasis, R. (eds), *Asceticism*, Oxford: Oxford University Press, 1995.

Wurz, E., 'Das Mysterium der Tränen und der Salbe,' *Frauen im Bann-Kreis Christi* (Limburg/Lahn, 1964).

Zaehner, R. C., *At Sundry Times. An Essay in the Comparison of Religions*, London: 1958.

Zizioulas, J. D., 'Apo to Prosopeion eis to Prosopon,' *Charisteria eis Timen tou Metropolitou Gerontos Chalkedonos Melitonos* (in Greek: Thessalonika, 1977), 287–323. English translation in *Being as Communion*, New York: St Vladimir's Seminary Press, 1985, 27–65.

Name Index

Subject Index